United States Government Information

Library and Information Science Text Series

United States Government Information
Policies and Sources

Peter Hernon
Simmons College

Harold C. Relyea
Congressional Research Service
Library of Congress

Robert E. Dugan
Suffolk University

Joan F. Cheverie
Georgetown University

2002
LIBRARIES UNLIMITED
A Division of Greenwood Publishing Group, Inc.
Westport, Connecticut

LIBRARIES UNLIMITED
A Division of Greenwood Publishing Group, Inc.
88 Post Road West
Westport, CT 06881
1-800-225-5800
www.lu.com

Library of Congress Cataloging-in-Publication Data

United States government information : policies and sources /
    Peter Hernon ... [et al.].
      p. cm. -- (Library and information science text series)
    Includes bibliographical references and index.
    ISBN 1-56308-978-5 -- ISBN 1-56308-979-3 (pbk.)
    1. Government information--United States. 2. Government in-
formation agencies--United States. 3. Government publications
--United States. 4. Electronic government information--United
States. 5. Information policy--

—United States.   I. Hernon, Peter.
    II. Series.
    ZA5055.U6U55 2002
    025.17'34'0973--dc21

2002009458

Contents

Chapter 16: Electronic Government (*cont.*)

List of Figures

 Preface

In America, information continues to be the currency of our democracy. Almost a quarter of a century ago, before the advent of electronic government, Dean Bernard M. Fry of the Indiana University Graduate Library School observed that "government publications at all levels . . . are today a major source of information in practically every field of endeavor and are crucial to informed public decision-making."[1] He also noted that these same "government publications are recognized as probably the most neglected and underutilized information resource available to the public. The root cause of this paradox lies in the diversity and confusion of government policies and in the widespread lack of public awareness of the existence of government publications which might be of value to them."[2]

Undoubtedly, the emergence of the Internet and the World Wide Web, to some extent, challenges the view of government sources, as well as services, as "most neglected and underutilized." Presidents William J. Clinton and George W. Bush, as well as Congresses of the recent past and the present, favor a customer-focused or citizen-centric government, one that is responsible to the public in a digital environment. However, Dean Fry's identification of the "root cause" still has some validity.

This book, which will be subsequently revised and updated periodically, combines a presentation of government information policies with identification of basic sources and, in some instances, their use. The discussion of these sources should enable readers to update the discussion of policies in the various chapters, as well as unlock vast sources that the federal government produces and makes available—distributes or disseminates—that are not associated with information policies. We have also placed present-day discussions within an historical context, thus avoiding an ahistorical perspective on the presentation of policies and sources. Using the sources identified, readers can trace previous policies and uncover more than two centuries of government publications in the nation's libraries and in repositories such as the National Archives and Records Administration.

As Laurence F. Schmeckebier and Roy B. Eastin noted thirty years ago, "special problems arise in searching for information to be found in older government publications."[3] Although *United States Government Information: Policies and Sources* cannot address all of these problems, it identifies various sources that will help in these instances.

As chapter presentations progress and focus on the present day, there is a clear shift from a print to a digital environment. Most dramatically, we see that the federal government has not limited its dissemination of sources to those relevant only to today; a number of them, available on the Web, pertain to yesterday. Recognizing the utility of the Web for the provision of government information sources, we have tried to minimize the extent of overlap with the companion volume, *U.S. Government on the Web* (Libraries Unlimited, 2001), now in its second edition. *U.S. Government on the Web*, which will continue to appear biannually, will identify many more Web sites than this book does but will lack the detailed presentation of topics, such as tracing a legislative history, found here.

United States Government Information: Policies and Sources has a companion CD-ROM, which, if it appeared as a supplementary print volume, would contain more than 1,800 pages. The CD-ROM

- Reprints some of the key documents discussed in the chapters;

- Digitizes some historically significant documents that are currently out-of-print (e.g., in Chapter 1, *Electronic Collection and Dissemination of Information by Federal Agencies: A Policy Overview* (House Committee on Government Operations));

- Presents examples to clarify the text (e.g., in Chapter 8, the position description for the chief information officer for the Department of Agriculture);

- Offers tutorials (e.g., using the retrospective indexes discussed in Chapter 2, the legislative history of the Paperwork Reduction Act of 1995 in Chapter 3, and searching the *Code of Federal Regulations* on the Web in Chapter 10);

- Provides exercises (e.g., in Chapter 15, enabling libraries to determine the costs of depository library status and the program itself to set a standard measure for identifying the cost contribution of the library community to public access to government information); and

- Supplies 100 practice questions and their answers for readers to use as they gain familiarity in searching for sources discussed in various chapters.

We are most grateful to Joe Morehead, author of *Introduction to United States Government Information Sources* (Libraries Unlimited) for giving us most of these practice questions, which he used in his teaching.

United States Government Information: Policies and Sources is intended to serve a wide audience: practicing information professionals needing a guide to policies and sources, such as those related to the ways in which the president communicates policy (see Chapter 5); students in programs in the fields of public administration, public policy, journalism, political science, and library and information science; and members of the public trying to navigate the myriad sources and producers of government information.

Similar to *U.S. Government on the Web*, the publisher's Web site (http://www.lu.com) will regularly update the Web sites listed at the end of chapters. In an era before the existence of Web sites, Schmeckebier and Eastin counseled that "persons new to the field of government publishing should not become discouraged by the apparent complexity, for, after a relatively brief exploration and exposure to the guides available, they will become proficient in availing themselves of the wealth of information to be found in no other sources."[4] This book, supported by a companion CD-ROM and Web site, seeks to provide a guide for those venturing into the information domain of the federal government's terminology, activities, and sources.

Peter Hernon

NOTES

1. National Commission on Libraries and Information Science, *Government Publications: Their Role in the National Program for Library and Information Services*, by Bernard M. Fry (Washington, D.C.: GPO, 1970), 1.

2. Ibid.

3. Laurence F. Schmeckebier and Roy B. Eastin, *Government Publications and Their Use* (Washington, D.C.: The Brookings Institution, 1969), 5.

4. Ibid.

Chapter 1

Government Publishing

Government publishing has at least three major components. First, it occurs within a context of governance; that is, it is conducted by some type of governmental system (e.g., democratic or totalitarian). Second, it involves the production of information through the application of ink to paper and, more recently, the use of digital technologies for the creation of portable document formats and other electronic forms and formats. The third component is dissemination of the information product to the public. Although the word "publishing" derives from a Latin root meaning "all of the people," the extent to which government publishing results in making government-produced information products readily accessible to the nation or a global population is determined by the form of government involved and the purpose of publication—its integrity (accurate or erroneous, reliable or propaganda). At the same time, some information is special, and its unauthorized disclosure could damage national security: "It is very important that classified information be correctly identified as such as soon as it comes into existence and that unnecessary classification is curtailed."[1] Restrictions on access can slow national progress, for example, in science and technology and "fail to keep the citizenry from being fully informed about matters of national significance."[2] The nation is founded on the principle that the public has the right and need to be informed about governmental matters. "Finally, unnecessary classification tends to decrease the actual protection for correctly classified information by lessening the credibility of (respect for) classification."[3]

PUBLICATION AS SPECIFIED IN THE CONSTITUTION

The U.S. Constitution specifies that each chamber of Congress "shall keep a Journal of its Proceedings, and from time to time publish the same, excepting such Parts as may in their Judgment require Secrecy" (Article I, section 5, clause 3). As for the electors, "they shall make distinct lists of all persons voted for as President, and of all persons voted for as Vice-President, and the number of votes for each, which lists they shall sign and certify" (Article II, section 1,

1

clause 3). Concerning the subnational level of government, the Constitution states: "Full faith and Credit shall be given in each state to the Public Acts, Records, and Judicial Proceedings of every other State" (Article IV, Section 1, clause 1).

With its system of checks and balances, the Constitution anticipated that the three branches of government would be cognizant of the activities and interests of the other two. In this regard, the Constitution specifically provides that, when the president vetoes a bill, "he shall return it, with his Objections to that House in which it shall have originated, who shall enter the Objections at large on their Journal and proceed to reconsider it" (Article I, section 7, clause 2). Concerning interbranch accountability, provision is made for the president to "require the Opinion in writing, of the principal officer in each of the executive Departments, upon any Subject relating to the Duties of their respective Offices" (Article II, section 2, clause 1). Finally, the Constitution indicates that the president "shall from time to time give to the Congress information of the State of the Union, and recommend to their Consideration such Measures as he shall judge necessary and expedient" (Article II, section 3).

These constitutional references to information matters indicate some fundamental expectations regarding government accountability and communication, the exercise of certain popular rights regarding government information, and subsequent legislation detailing and refining a few particular information policies. Historically, experience and practice, together with constitutional considerations, have guided the legislative process.

THE FOUNDATION FOR PUBLICATION

During the Constitutional Convention of 1787, James Wilson of Pennsylvania stressed the importance of official printing and publication by the new government. Addressing a proposal to allow each congressional chamber discretion as to the parts of its journal that would be published, he told the delegates: "The people have the right to know what their Agents are doing or have done, and it should not be in the option of the Legislature to conceal their proceedings."[4] The following year, James Madison and George Mason raised a similar consideration during the Virginia Convention on the proposed Constitution when speaking about the importance of publishing all receipts and expenditures of public money under the new government.

In deference to views such as these, Congress provided for the printing and public distribution of both the laws and treaties, the preservation of papers of state, and the maintenance of official files in the newly created departments. In 1813, the printing and distribution of both the Senate and House journals was authorized. Congress arranged for a contemporary summary of each chamber's floor proceedings to be published in the *Register of Debates*, beginning in 1824. It then switched, in 1833, to the weekly *Congressional Globe*, which sought to chronicle every step in the legislative proceedings of the two houses. A daily publication schedule was established for the *Globe* in 1865. Subsequently, the *Congressional Record* succeeded the *Globe* in March 1873 as the official congressional gazette.[5] It was produced by the newly created congressional printing agency, the Government Printing Office (GPO).

Provision was initially made in 1846 for the routine printing of all congressional reports, special documents, and bills. These responsibilities were met for many years through the use of contract printers, but such arrangements proved to be subject to considerable political abuse. Consequently, in 1860, Congress established GPO to produce all of its literature (including, eventually, the *Congressional Record*) and also to serve the printing needs of the executive branch. Additional aspects of governmentwide printing and publication policy were set with the 1895 Printing Act, which is the source of much of the basic policy still found in the printing chapters of Title 44, *United States Code*.

Congress mandated the publication of the statutes and a variety of legislative branch literature (including executive branch materials that were initially produced as Senate or House documents), authorized newspaper reprinting of the laws and treaties, and promoted circulating printed documents through official sources. Among other developments, Congress, with the 1895 Printing Act, established the Superintendent of Documents within GPO, who (among other duties) was given responsibility for managing the sale of public documents and preparing the *Monthly Catalog of United States Government Publications* as a record of government publications. Until 1904 the sales stock available to the Superintendent derived entirely from such materials as were provided for this purpose by the departments and agencies or were returned from depository libraries. The situation was changed when the Superintendent received authority in that year to reprint any departmental publication, with the consent of the pertinent secretary, for public sale. Congress legislated comparable discretion to reproduce its documents in 1922.

THE ADMINISTRATIVE STATE

In the early twentieth century, the federal government entered a new phase with the rise of the administrative state. Among the forces contributing to this development was the Progressive Movement, which sought greater government intervention into, and regulation of, various sections of American society and economic intercourse. In 1913, an autonomous Department of Labor and the Federal Reserve were established, and, in the following year, the Federal Trade Commission was created. With U.S. entry into the First World War, regulatory activities further expanded and the number of administrative agencies increased. In the postwar era government expansion momentarily slowed, but it resumed with the onset of the Great Depression and the arrival of the New Deal administration of Franklin D. Roosevelt in 1933.

As federal regulatory powers and administrative entities grew dramatically during this period, there was a concomitant increase in both the number and variety of controlling directives, regulations, and requirements. One contemporary observer, John A. Fairlie of the Army General Staff, characterized the operative situation in 1920 as one of "confusion," and another, Harvard Law School professor Erwin N. Griswold, described the deteriorating conditions in 1934 as "chaos." During the early days of the New Deal, administrative law pronouncements were in such disarray that, on one occasion, federal attorneys arguing a lawsuit before the U.S. Supreme Court were embarrassed to discover that their case was based on a nonexistent regulation; in another case, they found they were pursuing litigation based on a revoked executive order.

To address the need for accountability, Congress established an executive branch gazette. Such a publication had been temporarily produced during the time of U.S. involvement in World War I. Printed as a tabloid newspaper, the *Official Bulletin* contained presidential orders and proclamations along with department and agency directives, as well as various news items pertaining to the European hostilities.

The new gazette, statutorily authorized in July 1935, was named the *Federal Register*. It provides a variety of presidential directives and agency regulations, and eventually came to be published each workday. In 1937, Congress inaugurated the *Code of Federal Regulations*, a useful supplement to the *Federal Register*. This cumulation of the instruments and authorities appearing in the gazette contains most operative agency regulations.

Later, the general statutory authority underlying the *Federal Register* was relied on for the creation of other series of publications. The annual *United States Government Manual*, a catalog of government bodies that has been available for public purchase since 1939, is now available online from the Office of the Federal Register (see Chapter 10); the *Public Papers of the Presidents*, an official documents series, was launched in 1960 and covers the administrations of President Herbert Hoover, President Harry S. Truman, and subsequent presidents; and the *Weekly Compilation of Presidential Documents*, a presidential gazette, originated in mid-1965.[6]

THE JUDICIAL SETTING

Whereas GPO prints a significant portion of legislative and executive branch literature, much of which is made available to the public through its sales and depository library distribution, judicial branch materials are published in a somewhat different manner. During the early years of the federal government, the judicial branch had little to publish. Oral argument in the trial and appellate courts was the general practice. Attorneys were unaccustomed to preparing written briefs, and judges did not write many decisions or opinions. Final determinations in a lawsuit were rendered through entry upon the log or journal of the clerk of the court, a brief order, or an occasional handwritten note.

With the passage of time, however, the quantity and importance of federal judgments began to grow, as did interest in reading these decisions. A commercial response resulted; during the nineteenth century, more than 200 separate case reporters, most covering only a single court, published decisions from various federal courts other than the Supreme Court. Not only was this reporting unsystematic, but the private reporters also sometimes presented varying texts of the same decision.

Private enterprise retained its hold, and efforts were made to improve the quality of reporting. West Publishing Company became a leader in the field. West began to publish the *Federal Reporter* series in 1880, which systematically reproduced the written decisions rendered by judges of the federal trial and lower appellate courts. Using the collected products of the various early reporters, as well as materials gathered under its own auspices, between 1894 and 1897 the firm produced *Federal Cases*, a thirty-volume compilation of all available lower federal court case law to 1882. In 1932 West inaugurated the *Federal Supplement* series, which contains only trial court decisions. *Federal Rules Decisions*, launched by West in 1940, selectively reports federal court decisions concerning procedural matters.

Over the past sixty years a number of specialized topical reporters have been commercially produced. However, single copies of lower federal court decisions are publicly available from the issuing court in typescript or, sometimes, printed versions called slip opinions.

The publication of Supreme Court decisions has followed a different course. The task was begun as a private venture, in 1790, by Alexander J. Dallas, a noted Pennsylvania attorney. When the Court relocated from the temporary capital in Philadelphia to the federal district (Washington, D.C.) in 1800, William Cranch, then chief justice of the circuit court of the district, took over from Dallas. Subsequently, in March 1817, Congress authorized the Court to appoint and compensate a reporter to handle the publication of its decisions. This employee could secure the services of a private contract printer to produce each compilation, but a statutorily specified number of copies was to be supplied, "without any expense to the United States" to certain designated federal officials. This so-called nominative reporter system was discontinued with the decisions of the 1874 term.

Almost fifty years elapsed before contemporary practice was inaugurated in 1922. The Supreme Court reporter was divested of all interest in the publication of the reports; GPO was given responsibility for producing the Court's printing, including the production of the *United States Reports*, as the published series is entitled; and the Superintendent of Documents was authorized to sell copies of the series to the public. However, commercial publishers did not abandon the area, and they have continued to produce their own reportorial series of Court decisions with research features as well as particular specialized collections of Court opinions.

THE ELECTRONIC INFORMATION AGE

Clinton was the first president of the Internet age. There was press coverage of his use of e-mail to correspond with his daughter entering college, and shortly thereafter, the White House and other agency home pages evolved. They became easier to navigate, improved the linkage among the sources included, and offered more types of information resources than are found in a paper environment. Chapter 16 discusses the policy instruments essential to the evolution of information technologies and the emerging electronic government. These technologies and the World Wide Web have combined to provide a means of global communication, information access, response to crises, service delivery, and procurement. At the same time, issues of privacy and security have arisen, clearly indicating that Web system maintenance and management in the electronic Information Age will require a whole new set of information policies and delivery mechanisms.

Both the executive and legislative branches embraced those technologies and the Web but wanted greater management and oversight of related government activities. Clearly, continued maintenance of information technologies that underlie electronic government will require highly qualified and trained personnel. These personnel may not constitute an addition to the federal workforce; rather, there might be greater outsourcing. In addition, computer hardware and software will require continuous updating and replacement.

In the early 1990s the Government Printing Office created GPO Access, and the National Technical Information Service (NTIS) put forth its portal, FedWorld. The Library of Congress created THOMAS, named after the third president of the United States, as a portal leading to congressional material. Congress and the Clinton administration saw the Internet as a means for electronic commerce as well as for communicating with the public, providing them with information and services and conducting business with an agency's clientele.

A good indication of how far government policy moved in a few short years can be found by examining *Electronic Collection and Dissemination of Information by Federal Agencies*[7] and the policies presented in Chapter 8. The coverage, in effect, reflects the before and during stages. One of the later laws, the Government Paperwork Elimination Act of 1998 (PL 105-277), deals with the transition to electronic government. That transition, to a large extent, relies on agencies' use of the Internet and other electronic methods to receive and deliver information and services. More specifically, the Act requires that, by October 21, 2003, federal agencies provide the public, when practicable, with the option of submitting, maintaining, and disclosing required information electronically instead of on paper.

In July 2000 the Office of Management and Budget issued a memorandum for chief information officers on the subject of "achieving electronic government." According to that memorandum, "careful agency planning is critical to ensure that this transition succeeds. As part of this planning, agencies should re-evaluate how they do business by updating business processes to take advantage of the automation. Agencies should also consider automating groups of processes that service a common customer . . . , and coordinating with other agencies, to achieve *customer-centric* approaches to electronic government" (emphasis added).[8]

The final chapter of this book examines electronic government. Needless to say, electronic communication between the government and the public is extensive and growing. Agencies record high numbers of hits on the Web sites that they rely on to demonstrate the level of their contact with, and service delivery to, the public. Such communication is all the more necessary as the size of the federal workforce shrinks but the amount of work itself does not.

DEFINITION OF KEY TERMS

According to Title 44, *United States Code*, section 1901, a "government publication . . . means information matter which is published as an individual document at Government expense, or as required by law." Section 1902 states that, except for those publications "determined by their issuing components to be required for official use only or for strictly administrative or operational purposes which have no public interest or educational value and publications classified for reasons of national security . . . [government publications] shall be made available to depository libraries." This definition and declaration of the scope of public availability have become the standard for what makes up a government publication to which the public should have access. In fact, the word "product" has been substituted for "publication," and placement on the World Wide Web and in electronic form constitutes a form of publication.

In Circular A-130, most recently revised in 2000, the Office of Management and Budget defined:

- *Government information* as "information, created, collected, processed, disseminated, or disposed of by or for the Federal government";

- *Government publication* in terms of 44 U.S.C. 1901;

- *Information* as "any communication or representation of knowledge such as facts, data, or opinions in any medium or form, including textual, numerical, graphic, cartographic, narrative, or audiovisual forms";

- *Information dissemination product* as "any book, paper, map, machine-readable material, audiovisual production, or other documentary material, regardless of physical form or characteristics, disseminated by an agency to the public";

- *Information resources* as referring to "both government information and information technology"; and

- *Information resources management* as "the process of managing information resources to accomplish agency missions. The term encompasses both information itself and the related resources, such as personnel, equipment, funds, and information technology."[9]

Another type of government information is a *record*, which is created in the conduct of government (agency, court, legislative, or presidential) business and is communicated to the parties involved. Further,

- Records are evidence of transactions (relationships of acts), means of action, and information about acts;

- Records are known for their metadata—for example, forms documentation;

- Ideal records metadata can be defined from societal understanding of recordness;

- Any given record will be a better/worse (more/less risky) record for having complete/incomplete metadata; and

- The metadata is about content, context, and structure.[10]

Federal records are subject to the provisions of the Federal Records Act, as set forth in chapters 29, 31, and 33 of Title 44, *United States Code*. That Act requires the heads of federal agencies to make and preserve records documenting the official activities of the agency. It also directs federal agencies to establish a program for the management of agency records; put into place effective controls over the creation, maintenance, and use of records; and create safeguards against the removal or loss of records. The Archivist of the United States promulgates standards and guidance for implementation of the Federal Records Act, which, for instance, are found in Title 36 of the *Code of Federal Regulations*.

In a report on electronic records, the General Accounting Office pointed out that the Office of Management and Budget issued Circulars A-123, "Management Accountability and Control," and A-130, "Management of Federal Information Resources," "to ensure the adequacy of management and control of federal information systems." Appendix III of the latter directive "requires that federal agencies periodically test system controls meant to ensure the integrity, confidentiality, and availability of information resources."[11]

INFORMATION POLICY

Information policy is a set of interrelated laws, regulations, guidelines, and other policy "instruments" concerned with the life cycle of government information. These instruments shape agency responsibilities during that life cycle. There are a number of different opinions about what stages the life cycle comprises, but the most basic ones appear to be information

1. Creation, collection, and gathering;
2. Production, processing, and publication;
3. Transmission, including distribution and dissemination;
4. Retrieval and use; and
5. Retention or disposal, including storage and archival management.

Transmission might be limited to authorized personnel within an agency or to other groups, or a publication might contain sensitive defense, diplomatic, law enforcement, or technological information bearing on the security of the country. However, restricted availability within the executive branch might be challenged under the Freedom of Information Act (see Chapter 7). "The term 'dissemination' means the government initiated distribution of information to the public."[12] Planning and security management, including privacy protection, cut across stages and, in a digital environment, stages may not follow sequentially. For example, using a geographical information system in which data are geo-coded (coded to specific longitude and latitude) (see Chapter 14), it is possible to have the information retrieved from relational databases (stage four) result in the creation of new information (back to stage one).

Essential to this book are those policies that guide information management and public access. Retention involves the National Archives and Records Administration (NARA), because the Archivist of the United States has discretionary authority to accept and retrieve for deposit at NARA the records of federal entities determined by that official to have sufficient historical or other value to warrant their continued preservation by the federal government. Of course, many kinds of government publications are collected and preserved elsewhere. For example, the NTIS preserves scientific and technical reports and papers assigned to it; consequently, NARA's holdings consist primarily of unpublished federal records.

Another type of life cycle relates to information systems and focuses on the phases through which an information system—"a discrete set of information resources organized for the collection, processing, maintenance, transmission, and dissemination of information, in accordance with defined procedures, whether automated or manual"—passes, typically characterized as initiation, development, operation, and termination.[13]

Public Access

Public access, a widely used but little analyzed concept, applies to stages three and four, and it includes accessibility, availability, and acceptability. *Accessibility* refers to the extent to which (1) government information is accurately identified bibliographically in finding aids (e.g., those discussed in Chapter 2) and (2) the information is publicly known. It also requires the resolution of economic, political, social, and technological barriers encountered in gaining access to information. Accessibility diminishes if the public cannot locate information (including the burial of information in the "library" portion of an agency's Web site); information is contained in a format requiring the use of special tools (in some instances, the tools no longer exist to access historical information appearing in a digital format); information can be located, but not obtained, within an acceptable time frame; information is priced higher than individuals can afford to pay; and government departments lose, misplace, or do not make information available. Price involves more than money; it may include, for instance, the amount of time a person is willing to invest in locating information.

Educator Michael K. Buckland noted that accessibility includes "understanding" or "cognitive access": "[T]he inquirer . . . [needs] sufficient expertise to understand . . . [the information]."[14] When there is an insufficient level of understanding, explanation and education become important, but whose responsibility are these functions?

Availability refers to what information exists and what the government will release, either voluntarily or by legal recourse. It refers to physical access and document delivery, as well as to issues such as whether the information can be obtained in a convenient and user-friendly format, in a language understandable to the user, and in a time frame in which the information is relevant and timely and has utility.

Acceptability relates to credibility, user preferences and expectations, and, for the private sector, sales potential. With the war on terrorism following September 11, 2001, there is probably greater acceptance of the value of government as a protector of the public and greater willingness to use the World Wide Web as a means of direct communication between those who govern and those who are governed. The Web also provides information (data, reports and other documentation, and images) and services. The public prefers to receive the actual service online as opposed to merely information about the services offered. Acceptability also deals with issues such as misinformation, disinformation, and the fact that the public might trust government information in some situations more than others.

Government Publications and Propaganda

The content of a government publication is, of course, determined by government officials. Even a verbatim hearing transcript resulting from a proceeding organized by such officials can be influenced by the questions and exchanges they and their staff have developed ahead of time and may be edited prior to publication. In the production of a narrative product, the subject matter, data content, and writing style are all subject to control by government officials. Manipulation and censorship can replace fair and objective management in these situations. Furthermore, propaganda, which might constitute selected truths, intentional distortions or exaggerations, and outright lies, can result.

Sometimes publication is itself a check on the validity or acceptability of government information, particularly in the case of a policy pronouncement. To have legal effect, most presidential proclamations and executive orders must be published in the *Federal Register*, which permits their scrutiny by the public or by surrogates of the public such as the press and public interest groups. Proposed, new, or revised agency regulations often are published in the *Federal Register,* and public comment on them is invited during a period of time prior to their final issuance. Some other checks might be the appropriations process and the elimi- nation of funds, the Gillette Act of 1915 that prohibits agencies from hiring a public relations expert, and data quality regulations issued by the Office of Man- agement and Budget.

The veracity of information provided at congressional hearings and appear- ing in the published transcripts of such proceedings can be reinforced by requir- ing witnesses to swear an oath of truthfulness, regardless of their testimony. Congressional committee reports on legislation and Senate committee reports on nominations, whether approving or disapproving, must be sustained by a major- ity of committee members before being filed for publication. When interpreting a statute, federal judges may turn to the pertinent House or Senate legislative re- ports on it, knowing they represent the views of a majority of committee mem- bers who voted on the report; these reports are often useful to understand the meaning or the intent of a law. Committee prints, which are another type of con- gressional publication, do not enjoy the same authoritative status as committee reports because they do not directly convey legislators' considered understand- ing of legislation and are issued without an approving vote.

Federal judges may also turn to the *Congressional Record* for House and Senate floor debate on legislation enacted into law to gain a better understanding of the meaning or intent of a statute. It is the factor of debate, opposing points of view checking each other, that gives this particular type of information a higher degree of reliability.

Adequacy of Public Access

In discussing the adequacy of public access, Peter Hernon and Charles R. McClure identified six factors:

1. *Political and organizational*: What are the views, value assumptions, and objectives of the federal workforce about the government's role in the provision of government information, even that potentially re- lating to homeland security? Another question is, To what extent does the management of information enhance the accomplishment of political goals and objectives? As Chapter 16 indicates, Web-deliv- ered information and services enhance the Bush administration's view of a citizen-centric government.

2. *Information release*: Which information should be made available, and how will that determination be made?

3. *Bibliographic control*: To what degree is information identified ac- curately, indexed, and included in appropriate finding aids?

4. *Dissemination*: What methods are used? How effective are they in reaching their target audiences?

5. *Publication formats*: Multiple formats exist. Do any present barriers to access and use?

6. *User awareness*: How aware is the public (or target audiences) that government information and services exist? What do they use? How do they gather the information? What are their preferences?[15]

ASSESSMENT OF WEB SITES

With the government increasingly relying on the Web as a primary means of information dissemination and service provision, an assessment of government Web sites becomes more essential to ensure that they conform to the requirements specified in existing information policies and can be navigated in a clear and logical way.[16] Successful navigation may also involve the availability of a site map and a series of frequently asked questions, as well as identification of the most frequently used sites of that department or agency. Considering the extent to which government sites have been the target of hackers seeking to spread misinformation, the question arises, "How trusting should the public be of the information they take from any Web site?" Further, "What administrative procedures and technical safeguards have government bodies taken to ensure the integrity of the information posted on their sites?" Of course, anyone answering these questions must realize that information does not constitute knowledge. It is outside the scope of this chapter and book to discuss the conversion of information into knowledge.

Anyone conducting an assessment of government and other Web sites might appreciate a list of relevant criteria. Kristin R. Eschenfelder, John C. Beachboard, Charles R. McClure, and Steven K. Wyman have produced a useful set of criteria, many of which, however, are not set in information policies.[17] These criteria are grouped into

- Information content criteria (the substantive aspects of the Web site): "orientation to Website," "Content," "Currency," "Bibliographic Control," "Services (if provided)," "Accuracy," and "Privacy" and

- Ease-of-use criteria (physical movement through the Web site): "Quality of Links," "Feedback Mechanisms," "Accessibility," "Design," and "Navigability."

McClure adds to the criteria by developing a "checklist of legal and policy conditions pertaining to federal agency Websites" and identifying "management and infrastructure factors pertaining to federal agency Websites."[18]

A survey of some users of congressional Web sites disclosed a preference for "clear, easy-to-use Web sites that tell how their representatives voted on key issues, what bills they have introduced, what committees they serve on, and how citizens can access government services." Other desired information included "how to solve government-related problems, [members'] phone numbers [and] district offices and . . . [how] a bill becomes law." They did not "want 'show-off Web sites' or self-promotion"; they "disliked seeing a lot of pictures of their representatives."[19]

Some additional criteria must be offered. For example, how often does a government body change URLs, and has it made them more complex? (See Chapter 16.) To what extent is access to information seamless, and does it require minimal need for the public to understand terminology and differences among types of publications? Is there a good site map that leads to the types of resources available on the home page? How visually appealing are the screen image and the colors displayed?[20]

PRESERVATION OF ELECTRONIC INFORMATION RESOURCES

As the amount of electronic information proliferates, enters, and leaves a prominent position within a home page (e.g., buried in a Web site "library"), some important questions arise:

- Which information resources merit retention, for how long, and where are they located?

- How easy is it to navigate a "library" and locate needed information?

- How is the decision about retention made, by whom, and following what criteria?

- How can the government ensure that the technology of tomorrow can read and handle the files and information of today and yesterday?

- What types of provisions must agencies make for the review and preservation of electronic information resources?

Without satisfactory policy answers to such questions, information will be lost. The result will be a loss of agency memory or history, as it becomes difficult, if not impossible, to reconstruct the development of a particular policy or to locate data. Clearly, it is important to realize that decisions of today may have an impact on tomorrow and tracking those of yesterday.

CONCLUSION

According to historian Culver H. Smith, during the first century of the American republic, an "extraordinary relationship" emerged between newspapers and the federal government, political leaders, and political parties. As part of that relationship, the State Department encouraged newspapers to "publish the laws, orders, and resolutions of Congress."[21] We now see the Internet filling much of the same role as the government uses it for official purposes, and this new relationship has gained popular acceptance. Currently, there are at least twenty-six types of government publications available through government Web sites.[22] The relationship, however, is not limited to the dissemination of information. It also includes an opportunity for input into policy development and the conveyance of services.

NOTES

1. Arvin S. Quist, *Security Classification of Information,* vol. 1, *Introduction, History, and Adverse Impacts.* Prepared by the Oak Ridge Gaseous Diffusion Plant (Oak Ridge, Tenn.: Department of Energy, 1989), ix.

2. Ibid.

3. Ibid.

4. See Harold C. Relyea, "Historical Development of Federal Information Policy," in *United States Government Information Policies,* ed. Charles R. McClure, Peter Hernon, and Harold C. Relyea (Norwood, N.J.: Ablex, 1989), 25–48.

5. THOMAS, the congressional portal (http://thomas.loc.gov), provides access to the historical registers prior to 1987.

6. Compilations for President Franklin D. Roosevelt and earlier presidents have been published commercially (see coverage of *Public Papers of the President* in Chapter 5).

7. House Committee on Government Operations, *Electronic Collection and Dissemination of Information by Federal Agencies*: *A Policy Overview,* H. Rept. 99-560 (Washington, D.C.: GPO, 1986).

8. Office of Management and Budget, "Memorandum for Chief Information Officers: Achieving Electronic Government: Instruction for Plans to Implement the Government Paperwork Elimination Act" (Washington, D.C., July 25, 2000), 1.

9. Office of Management and Budget, "Circular A-130: Management of Federal Information Resources" (Washington, D.C., November 30, 2000), 3–4.

10. David Bearman and Jennifer Trant, "Electronic Records Research Working Meeting, May 28-30, 1997: A Report from the Archives Community," *Bulletin of the American Society for Information Science* 24 (February/March 1998): 14.

11. General Accounting Office, *Electronic Records: Clinton Administration's Management of Executive Office of the President's E-Mail System,* GAO-01-446 (Washington, D.C., April 2001), 5, 6.

12. Office of Management and Budget, "Circular A-130," 1.

13. Ibid., 4.

14. Michael K. Buckland, *Information and Information Systems* (New York: Greenwood Press, 1991), 78.

15. Peter Hernon and Charles R. McClure, *Federal Information Policies in the 1980s* (Norwood, N.J.: Ablex, 1987), 11–12.

16. Examples of such policy are the Federal Records Act (44 U.S.C. chs. 29, 31, 33, and 35), the Paperwork Reduction Act (44 U.S.C. ch. 35), and the Electronic Freedom of Information Improvement Act of 1996 (see Chapter 7).

17. Kristin R. Eschenfelder, John C. Beachboard, Charles R. McClure, and Steven K. Wyman, "Assessing U.S. Federal Government Websites," *Government Information Quarterly* 14 (1997): 173–89.

18. Charles R. McClure, "Assessing Federal Websites: Preliminary Findings and Key Issues," *Documents to the People* 29 (Spring 2001): 13–14.

19. William Matthews, "Keep Web Sites Simple," *Federal Computer Week* 15, no. 38 (November 12, 2001): 67.

20. See also William Matthews, "Dot-gov by Design," *Federal Computer Week* 15, no. 40 (December 10, 2001): 16–18, 20–21.

21. Culver H. Smith, *The Press, Politics, and Patronage: The American Government's Use of Newspapers, 1789–1875* (Athens, Ga.: University of Georgia Press, 1977), xi.

22. See Peter Hernon, Robert E. Dugan, and John A. Shuler, *U.S. Government on the Web: Getting the Information You Need* (Englewood, Colo.: Libraries Unlimited, 2000), 34–42.

URL SITE GUIDE

THOMAS
    http://thomas.loc.gov/

Chapter 2

Access to Government Information (Finding Aids)

This chapter identifies key finding aids (indexing tools and guides) that readers can use to update the policy instruments discussed in this book as well as to move the search for government information in new directions. It highlights access to government information from the formation of the new republic to the present. There is a discussion of printed indexes as well as electronic finding aids. The Appendix identifies how to locate scholarly literature and other policy analyses.

BACKGROUND

On December 8, 1813, the House of Representatives passed a resolution ordering the uniform printing of "all messages and communications from the President of the United States, all letters from the several departments of the Government, all motions and resolutions offered for the consideration of the House, all reports of committees of the House, and all other papers which [are produced] in the usual course of proceeding or by special order of the House." As a result of this resolution and similar congressional directives, the Serial Set (first known as the Congressional Set)[1] contains a shifting composition of publications from Congress, the executive branch, and some nongovernmental organizations chartered by Congress or for which Congress had agreed to provide printing services. The congressional material includes committee reports, journals, administrative reports, orations, special publications, and so forth.

Classification of congressional publications began with the first session of the 15th Congress. For that Congress (1817–1819), the Serial Set consisted of two series, House Documents and Senate Documents. There were no publications entitled "reports." From 1819 to 1847 (16th–29th Congresses), there were House and Senate Documents (including reports of the executive departments transmitted to Congress and miscellaneous publications originating in Congress, other than House committee reports). The reports of Senate committees were issued as Senate Documents, but reports of House committees were issued as House Reports.

17

From 1847 to 1895 (30th–53rd Congresses), the publications were known as House Reports and Senate Reports (committee reports), House Executive Documents and Senate Executive Documents (reports made to Congress by the executive branch), and House Miscellaneous Documents and Senate Miscellaneous Documents (all other publications except reports ordered by Congress or either house).

In 1895 Congress discontinued the distinction between the two types of Documents. Until 1952, there were only two congressional series: Documents and Reports. At that time, the Serial Set was consolidated into House and Senate Documents and Reports.

In addition to the series of publications already mentioned, constitutionally mandated House and Senate journals were also published. The Constitution (Article I, section 5, clause 30) states that "Each House shall keep a Journal of its Proceedings, and from time to time publish the same." Therefore, the proceedings of each chamber are published annually in their respective Journals. These Journals contain the minutes of meetings and a concise record of congressional action on bills, resolutions, memorials, and petitions, together with acknowledgment of communications from the president of the United States.

Publications from the time of the founding of the nation (and even before) might be available in depository libraries as either part of the Serial Set or the Superintendent of Documents (SuDocs) Classification Scheme. For earlier periods, these libraries might be more likely to have executive branch publications in the Serial Set, either paper copy or microformat, because the depository program was originally established to distribute the Serial Set to the public. Furthermore, Congress might take executive publications (e.g., annual reports) and reissue them as part of the Serial Set.

HISTORICAL INDEXES

None of the indexes identified in Figure 2.1 is comprehensive, and, even those covering the same time period (see Figure 2.2) might list different publications. Furthermore, whereas some of the indexes only cover the Serial Set, others emphasize access to agency publications through the agency-focused SuDocs Classification Scheme, and yet others cover both methods of access (Serial Set and agency access). In some instances, a couple of indexes must be used in combination to identify the requisite number to retrieve the publication in a depository library. (Prior to using the early indexes, it would be beneficial to consult Laurence F. Schmeckebier and Roy B. Eastin's coverage of them in *Government Publications and Their Use*[2] as well as to review the preface of each index.)

Ames, John G. *Comprehensive Index to the Publications of the United States Government, 1881–1893*. 2 vols. Washington, D.C.: GPO, 1905. 58th Cong., 2d sess. H. Doc. 745. Serial **4745** and **4746**).

Congressional Information Service. *CIS U.S. Serial Set Index, 1789–1969*. Bethesda, Md.: Congressional Information Service. 14 parts.

Congressional Information Service. *CIS Index to US Executive Branch Documents, 1789–1909; 1910–1932*. Bethesda, Md.: LexisNexis Academic & Library Solutions. 7 parts.

Greely, Adolphus Washington. *Public Documents of the First Fourteen Congresses, 1789–1817. Papers Relating to Early Congressional Documents*. Washington, D.C.: GPO, 1900. 56th Cong., 1st sess. S. Doc. 428. Serial **3879**.

Poole, Mary Elizabeth. *Document Office Classification*. 4th ed. Ann Arbor, Mich.: Edwards Brothers, 1945. Reprinted by U.S. Historical Documents Institute.

Poole, Mary Elizabeth, and Ella Frances Smith. *Documents Office Classification Numbers for Cuttered Documents, 1910–1924*. 2 vols. Ann Arbor, Mich.: University Microfilms, Inc., 1960.

Poore, Benjamin Perley. *A Descriptive Catalogue of Government Publications of the United States . . . September 5, 1774–March 4, 1881*. 2 vols. Washington, D.C.: GPO, 1885. 48th Cong., 2d sess. S. Misc. Doc. 67. Serial **2268**.

U.S. Document Office. *Tables of and Annotated Index to the Congressional Series of U.S. Public Documents*. Washington, D.C.: GPO, 1902.

U.S. Superintendent of Documents. *Catalog of the Public Documents of the 53rd to 76th Congress and All Departments of the Government of the United States for the Period from March 4, 1893 to December 31, 1940*. 25 vols. Washington, D.C.: GPO, 1896–1945. (Short title: *Document Catalog*).

U.S. Superintendent of Documents. *Checklist of United States Public Documents, 1789–1909*. 3d ed. Washington, D.C.: GPO, 1911.

U.S. Superintendent of Documents. *Index to Reports and Documents of the 54th Congress, 1st Session–72nd Congress, 2nd Session; December 2, 1895–March 4, 1933*. 43 vols. Washington, D.C.: GPO, 1895–1933. (Short title: *Document Index*).

U.S. Superintendent of Documents. *Monthly Catalog of United States Government Publications*. Washington, D.C.: GPO, 1895– . (Short Title: *Monthly Catalog*). Currently known as *Catalog of United States Government Publications*.

U.S. Superintendent of Documents. *Numerical Lists and Schedule of Volumes of the Reports and Documents of the 73rd Congress*. Washington, D.C.: GPO, 1934–1980. (Short title: *Numerical Lists*). From 1983 to 1994, the *Monthly Catalog of United States Government Publications* contained a special supplement for the *Numerical Lists*.

Figure 2.1. Historical Indexes.

```
Poore's   1774...............................1881
Checklist       1789..............................................1909
Greely          1789..1817
Tables of and
Annotated Index       1817.........................1893
Ames                          1881......1893
Document Catalog                          1893.........................1940
Document Index                          1895.............1933
Numerical List                                          1933.......................1981*
Monthly Catalog/
  Catalog of United States
  Government Publications                    1895 .......................................................
CIS U.S. Serial
  Set Index      1789...........................................................................1969
CIS Index to US Executive Branch
  Documents   1789.............................................1909
CIS Index to US Executive Branch Documents   1910........1932
CIS U.S. Congressional
  Committee Hearing Index 1830..........................................................1969
CIS U.S. Congressional
  Committee Prints Index      1830...........................................................1969
```

* **Replaced by coverage in the** *Monthly Catalog of United States Government Publications*
and *Catalog of United States Government Publications*.

Figure 2.2. Chronological Chart of the Indexes.

Poore

A Descriptive Catalogue of Government Publications of the United States . . . , produced by Benjamin Perley Poore, clerk of the Senate Committee on Printing, together with his staff, identifies publications for all three branches of the federal government (although it is particularly weak in its coverage of executive departments). Some of them, however, predate the establishment of the new government in 1789, and others are state and nongovernment publications, including some produced in Europe. The chronologically arranged list has an index (of authors, agencies, and subjects) that contains numerous errors and omissions. Entries in the list describe the publications but do not provide the Serial Set number; *A Descriptive Catalogue of Government Publications of the United States* only covers the Serial Set. As a result, it is necessary to consult the charts in the front of either the *Checklist* or *Tables of and Index*. (The examples below and the CD-ROM illustrate the process for finding the Serial Set number.)

Ames

Dr. John Griffith Ames, the Superintendent of Documents who developed the numbering system for the Serial Set, extended the work of Poore and his team for 1881–1893.[3] His index is considered an improvement over that of *A Descriptive Catalogue*. At the back of Ames's index is a personal name index. For each entry, there is a page number. The rest of the index is divided into three columns:

1. Personal name (corresponding to the index in volume 2);

2. An alphabetically arranged subject index; and

3. Identification of the publication by Congress, session, series, document number, and volume number.

Similar to *A Descriptive Catalogue,* the Ames index only covers the Serial Set, and users must turn to the charts at the front of either the *Checklist* or *Tables of and Index* to translate that information into a Serial Set number. (The examples below and the CD-ROM illustrate the process for finding the Serial Set number.)

Greely

Adolphus Washington Greely supervised a compilation of congressional publications for the early Congresses. His work, *Public Documents of the First Fourteen Congresses, 1789–1817—Papers Relating to Early Congressional Documents*, partially overlaps with *A Descriptive Catalogue* but includes only departmental publications that Congress reissued. The arrangement is chronological by Congress, followed by a name index. A supplement was published in volume 1 of the 1903 *Annual Report of the American Historical Association* (58th Cong., 2d sess.. H. Doc. 745, 343–406).

Tables of and Annotated Index

As previously mentioned, this index contains the charts at the front to facilitate the retrieval of information contained in *A Descriptive Catalogue* or the Ames index. However, the rest of the index provides subject access to portions of the Serial Set. The first column represents the subject, the second column gives the Serial Set number, and the third column covers the document number. Thus, there is no need to look elsewhere for this information. For example, if we seek a document on the "construction of ironclads for the Navy," we find that it is document 70 in Serial no. 1124 (p. 423 of the index). Furthermore, the next line says "same," which means that the document is also Serial no. 1317 (document 86).

Checklist of United States Public Documents

Known simply as the *Checklist*, this work includes charts for the first sixty Congresses that enables users of *A Descriptive Catalogue* and the Ames index to locate Serial Set numbers. Moreover, the *Checklist* is a most useful retrospective bibliography for executive branch publications. There are informative notes on the history of departments and their publications. A second volume was planned, but never produced; it would have included the index. Thus, access is through the "List of Departments, Bureaus, etc." at the end of the volume. For example, anyone searching for the Ethnology Bureau would find that coverage of it begins on page 990 under SI2.1. In other words, the *Checklist* leads to executive branch publications arranged by the SuDocs Classification Scheme. However, in the case of annual reports, there is often a set of brackets with some numbers in it. The numbers are the Serial Set number, thereby showing that the annual report is available in two places: the position of the agency within the SuDocs scheme and the Serial Set. For example, if we wanted the 1900 annual report of the secretary of war covering civil affairs in the Philippine Islands, it is available as W1.1: 1900/v.1, pt.10 and 4079-2.

Finally, it merits mention that the opening charts at the front of the volume (as well as the front of *Tables of and Annotated Index*) contain the *American State Papers*. These congressional publications, considered the most important for the earliest Congresses, are arranged into ten classes (e.g., Foreign Relations, Indian Affairs, Finance, and Military Affairs) and subtitles, and dates. Within the Serial Set, they constitute numbers 01 to 038.[4]

Document Catalog/Monthly Catalog/ Documents Index/Numerical Lists

Moving forward in time, there are the *Document Catalog* (1893–1940) and the *Monthly Catalog* (with the placement of this index on the World Wide Web, "monthly" was dropped from the title). The *Document Catalog* is the first and most comprehensive dictionary catalog of federal publications. It was established by the Printing Act of 1895, which required the Superintendent of Documents to publish a comprehensive index of public documents at the end of each congressional session. Entries are by subject, author, agency, and, often, title. They give reference to the Serial Set for congressional publications. For publications of the executive branch, there is a description, but no SuDocs number is provided. When the next entry says "same," it means that the publication is available through the Serial Set. For example,

Same. (H. Doc. 131, 60th Cong. 2d sess. In v. 101; **8462**.)

The 8462 is the Serial Set number. To identify the SuDocs number, we need to look elsewhere (see below).

The *Monthly Catalog* does the opposite of the *Document Catalog*. It provides the SuDocs number for agency publications (as of 1924), but describes items in the Serial Set; no Serial Set number is provided. Thus, a user would need to check the *Document Catalog* for the Serial Set number.

The *Documents Index* and the *Numerical List* both deal with the Serial Set and are arranged by Congress, session, chamber (House and Senate), document type (e.g., report), and document number. Then, for each entry, they provide the Serial Set number.

As a general guide, anyone searching for the Serial Set can turn to the

Document Catalog;

Monthly Catalog;

Document Index or *Numerical List* (depending on the year); and

CIS U.S. Serial Set Index.

For executive branch publications arranged by the SuDocs scheme,

The *Document Catalog* describes the publication, but does not provide the retrieval number; and

the *Monthly Catalog* provides the number, but only as of 1924. (*Classes Added Reprint Edition of the Monthly Catalog of U.S. Government Publications, 1895–1924,* compiled by Mary Elizabeth Poole [Carrollton Press], added the SuDocs classification numbers for the earlier years.

As a consequence, for anyone seeking a publication in the *Document Catalog* from 1893 to 1924, there are the following options for locating the SuDocs number:

- Up to 1911, check the *Checklist.* Look up the agency in "List of Departments, Bureaus, etc.," and turn to the agency coverage of publications to find the retrieval number.

- From 1924 forward, look in the *Monthly Catalog.* (Some libraries may have a reprinted edition of the *Monthly Catalog* in which Mary Elizabeth Poole, a former documents librarian, used the GPO's shelflist to locate the retrieval number. Poole's reprinted edition contains those numbers.);

- From 1912 to 1924,

  - Look up the agency in Mary Elizabeth Poole's *Document Office Classification* (see Figure 2.1) or John Andriot's *Guide to U.S. Government Publications* (McLean, Va.: Documents Index, 1973–) and find the beginning portion (letter and initial number) of the SuDocs Scheme; and
  - Then, refer to Mary Elizabeth Poole and Ella Frances Smith's *Documents Office Classification Numbers for Cuttered Documents* (see Figure 2.1), which will contain the retrieval number.

Finally, beginning with the 97th Congress (1981–1982), the *Numerical Lists* were renamed, reformatted, and published as a supplement to the *Monthly Catalog*: *Monthly Catalog—U.S. Congressional Serial Set Supplement, 97th Congress, 1981–1982.* With the next Congress, the title was changed to *United States Congressional Serial Set Catalog: Numerical Lists and Schedule of Volumes, 98th Congress: 1983–1984, Entries and Indexes.* Subsequent biennial issues retained this title. Beginning with the 105th Congress (1997–1998), as part of cost saving, Congress directed GPO to discontinue distribution of the bound

Serial Set, except to regional depositories and one library in each state not having a regional depository.

Miscellaneous Sources

The *Checklist of United States Public Documents, 1789–1976*, known as *Checklist '76*, includes the entries found in the 1909 *Checklist*, the *Document Catalog*, and the *Monthly Catalog*. Because it is the shelflist of GPO's old Public Documents Library, which, in 1972, became part of the Printed Archives Branch of the National Archives and Records Administration, there are entries that were never included in any index or catalog. The sixteen-volume *Cumulative Title Index to United States Public Documents, 1789–1976*, a spin-off of *Checklist '76*, was compiled by Daniel Lester, Marilyn Lester, and Sandra Faull. Joe Morehead, in his *Introduction to United States Government Information Sources*, identifies other sources for "assessing older primary sources."[5]

The three-volume *Cumulative Index to Hickcox's Monthly Catalog of U.S. Government Publications, 1885–1894*, compiled by Edna A. Kanely, has cumulative subject and author entries to John H. Hickcox's privately published ten annual catalogs. In addition, Mary Elizabeth Poole compiled a six-volume "Classes Added" *Reprint Edition of Hickcox's Monthly Catalog of U.S. Government Publications, 1895–1899* (Carrollton Press, 1977).

Examples

Let us assume that someone is seeking government publications on the use of camels in military operations of the 1850s. For that time period (see Figure 2.2, page 20), the following indexes might contain useful sources:

A Descriptive Catalogue of Government Publications of the United States

Tables of and Annotated Index to the Congressional Series of U.S. Public Documents

Checklist of United States Public Documents

Taking the first source, *A Descriptive Catalogue of Government Publications of the United States*, we see that on page 1261 (the index), there are two page references (709 and 737) to "Camels, use of, in military operations." Looking at the top of those pages will indicate if either or both covered the 1850s. Since they do, we examine every entry on a page to locate the reference to camels. For example, page 738 covers 1858 and the following entry:

> Letter on Treatment and Use of the Dromedary June 11, 1858
> Senate Mis. Docs. No. 271. 35th Cong., 1st Sess. Vol. IV 35pp.
> Account on the habits, powers, and use of camels; Descriptions of different breeds; The food and drink of camels; Use of dromedaries in military operations, etc.

Note that the first line identifies the document, while lines three through five provide a brief abstract. Line two is most important because it identifies the Serial Set publication by Congress, session, series, and number: 35th Congress, 1st session, Senate Miscellaneous Document, and no. 271. We then take this information to the charts appearing in the front of either the *Checklist* or the *Tables and Index*. For example, page 33 of the *Checklist* contains a chart for the first session of the 35th Congress. The fourth column is for Series. Under it, we see "S. mis docs" followed by three listings of "do" (do is similar to ditto). The fifth column is for document number, and 271 falls within the range "251-273." The last column, "Notes," might indicate that a particular source was not printed or is available elsewhere in the Serial Set, or the note might provide other useful information. Turning to the first column for that entry, we see 987 and column two contains a 4 (for the volume number). Since our publication on camels is in the fourth volume, we confirm the Serial Set number as 987. Thus, assuming that the depository library has a good historical collection for this time period, we can locate Serial Set volume 987 in either the paper or microform collection and within it number 271.

Since the Ames index is an extension of Poore's *A Descriptive Catalogue*, we can search the middle column of both volumes by subject. Once we find a relevant entry, we can see that the third column might say, for instance, S.R. 47-2, vol. 1. No. 883; 14, 10p. This time we would check either the *Checklist* or *Tables and Index* for the chart covering the 47th Congress, 2d session. The series is S.R. (Senate Report) and the document number is 883. If there is no information to the contrary in the Notes, the document is in volume 14 of Senate reports. Turning to the first column, we discover the Serial Set number. A note of caution: If the volume number of the entry does not match what you find in the chart, you have made a mistake. Most likely, you are either looking at a chart of the wrong Congress or session, or the wrong series (e.g., H.R., not the required S.R.).

As another example, in *Magnificence and Misery*, Randall M. Dodd, who edited E. Harzard Wells's "firsthand account of the 1897 Klondike Gold Rush," mentioned the need for a relief expedition and congressional action. The secretary of war was "authorized to purchase and import reindeer, and employ and bring into the country reindeer drivers, not citizens of the United States." The secretary "hired Dr. Sheldon Jackson, an officer of the Interior Department, and instructed him to proceed to Norway and Sweden to purchase 500 domestic reindeer, with sleds, harness and drivers, and transport them to the United States."[6] Assuming an interest in learning more about the introduction of domestic reindeer into Alaska, we turn to the *Document Catalog* (July 1, 1903 to June 30, 1905) and find, for example, the following under "Reindeer:"

1. Education Bureau. 13th annual report on introduction of domestic reindeer into Alaska by Sheldon Jackson, 1903. Mar. 16, 1904. . . . (S.doc. 210, 58th Congress 2d sess. In v. 14; **4599**);

2. Same, without appendix and plates. (In Education Bureau. Report, 1903, 1905. v.2. p. 2365-84);

3. ___ Same, with 4 plates. (In Education Bureau. Education and reindeer in Alaska, 1903, 1904 p. 2365-84); and

4. ___14th same, 1904. Jan 4, 1905 . . . (S. doc. 61, 58th Cong. 3d sess. In v. 2; **4764**).

The first and fourth entries are in the Serial Set, numbers 4599 and 4764. The second and third entry are not; given the time period, we could find the Education Bureau in the *Checklist*'s "List of Departments, Bureaus, etc.," which leads us to the Education Bureau (I16.) and a series of reports on the "introduction of domestic reindeer into Alaska" (I16.8:). Thus, for the 1905 report, the SuDocs number is I16.8: (date), or I16.8:1905 and volume 2. Following this entry in the *Checklist* we see [4931-499], which indicates that this publication is also available in the Congressional Set, or generic Serial Set.

The introduction to the section in the *Checklist* is most informative. It identifies other areas of the Serial Set and the SuDocs classification to check for additional coverage on the introduction of reindeer. For example,

From 1897 to 1906, information relative to reindeer in Alaska is included in annual reports of Education Bureau . . . and also in annual reports of Interior Department . . . as part of the reports of the commissioner of education. The information so included is usually the report of Dr. [Sheldon] Jackson with some alterations without appendixes; for 1904 and 1906, only an epitome appears.

CIS U.S. Serial Set Index

Because this monumental index of the Congressional Information Service (CIS) covers the Serial Set from 1789 to 1969, it includes the *American State Papers* and, on the surface, supersedes other indexes to the Serial Set for all these years. In effect, it appears to be a "one-stop shop." Yet because the index contains numerous errors and omissions, it does not completely replace the other indexes mentioned in this chapter.

The index has two parts, a subject index and a finding list. The subject index has keyword terms derived from the individual reports and document titles. The finding list contains the numerical lists and schedule of volumes, plus an index to individuals and organizations cited in reports on private bills.

CIS Index to US Executive Branch Documents

Similar to other CIS products, the *CIS Index to US Executive Branch Documents* offers both an indexing and a microfiche collection The index consists of twenty-six volumes covering the years 1789 to 1909 and another seven-volume set for the years 1910 to 1932. These indexes complement the *CIS US Serial Set Index* by focusing on the executive branch and its publications, thereby, the publisher would hope, replacing the other retrospective indexes discussed in this section of the chapter.

Summary

There never has been, and probably never will be, a comprehensive index of all publications of the U.S. government. It is important to use Figure 2.2 (page 20) as a guide when using the indexes discussed in this chapter. For any year, make a list of the indexes that apply and then search each for relevant material. An example follows:

- *Education Bureau, Bulletin 34 (1914). Library instruction in universities, colleges, and normal schools. Compiled by Henry R. Evans.* We know that this is a bulletin of the Education Bureau and that it was published in 1914. Thus, we have the following sources to consider: the *Monthly Catalog* and *Document Catalog*.

  Assuming that we do not have access to the reprinted edition of the *Monthly Catalog*, we merely gain confirmation of our entry in the *Monthly Catalog* but see that the bulletin is not part of the Serial Set. Thus, to retrieve the SuDocs number, our date is in the period between the *Checklist* and the *Monthly Catalog* when it began to include SuDocs numbers. Thus, we can turn to Poole or Andriot and see that they explain that I16.3: equals bulletins of the Education Bureau and that we need to insert the year and bulletin number after the colon. Poole and Smith would confirm this fact.

  Note that, if we had access to the reprinted *Monthly Catalog* for the entry, it would say I16.3: 914/45. But our bulletin number is actually 34. Clearly there is a typographical error; we replace 45 with 34: I 16.3: 914/34.

  Note: The indexes might refer to "whole no." Do not confuse this with a SuDocs Number; a whole number is assigned to a serial publication, and it continues from the first issue.

- Next we are seeking a publication on *Christian conditions of Indians* (1822–23). Our pool of indexes includes the *American State Papers*, the *Checklist, Tables of and Annotated Index, A Descriptive Catalogue of Government Publications of the United States,* and *CIS U.S. Serial Set Index.*

  Looking in *Tables of and Annotated Index*, we do not find anything under "Indian," but we locate the entry under "Indians!" It is in the Serial Set: 73(3) and 74(29).

We encourage you to spend some time with the indexes and the CD-ROM accompanying this book as you develop your expertise in the search for publications for the period prior to 1940.

MORE RECENT INDEXES
(PRIOR TO THE ADVENT OF THE INTERNET)

For more recent years (1940 to around 1990), comprehensive bibliographic control of government publications also remained illusive. Access to government publications was still fragmented, with different parties (agencies and the private sector) identifying different sources and deciding on their organization and level of description, how to include them in their products (e.g., indexes) and when, and how to provide access to them (e.g., gratis through a depository program or by subscription from their private sector). Agencies such as GPO and the National Technical Information Service (NTIS) released sources that fell within their jurisdiction, with only a small percentage of overlap. Clearinghouses and the private sector also offered other segments of what the government produced. Thus, anyone seeking access to government publications had to be familiar with the range of sources and changes in them over time.

Monthly Catalog

In the 1940s the *Monthly Catalog of United States Government Publications* was the major general index, and the *Numerical List* served as a companion resource to identify Serial Set numbers. To make searching the various issues and volumes of the *Monthly Catalog* easier, the private sector produced value-added enhancements. For example, in 1975 Carrollton Press issued the *Cumulative Subject Index to the Monthly Catalog of the United States Government Publications, 1900–71* (15 vols.) to assist those trying to conduct a general subject search over time. Two years later, this company offered the *Cumulative Subject Index to the Monthly Catalog of United States Government Publications, 1895–1899* (2 vols.). Perian Press provided *Cumulative Personal Author Indexes to the Monthly Catalog, 1941–1975*. Oryx Press produced five-year cumulative indexes for the *Monthly Catalog* for 1976–1980 and 1981–1985. As Morehead has observed:

> These indexes are invaluable because from September 1946 to December 1962 personal authors were omitted from the ... [*Monthly Catalog*] indexes, including the two decennial cumulative indexes (1941–1950 and 1951–1960). In other years, the *Monthly Catalog* indexed first author only. The Document Catalog includes personal authors, and since July 1976 the *Monthly Catalog* has been thoroughly indexing authorial relationships.[7]

In 1976, GPO joined OCLC, abandoned its old cataloging practices, complied with AACR2 (the Anglo American Cataloging Rules), and adopted Library of Congress subject headings. In July of that year, GPO launched a new and improved version of the *Monthly Catalog*. The publication records that the agency created would subsequently migrate to the private sector, and companies such as Marcive (San Antonio, Texas) began to offer electronic products. One such product is magnetic tapes that individual libraries can use to load depository publications into their online catalog. Another is a CD-ROM version of the *Monthly Catalog* that libraries can use to improve access to their depository collections. The advantage of using a CD-ROM product is that information seekers can search the index across a number of years; in some instances, some of the products permit searching back to mid-1976.

Complementary Sources for Hearings

For congressional hearings published prior to the issuance of the *CIS Index* (see below) or not included in the *Monthly Catalog*, there are the following:

* *Cumulative Index of Congressional Committee Hearings (not confidential in character) from the Ninetieth Congress (January 10, 1967) through Ninety-First Congress (January 2, 1971). Together with Selected Committee Prints in the U.S. Senate Library* (1971). Y1.3:H35/2/959/supp.2.

* *Quadrennial Supplement to Cumulative Index of Congressional Committee Hearings (not confidential in character) from Eighty-Sixth Congress (January 7, 1959) through Eighty-Seventh Congress (January 3, 1963) together with Selected Committee Prints in the U.S. Senate Library* (1963). Y1.3:H35/2/959/supp.2.

* *Cumulative Index of Congressional Committee hearings (not confidential in character) from Seventy-Fourth Congress (January 3, 1935) through Eighty-Fifth Congress (January 3, 1959) in the U.S. Senate Library* (1959).

* *Shelf List of Congressional Committee hearings (not confidential in character) in the U.S. Senate Library from Seventy-Fourth Congress (January 3, 1935) through Eight-Fifth Congress (January 3, 1959)* (Greenwood Press, 1973).

* *Index to Congressional Committee Hearings in the Library of the U.S. House of Representative. Prior to January 1, 1951* (1954). Y1.2:H35/951.

* *Index to Congressional Committee Hearings . . . Prior to March 4, 1935 in the U.S. Senate Library* (1935).

The Later Serial Set

The *Numerical Lists* served as a retrieval guide to the bound volumes of the Serial Set until 1980, when, for a while, special editions of the *Monthly Catalog* covered a Congress (two sessions), provided complete bibliographic information on these publications, and organized entries by SuDocs classification. Beginning in the 1980s, the *Monthly Catalog* included the Serial Set as Y1. publications, and there is no longer a bound set.

The Readex Collection

In 1953 the Readex Microprint Corporation began microfilming and selling the text of nondepository titles in the *Monthly Catalog* as a microprint, and in 1956 the company added depository titles to its collection. Beginning in 1981, Readex switched to the more widely used microfiche medium. Depository libraries may have purchased one or both sets to supplement the holdings they received from GPO. For older publications, librarians and the public may have to use microprint and the special readers (and printers) required to access their content.

National Technical Information Service

The National Technical Information Service (NTIS), an agency of the Department of Commerce and its predecessor agencies, is a clearinghouse. As such, it "serves as a repository for publications on subjects defined as falling within the scope of its acquisition policy," "actively solicits publications that fit its subject profile," "evaluates the publications it has received to determine whether or not their quality and significance merit their inclusion in the archival collection," "provides a mechanism for the announcement of publication in its collection through an abstracting and indexing service," and "actively engages in a dissemination process through various marketing mechanisms."[8] Although NTIS has expanded the types of information products and services it offers, historically its collections and services have focused on technical reports—research and development reports—typically aimed at the scientific, technical, engineering, and business communities. *Government Reports Announcements and Index* (*GRA&I*), prior to the Internet age, was the agency's major indexing and abstracting service.

Congressional Information Service

In 1970, CIS began to produce the *CIS Index* for congressional publications. This indexing and abstracting service covers the literature of Congress: hearings, prints, documents, reports, and special publications. These publications might be available from the government (e.g., issuing committee or GPO) or for purchase from the CIS microfiche collection; depository libraries might have subscribed to both the indexing/abstracting service and the microfiche collection. Most important, the *CIS U.S. Serial Set Index* covers through 1969 for reports and documents (but not for hearings and committee prints), and the *CIS Index* provides coverage of reports, documents, hearings, and committee prints since then.

In 1974, CIS began offering the *American Statistics Index*, another indexing and abstracting service, which covers statistical publications of the three branches of government dating back to 1973. Because the federal government is undoubtedly the largest producer of statistical data in the world, this product covers such areas as demographics, crime, economics, health, education, international trade, labor, the environment, and energy. Similar to the *CIS Index*, the holdings for both depository and nondepository publications are available in microfiche.

ERIC Clearinghouses

Established in 1966, the Educational Resources Information Center (ERIC), which is located within the Department of Education, manages a nationwide network that acquires, catalogs, summarizes, and provides access to education literature and resources from a broad range of sources. The network includes sixteen subject-specific clearinghouses and an ERIC Processing and Reference facility. Two of the products produced by ERIC are *Resources in Education* (RIE), which announces "document" literature (e.g., reports of studies funded by the federal government and state governments), and *Current Index to Journals in Education*, which covers the "journal" literature.

Currently, the part of the ERIC collection for the years since 1980 can be searched and ordered online (http://www.ed.gov/pubs/pubsdb.html). Other services include

- AskERIC, which "is a personalized, Internet-based service providing education information to teachers, librarians, students, counselors, administrators, parents, and others" (http://www.askeric.org);

- National Parent Information Network, which "is a pilot project led by the ERIC Clearinghouse on Urban Education at Teachers College and the ERIC Clearinghouse on Elementary and Early Childhood Education to provide information and communications capabilities to parents and those who work with them";

- ERIC News, which covers new products, systemwide administrative announcements, and more (http://www.eric.ed.gov); and

- Resources of individual ERIC clearinghouses and associated Adjunct Clearinghouses (http://www.ed.gov/EdRes/EDFed/ERIC.html) (see also http://search.ed.gov/csi/eric.html).

The Office of Educational Research and Improvement (OERI) and the major OERI-funded institutions (i.e., centers, laboratories, and ERIC) offer

- *ERIC Digests*, which are a series of "two page syntheses of the best, most current research on a topic. . . . A full-text searchable collection of . . .

ERIC Digests is maintained at the Department of Education" (http://www.ed.gov/pubs/collect.html);

- *Research Today*, which "is a series of concise research summaries on current topics of national significance, such as charter schools and professional development" (http://www.ed.gov/pubs/ResearchToday);

- *Education Consumer Guides* and *Education Research Reports*, which "are brief, research-based explanations of current concepts and topics such as school-based management and cooperative learning" (http://www.ed.gov/pubs/collect.html); and

- *CPRE* [Consortium for Policy Research in Education] *Policy Briefs* and *CPRE Finance Briefs*, which "are 8–12 page papers reporting on issues and research in education finance and policy" (http://www.cpre.org/Publications/Publications_Policy_Briefs.htm).

PAIS

Begun in the second decade of the twentieth century by the New York Public Library, *Public Affairs Information Service (PAIS)* is an index that, among its various listings, includes citations to government publications, from the local to the national level in the United States, as well as from international organizations. The index is now available online through FirstSearch, as a fee-based service.

Topical Examples

When searching for publications, for example, relating to "acid rain" or "strip mining," it would be appropriate to check the following indexes (but not necessarily in the following order):

Monthly Catalog

Government Reports Announcements and Index

CIS Index

American Statistics Index

Or when looking for information on the 1962 Cuban Missile Crisis, indexes such as the *Monthly Catalog* and *CIS Index* would provide publications available at that time, and the *Declassified Documents Reference System* contains records subsequently declassified (see Chapter 8).

INDEXES (ELECTRONIC INFORMATION AGE)

During the presidency of William Clinton, agency use of the Internet moved from being a curiosity or experiment to the primary means of agency distribution and dissemination of information resources and services to the public. As a result, the value or importance of traditional indexes to identify what the government produced decreased as people demanded more full-text retrieval from remote sites and as agencies placed a wide collection of information, data, images, and other resources on their Web sites.

FirstGov

Launched in September 2000, FirstGov (http://www.firstgov.gov) is an essential building block in the effort of the Clinton administration and subsequently the Bush administration to create a "citizen-centric government" that provides seamless access to federal government information, services, and online transactions. It "is a public-private partnership, led by a cross-agency board and administered by the Office of FirstGov in the General Services Administration (GSA)'s Office of Governmentwide Policy." Using FirstGov, it is possible to do a basic or advanced search of federal and state government Web sites or to browse government sources and services by topic, such as the following:

- Online Services for Citizens (e.g., "Change Your Address," "Shopping & Auctions," "Find Government Benefit," "Find a Government Job," "Social Security Online," "Apply for Student Loans," "Zip Code Look-Up," "Recreation One-Stop," and much more);

- Online Services for Business ("Business Opportunities," "Business Laws & Regs," "Subcontracting Opportunities," "File Patents & Trademarks," and much more);

- Online Services for Governments (e.g., "Grants," "Geographic Information," "Per Diem Rates," and much more).

FirstGov also provides access to news releases, free e-mail newsletters, federal forms, laws and regulations, telephone directories, answers to questions about government, international resources, and cross-agency portals for sources and services related to senior citizens, students, people with disabilities, workers, and exporters.

GSA officials want to replace the existing search engine with a more powerful one in 2003. The current search engine, which "can search 500 million documents in less than a quarter of a second" and "can handle about 100 million searches a day," "enables Internet users to access 31 million Web pages posted by the federal government and 16 million pages posted by the states and Washington, D.C. But free use is limited, and the government must start paying for FirstGov's search capability by August 2003."[9] The expectation is that the replacement search engine will be able to handle "'unstructured government databases,' such as large databases of geographic or number information," as well as "map occurrences and clusters of keywords" (to identify which departments and agencies are working on related topics) and map concepts (to analyze natural language).[10]

FirstGov offers the hope that comprehensive bibliographic control of federal information products may be realized some time in the future. However, to reach this goal, significant hurdles will have to be overcome (see Chapter 16). Until then, searches of popular topics may identify more than 1,000 sources. In such instances, FirstGov offers search tips so that the information seeker might be able to refine the scope of the search.

Catalog of U.S. Government Publications

In 1999, the *Catalog of U.S. Government Publications* replaced the *Monthly Catalog* on the Internet. However, the *Monthly Catalog* is still produced. Available on GPO Access, the electronic *Catalog*

> is a search and retrieval service that provides bibliographic records of U.S. Government information products—those distributed to Federal Depository Libraries. Coverage begins with January 1994 and new records are added daily. New Electronic Titles [http://www.access.gpo.gov/su_docs/locators/ net/index.html] contains online titles that are the latest entries in the catalog or are in the queue to be added to it. (http://www.access.gpo.gov/su_docs/locators/ cgp/index.html)

The *Catalog* can be searched by keyword (retrieving a maximum of 200 records), title, SuDocs class number, depository item number, GPO stock number, publication date, and cataloging date, or by multiple fields. Some of the products retrieved might be available online through the portable document format (PDF) and linked to an agency URL.

As an example, a search of "campaign finance reform" leads to:

> Term limits on campaign finance reform: which provides true political reform?: hearing before the Subcommittee on the Constitution, Federalism, and Property Rights of the Committee on the Judiciary, United States Senate, One Hundred Fifth Congress, second session, on S.J. Res. 16 . . . and S. 25 . . . February 24, 1998. 1998. United States. Y4.J89/2:S.HRG105-511. [[1042-A]]. Rank: 903 Locate Libraries [Short Record], [Full Record]

The SuDocs number to retrieve the document in a depository library is Y4.J89/2:S.HRG105-511, and 1042-A is the item number, which selective depositories use to identify the categories they want to receive gratis through the depository program.

"Locate Libraries" enables searchers to identify those depository libraries near them likely to have the publication or the item number. The cataloging information on a publication is available at either "Short Record" ("for the user-friendly display") or "Full Record" ("for the full cataloging record"). Those publications for which the record gives a GPO Stock Number may be available for purchase (see the U.S. Government Online Bookstore, http://bookstore.gpo.gov).

Sales Product Catalog

The *Sales Product Catalog* (*SPC*), which replaced the *Publications Reference File* (1976–1997), provides access to publications in the SuDocs sales program. The Online Bookstore, available through GPO Access, leads to the *SPC* (http://bookstore.gpo.gov/index.html), which can be searched by keyword or topic. The Online Bookstore provides access to "best sellers" and new titles. It also identifies the location of the few remaining government bookstores around the nation should the public want to visit them or contact them for access to local sales collections. Furthermore, the bookstore provides ordering information, some CD-ROM and other electronic products, a *Subscription Catalog*, and "a free fax-on-demand service that provides information 24 hours a day, 7 days a week on the products and services available from the Superintendent of Documents" (http://bookstore.gpo.gov) for customers within the United States and Canada. GPO's *Subject Bibliographies*, and an index to the series, are available there.

Browse Topics

Browse Topics, which the University of Central Oklahoma Chambers Library maintains in partnership with the Federal Depository Library Program, provides topical pathfinders to federal government information products. The list (see http://library.ucok.edu/gov/browsetopics) is derived from the subject bibliographies "that are used to categorize the publications, subscriptions, and electronic products for sale by the Superintendent of Documents" (http://www.access.gpo.gov/su_docs/locators/topics/index.html). These bibliographies are available through the *SPC*.

FedWorld

In 1992, NTIS established its portal, FedWorld (http://www.fedworld.gov), which can be browsed by database or searched by keyword (for reports and Web pages). NTIS's home page (http://www.ntis.gov) provides access to the *NTIS Database Search Guide* (http://www.ntis.gov/prs/search/index.asp?), which is useful in understanding the database and structure.

ERIC Clearinghouse

As mentioned previously, ERIC has sixteen subject-specific clearinghouses (see http://www.ed.gov/EdRes/EdFed/ERIC.html), as well as some affiliated clearinghouses and AskERIC, a service on education information for teachers, librarians, students, counselors, parents, and others. The ERIC Clearinghouse on Urban Education at Teachers College and the Clearinghouse on Elementary and Early Childhood Education maintain the National Parent Information Network (NPIN), which provides information for parents. The ERIC Document Reproduction Services (EDRS) is a document delivery service for microfiche documents. Through http://www.eric.ed.gov/searchdb/searchdb.html, it is possible to search the ERIC databases for relevant educational resources.

Congressional Information Service

In an effort to assist libraries and their users in navigating the diverse array of information resources produced in both a print and electronic environment, the Congressional Information Service (http://www.lexisnexis.com), a wholly-owned subsidiary of LEXIS-NEXIS, developed a "most comprehensive, one-stop Website" entitled Statistical Universe™ that includes the *American Statistics Index*, as well as *Statistical Reference Index*, for publications from the private sector and state governments since 1980, and the *Index to International Statistics* for titles from international intergovernmental organizations dating back to 1983. The database, to which institutional libraries subscribe, permits online (Web) searching and full-text retrieval from an archival collection.

One product, Congressional Universe, covers the following items:

- *CIS Index* (since 1970)

- *National Journal* (since 1977)

- *Federal Register* (since 1980)

- CIS legislative histories (since 1984)

- *Congressional Record*, voting records (since 1985)

- Floor votes, campaign contributions from individuals and PACS (since 1987)

- Hearing transcripts, submitted testimony, public laws (since 1988) (Note: With purchase of *Statutes-at-Large* module, public law coverage extends back to 1789.)

- Committee reports, campaign financial data, bills (all versions), bill tracking reports (including Congressional Research Service's Bill Digest) (since 1989)

- *Congress Daily,* member financial disclosures (since 1991)

- Selected committee prints, congressional documents (since 1995)

- Congressional committee schedules (since 1996)

- *United States Code, Code of Federal Regulations*, congressional rules, hot bills and hot topics, committee information (current only) (see http://www.lexisnexis.com/academic/1univ/cong/time_linewhat.htm)

The *Government Periodicals Universe*, which replaced *the US Government Periodicals Index on CD-ROM*, covers articles in approximately 170 current federal publications. It includes retrospective coverage through 1988. Each quarterly update adds approximately 2,500 articles to the *Government Periodicals Universe*.

Some other services that CIS offers on the national government are the following:

- *Reports Required by Congress: CIS Guide to Executive Communication* is published quarterly. "The fourth quarterly printed index is hardbound and cumulates entries for the preceding year" (dating back to 1994). Many of these publications were not sent to depository libraries. Thus, these libraries might purchase the microfiche collection.

- *CIS Index to Presidential Executive Orders & Proclamations*, a twenty-two-volume index that covers these orders and proclamations from 1798 to 1982. Starting with 1983, CIS's *Federal Register Index* covers these resources.

Other Sources

Google is one of the most popular portals, and it has a component for searching federal government sites, those ending in the extension .gov or .mil (http://www.google.com/unclesam). It is not as complete as FirstGov, which has a special relationship with the government. Finally, some indexes described in the previous section and other chapters apply in the Internet age; see Chapter 3 of *U.S. Government on the Web* (2d ed., Libraries Unlimited, 2001), by Peter Hernon, Robert E. Dugan, and John A. Shuler.

GUIDES

In 1936, the Brookings Institution published the first edition of Schmeckebier's *Government Publications and Their Use*. In the 1950s, aided by Roy B. Eastin, Schmeckebier revised the monumental work, which was published in 1961 and republished in 1969.[11] Although parts are long outdated, there is still ample guidance to locating source material produced in the eighteenth and nineteenth centuries. More recently, in 1975, Morehead began his *Introduction to United States Government Information Sources*. The latest edition was published by Libraries Unlimited in 1999. The six editions document the types of publications that GPO depository libraries provide to the public. Morehead also documents the shift from paper publication to microfiche and to electronic products.

Some other guides are the following:

- Anne M. Boyd's *United States Government Publications*, which was revised in 1949 by Rae E. Rips (New York: H. W. Wilson).

- J. H. Powell, *The Books of a New Nation: United States Government Publications, 1774–1814* (Philadelphia: University of Pennsylvania Press, 1957).

- LeRoy C. Merritt, *The United States Government as Publisher* (Chicago: University of Chicago Press, 1943).

- James Bennett Childs, *Government Publications: A Guide to Bibliographic Tools* (Washington, D.C.: GPO, 1942).

- Vladimir M. Palic, *Government Publications: A Guide to Bibliographic Tools* (Washington, D.C.: Library of Congress, 1975). Although the work covers official publications worldwide, there is extensive coverage of the United States.

CONCLUSION

In its more than two centuries of existence, the U.S. federal government has produced a vast array of publications. No single source captures all of them. However, in the future, FirstGov might have the best chance of doing so, although only for certain types of information resources: those placed or retained on the Web. However, such bibliographic control would be for that date forward, not retrospective, and, as resources are removed from Web sites, FirstGov would not necessarily have archival capacity. Thus, anyone searching for government information must be aware of the types of sources mentioned in this chapter and the fact that federal law limits depository distribution to those publications having educational value and general interest to the public. (Incidentally, the Readex collection goes beyond this limitation.)

Searching for government information involves familiarity with special terminology, which other chapters in this book address. Indexes alone do not provide the contents of all resources produced and distributed by the government and aided by the private and nonprofit sectors. Moreover, a real danger with the use of indexes, and especially portals, is that they can create information overload, the availability of more information than the information seeker wants and is willing to consider. Whatever information is discovered must still be evaluated and filtered.

NOTES

1. "The United States Congressional Serial Set has been known by different short or popular names including the serial number set, congressional edition, congressional set, congressional series, and sheep, or sheep-bound, set (owing to its distinctive sheepskin binding)." Joe Morehead, *Introduction to United States Government Information Sources* (Englewood, Colo.: Libraries Unlimited, 1999), 146.

2. See Laurence F. Schmeckebier and Roy B. Eastin, *Government Publications and Their Use* (Washington, D.C.: Brookings Institution, 1969), 6–64.

3. Ames also produced a *Comprehensive Index* ..., which covered the years 1889–1893 (GPO, 1894). It is similar to the 1881–1893 compilation, which was replaced by the biennial *Document Catalog.*

4. Morehead, *Introduction to US Government Information Sources*, 188–89.

5. Ibid., 92–93, 95–97.

6. E. Hazard Wells, *Magnificence and Misery*, ed. Randall M. Dood (Garden City, N.Y.: Doubleday, 1984), 224.

7. Morehead, *Introduction to US Government Information Sources*, 93.

8. Charles R. McClure, Peter Hernon, and Gary R. Purcell, *Linking the U.S. National Technical Information Service with Academic and Public Libraries* (Norwood, N.J.: Ablex, 1986), 3.

9. William Matthews, "Search on for Search Engine," *Federal Computer Week* (July 2, 2001): 14.

10. Ibid.

11. Schmeckebier and Eastin, *Government Publications and Their Use.*

URL SITE GUIDE

Congressional Information Service
    http://www.lexisnexis.com/

ERIC (Department of Education)
    AskERIC
        http://www.askeric.org/

    Clearinghouses
        http://www.ed.gov/EdRes/EdFed/ERIC.html
        http://search.ed.gov/csi/eric.html

    CPRE Policy Briefs

    CPRE Finance Briefs
        http://www.cpre.org/Publications/Publications_Policy_Briefs.htm

    Education Consumer Guides

    Education Research Reports
        http://www.ed.gov/pubs/collect.html

ERIC Digests
    http://www.ed.gov/pubs/collect.html

ERIC News
    http://www.eric.ed.gov/

Research Today
    http://www.ed.gov/pubs/ResearchToday

Searching and Ordering
    http://www.eric.ed.gov/searchdb/searchdb.html

FirstGov
    http://www.firstgov.gov/

Google
    http://www.google.com/unclesam

Government Printing Office
    Bookstore
        http://bookstore.gpo.gov/

    Browse Topics
        http://library.ucok.edu/gov/browsetopics/

    Catalog of United States Government Publications
        http://www.access.gpo.gov/su_docs/locators/cgp/index.html

    GPO Access
        http://www.access.gpo.gov/su_docs/index.html

    New Electronic Titles
        http://www.access.gpo.gov/su_docs/locators/net/index.html

    Sales Product Catalog
        http://bookstore.gpo.gov/index.html

    Subject Bibliographies
        http://www.access.gpo.gov/su_docs/locators/topics/index.html

National Technical Information Service
    http://www.ntis.gov/

    FedWorld
        http://www.fedworld.gov/

    NTIS Database Search Guide
        http://www.ntis.gov/search/index.asp?

Chapter 3

Congress and the Legislative Process

Congress, characterized as "the first branch of government"[1] because it is mandated by the first article of the Constitution, acts through the legislative process, the appropriations process, and oversight activities, as well as its provision of constituent services. Legislation mandates government programs and their administration and establishes the boundaries and functions of government organizations. Each year, Congress creates its own budget, using the president's budget as the starting point of a long and complex process that determines federal spending. Congress sees itself as a watchdog of the public purse and guardian of the public trust. As Roger L. Sperry notes,

> each congressional committee is formally required to continuously oversee the programs under its jurisdiction, and many committees have established oversight subcommittees whose sole responsibility is to perform this task. In addition, each house of Congress has a government operations committee whose primary task is oversight. These committees' efforts are supplemented by those of the auditors, evaluators, and investigators in the GAO [General Accounting Office], as well as by the efforts of a multitude of investigative reporters working for the newspapers and television networks [and organizations on the Internet].[2]

The *legislative process* specifically refers to the process by which a bill becomes public law. Legislation may originate with the president, executive branch departments and agencies, or special interest groups if members of Congress are willing to introduce it, or it may come from the members themselves. Most measures introduced in Congress do not become public law and usually die in committee. Those that do not complete the legislative process by the end of a Congress (two sessions or years) automatically die and must be reintroduced in a subsequent Congress to be considered.

There are differences in the operational arrangements of the two houses of Congress:

The order of business in the Senate is simpler than that of the House. While the procedure of both bodies is basically founded on Jefferson's *Manual of Parliamentary Practice*, the practices of the two bodies are at considerable variance. The order and privileged status of motions and the amending procedure of the two are at less variance than their method of calling up business. The business of the Senate (bills and resolutions) is not divided into classes as a basis for their consideration, nor are there calendar days set aside each month in the Senate for the consideration of particular bills and resolutions. The nature of bills has no effect on the order or time of their initial consideration. (http://thomas.loc.gov/home/enactment/contrasting.html)

TERMINOLOGY

Legislation takes the form of bills and resolutions (joint, concurrent, and simple), and they may be introduced in either chamber, with the exception of measures to raise revenue; according to Article I, section 7 of the Constitution: "All Bills for raising revenue shall originate in the House of Representatives; but the Senate may propose or concur with Amendments as on other Bills." Joint resolutions, like bills, must be passed by both chambers and be signed by the president or vetoed. Concurrent and simple resolutions must be passed by one or both chambers, but they do not require presidential concurrence because they usually relate to procedural matters or express the "sense" of the chamber(s) on a matter.

Most legislative proposals before Congress are in the form of bills and are designated as H.R. (for the House of Representatives) or S. (for Senate) according to the chamber in which they originate, as well as by a number assigned in the order in which they are introduced, from the beginning of each Congress. "Public Bills" deal with policy matters and become public laws if Congress approves them and the president concurs, or if Congress overrides the president's veto. "Private bills" deal with individual relief matters (e.g., immigration and naturalization cases and claims against the government) and also require approval by Congress and the president or congressional override of the presidential veto.

Both bills and joint resolutions (H.J. Res., S.J. Res.) have the same effect; however, joint resolutions are always used to propose amendments to the Constitution. This type of resolution generally deals with a limited matter (e.g., a single appropriation for a specific purpose, or the granting of congressional approval on an executive action). A concurrent resolution (H. Con. Res., S. Con. Res.) expresses the sentiment of Congress to the president or other parties or attends to "housekeeping" matters that affect both chambers (e.g., creation of a joint committee).

A simple resolution (H. Res., S. Res.) deals with matters entirely within the prerogative of one chamber. Most often, such resolutions deal with the rules of a chamber, but they can also be used to express sentiments (e.g., condolences to the family of a deceased member), to offer advice on foreign policy or other executive business, or to create a select (temporary) committee.

STAGES (AND TYPES OF SOURCES) IN THE LEGISLATIVE PROCESS

This section provides an overview of the stages in the legislative process, from the introduction of legislation in Congress to its enactment as public law, and discusses the types of documentation produced at each stage of the process. As congressional analyst Ilona B. Nickels has observed:

> Forwarding a bill successfully through the numerous stages of the legislative process is an art, not a science. The unpredictability of events in the political area and the often unforeseen consequences of any one action can frustrate the most brilliantly conceived legislative strategy. Moreover, the fate of a bill is likely to be affected by factors of policy, personality, procedure and politics that an individual legislative assistant may not be able to influence directly. For example, the involvement or lack of involvement of the President or other executive branch officials, the policies of the congressional leadership, and the seniority and political standing of the Member introducing a bill may all bear on the legislative outcome of a measure.[3]

Introduction

As shown in Figure 3.1 (page 44), a member of either the House or Senate introduces a bill. The motivation of the member might be to see that measure enacted into law. However,

> [a]t times, . . . a bill may be introduced as a means by which an issue can be publicized and interest generated without enactment into law as an objective. In cases where the subject matter is not well known, introducing a measure can germinate the seed of an issue in one Congress with the expectation that this will set the stage for action in a potentially more receptive future session of Congress. A bill may also be introduced to establish a position on a controversial issue, spur desired executive or judicial action, or be introduced at the request of a constituent, interest group, or executive branch official.

> Introducing a new bill may not be necessary in all cases. Given the low percentage of bills introduced which are enacted into law and the trend in recent Congresses to enact fewer laws altogether, a Member may choose to concentrate on amending a measure already receiving active consideration rather than working to get a separate bill enacted. In the House, however, following this course of action requires attention to the rule of germaneness. Other alternatives to developing new legislative exist. Measures that have already seen some action in a previous Congress could provide a Member with a blueprint to follow; or a Member might choose to co-sponsor and actively support an existing House bill; or a Senator with a viable legislative proposal in that chamber might welcome a companion bill in the House.[4]

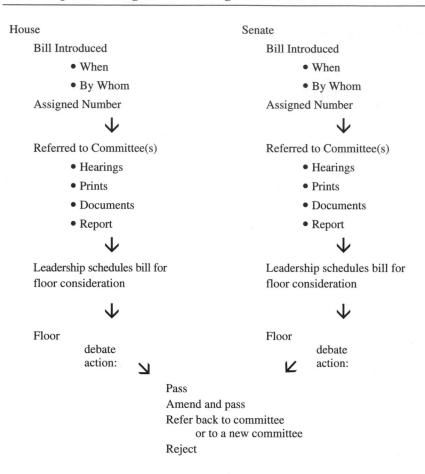

Before the bill is presented to the president both chambers must pass *identical* versions. Thus, they might do one of the following:
- One chamber concurs with the version of the other chamber.
- Each chamber exchanges amendments to a bill and reaches agreement.
- Each chamber can call for a conference committee and appoint members to that committee. The committee then meets and reaches agreement (stated in a conference report). That report is then approved in the House and Senate.

Legislation is then presented to the president, who has the following options (Article I, section 7 of the Constitution):
- Sign the bill into law.
- Not sign the bill but, if Congress is in session, let it become law after 10 days.
- Not sign the bill but, if Congress is not in session, let it fail to become law after 10 days (pocket veto).
- Veto the bill (requires two-thirds vote of Congress in each chamber to override the veto).

Figure 3.1. How a Bill Becomes Law.

Committee Stage

Once introduced, legislation is referred to a congressional committee having jurisdiction over that policy area. Standing committees decide what legislation they will consider; they often do this through subcommittees, which study the legislation, hold hearings and revise it, and report it back to the full committee. Only the full committee can report legislation to the floor of the chamber. In addition to standing committees, there are select, joint, and special committees, but most of these do not have legislative authority.

A committee or subcommittee may decide to hold a public hearing and involve witnesses (other members of Congress, government officials, specialists, interest group representatives, and spokespersons for those affected by the legislation being studied). Such hearings can serve various purposes. They

> may signal a committee's serious intent to report legislation. They can be organized to help a committee gain specific information and advice in order to perfect the policies and the language of legislation it wishes to report. Some hearings are designed to explore whether or not legislation in a given area is necessary. Hearings also can be structured to explore how much public interest in an issue exists, to increase public awareness of the issues involved, or to provide a forum for members so the public . . . [can] express their views or frustration with government policies. Hearings may also be scheduled to investigate problems or to conduct an oversight review of executive branch actions.[5]

After holding hearings, the committee or subcommittee engages in a "markup," a section-by-section review of the measure at which time there might be some revision. If the bill is extensively rewritten, it may be reintroduced as a "clean bill" with a new bill number. Usually hearing transcripts of the committee or subcommittee proceedings are published.

A committee or subcommittee may utilize a "committee print," a publication of varying content and practical value, which is used during consideration of a bill. That print might be prepared by committee staff or outside specialists (e.g., the Congressional Research Service of the Library of Congress).[6] Further, the committee or subcommittee may produce documents or papers, other than hearings and reports (see below) that either chamber orders printed. These documents may be miscellaneous resources compiled by committee or subcommittee staff or requested by members, or they may be reports from (or information provided by) the executive branch. When a committee favorably reports a bill (releases it from committee consideration), it usually produces a written report (H. Rept., S. Rept.) providing the committee's explanation of its action. That report may also contain the views of those in opposition to the legislation. The report language is an important part of a bill's legislative history, and both the judiciary and executive branch may view it as a statement of congressional intent on how public laws are to be implemented. Often judges will refer to committee reports as rationales for their decisions.

It merits mention that

> [c]ommittee consideration may provide a bill's sponsors an opportunity to gauge the extent of conflicting views on the measure, to negotiate reconciliation of disagreements prior to floor action and to prepare counter-arguments or contingency tactics which may be needed if floor action follows. If the committee chooses to report the bill favorably, legislative leadership of the measure could transfer from the original sponsor to the chairman of the committee. In other instances, the committee may choose to consider an alternative measure or to report a clean bill of its own. At times, then, [the] legislative progress may entail a Member's loss of the primary sponsorship of a measure.[7]

It is important to note that the first printing of a bill is known as the *introduced print*, but when the bill is reported out of committee, there is a *reported print* that contains a calendar number and report number. When reported out of a Senate committee, the bill is a *Senate reported print* and has a calendar and report number. A republished bill correcting an error is called a *star print*.

Floor Action (House and Senate)

The next step involves making the decision about which legislation will be considered on the floor, and when. Once the legislation makes it to the floor, it is debated and acted upon (however, within the Senate a filibuster may delay or prevent action). As shown in Figure 3.1 (page 44), action may take different forms. For example, the measure may change through the amendment process. This process may strengthen the legislation, thereby increasing the likelihood of passage.

Both chambers must agree to identical versions of a measure before it can proceed to the president for signature and enactment into law. When passed by one chamber and sent to the other one, the bill becomes a referred (Act) print. When the House passes a bill, an enrolling clerk in that chamber prepares an "engrossed bill" that contains all the amendments agreed to. It is then referred to the appropriate committee, reprinted, and labeled an "Act Print."

Differences between House and Senate versions of a measure might be resolved when one chamber adopts the other's version of a bill. As an alternative, amendments might be effected by both chambers until differences are resolved. The greater the disagreements between the chambers and between Congress and the president, the more likely it is that the bill will go to conference. The conferees are appointed and meet to reach agreement:

> Since the conferees of each house vote as a unit, the House, like the Senate, may appoint as many conferees as it chooses to meet with the Senate conferees to reconcile the difference between the two Houses—the sole purpose of a conference. . . . After deliberation, the conferees may make one or more recommendations; for example, (1) that the House recede from all or certain of

its amendments; (2) that the Senate recede from its disagreement to all or certain of the House amendments and agree to the same; or (3) that the conference committee report any inability to agree in all or in part. Usually, however, there is a compromise. (http://thomas.loc.gov/home/enactment/confcomm.html)

That compromise is relayed to both chambers in the form of a conference report. "Because rejecting a conference committee report would mean either renewing House-Senate negotiations or killing a bill for which considerable momentum toward passage has been demonstrated, most conference reports are adopted."[8]

Final Stage (Enactment)

After a bill is signed by the president or Congress has successfully overridden a veto, it is forwarded to the Office of the Federal Register, National Archives and Records Administration, for registration and publication. A slip law is the first official published form of an enacted bill.[9] Each slip law is published in unbound single-sheet or pamphlet form; nowadays that slip law also appears on the Web. Later, the individual enacted bills appear in the *Statutes at Large*, a chronological arrangement of the public laws for each session of Congress. This bound set has a subject index, a name index for access to private laws, and, since 1991, a popular name index. The *United States Code* is a consolidation and systematic codification of these laws arranged in fifty titles. The *Code* is revised every six years, and a supplement is produced after each Congress.

SOURCES ON THE LEGISLATIVE PROCESS

This section and Figure 3.2 (pages 48–51) identify the sources appropriate to each stage in the legislative process. The figure demonstrates that, over time, these sources have changed. There has been a shift from print to electronic sources for the present-day legislative process. Retrospective coverage may still depend on printed sources, such as those held in depository and other libraries.

THOMAS

Figure 3.3 (page 52) shows the home page for THOMAS (http://thomas.loc.gov), which was inaugurated January 5, 1995, by the Library of Congress at the request of then Speaker of the House Newt Gingrich as the portal for "legislative information on the Internet." This portal permits a search of bills (for the current Congress) by bill number or word/phrase. The center part of the page covers

- Legislation

  - Bill Summary and Status, 93rd–107th Congresses
  - Bill Text, 101st–107th Congresses
  - Public Laws by Law Number, 93rd–107th Congresses

Text continued on page 52.

Present Day*

Date Introduced

THOMAS (*Congressional Record*); GPO Access; and commercial sources such as WESTLAW, LEXIS-NEXIS, CQ Washington Alert, Legi-Slate, *CQ Weekly* (http://libraryip.cq.com), and Congressional Universe

Bill Sponsors

THOMAS (*Congressional Record*); GPO Access; and commercial sources such as WESTLAW, LEXIS-NEXIS, CQ Washington Alert, Legi-Slate, *CQ Weekly* (http://libraryip.cq.com), and Congressional Universe

Bill/Resolutions Text

THOMAS (103rd Congress–); the journals of both chambers; microfiche in depository libraries; *Congressional Record;* GPO Access; and commercial sources such as WESTLAW, LEXIS-NEXIS, CQ Washington Alert, Legi-Slate, and Congressional Universe

Committee Referred to

THOMAS (*Congressional Record*), *CQ Weekly*, *National Journal*, WESTLAW, LEXIS-NEXIS, CQ Washington Alert, Legi-Slate, and Congressional Universe

Committee Hearings

THOMAS (hearing transcripts) (105th Congress–), Web sites of committees for current Congress, *Catalog of United States Government Publications* and GPO Access (printed hearings), Congressional Universe, WESTLAW, LEXIS-NEXIS, Washington Alert, and Legi-Slate

Committee Prints

THOMAS (105th Congress–), GPO Access (Page on "Legislative" publications), including the *Catalog of United States Government Publications*, and Congressional Universe. On occasion, some prints are included in the *Congressional Record.*

Committee Documents

THOMAS (104th Congress–), GPO Access, *Monthly Catalog, Catalog of U.S. Government Publications,* and Congressional Universe

Committee Reports

THOMAS (104th Congress–); GPO Access, including the *Catalog of United States Government Publications;* CIS Congressional Universe; CQ Washington Alert, WESTLAW, LEXIS-NEXIS, and Legi-Slate. Report numbers can be traced through the Calendar of the House of Representatives and History of Legislation, House Journal, Senate Journal, *Congressional Record*, and *Congressional Universe.*

Floor Debate/Action

Congressional Record (THOMAS: 1994; index, 1983– ; history of bills, 1983– ; etc.)

Roll Call Vote

Congressional Record (THOMAS, etc.), GPO Access, Clerk of the House (http://clerkweb.house.gov/), Senate Web site (http://www.senate.gov/legislative/index.html), CIS Congressional Universe, CQ Washington Alert, *CQ Weekly*

(formerly *CQ Weekly Report*) and *CQ Almanac*, Legi-Slate, Congressional Universe, *National Journal*, and *Congressional Roll Call* (Congressional Quarterly, annual)

Conference Committee Report
Clerk of the House (http://clerkweb.house.gov/), beginning with 107th Congress; *Catalog of U.S. Government Publications;* and Congressional Universe

Presidential Decision (Signs or Vetoes)
Weekly Compilation of Presidential Documents, Public Papers of the President, White House Web site (http://www.whitehouse.gov), *Federal Register, Catalog of United States Government Publications*, and *Presidential Vetoes, 1989–1996*, S. Pub. 105-22 (GPO, 1997)

Veto Upheld/Overturned
Congressional Record, CQ Weekly, and *National Journal*

Public Law (Slip Laws)
THOMAS, GPO's Online Bookstore (http://bookstore.gpo.gov/), depository libraries, *United States Law Week* (Bureau of National Affairs) on a selective basis, *United States Code Congressional and Administrative News* (West Group), WESTLAW, LEXIS-NEXIS, Legi-Slate, CQ Washington Alert, and Congressional Universe

Chronological Arrangement of Slip Laws by Congressional Session
Statutes at Large (THOMAS, depository libraries, or GPO's Online Bookstore)

Consolidation and Codification of General and Permanent Laws
United States Code (GPO Access and depository libraries)

1970 up to Electronic Coverage Above

Date Introduced
Congressional Record and *CQ Weekly*

Bill Sponsors
Congressional Record and *CQ Weekly*

Bill/Resolutions Text
Congressional Record, the journals of both chambers, depository libraries (before 1979 they received them in paper copy), *Digest of Public General Bills and Resolutions* (Congressional Research Service, 1936–); however, with the 101st Congress, second session, the print edition ended and was replaced with coverage on THOMAS.

Committee Referred to
Congressional Record, CQ Weekly, and *National Journal*

Committee Hearings
Monthly Catalog of United States Government Publications and then *Catalog of United States Government Publications*, and CIS Index (CIS Congressional Universe)—printed hearings, not transcripts. Note that, except for the *Monthly Catalog* and *CIS Index*, the others listed for the "present day" tend not to cover hearings before 1990. *Checklist & Index of Congressional Hearings, 1958–1960*, by Jeanne K. Androit and John L. Androit (McLean, Va.: Documents Index, 1967).

Committee Prints
> Documents Expediting Project (Library of Congress) collected and distributed prints to its subscribers (prints have eluded depository distribution because committee chairpersons have not been obligated to authorize their distribution or sale). On occasion, some prints are included in the *Congressional Record.*

Committee Documents
> *Monthly Catalog, Numerical Lists*, and *CIS Index*

Committee Reports
> *Monthly Catalog ,Numerical Lists*, and *CIS Index*

Floor Debate/Action
> *Congressional Record, CQ Weekly*, and *National Journal*

Roll Call Vote
> *Congressional Record, CQ Weekly*, and *National Journal*

Conference Committee (report)
> *Monthly Catalog, Numerical Lists*, and *CIS Index*

Presidential Decision (including Veto Message)
> *Weekly Compilation of Presidential Documents; Public Papers of the President; Federal Register;* Web sites for presidential libraries and projects (see http://www.archives.gov/presidential_libraries/index.html); *Monthly Catalog; CIS Index; Presidential Vetoes, 1789–1988*, S. Pub. 102-12 (GPO, 1992); and *Presidential Vetoes, 1989–1996*, S. Pub. 105-22 (GPO, 1997)

Veto Upheld/Overturned
> *Congressional Record*

Public Law
> *Statutes at Large* and *United States Code*. The *Monthly Catalog* includes slip laws.

1780–1970

Date Introduced
> *Congressional Record*

Bill Sponsors
> *Congressional Record*

Bill/Resolutions Text
> *Congressional Record*, the journals of both chambers, *Digest of Public General Bills and Resolutions* (Congressional Research Service, 1936–)

Committee Referred to
> *Congressional Record*

Committee Hearings
> *Monthly Catalog* and the retrospective indexes and bibliographic aids covered in Chapter 3

Committee Prints
> *CIS US Congressional Committee Prints Index* (1830–1969)

Committee Documents
> Indexes to the Serial Set (See Chapter 2.)

Committee Reports
> *Monthly Catalog of United States Government Publications, CIS US Serial Set Index*, and other retrospective indexes to the Serial Set

Journals
> See "A Century of Lawmaking for a New Nation, 1774–1873" on THOMAS.

Floor Debate/Action
> *Congressional Record* and predecessors (see "A Century of Lawmaking for a New Nation, 1774–1873" on THOMAS), *Annals of Congress, Register of Debates*, and *Congressional Globe*

Roll Call Vote
> *Congressional Record*

Conference Committee Report
> *Monthly Catalog, Numerical Lists*, and other historical indexes to the Serial Set

Presidential Decision (including Veto Message)
> Presidential veto messages are published as either House or Senate documents depending on the origin of the bill. Thus they are in the Serial Set. Also *Public Papers of the President, A Compilation of the Messages and Papers of the Presidents, 1789–1897* . . . (53d Cong., 2d sess., H. Misc. Doc. 210) (popularly known after its compiler James D. Richardson); *The Presidential Papers: Washington–Taft* (Provo, Utah: CDex Information Group, 1995) (CD-ROM); presidential paper collections (e.g., the published papers of George Washington); *Veto Messages of Presidents of the United States, with the Action of Congress Thereon* (49th Cong., 2d sess., S. Misc. Doc. 53), compiled by Ben Perley Poore; *Presidential Vetoes: List of Bills Vetoed and Action Taken Thereon by the Senate and House of Representatives*, 1st Congress through 86th Congress, 1789–1961 (1961), compiled by Richard D. Hupman and staff of the Senate Library; *Presidential Vetoes, 1789–1988*, S. Pub. 102-12 (GPO, 1992); *Congressional Record* (lists vetoes and gives the reasons for pocket veto)

Veto Upheld/Overturned
> *Congressional Record* and its predecessors (see "A Century of Lawmaking for a New Nation, 1774–1873" on THOMAS)

Public Law
> *Statutes at Large* (see also "A Century of Lawmaking for a New Nation, 1774-1873" on THOMAS) and *United States Code* (produced since 1926). Slip laws were included in the *Monthly Catalog* and *Document Catalog*.

> *Some useful Web sites are Library of Congress, "United States Legislative Branch" (http://lcweb.loc.gov.global.legislative/congress.html); Office of the Clerk of the House (http://clerkweb.house.gov/); and coverage of legislation by the Library of Congress (http://www.loc.gov/law/glin/GLINv1/glintro.htm).

Figure 3.2. Sources for Tracing the Legislative Process.

- *Congressional Record*
    - Most Recent Issue
    - Text Search, 101st–107th Congresses
    - Roll Call Votes: House (back to 1990), Senate (back to 1989)
- Committee Information
    - Committee Reports, 104th–107th Congresses
    - House Committees: Home Pages, Schedules, and Hearings
    - Senate Committees: Home Pages, Schedules, and Hearings

There is also a link to FirstGov (see Chapter 2) and some high profile bills and reports.

The Library of Congress

THOMAS
Legislative Information on the Internet

In the Spirit of Thomas Jefferson, a service of The Library of Congress

Congress Now: House Floor This Week I House Floor Now I Senate Schedule

Search Bill Text 107th Congress (2001-2002):
Bill Number [ ] Word/Phrase [ ] [Search] [Clear]

Quick Links: House of Representatives I House Directory I Senate I Senate Directory I GPO

LINKS	LEGISLATION	*CONGRESSIONAL RECORD*	COMMITTEE INFORMATION
About THOMAS	**Bill Summary & Status** 93rd - 107th	**Most Recent Issue**	**Committee Reports** 104th - 107th
THOMAS FAQ		**Text Search** 101st - 107th	**House Committees:** Home Pages, Schedules, and Hearings
Congress & Legislative Agencies	**Bill Text** 101st - 107th	**Index** 104th - 107th	
Legislation Related to the Attack of September 11, 2001	**Public Laws By Law Number** 93rd - 107th	**Roll Call Votes:** House Senate	**Senate Committees:** Home Pages, Schedules, and Hearings
How Congress Makes Laws: House I Senate			

Résumés of Congressional Activity

Days in Session Calendar

Executive Branch

Judicial Branch

State/Local

Historical Documents

Status of FY2002 Appropriations Bills

Appropriations Legislation FY1999-FY2001

Legislation Related to the Attack of September 11, 2001

National Bipartisan Commission on the Future of Medicare

The Library of Congress   Contact Us   Please Read Our Legal Notices

Figure 3.3. THOMAS (http://thomas.loc.gov).

The left side of the page explains "About THOMAS?"; answers "Frequently Asked Questions," and links to the home pages of the House and the Senate for the current Congress; covers legislative agencies; and links to the Web sites of the legislative, executive, and judicial branches, as well as state and local governments. Other sources include "Résumés of Congressional Activity," an overview of the legislative process for each chamber, and "Historical Documents." Located within the "Résumés of Congressional Activity" is the *Résumé of Congressional Activity*, which "displays quantitative measures of the workload of each Congress. It is divided into two parts: Data on Legislative Activity and Disposition of Executive Nominations":

> **Résumés** have been printed in the **Congressional Record** since the 80th Congress (1947–1948, though THOMAS has data only from the 91st (1969-1970). A **Résumé** appears in the first issue of the Daily Digest each month and accumulates data from all previous months of the current annual session. Sometime in January after a session is completed, a final **Résumé** for that session appears. THOMAS links to the most recent Daily Digest **Résumé** for the current session of Congress and to the final **Résumés** for all preceding Congresses. (http://thomas.loc.gov/home/summary.html)

The "Days in Session Calendar," which shows those days on which each chamber was in session. THOMAS has these calendars from the 94th Congress (for the House) and the 95th Congress, 2d session (for the Senate) through the 1st session of the 107th Congress.

Included among the historical documents is "A Century of Lawmaking for a New Nation, 1774–1873" (http://lcweb2.loc.gov/ammem/amlaw/lawhome.html), which covers

- Continental Congress and the Constitutional Convention
    - Journals of the Continental Congress
    - Elliot's Debates
    - Farrand's Records
- Statutes and Documents
    - *Statutes at Large*
    - U.S. Serial Set
- Journals of Congress
    - House Journal
    - Senate Executive Journal
    - MaClay's Journal

- Debates of Congress
  - Annals of Congress
  - Register of Debates
  - Congressional Globe

This set of documents also includes "Early Congressional Documents," including the *Federalist Papers,* the Constitution and its amendments, and papers of Thomas Jefferson. Obviously, these documents "comprise a rich documentary history of the construction of the nation, the development of the federal government, and its role in the national life. These documents record American history in the words of those who build our government" (http://lcweb2.loc.gov/ammem/amlaw/lawhome.html).

Public Laws

THOMAS offers coverage of public laws enacted since 1993. These can be searched in "law number sequence" and "bill number sequence." GPO Access (see below), on the other hand, covers public laws beginning with the 104th Congress (1995–1996), and permits searching by Congress or search term (104th Congress–) (http://www.access.gpo.gov/nara/nara005.html). This page also contains "helpful hints for searching Public Laws."

GPO Access

Under "Legislative" publications, GPO Access (http://www.access.gpo.gov/su_docs/legislative.html) covers the following:

Congressional Bills (103rd Congress–)

Congressional Committee Prints (105th Congress–)

Congressional Documents (104th Congress–)

Congressional Hearings (105th Congress–)

Congressional Record (1994–) and *Congressional Record Index* (1983–)

Congressional Reports (104th Congress–)

History of Bills (1983–)

House Calendar (104th Congress–)

House Journal, 1991–1995

House, Senate, and Executive Reports (104th Congress–)

House, Senate, and Treaty Documents (104th Congress–)

Senate Calendar (104th Congress–)

United States Code (2000 and supplements)

Miscellaneous Publications of the House and Senate

GPO Access, at this page, covers House and Senate Manuals, which convey the procedures or rules that each chamber follows. These manuals also appear as part of the Serial Set and, therefore, libraries may have them in either their hardcopy or microform collections. It should be noted that GPO Access is the official source for the materials it covers.

Congressional Record

The official gazette of Congress, the *Congressional Record*, dating from 1873, is the primary written source for a daily account of the floor proceedings of the Senate and the House of Representatives. Not to be confused with the constitutionally mandated journals of the two legislative chambers, which are essentially minute books summarizing the procedural actions of the Senate and the House, the *Congressional Record* serves to inform not only the public about congressional activities, but also the federal courts and agencies, as well as scholars, regarding legislative intent. The need for such a publication was recognized during the Constitutional Convention. James Wilson of Pennsylvania, addressing a proposal that would allow each house of Congress discretion as to the parts of its journal that would be published, told the delegates: "The people have the right to know what their Agents are doing or have done, and it should not be in the option of the Legislature to conceal their proceedings."[10] The secrecy option was retained for each house in the ratified Constitution, and Congress continued to struggle with the reporting issue. Although the House immediately opened its doors to the public to observe its debates and to reporters to unofficially record them, the Senate met in virtual secrecy during its first five years, finally shedding its cloak in February 1794. By 1802, the Senate, in response to a petition from Samuel Smith, voted to permit stenographers and note-takers on the floor, following the practice of the House. Smith was the publisher of the *National Intelligencer*, a thrice-weekly Washington newspaper of growing influence both politically and as a source for other newspapers that reprinted *Intelligencer* accounts of congressional news.

Smith subsequently sold his newspaper to one of his printers, Joseph Gales, who was later joined by his brother-in-law, William Seaton, to form one of the more renowned publishing enterprises in the capital, Gales and Seaton. When Congress decided to embark on production of a contemporary summary of each chamber's floor proceedings, Gales and Seaton received the contract and began publishing the *Registry of Debates* in 1824. Gales handled reporting on the Senate while Seaton acted as his counterpart in the House. Their accounts, written in the first and third persons, covered from the second session of the 18th Congress to the first session of the 25th Congress (1824–1837). After losing their congressional contract, Gales and Seaton embarked on another publication venture in 1834, the *Annals of Congress*. Compiled from newspaper accounts about Congress, the journals of each chamber, stenographic reports of important debates, and unpublished accounts of debates, the *Annals* provided reconstructive abstracts covering the 1st Congress through the 1st session of the 18th Congress

(1789–1824). Funding for the project came from Congress, and the final volumes of the *Annals* were produced in 1856.

In 1833, the year that work on the *Annals* was begun, a rival printing firm operated by Francis Blair and John Rives obtained the congressional printing contract and launched the *Congressional Globe*, displacing the *Register*, which continued publication for a few years thereafter. Thus, between December 2, 1833, and October 16, 1837, when the *Register* was suspended, there were two simultaneous publications of congressional proceedings. During its early years, the *Globe* used an abstract format much like its predecessor but also sought to chronicle every step in the legislative process of the two houses. Subsequently, beginning with the 32nd Congress in 1851, it was written in the first person and was more nearly a verbatim account. Originally a weekly, the *Globe* was required to become a daily, delivered to members of Congress at the time of their next meeting, by a statutory requirement enacted in 1865 (13 Stat. 460). By this time, complaints were being heard about the *Globe's* inability to produce the proceedings of the Civil War and Reconstruction Congress in a timely manner. Moreover, some in Congress favored production of the gazette by the newly established Government Printing Office (GPO) (12 Stat. 117). After a few more years, Congress reached a compromise: For reasons of efficiency and economy, GPO would take over production of the congressional gazette when the *Globe* contract expired at the end of the 42nd Congress (17 Stat. 510). Thus, on March 4, 1873, the *Congressional Record* made its debut, retaining the two-column style of its predecessor until 1941, and has seen modest modifications in the ensuing years, such as the addition of a résumé of congressional activity—the Daily Digest—in 1947.

The *Congressional Record* is divided into four sections: proceedings and debates for each chamber, the Extension of Remarks, and the Daily Digest, a summary of the daily proceedings in each chamber and before each committee and subcommittee (see Figure 3.4). A permanent edition is available to selective depository libraries on microfiche; since 1985, only regional depositories receive the bound edition. At the time of writing, the 1996 volume (volume 142) is in the process of distribution. However, the Congressional Information Service films the bound edition and makes it (and the earlier volumes) available for purchase. Due to revision and rearrangement, the pagination of the final bound edition differs from that of the daily edition. The permanent edition is organized chronologically, with an index volume and a cumulative daily digest volume. The index includes a cumulative history of bills and resolutions. Furthermore, the permanent edition is a revised version. There are numerous instances when members of Congress have exercised their prerogative to revise and extend their remarks. For example, in late September 1986, during a Senate debate over "dial-for-sex" pornographic telephone messages, Jesse Helms inserted a legal brief into the *Record* to support his claim that over-the-phone sex could be banned under the Constitution. That brief, however, contained an unedited transcript of an X-rated message. The permanent edition was revised to remove it.[11]

For each Congress (101st forward), the *Congressional Record* on THOMAS can be searched by word/phrase, member (House or Senate), time period, or part (Senate or House section, Extension of Remarks, or Daily Digest). It is also possible to search the entire database and to specify the number of documents to be retrieved. Those retrieved can be sorted by date.

Daily updates to the *Congressional Record Index*—unedited and unproofed—are made in preparation for publishing the final biweekly edition. Until the final biweekly edition is published, cumulative daily updates are available from the GPO Access system.

There is also a "List of All Index Topics in the Congressional Record Index: Select one of the alphabetical ranges below in which your topic falls. When you have located your topic entry, select it to see *Congressional Record* page references or bill number(s) relevant to your subject. Clicking on a page number will take you to a listing which contains the relevant document in the *Record*. Clicking on a bill number will take you to all of the versions of the full text of that bill." (http://thomas.loc.gov/j107/j107index1.html)

Figure 3.4. Using the *Congressional Record* (THOMAS).

The *Congressional Record* is available on THOMAS, GPO Access, and elsewhere (e.g., LEXIS-NEXIS, including Congressional Universe, CQ Washington Alert, WESTLAW, and Legi-Slate). THOMAS has the *Congressional Record* and full text of legislation from 1989 (101st Congress) to the present. It also has summaries (not the full text) of legislation to 1975 (94th Congress). Congress might cease publication of this edition once the version available through THOMAS (and other distributors) is secure and can be easily and fully searched for specific information.[12]

C-SPAN

The cable television station C-SPAN I carries same day coverage of House debates, and C-SPAN II does the same for the Senate. They may also cover committee hearings, public policy conferences, and so forth.

United States Code

The Office of the Law Revision Counsel, House of Representatives, prepares and publishes the *Code*, which, as already noted, is a consolidation and systematic codification of the general and permanent laws of the nation. Depository libraries receive the bound edition in hard copy and the annual supplements in either hard copy or CD-ROM. The *United States Code*, in electronic form (2000 plus supplements), is available at http://uscode.house.gov/ and GPO Access (http://www.access.gpo.gov/su_docs/legislative.html). It can also be searched through Congressional Universe.

The *United States Code* was first published in 1926. The first codification of laws was in 1875. Because the *Revised Statutes of the United States* contained numerous inaccuracies, a second edition was authorized three years later.

Journals

According to Article I, section 5 of the Constitution, "Each House shall keep a Journal of its Proceedings, and from time to time publish the same, excepting such Parts as may in their Judgment require Secrecy; and the Yeas and Nays of the Members of either House on any questions shall, at the Desire of one fifth of those Present, be entered on the Journal." As a consequence, each Journal is the official record of that chamber's proceedings, but it does not include the verbatim floor debates contained in the *Congressional Record*. As noted above, GPO Access offers the *House Journal*, 1991–1995. The Congressional Information Service produced *CIS Congressional Journals on Microfiche, 1789–1978*, a resource that enabled libraries to fill the gaps in their collections. Also valuable is "A Century of Lawmaking for a New Nation, 1774–1873" on THOMAS.

Other Sources

Congressional Quarterly, Inc. (Washington, D.C.) produces some important publications and an online service, CQ Washington Alert. For example, *CQ Weekly* (formerly *CQ Weekly Report*) contains essays on significant legislation, various public policies, updates on committee activities (e.g, bill status), comparisons of competing versions of bills, voting records, and such. *CQ Almanac* provides a distillation of the information in the weekly service. Both guides cover the current status of legislation and provide retrospective legislative histories. For these and other products and services that the company offers, see http://www.cq.com/products/products.jsp. Furthermore, CQ Press, a division of Congressional Quarterly, Inc., offers assorted guides and other sources on Congress and the federal government.

National Journal Group's Policy Central covers politics and policy. Updated ten times daily, it covers the *National Journal*, a weekly publication; the *Hotline*, a daily news briefing culled from various sources; *Congress Daily*, published twice daily and providing current congressional news; *Technology Daily*, a news source on information technology; the *Almanac of American Politics*, a reference source; and *Research Databases*, providing items such as markup reports and bill status. Information on this product is available by calling (800) 424-2921 or visiting http://nationaljournal.com/about/policycentral.

West Group publishes the *United States Code Annotated* (U.S.C.A.), and LEXIS Law Publishing produces the *United States Code Service* (U.S.C.S.). Both of these products contain the type of information found in the *United States Code*, as well as editorial enhancements, such as cross-references and historical notes.

FedNet provides broadcast coverage of the White House and congressional committees (see http://www.fednet.net). There is a daily schedule for live broadcasts, as well as an archive of past broadcasts and a schedule of future ones. Radio and television broadcasts are available through C-SPAN.org (http://www.c-span.org), which also includes coverage of issues, current events, the Lyndon B. Johnson White House tapes, the *Washington Journal*, and other items.

PERSONAL COPIES

Today, a personal (printed) copy of a House publication might be obtained from "a limited quantity . . . available through the Legislative Resource Center at B 106 Cannon HOB [House Office Building, Washington, DC]. The public may also order documents by phone at (202) 226-5200 for delivery via postal mail." (See http://clerk.house.gov/clerk/Offices_Services/lrc.php for a link to the Legislative Resource Center.) Paper copies of some publications may be available through GPO's Online Bookstore (http://bookstore.gpo.gov) or *FedWorld* (National Technical Information Service), as well as, in some instances, congressional committees.

PRIVATE LEGISLATION

As noted previously, private bills seek relief for one or more individuals, institutions, corporations, and so forth. When a member introduces a private bill for a constituent, it is referred to the House or Senate Judiciary Committee. If reported out of committee favorably, a private bill is considered on the floor on predetermined days of the month. Before final passage, either chamber might refer the claim to the United States Court of Federal Claims for guidance in determining the "facts." Once there is final passage, the president either approves or vetoes the bill (congressional overturn of the veto would be required). When such a bill becomes law, it is assigned a separate slip law number and placed in a separate section of the *Statutes at Large*.

Sources of Information

Relevant sources for private bills are the *Monthly Catalog* (since July 1976); the *House Calendar,* the *House Journal*, and the *Senate Calendar* (see GPO Access); and the *Congressional Record* (see, e.g., THOMAS). For prior years, such legislation was included in the Serial Set and the historical indexes discussed in Chapter 2. The text of private laws is included in the sessional volumes of the *Statutes at Large*, but, since they are not of a permanent or general nature, they are excluded from the *United States Code*.

BILL TRACKING

A number of sources are useful for tracking the status and stage of legislation. Obviously, electronic sources, updated on a regular basis, provide the most current information. THOMAS, with its coverage of the *Congressional Record*, is a very useful source, as are WESTLAW, LEXIS-NEXIS, CQ Washington Alert, Congressional Universe, and Legi-Slate. *CQ Week*, *National Journal*, and *Congressional Index* (Commerce Clearinghouse) provide brief coverage. Slip laws and *United States Code Congressional and Administrative News* give partial coverage of legislative histories.

The bound edition of the *Congressional Record* has an index volume that has a section on House and Senate bills, which provides a brief synopsis of the legislative histories of all bills, both those enacted and those not. In addition, the volume known as the Daily Digest provides supplementary information. Other official sources that provide legislative histories are the *House Journal*, *Senate Journal*, and LOCIS (Library of Congress Information System) (http://lcweb.loc.gov).[13]

Nancy P. Johnson's *Sources of Compiled Legislative Histories: A Bibliography of Government Documents, Periodical Articles, and Books, 1st Congress to 102nd Congress* (Littleton, Colo.: Fred B. Rothman, 1996), provides selective compilations of legislative histories.

The *CIS Index*, from 1970 through 1983, includes legislative history citations in the volume of "Abstracts." Beginning in 1984, detailed legislative history citations are published in a separate volume, *CIS Annual: Legislative Histories of U.S. Public Laws*.

DECIPHERING THE HISTORY OF A BILL IN THE *CONGRESSIONAL RECORD*

The bound edition of the *Congressional Record* contains many parts and issues for one session of a Congress. The final parts include an index volume and a Daily Digest. The index volume contains a subject index that leads to remarks of the members, as well as indexes by House bill number and Senate bill number. If we do not know the bill number, we could turn to THOMAS (for the appropriate years), the *Statutes at Large*, or one of the sources produced by the commercial sector (e.g., *Congressional Index*, *National Journal*, or *CQ Week*).

For example, as already noted, the *Statutes at Large* is arranged, for each year, by public law number, but there is a subject index to the contents. Once we locate the desired act, there is provided, at the top of the page, the Public Law (PL) number and date on which that measure became law. On the left side of the page (in brackets) is the major bill number. Using the bill number, we can turn to the index volume of the *Congressional Record*. If our number begins with H., we turn to the House section; if it is S., we would look in the Senate section. Note that much legislation does not move through the entire process (from introduction to enactment) during one session. As a consequence, our search, most likely, is through two sessions. We might not know if the bill we are tracing became public law; it might be one of the many bills that died in committee or on the floor of one chamber. On the other hand, the bill that we are tracing might be replaced by another measure; it might then be this new measure we want to trace.

For illustrative purposes, let us examine H.R. 2434 for a specific Congress, and the House bills section of the *Congressional Record*, which identifies the bill and provides a brief explanation of it. Then the following abstract appears:

> —Reported with amendments (S. Rept. 104-305), 11314—Amended and passed Senate, 12926—House concurs in Senate amendment with amendments, 28120—Senate concurs win House amendments, 33120—Presented to the President, 33700—Examined and signed in the House, 33701—Examined and signed in the Senate, 33873—Approved [Public Law 104-607].

What does this tell us? First, we see that there is a Senate Report (104-305). Second, the measure passed the Senate, but only after it was amended on the floor. Third, through an exchange of amendments, both chambers agreed to an identical version. There was no need for a conference; we saw no mention of the following:

> House disagreed to Senate amendment and asked for a conference. Conferees appointed, 28116—Senate insisted on its amendments and agreed to a conference. Conferees appointed, 32110—Conference report (H. Rept. 104-487) submitted in the Senate and agreed to, 38133—Conference report submitted in the House and agreed to, 38455—Examined and signed in the Senate, 41000—Examined and signed in the House, 42455—Presented to the President, 44677—Approved (Public Law 104-606), 45551.

Note the references to a conference and the resulting report (104-487). Further, that report was submitted to each chamber and agreed to. Now the bill can proceed to the president.

What else do we learn from the first abstract? First, there is no mention of the early stages of the legislative process: who introduced the measure and when; what committee it went to; whether there were hearings, prints, and documents; or if there was a companion Senate bill. The absence of such information reminds us to look in the previous session's index under the bill number. Here, we should find the answers to most of these questions. If there is mention of "in lieu of," we now have reference to a companion bill. Note that the *Congressional Record* does not identify prints, documents, and hearings. For such information, we need to turn to sources such as the *Monthly Catalog* (or *Catalog of United States Government Publications*), *CIS Index* or CIS Congressional Universe, or GPO Access.

Finally, for both abstracts, each entry is followed by a number (the page number in the *Congressional Record* that covers the specific point). For each page, there is a corresponding date; however, we would have to look at each of these pages to find the date.

If the abstract for both sessions only provides who introduced (sponsored) the measure and listed the committee to which it was referred, that measure failed. It died in committee. Also, if the measure was passed by both chambers in one Congress (two sessions), but in different forms, it would have to be reintroduced if members are to consider it in the next Congress.

The above discussion applies to the bound edition. The paper edition of the *Congressional Record* has a separate, biweekly *Congressional Record Index* that records the legislative history that occurred during that time frame. Information seekers would have to examine all the individual indexes during the duration of Congress's consideration of the legislation and piece together the entire abstract. As an alternative, they could consult one of the other sources on legislative histories previously discussed.

Serial Set and SuDocs Classification Scheme

Some reminders are in order for those preparing a legislative history in a depository library or seeking some of the documentation in these libraries. First, congressional reports, including those emanating from a conference committee, and documents make up part of the Serial Set. Before the 96th Congress, the Serial Set had a numerical designation. Since then, these publications have a SuDocs classification designation within Y1.

Second, congressional hearings and committee prints have a SuDocs classification designation. They are placed in Y4. Moreover, a library's holdings of reports, documents, prints, and hearings might be located in either (or both) a hard copy or microform collection.

TRACING TWO EXAMPLES

This section traces aspects of two legislative histories and the accompanying CD-ROM covers a third one. The purpose of these thumbnail sketches is to illustrate various components of Figure 3.1 (page 44).

The Flag Protection Act

The Flag Protection Act, which was enacted on October 28, 1989 (PL 101-131, 103 Stat. 777), protects the physical integrity of the U.S. flag and provides criminal penalties for the mutilation, defacement, burning, or trampling of the flag. The Act includes an exemption for the disposal of worn or soiled flags, and amends the definition of the flag. It also provides for Supreme Court jurisdiction and expedited procedures in the event of a court challenge to the constitutionality of the Act.

First, various bills and resolutions (S. 607, S. 1338, S.J. Res. 180, H. J. Res. 350, H. R. 2855, H.R. 2978) were introduced in the 101st Congress. On July 13,

18–20, 1989, the Subcommittee on Civil and Constitutional Rights, House Committee on the Judiciary, held hearings (SuDocs: Y4.J89/1:101/24) and, on August 1, 14, September 13–14, 1989, the Senate Committee on Judiciary likewise held hearings (Y4.J89/2:S.hrg.101-355). On September 7, 1989, the House Committee issued a report (H. Rept.101-231) on H. R. 2978 (Y1.1/8: 101-231). The Senate issued two reports (S. Rept. 101-152 on S. 1338 (Y1.1/5: 101-152) on September 29, 1989, and S. Rept. 101-162 on S.J. 180 (Y1.1/5: 101-162) on October 6, 1989).

Turning to the *Congressional Record*, the Senate considered and passed S. 607 on March 16, 1989, and the House did the same for H. R. 2978 on September 12, 1989. The Senate then considered the House bill and passed it on October 5 with amendments. On October 12, the House concurred in those amendments. Because an identical version of the bill (H.R. 2978) cleared both chambers, the legislation proceeded to the president, who allowed it to become law without his signature. In a statement of October 26, 1989, he declared a preference to deal with protecting the nation's symbol by constitutional amendment and not by statute *(Weekly Compilation of Presidential Documents* 25 (October 26, 1989); *Public Papers of the President* (vol. 2, 1989, 1403); Public Papers at http://bushlibrary.tamu.edu/papers). The Act amended 18 U.S.C. 700.

Government Printing Office Electronic Information Access Enhancement Act of 1993

This Act (P. L. 103-40, 107 Stat. 112), which the president signed into law on June 8, 1993, established within GPO a means of enhancing electronic public access to a wide range of federal electronic information; required GPO to establish and maintain an online directory of federal publications stored in electronic format, and to provide online computer access to the *Congressional Record* and the *Federal Register*; and authorized GPO to charge user fees to cover incremental costs of providing federal documents in electronic format, but required that access to the directory and documents be made available to depository libraries without charge.

A series of bills were introduced into both chambers of Congress in the 101st Congress (H. R. 3849), the 102nd Congress (H.R. 2772, H. R. 5983, and S. 2813), and the 103rd Congress (H. R. 1328, S. 564). Some of these bills resulted in hearings before the Subcommittee on Government Information, Justice, and Agriculture, House Committee on Government Operations (Y4.G74/7: In3/22); the Subcommittee on Procurement and Printing, House Committee on House Administration (Y4.H81/3:T53); the Subcommittee on Procurement and Printing, House Committee on House Administration (Y4.H81/3:G74); the Joint Committee on Printing (Y4.P93/1:G74/12 and Y4.P93/1:T22); and the House Committee on House Administration and the Senate Committee on Rules and Administration (Y4.H81/3:IN3/4).

S. 564, which became the enacted bill, was guided by S. Rept. 103-27 (Y1.1/5: 103-27) and H. Rept. 103-108 (Y1.1/8: 103-108). H.R. 1328 was attended by H. Rept. 103-51 (Y1.1/8: 103-51).

On March 22, 1993, the Senate considered and passed S. 564, and the House did the same on May 25. The legislation, therefore, proceeded to the president, who concurred *(Weekly Compilation of Presidential Documents* 29 (June 8, 1993); *Public Papers of the President* (vol. 1, 1993, 820), the electronic version of the Public Papers available through GPO Access, or http://www.clinton.archives.gov).

CONCLUSION

THOMAS provides access to basic publications that explain the legislative process in more detail than is provided in this chapter. In addition, a number of reports from the Congressional Research Service (Library of Congress) provide similar coverage and may be available through the House Rules Committee (http://www.house.gov/rules/crs_reports.htm). Another excellent Web site on the legislative process is "United States Legislative Branch," which the Library of Congress produces (http://lcweb.loc.gov/global/legislative/congress.html). The Documents Center at the University of Michigan Libraries (http://www.lib.umich.edu/govdocs), among its many choices, provides access to a series of choices under the umbrella term "Class Assignments." Some of these relate to legislative histories, including a tutorial.

The next chapter provides additional information about Congress. It focuses on resources not directly related to the legislative process and to the support agencies of the legislative branch.

NOTES

1. Louis Fisher, *The Politics of Shared Power: Congress and the Executive* (Washington, D.C.: Congressional Quarterly Press, 1981).

2. Roger L. Sperry, "Developing Effective Relations with Legislatures," in *Handbook of Public Administration*, ed. James L. Perry (San Francisco: Jossey-Bass, 1989), 184–85.

3. Ilona B. Nickels, *Guiding a Bill through the Legislative Process: Consideration for Legislative Staff.* CRS Report for Congress, 87-288 GOV (Washington, D.C.: Library of Congress, Congressional Research Service, 1987), 1.

4. Ibid., 5–6.

5. Ibid., 22.

6. In a few instances, committee prints have appeared in the *Congressional Record.* One example is "Instances of Use of United States Armed Forces Abroad, 1789–1989," prepared by the Congressional Research Service prepared and entered into the *Congressional Record* (January 3, 1991).

7. Nickels, *Guiding a Bill through the Legislative Process,* 22.

8. Nickels, *Guiding a Bill through the Legislative Process,* 35.

9. The threat of a presidential veto is not an idle threat, as Congress seldom overrides a veto. For example, Congress only did so in eight instances for President Ronald Reagan, one instance for President George H. W. Bush, and two instances for President William Jefferson Clinton.

10. Geoffrey Seed, *James Wilson* (Millwood, N.Y.: KTO Press, 1978), 55.

11. In "Kennedy Becomes Target of Republican Gibes," which appeared in the *Boston Globe* (October 16, 1991), reporter John Aloysius Farrell noted that Senator Orrin Hatch inadvertently referred to a "bridge up in Massachusetts." He later asked that "the reference to Kennedy be stricken from the record and that the bridge in question be changed to a 'bridge in Brooklyn' " (6). See also "Legislator Says Clinton 'Gave Aid to the Enemy'," *Boston Globe* (January 26, 1995); and Michael Wines, "How the Record Tells the Truth Now," *The New York Times* (January 22, 1995).

12. According to GPO, the bound edition of the *Congressional Record* will continue to be printed and distributed to depository libraries.

13. For other examples of sources pertinent for locating citations to legislative histories, see Joe Morehead, *Introduction to United States Government Information Sources* (Littleton, Colo.: Libraries Unlimited, 1999), 162–64.

URL SITE GUIDE

Clerk of the House
House of Representatives
 http://clerkweb.house.gov/
 Legislative Resource Center
  http://clerk.house.gov/clerk/Offices_Services/lrc.php

Congressional Quarterly, Inc.
 http://www.cq.com/products/products.jsp

 CQ Press
  http://www.congress.com

CRS Reports
 http://www.house.gov/rules/crs_reports.htm

C-SPAN.org
 http://www.c-span.org/

Documents Center
 University of Michigan Libraries
  http://www.lib.umich.edu/govdocs

FedNet
 http://www.fednet.net/

FedWorld
 National Technical Information Service
  http://www.fedworld.gov/

GPO Access
> http://www.access.gpo.gov

> Legislative Publications
>> http://www.access.gpo.gov/su_docs/legislative.html

> Online Bookstore
>> http://bookstore.gpo.gov

> Public Laws
>> http://www.access.gpo.gov/nara/nara005.html

LOCIS Library of Congress Information System
> http://lcweb.loc.gov

National Archives and Records Administration
> http://www.archives.gov/index.html

> Presidential Libraries
>> http://www.archives.gov/presidential_libraries/index.html

National Journal Group
Policy Central
> http://nationaljournal.com/about/policycentral

Public Papers (George Bush)
> http://bushlibrary.tamu.edu/papers/1989/89/102607.html

Public Papers (William Clinton)
> http://www.clinton.archives.gov/

THOMAS
> http://thomas.loc.gov/

> A Century of Lawmaking for a New Nation
>> http://lcweb2.loc.gov/ammem/amlaw/lawhome.html

> Congressional Record
>> http://www.access.gpo.gov/su_docs/aces/aces150.html
>> http://thomas.loc.gov

> Early Congressional Documents
>> http://lcweb2.loc.gov/ammem/amlaw/lawhome.html

> Public Laws
>> http://www.access.gpo.gov/nara/nara005.html

United States Code
> http://uscode.house.gov/

> http://www.access.gpo.gov/su_docs/legislative.html

United States Legislative Branch
Library of Congress
> http://lcweb.loc.gov/global/legislative/congress.html

White House
> http://www.whitehouse.gov/

 **Chapter 4**

More on the Legislative Branch

The previous chapter focused on Congress and legislative histories; this chapter examines other aspects of Congress and discusses some of the support agencies: Government Printing Office (GPO), General Accounting Office (GAO), Library of Congress (LC), and Congressional Budget Office (CBO). The LC is also discussed in other chapters, especially 13 and 15. The companion to this volume, *U.S. Government on the Web*, also covers some congressional agencies that are now defunct but whose publications have been preserved on the Web.[1]

CONGRESS

Congress plays a central role in oversight of the executive branch and in the budgetary process. Oversight responsibility rests with congressional committees (those presented in the previous chapter; see http://www.house.gov, http://www.senate.gov). This section briefly highlights the budgetary process and related source material and some other congressional publications, including publications about Congress.

Budgetary Process

In early February, the president submits a comprehensive budget request to Congress outlining the administration's policy and funding priorities and the economic outlook for the coming fiscal year (October 1 to October 1). Compiled by the Office of Management and Budget, the budget estimates spending, revenue, and borrowing levels.

Within Congress, House and Senate budget committees hold hearings and report a concurrent resolution that sets spending authority for the next fiscal year and aggregate spending and revenue levels for the next five years. The resolution also provides aggregate totals with respect to revenues and spending for the federal budget. Once adopted, the resolution does not become public law, as the president does not sign it, but its allocations establish a basis to consider spending and revenue bills on the floors of both chambers.

Appropriations originate in the House and proceed through the Senate. Congress generally passes three types of appropriations measures:

- General appropriation bills allocating funds for the agencies for the next fiscal year;

- Supplemental appropriations bills providing additional funds during the current fiscal year; and

- Continuing appropriation bills providing temporary (or full-year) funding for those agencies whose regular appropriation has not yet been enacted by the start of that fiscal year. (http://www.house.gov/rules/approps_proc.htm)

In May, the House begins consideration of the annual appropriations bills for the next fiscal year based on the discretionary spending allocation specified in the budget resolution and the recommended funding of the appropriations committee. As these bills move through hearings, markup, floor consideration, and conference, they are constrained by the levels and allocations in the budget resolution and through a special rule in the House.

The sources discussed in the previous chapter also pertain to the budget process. They include THOMAS, GPO Access, and the *Congressional Record*, as well as relevant committee and conference reports (Serial Set) and hearings. The Congressional Budget Office (see below) produces an annual analysis of the president's budget at the request of the Senate Committee on Appropriations. Some other reports of the agency analyze programmatic or policy issues that affect the budget and examine the economic outlook (the winter report and the summer update). For an excellent introduction to the budget process, see http://www.house.gov/rules/bud_procres.htm.

Authorization and Appropriations Process

Each chamber of Congress requires this two-step process for establishing and funding federal agencies and programs. First, there must be enactment of authorizing legislation that creates or continues an agency or program. Second, there is enactment of appropriations legislation that provides funds for the authorized agency or program.

The rules for each chamber differ. There are four basic prohibitions in the House: (1) no appropriation without an authorization in law; (2) no authorizing language in a general appropriation bill; (3) no appropriation in an authorizing bill; and (4) no appropriation larger than the amount, if any, specified in the authorization. The Senate, however, allows appropriations for authorizations that it has passed in the same session of Congress (i.e., not only for measures enacted into law, as required by the House). It also permits appropriations for authorized purposes, if proposed by its appropriations committee, by any committee with jurisdiction over that purpose or by a senator if the appropriation appears in the president's budget estimates. Appropriations are also allowed in authorizing measures. Both houses agree that Congress may appropriate less than the authorized amount or no amount at all. The historical rationale for the process has been to prevent delay of appropriation bills caused by disputes over substantive policy. However, disputes still arise because the House and Senate often circumvent the rules of the process.

Financial Disclosure Information

Elected officials are required to file personal financial disclosure reports every year, based on the principle that information concerning possible conflicts of interest should be available to the public. For information on public disclosure, see the Office of the Clerk of the House (http://clerkweb.house.gov/pd/fds.htm). The *Financial Disclosure Reports*, which are available at that site, include information about the source, type, amount, or value of the income of members, officers, some employees of the House, legislative agencies, and candidates for the House. Public disclosure documents filed with the Office of the Clerk are available for inspection at the Legislative Resources Center, B-10 Cannon House Office Building, during normal office hours.

The Federal Election Commission (http://www.fec.gov), an independent executive agency, is responsible for, among other things, ensuring public disclosure of the campaign finance activities reported by political committees supporting federal candidates.

The Center for Responsive Politics, a nonpartisan, nonprofit research group based in Washington, D.C., provides information on public policy issues, in particular those relating to the role that money plays in politics. The Center's Web site (http://www.opensecrets.org) tracks campaign contributions and other issues. Other Web sites, such as http://www.tray.com/fecinfo, also track campaign donations.

Cancellation of a Proposed Rule or Regulation

The Congressional Review Act was part of a package of proposals offered in the Contract with America in 1995. Basically, it authorizes the cancellation of a proposed rule or regulation through the enactment of a joint resolution of disapproval by each house of Congress with presentment to the president for signature—the constitutional process of lawmaking. By applying the Act, Congress can seek to overturn federal rules it opposes within sixty days of being notified of them. The *Chadha* decision (covered later in this chapter) struck the one house veto of executive branch policies, rules, and regulations. The cancellation of an ergonomics regulation was the first actual use of the statute's procedures.

Congressional History

The *Biographical Directory of the United States Congress* has undergone several cumulative editions. One edition covers the years 1774–1989 (S. Doc. 100-34, Serial 13849). The Office of the Clerk of the House (http://clerk.house. gov/histHigh/index.php) provides "Historical Facts," biographical information for past members, and a list of those institutions that maintain collections of papers on former members of Congress. The biographical information "includes biographies of the more than 11,500 individuals who have served in the U.S. House . . . and Senate since 1789 as well as those Members who served during the Continental Congress from 1774 to 1789." There is a list of Speakers of the House since 1789, with links to the biographical directory, as well as a list of women who have served in Congress. Clearly the Web-based source updates the print edition and makes it easy to retrieve biographical information on those serving in the Continental Congress and, later, in the federal Congress.

The Office of the Clerk is "working to make *A Guide to Research Collections of Former Members of the United States House of Representatives* available electronically on the Internet." The *Guide* was originally published during the celebration of the bicentennial of Congress, and the Clerk has continued to collect information as it has been provided by various institutions (http://clerk.house.gov/histHigh/Congressional_History/index.php).

In the Senate, Robert Byrd (D-W.Va.) is well known as a historian of that chamber. He has read his history into the *Congressional Record* and it has been published separately by the Government Printing Office in four volumes. Other pertinent information is available from the Senate Web site (see "Explore the Senate's Past," http://www.senate.gov/learning/learn_history.html). The offerings at the site include the following:

Biographical Directory of the U.S. Congress: archival, biographical, and bibliographic information on all Senators

Oral History Project of the Senate Historical Office: oral histories with former senators, officers, and staff members

Senate Statistics: Majority and Minority Parties (Party Division): coverage begins with the 1st Congress (1789–1791)

Minutes of the Senate Republican Conference, 1911–1964

Minutes of the Senate Democratic Conference, 1903–1964

Key Publications and Publishers

The home pages for the House (http://www.house.gov) and Senate (http://www.senate.gov) provide links to directory information on the members in the current Congress, including their home pages and those of committees and the leadership. Compiled for each Congress, the *Congressional Directory* contains an alphabetical list of members of Congress and their biographies, office listings and district descriptions, state delegations, and committee assignments. It also lists standing committees, and their subcommittees, for both chambers; congressional advisory boards; commissions; terms of service for members; and the Cabinet and principal officers of the executive departments and agencies, the agencies of the Executive Office of the President, independent agencies, and selected boards and commissions. Since the 104th Congress, it has been available online (see GPO Access or http://www.access.gpo/congress/107_pictorial/index.html).

Both Web sites also offer the *Congressional Pictorial Directory*. The online version has a series of files in Adobe Portable Document Format (PDF). These files contain photographs; there is no ASCII text equivalent.

Congressional Quarterly (CQ), founded in 1945, is a leading private sector publisher on Congress. It provides the *Congressional Staff Directory* in both print and electronic forms (http://www.csd.cq.com). The Web version, which is free to CQ service subscribers, contains more than 40,000 names of members and their staffs, as well as support agency personnel. House and Senate members can be found by name, committee, party affiliation, city, country, state, or zip code. Full member listings include photographs, addresses, phone and fax numbers, hyperlinked e-mail and Web addresses, and extensive biographical information. Member pages also have comprehensive staff listings that include legislative responsibilities, e-mail addresses, and biographical information. Committee assignments for members are hyperlinked to committee pages that contain detailed descriptions, majority/minority member rankings, and committee staff. Other searches can be performed by staff name and keyword.

Examples of other CQ products are the following:

- *GovStaff.com*, a Web and CD-ROM product, provides contact information for approximately 100,000 government leaders and staff in all three branches of government.

- *Federal Staff Directory* covers the executive branch, including the independent and quasi-official agencies. It lists senior officials, staff, telephone and departmental fax numbers, biographies, and so forth.

- *Judicial Staff Directory* is similar to the other products in its type of coverage.

Bernan Press (Lanham, Md.), a distributor and publisher of works on the U.S. government and international organizations (see http://www.bernan.com), puts out *The Almanac of the Unelected*, which contains more than 700 personal profiles of senior congressional staff, including those working for the leadership of the House and Senate. *The Almanac of the Executive Branch* is a similar work. There is also *The New Members of Congress Almanac*, which profiles each new member by providing biographical information covering education and other topics and a photograph. Further, it includes election statistics, district data, voter registration statistics, and political analyses. A *Telephone Directory* for each chamber gives telephone numbers and office addresses for members and their staff, committee members and staff, and more. Clearly, these are only some of the many guides and directories available.

GOVERNMENT PRINTING OFFICE

This section provides an overview of information policies relevant to GPO, as well as a discussion of GPO today. The next section reviews GPO's Office of the Superintendent of Documents.

Policy Context

Statutory provisions governing public printing by the federal government, including production, dissemination, management, and oversight, are largely concentrated in the opening chapters of Title 44 of the *United States Code* (chapters 1, 3, 5, 7, 9, 11, 13, 15, 17, 19, 39, and 41). The Government Printing Office, established in 1860, is the principal agent for all printing for "Congress, the Executive Office, the Judiciary, other than the Supreme Court of the United States, and every executive department, independent office and establishment of the Government." Furthermore, such printing "may be done at the Government Printing Office only when authorized by law" (44 U.S.C. 501 (1994)).

Oversight responsibility for the GPO printing system is vested principally in the Joint Committee on Printing (JCP), which was statutorily established in 1846. Composed of the senior members of the House Committee on House Administration and the Senate Committee on Rules and Administration, the JCP is empowered to "use any measures it considers necessary to remedy neglect, delay, duplication, or waste in the public printing and binding and the distribution of Government publications" (44 U.S.C. 103). Although it is not a legislative committee, the JCP contributes to the management of the GPO printing system through the exercise of statutory functions.

Much of the content of the public printing chapters of Title 44 derives from the Printing Act of 1895, the first comprehensive government printing statute (28 Stat. 601). This body of law has been amended and modified by Congress from time to time to accommodate changing technology and policy developments. Since the 1970s, however, monumental challenges have arisen that have prompted a reconsideration of government printing policy and practice and the provisions of Title 44 prescribing them. These challenges include the rise of electronic information; the erosion of the Public Printer's authority to supervise the public printing system; constitutional challenges; and, against a background of budget reduction and government downsizing, the desire for greater efficiency and economy in the production and dissemination of government information products.

Electronic Information

Informing the Nation, an important report produced by the now defunct Office of Technology Assessment, was one voice that called explicitly for defining "GPO's role in the dissemination of electronic formats" and "GPO's role relative to the growth in agency desktop and high-end electronic publishing systems."[2] A response to the recommendations of this report was the passage of the Government Printing Office Electronic Information Access Enhancement Act of 1993 (107 Stat. 112; 44 U.S.C. 4101–4104), which directed the GPO's Superintendent of Documents to provide a system of online access to the *Congressional Record* and the *Federal Register* by June 1994. The Superintendent was given discretion to make available other appropriate publications and responsibility for maintaining an electronic directory of federal electronic information, as well as for operating an electronic storage facility for federal electronic information. In addition to the online *Congressional Record* and *Federal Register*, GPO also created a legislation database containing all published versions of House and Senate bills introduced since the 103rd Congress. The act provided free online access for all depository libraries and cost recovery based on the marginal cost of dissemination for all other users. Subsequently, in December 1995, GPO announced that it was making the GPO Access service directly available over the Internet and that it was dropping the subscription fee.

Erosion of Supervisory Authority

As the GAO reported in April 1994, "for all practical purposes, the framework of laws and regulations used to manage many aspects of government publishing has become outdated" as a consequence of the emergence and use of various new electronic information technologies.[3] GPO was deemed ill-equipped to continue to exercise monopoly control over agency printing-like operations. Moreover, noted the GAO report, "some agencies want to publish their work independent of GPO involvement" and can do so as a "result of significant advances in publishing technologies."[4]

Constitutional Challenges

A third development prompting congressional reconsideration of government publication arrangements is rooted in the Supreme Court's 1983 invalidation of the legislative veto authority of Congress. In the aftermath of the ruling, the executive branch sought more independence to set publication policy and to procure its own printing and information products. In the *Chadha* decision of June 23, 1983,[5] the U.S. Supreme Court found adoption of a simple resolution by one congressional chamber to veto executive action or policy unconstitutional because it was an exercise of legislative power that did not follow the constitutionally prescribed lawmaking process: bicameral consideration and presentation of a bill or joint resolution to the president for signature or veto. The potential breadth of the Court's ruling was signaled by its definition of a legislative act. Whether an action is an exercise of legislative power will depend on its purpose and effect. This ruling concluded that, where such action has "the purpose and effect of altering legal rights, duties and relations of persons . . . outside the legislative branch," it must be effected through the constitutionally-mandated lawmaking process.[6] The broad reach of the Court's rationale was shortly confirmed by its summary affirmation of two appeals court rulings invalidating one- and two-house vetoes of agency rulemaking, and was shortly recognized by the Department of Justice as an effective vehicle to challenge the very foundation of Congress's control of federal printing.[7]

Until *Chadha*, the historic prerogative of Congress to control public printing through the JCP was virtually unquestioned. The basic authority of this committee—to "use any measures it considers necessary to remedy neglect, delay, duplication, or waste in the public printing and binding and the distribution of Government publications"—is sweeping and unqualified (44 U.S.C. 103). Its exercise extends beyond oversight and veto to affirmative direction and control. The JCP's role has been likened to that of the board of directors of a corporation, and it assumed powers of commensurate scope without any serious challenge.[8] This status was confirmed by a decision of the Court of Appeals for the District of Columbia Circuit announced shortly before *Chadha*.[9]

In sum, by 1983, the statutory scheme of Title 44, *United States Code*, as interpreted by the courts, GAO, and the attorney general, appeared to prescribe a predominant role for the JCP with respect to the central tasks of satisfying the printing needs of Congress and the other branches of government and making it possible for the broadest segment of the public to have direct access to government publications. To ensure accomplishment of those tasks, Congress previously had established the JCP to oversee the process and invested it with ample power to enforce compliance, whether directly pursuant to its remedial authority or indirectly through its general management agent, the Public Printer. The JCP had three kinds of authority it could exercise over government printing: (1) statutory requirements that the Public Printer and government agencies obtain JCP approval prior to taking action, (2) regulations promulgation, and (3) managerial and remedial power. In view of this, the authority of the JCP over the Public Printer and federal printing establishment was virtually plenary.

In the aftermath of the *Chadha* decision, the Department of Justice and the Office of Management and Budget (OMB) began to question the long-standing assumption that Congress, through the JCP, had plenary authority to control public printing throughout the federal government.[10] Three years later, the Department of Defense, the General Services Administration, and the National Aeronautics and Space Administration published notice of their intention to implement, on July 1, 1987, a final rule supplanting the current Federal Acquisition Rule (FAR) dealing with the acquisition of printing and related supplies.[11] The agencies explained that revision of the rule was made necessary by *Chadha's* implicit invalidation of the JCP's approval requirement under 44 U.S.C. 501(2), referencing the 1984 opinion of the Department of Justice.

Congress responded by placing an appropriations limitation in the FY1988 legislative branch appropriation measure, proscribing any executive agency procurement of commercial printing, with certain limited exceptions, unless authorized by GPO.[12] The proposed FAR was subsequently withdrawn.

Congress imposed the same limiting language in legislative branch appropriations acts for FY1989, FY1990, and FY 1991, the last making the provision permanent (PL 101-520, sec. 206; 104 Stat. 2274). The legislation for FY1993 repealed the FY1991 provision and substituted one that was broader.[13] In 1994, Congress again altered the limitation by requiring the executive branch agencies to obtain a certification from the Public Printer before procuring the production of certain documents outside of GPO and by expanding the types of materials that were to be produced by GPO (PL 103-283, sec. 207; 108 Stat. 1423, 1440). This modification prompted President Clinton to comment in his July 22, 1994, signing statement that the provision "raises serious constitutional concerns" and to declare that he would "interpret the amendments to the public printing provisions in a manner that minimizes the potential constitutional deficiencies in the Act."[14]

Later, as revealed in a September 19, 1994, memorandum from OMB Acting Director Alice Rivlin to department and agency heads, an accommodation between the two branches was reached concerning public printing: "The leadership of the Congressional committees of jurisdiction has agreed to work with the Administration to produce a legislative approach to solving this problem" of comprehensive reform of federal government printing. As a consequence, she directed the executive departments and agencies "to maintain the *status quo* regarding present printing and duplicating arrangements during Fiscal Year 1995 to allow this initiative to go forward."[15] However, the accommodation proved to be temporary; several weeks later, the Democrats lost majority control of both houses of Congress and congressional reconsideration of public printing arrangements came under new leadership.

Subsequently, some post-*Chadha* judicial rulings, which substantially narrowed the ways in which Congress may directly control executive agency decision making,[16] coupled with Congress's effort to expand the definition of "printing" subject to GPO control to include "duplicating," in the FY1995 Legislative Branch Appropriations Act and the collapse of the Rivlin accommodation after the fall 1994 congressional elections, prompted the Justice Department to issue its most direct legal challenge to congressional control of executive branch printing. In a May 31, 1996, opinion, the Department's Office of Legal Counsel (OLC) found that the current extent of congressional control over the printing operations of GPO, and, in particular, the printing needs of the executive branch, was an unconstitutional violation of the separation of powers doctrine. The OLC also assured all executive branch officers and employees who acted in conformity with its opinion that they would not be subject to liability or sanction even if their actions were contrary to the views and rulings of the Comptroller General.[17] The OLC opinion was a clear indication that challenges to congressional attempts to maintain direct control of executive branch printing were not likely to abate. Indeed, OLC's invitation to ignore the contrary views of the Comptroller General, which would ordinarily deter certifying and disbursing officers from acting contrary to his advice, reflected a serious deterioration of interbranch comity (see 31 U.S.C. 3522–3530).

Reinventing, Downsizing, and Economizing

Shortly after his inauguration, President Clinton initiated a National Performance Review (NPR) by a task force headed by Vice President Albert Gore Jr. The NPR's September report criticized federal government hiring, purchasing, decision-making structure, program duplication, and administrative procedures. To rectify the situation, more than 380 major recommendations were offered, including a proposal to eliminate GPO's monopoly over the procurement of government printing.[18] The NPR report also urged Congress to end JCP's oversight role concerning executive branch printing.[19]

In November 1994 the Democratic Party lost majority control in both chambers of Congress, and the new House leadership prepared to implement its "Contract with America." Formulated before the elections, this reform program sought dramatic changes in a government that was perceived to have become "too big and spends too much." Public printing reform was initially addressed in the 104th Congress with proposals (e.g., H. Res. 24 and H. R. 1924) to downsize GPO, reduce its resources, and privatize public printing.

A provision common to both initial reform proposals—abolition of the JCP—came under consideration at a February 22, 1995, hearing by the House Subcommittee on Legislative Appropriations. The chairman of the JCP recommended that the panel be eliminated and made a zero budget request for it for FY1996. Because the JCP is statutorily mandated, the chairman also proposed that the appropriate language for the panel's abolition be included in the legislative branch appropriations bill and suggested that some JCP responsibilities, staff, and funds be transferred to the Committee on House Oversight (Administration) and the Senate Committee on Rules and Administration. However, for various reasons, there was opposition to this course of action. When the legislative branch appropriations bill was marked up and reported in the House in mid-June, no funds were allocated to the JCP, and its proposed $1,414,000 FY1996 allocation was reduced to $750,000 and divided equally between the Committee on House Oversight and the Senate Committee on Rules and Administration. The Senate Committee on Rules and Administration disagreed with this action and allocated $1,164,000 for the JCP, given floor approval on July 20. Conferees agreed to appropriate $750,000 for the use of the JCP, which both chambers accepted.

A similar pattern of action had occurred earlier with the FY1995 rescission bill. Also, when reporting the nonbinding budget resolution, the House Committee on the Budget, in recommending that public printing currently produced in-house by GPO be performed through competitive bid by private contractors, proposed eliminating the JCP and assigning its oversight responsibilities to the Committee on House Oversight and the Senate Committee on Rules and Administration. However, because the committee had no actual jurisdiction over these matters, these views were offered only as illustrations of savings suggestions for bringing the budget into balance by FY2002.

In the closing days of the 104th Congress, a comprehensive public printing reform bill (H.R. 4280) was offered for discussion. Among the reforms it proposed were replacing the JCP and the Joint Committee on the Library with a new Joint Committee on Information, establishing new organizational and managerial arrangements for GPO, giving Congress greater flexibility in managing the production and dissemination of its publications, accommodating the production of publications in electronic forms and formats, and offering various innovations that promote greater efficiency and economy in the public printing system. At the same time, the Clinton administration continued to pursue a new printing policy that would address various problems to the satisfaction of both Congress and the administration.[20]

In the 105th Congress, Senator John Warner, as chairman of the Senate Committee on Rules and Administration, initiated an effort to develop a public printing reform bill. That effort resulted in the Wendell H. Ford Government Publications Reform Act of 1998 (S. 2288). Among its provisions were creation of a Government Publications Office, which would be an independent entity; and the elimination of the JCP. The bill, however, failed to receive floor consideration.

Later, the 106th Congress sought to make printing competitive in that agencies could seek the lowest cost for publishing and GPO would have to compete for publishing contracts. Even publication for Congress was approached from a position of competition. During the same time frame, the National Commission on Library and Information Science proposed a revision of Title 44 of the *United States Code* that would have reasserted the dominant role of GPO as a central printer and distributor, while requiring federal agencies to disseminate their publications through GPO's depository library program. This proposal, however, failed to be introduced in Congress. However, a background study reasserted seven principles to guide the relationship between the public and private sectors:

1. The federal government should take a leadership role in creating a framework that would facilitate the development and foster the use of information products and services.

2. The federal government should establish and enforce policies and procedures that encourage, and do not discourage, investment by the private sector in the development and use of information products and services.

3. The federal government should not provide information products and services in commerce except when there are compelling reasons to do so, and then only when it protects the private sector's every opportunity to assume the function(s) commercially.

4. The federal government, when it uses, reproduces, or distributes information available from the private sector as part of an information resource, product, or service, must assure that the property rights of the private sector sources are adequately protected.

5. The federal government should make governmentally distributable information openly available in readily reproducible form, without any constraints on subsequent use.

6. The federal government should set pricing policies for distributing information products or services that reflect the true cost of access and/or reproduction, any specific prices to be subject to review by an independent authority.

7. The federal government should actively use existing mechanisms, such as the libraries of the country, as primary channels for making governmentally distributable information available to the public.[21]

The federal government has implemented most of these recommendations with its embracing of electronic government. However, the Web, and not "mechanisms, such as the libraries of the country," has become a primary channel for distributing information and other resources and services to the public.

The GPO Today

An agency of Congress, GPO acquires, prints, and distributes government information. Traditionally, it did so "using conventional printing technologies. But the advent of electronic information technologies—of rapidly evolving computer and telecommunications capabilities—has awakened . . . [GPO] to a new awareness that government information—the content of books, reports, journals, and databases—has an intrinsic value independent of the format in which it is replicated and disseminated." Furthermore, GPO sees itself as being "transformed from an environment dedicated to traditional print technologies to an integrated information-processing operation distinguished by the electronic creation, replication, and dissemination of information."[22]

The Public Printer of the United States, the head of the agency, is an appointive position that requires Senate approval. Congress exercises its oversight through the JCP and the appropriations process. GPO is required by law to recover its printing costs. Its revolving fund for departmental printing "shall be reimbursed for the cost of all services and supplies furnished . . . at rates which include charges for overhead and related expenses" (44 U.S.C. 309). The next section of the *United States Code* (section 310) requires an ordering agency to pay GPO, upon its written request, all or part of the estimated or actual cost of the delivered work, and for GPO to adjust its billing on the basis of actual cost when a customer pays for delivered work in advance.

GPO Access, which emerged from PL 103-40 (the 1993 GPO Electronic Information Enhancement Act; see Chapter 3), is one of the primary portals for gaining access to government information. It provides free access to more than 1,500 databases of federal government publications and complements THOMAS (Library of Congress), which went online in January 1995.

OFFICE OF SUPERINTENDENT OF DOCUMENTS (GPO)

The position of Superintendent of Documents (SuDocs) was initially established in the Department of the Interior by an act of March 3, 1869 (15 Stat. 292) with the responsibility of distributing public documents to depository libraries and to other institutions and officials authorized by law. The position was transferred to GPO and renamed the Superintendent of Documents by the 1895 Printing Act, which also expanded the Superintendent's responsibilities to include bibliographic control and sale of government publications. Sections 62 and 63 of the act required the preparation of three catalogs: a "comprehensive index of public documents," a "consolidated index of Congressional documents," and a "catalog of Government publications . . . which shall show the documents printed during the preceding month, where obtainable and the price thereof." The comprehensive index became the *Document Catalog* (1893–1940), whereas the consolidated index became the *Document Index* (1895–1933) and the *Numerical Lists and Schedule of Volumes* (1933–1980). The monthly catalog became the *Monthly Catalog of United States Government Publications* and was later renamed the *Catalog of United States Government Publications*. In 1947, the JCP declared that the *Monthly Catalog* satisfied the statutory requirements for the comprehensive index.

Structure and Functions

The Office of Superintendent of Documents comprises six principal units: Documents Sales Service, Information Dissemination Policy, Office of Electronic Information Dissemination, Office of Marketing, Technical Support Group, and Library Programs Service (LPS). This last consists of two major components: the Library Division and the Depository Distribution Division. In turn, the Library Division has subdivisions that manage cataloging, depository services, and depository administration.

The major programs of SuDocs include GPO Access, sale cataloging and indexing of government publications, mailing of certain publications for Congress and executive branch entities according to specific provisions of law ("by law") or on a reimbursable basis, the depository library program, and the international exchange program. Under this last activity, pursuant to international compacts (and authorized at 44 U.S.C. 1719), federal government publications are distributed to libraries of other countries in exchange for copies of official publications of those nations, which are then shipped to the Library of Congress.

In fiscal year 2000, SuDocs made approximately 9,000 titles available to the public for purchase and maintained "a large inventory of these documents— about 5.2 million copies . . ., with a retail value of $74 million." However, "the number of titles available for sale and the inventory . . . dropped substantially over the last decade. From fiscal years 1991 to 2000, the number of titles dropped by 7,759, a reduction of 46 percent, and the number of copies in the inventory fell by about 4.8 million copies, a drop of 48 percent." Turning to the depository program, in the same fiscal year, GPO distributed approximately 28,000 publications to over 1,200 libraries.[23]

The Sales Program

The inventory in the sales program consists of various formats: print, CD-ROM, magnetic tape, microfiche, and videos. The prices of these products are governed by law (44 U.S.C. 1708); the formula is based on recovering only the incremental costs for reproducing and disseminating a product, plus a legislated 50 percent surcharge. In addition, designated book dealers and educational institution bookstores are authorized to receive a 25 percent discount on the domestic price of a product when delivered to the dealer's normal place of business. No discount is allowed if the item is shipped to a third party, unless the quantity shipped for a single title is at least 100 copies. These products are sold through mail-order operations in Laurel, Maryland, and Pueblo, Colorado; consigned sales agents from other federal agencies; and government bookstores.

In 1921, GPO opened its first bookstore in its main building. The first out-of-town bookstore opened in Chicago in 1967. A number of these bookstores have now closed. A list of the remaining bookstores, as well as online access to purchase products (through the *Sales Product Catalog*),[24] is available at http://bookstore.gpo.gov. An important product is a numbered series of Subject Bibliographies, issued irregularly and arranged by topic, series, and agency. Such bibliographies highlight products in the sales program. There is a Subject Bibliography Index that lists the titles and numbers of the individual bibliographies alphabetically.

GENERAL ACCOUNTING OFFICE

Established by the Budget and Accounting Act of 1921 (96 Stat. 887, 31 U.S.C. 702) as an independent agency, the General Accounting Office has experienced expanded authority, duties, and responsibilities. Today GAO, which serves as the auditing and investigative agency of Congress,

> exists to support the Congress in meeting its Constitutional responsibilities and to help improve the performance and accountability of the federal government for the American people. GAO examines the use of public funds, evaluates federal programs and activities, and provides analyses, options,

recommendations, and other assistance to help the Congress make effective oversight, policy, and funding decisions. In this context, GAO works to continuously improve the economy, efficiency, and effectiveness of the federal government through financial audits, program reviews and evaluations, analyses, legal opinions, investigations, and other services. GAO's activities are designed to ensure the executive branch's accountability to the Congress under the Constitution and the government's accountability to the American people. GAO is dedicated to good government through its commitment to the core values of accountability, integrity, and reliability. (http://www.gao.gov/main.html)

For coverage of the agency's history, see "The History of GAO," under the heading "About GAO" (http://www.gao.gov/about/history/splas.htm). Complementary works include Darrell H. Smith, *The General Accounting Office: Its History, Activities, and Organization* (Baltimore, Md: Johns Hopkins University Press, 1927); Roger R. Trask, *Defender of the Public Interest: The General Accounting Office, 1921–1966* (Washington, D.C.: General Accounting Office, 1996) (GA 1/2:D36); Frederick C. Mosher, *The GAO: The Quest for Accountability in American Government* (Boulder, Colo.: Westview Press, 1979); and Gerald G. Schulsinger, *The General Accounting Office: Two Glimpses* (Tuscaloosa: University of Alabama Press, 1956).

The Comptroller General of the United States, the head of GAO, serves a fifteen-year term. This long tenure secures for the agency a degree of independence from both the executive branch and Congress so that it can conduct audits and investigations of all other agencies.

The Web site (http://www.gao.gov/main.html) is divided into fourteen choices:

1. From the Comptroller General: The Comptroller General issues decisions and legal opinions.

2. GAO Reports: Updated daily, it is possible to subscribe to a daily e-mail alert for newly released products.

3. Order GAO Products: Order print copies of reports and request reference services

4. Other Publications: Policy, The Yellow Book, Methodology, Guidance, Performance and Accountability Report, Financial Report of the U.S. Government.

5. Employment Opportunities: Current job vacancies, recruitment information, teams, and offices with GAO.

6. About GAO: Its mission, history, annual report, access to records, organization, and photographs.

7. Help Using This Site: How to find reports, help for the visually disabled, privacy policy.

8. For the Press: Reporter's Guide; subscribe to daily e-mail alert, public affairs contacts.

9. GAO Legal Products: Updated daily, these decisions and opinions cover appropriations, bid protests, and major agency rules.

10. GAO's Performance and Accountability Series and High Risk Update: Briefing talking points.

11. GAO Congressional Presidential Transition Effort: GAO products about federal agencies' operations, challenges, and recent performance.

12. FraudNet: Report allegations of fraud, waste, abuse, or mismanagement of federal funds.

13. Commercial Activities Panel: A group to study the federal government's policies and procedures on outsourcing.

14. Market Mechanisms for Student Loans: A study group sponsored jointly by the GAO and the Department of Education.

Number two is an important resource because it provides access to the reports, correspondence, and congressional testimony that GAO has released. The page (http://www.gao.gov/audit.html) also provides special collections, such as reports on homeland security issued since 1980.

GAO reports and testimony are available to depository libraries on microfiche. The reports, in particular, are among the most requested items because of their timely subject matter and thorough analysis (e.g., *Terrorism, Reports from 1980 to Present*; and *Airport Security, Reports from 1980 to Present*). Many depositories retain these reports beyond the five-year retention requirement of the depository library program because of the comprehensiveness of the content.

Access to the reports and testimony has been enhanced through the Web. GAO provides both summaries and full text of the material on its home page back to FY1996. The GAO Archive (back to 1975) also is hosted by GPO Access. Usually within twenty-four hours of being publicly released, GAO reports and/or testimony are posted, in full text, on the Web site. A list of issued reports and testimony, "Today's Reports," is updated daily. It was formerly known as the "GAO Daybook." The full-text database of reports and testimony issued during the previous month is also updated daily.

LIBRARY OF CONGRESS

The Library of Congress (LC), the nation's oldest federal cultural institution, has a collection of nearly 121 million items, which includes printed books, maps, film and television collections, and other media. Several chapters of this book, such as those on intellectual property rights and maps, cover LC. One unit within the agency is the Congressional Research Service (CRS), which provides information, research support, and policy analysis for members and congressional staff as they carry out their various legislative, administrative, and oversight functions. Much of the information produced is not directly conveyed to the public, except as members and staff choose to make it available. Some CRS material is available on the Web sites of committees (e.g., the House Rules Committee and the Senate Democratic Leadership) and members, as well as in the *Congressional Record*, committee prints and documents, and hearing transcripts. University Publications of America (Bethesda, Md.) offers a collection of *Major Studies and Issue Briefs of the Congressional Research Service* from 1916 to date. This microfiche collection lags by one to two years.

Penny Hill Press (see http://www.pennyhill/com/aboutcrs.html) "is the only private supplier of all . . . CRS . . . publications and makes them available individually and by subscription." This publishing company has "all CRS documents issued since 1995, as well as most documents issued during 1993 and 1994, and some issued prior to 1993. Our collection is kept up-to-date at least weekly."

CRS provides *The Constitution of the United States of America: Analysis and Interpretation,* which contains "annotations of cases decided by the Supreme Court of the United States" (see http://www.access.gpo.gov/congress/senate/constitution/index.html).

LC's Law Library provides "research and legal information to the U.S. Congress as well as to U.S. Federal Courts and Executive Agencies, and . . . [offers] reference services to the public." The Law Library has a reading room and a rare book room (see http://lcweb.loc.gov/rr/law/collections.html).

LC's Science Reading Room has a Web page that discusses its collections, finding aids (e.g., Cold Regions Bibliography and Science Tracer Bullet Services Online: "research guides designed for those with only a general knowledge in specific science and technology subject areas"), and services. There is access to "Selected Internet Resources in Science and Technology" (see http://lcweb.loc.gov/rr/scitech).

LC maintains the Global Legal Information Network (GLIN), which "provides a database of laws, regulations, and other complementary legal sources. The documents included in the database are contributed by the governments of the member nations from the original official texts which are deposited . . . in a server initially at . . . [LC]" (see http://lcweb2.loc.gov/law/GLINv1/glintro.htm).

LC also maintains THOMAS (see Chapter 3). One section of this portal covers the "History of Congress" (http://thomas.loc.gov/home/legbranch/history. html). There are historical highlights for both chambers, biographies for past and present members, access to some past congressional documents, a guide to the personal papers of former members, and election statistics dating from 1920 (emanating from the Office of the Clerk). Another useful guide on THOMAS is "Information Sources for Legislative Research" (http://thomas. loc.gov/home/legbranch/otherleg.html). Examples of the listings are hyperlinks to the schedules of both chambers and committees; Federal News Service, which provides transcripts of hearings and statements; and news services (e.g., C-SPAN Web).

CONGRESSIONAL BUDGET OFFICE

The Congressional Budget Office (CBO) was created by the Congressional Budget and Impoundment Control Act of 1974 (88 Stat. 297, 31 U.S.C. 1301). Its "mission is to provide the Congress with the objective, timely, nonpartisan analyses needed for economic and budget decisions, and with the information and estimates required for the congressional budget process" (see http://www.cbo.gov/about.shtml; http://www.cbo.gov/respon.shtml).

CBO's Web site (http://www.cbo.gov) provides access to sources such as the following:

- *Publications.* These are arranged by topics such as "Economic and Budget Projections," "Environment and Natural Resources," "General Government," "Health and Human Resources," and "National Security."

- *Cost estimates.* The agency prepares cost estimates and mandates statements for all bills ordered reported by a full committee of Congress.

- *Testimony.* Here are agency testimony or statements before congressional committees.

- *Other documents.* Occasionally, the agency provide Congress with less formal documents, such as letters or simple tables.

- *Technical papers.* These papers "are preliminary and are circulated to stimulate discussion and critical comment . . . [and] are not subject to CBO's formal review and editing processes."

The Web site provides a list of CBO publications issued since 1975 and arranged by subject area.

CBO publications form a significant portion of the collection in many depository libraries. The most requested titles are *An Analysis of the President's Budgetary Proposal for Fiscal Year ___*; *Budget Options*; *The Budget and Economic Outlook: Fiscal Year ___*; and *The Budget and Economic Outlook: An Update*. CBO is well known for its objective and impartial analyses, which make its publications valuable to scholars, students, and the public.

All of the above-mentioned publications are also available on CBO's Web site, with some enhancements that users might find helpful. For example, the electronic version of *Budget Options* is an interactive version, which offers advanced search capabilities. Users can search the entire volume by word or phrase and specific numbered policy options by budget function, by spending category, and by federal agency; the tables contained in the report showing historical spending can be searched by budget function.

CONCLUSION

In recent years, the Internet and electronic government have expanded the amount and types of government information available to the public, as well as providing the public and special groups with services. Seeking to improve the bond between the public and the Internet, President Clinton spoke of agencies serving "customers," and the Bush administration has referred to "citizen-centric government." Consequently, agencies were instructed to factor these expectations into the delivery of service. At the same time, the new focus has meant an increased availability of legislative branch publications through the Internet, and the need for a congressional committee such as the Joint Committee on Printing that exercises authority over printing has declined. The future of GPO rests less with its role as a printer and more as an agency that operates GPO Access to improve public access to electronic products, maintains a selective sales program, and supports libraries to close the digital divide that exists in the United States. Undoubtedly, agencies such as GPO will continue to change, and replacement systems will likely emerge when there is no longer a need for a centralized printing facility.

NOTES

1. The congressional Office of Technology Assessment (OTA) operated from 1972 to 1995 and was a key resource for Congress in confronting technological issues while devising public policy. The reports it produced provided members of Congress with objective and authoritative analysis of complex scientific and technological issues. The hundreds of reports that it produced during its twenty-three-year history have been widely acknowledged to be nonpartisan and of enduring interest and relevance to policymakers, scholars, researchers, students, and citizens. The 104th Congress voted to withdraw funding for OTA, as part of the "Contract with America," which effectively closed the agency.

The agency's reports were made freely available through GPO's depository library program (FDLP) or for purchase from GPO and the National Technical Information Service. In order that its legacy not be lost, a CD-ROM product was produced. Known as *The OTA Legacy, 1972–1995*, it is available via the FDLP or from GPO's SuDocs. The set includes all reports produced by the agency, together with some other historical material. In addition, an electronic archive was established at the Woodrow Wilson School of Public and International Affairs, Princeton University (http://www.wws. princeton.edu/~ota). The site is mirrored at http//www.access.gpo.gov/ota (GPO).

2. Office of Technology Assessment, *Informing the Nation: Federal Information Dissemination in an Electronic Age* (Washington, D.C.: GPO, 1988), 8.

3. General Accounting Office, *Government Printing: Legal and Regulatory Framework Is Outdated for New Technological Environment*, GAO/NSIAD-94-157 (Washington, D.C.: General Accounting Office, 1994), 3.

4. Ibid., 2.

5. *INS v. Chadha*, 462 U.S. 919 (1983).

6. Ibid., 952.

7. *Process Gas Consumers Group v. Consumer Energy Council of America*, 463 U.S. 1216 (1983); and *United States Senate v. Federal Trade Commission*, 463 U.S. 1216 (1983).

8. See *Congressional Record* 65 (June 4, 1924): 10556; Congress, Senate Committee on Rules and Administration, *Report with Recommendations of the Committee on Rules and Administration on the Joint Committee on Printing*, 95th Cong., 1st sess., S. Rept. 327 (Washington, D.C.: GPO, 1977), 2, 41; *Op. Atty. Gen.* 282, 286–287 (1957).

9. *Lewis v. Sawyer*, 698 F.2d. 1261 (D.C. Cir. 1983). Lewis was decided immediately after three D.C. Circuit rulings overturning a variety of legislative veto provisions.

10. See Department of Justice, Office of Legal Counsel, Memorandum from Theodore B. Olsen, Assistant Attorney General, for William H. Taft IV, Deputy Secretary of Defense, Department of Defense, "Effect of INS v. Chadha on 44 U.S.C. 501, 'Public Printing and Documents' " (Washington, D.C., March 2, 1984);*Congressional Record* (daily edition) 129 (November 11, 1983): H9709; and *Congressional Record* (daily edition) 130 (June 26, 1984): H7075.

11. *Federal Register* 54 (March 20, 1987): 9037.

12. Congress, Conference Committees, *Making Further Continuing Appropriations for the Fiscal Year Ending September 30, 1988*, 100th Cong., 1st sess., H. Rept. 100-498, (Washington, D.C.: GPO, 1987), 1001.

13. See PL 102-392, sec. 207; 106 Stat. 1719–1720. Previous versions were narrower in that they applied only to printing "from commercial sources." The new version applied to virtually all spending by all executive agencies for any printing.

14. *Weekly Compilation of Presidential Documents* 30 (July 29, 1994): 1541–42.

15. Memorandum reprinted in *Congressional Record* (daily edition) 140 (September 29, 1994): E1997–98.

16. *Bowsher v. Synar*, 478 U.S. 714 (1986); *Metropolitan Washington Airport Authority v. Citizens for the Abatement of Aircraft Noise, Inc.*, 501 U.S. 252 (1991); *Federal Election Commission v. NRA Political Victory Fund*, 6 F.3d 821 (D.C. Cir. 1993), cert. dismissed for want of jurisdiction, 115 S. Ct. 537 (1994); *Hechinger v. Metropolitan Washington Airport Authority Board of Review*, 36 F.3d. 97 (D.C. Cir. 1994), cert. denied, 115 S. Ct. 934 (January 23, 1995).

17. Department of Justice, Office of Legal Counsel, Memorandum from Walter Dellinger, Assistant Attorney General for Emily C. Hewitt, General Counsel, General Services Administration, "Government Printing Office Involvement in Executive Branch Printing" (Washington, D.C., May 31, 1996).

18. In 1990, GAO had criticized GPO's monopoly status. See General Accounting Office, *Government Printing Office: Monopoly-Like Status Contributes to Inefficiency and Ineffectiveness*, GAO/GGD-90-107 (Washington, D.C.:General Accounting Office, 1990).

19. Office of the Vice President, *From Red Tape to Results: Creating a Government That Works Better & Costs Less, Report of the National Performance Review* (Washington, D.C.: GPO, 1993), 6–7.

20. See White House, Memorandum from Leon E. Panetta, Chief of Staff, for heads of executive departments and agencies, "Procurement of Printing and Duplication through the Government Printing Office" (Washington, D.C., April 11, 1996); and Department of Justice, Office of Legal Counsel, Memorandum from Walter Dellinger, Assistant Attorney General for Emily C. Hewitt, General Counsel, General Services Administration, "Government Printing Office Involvement in Executive Branch Printing" (Washington, D.C., May 31, 1996).

21. Robert M. Hayes, "An Invited Retrospective Appraisal of the 1982 NCLIS Public Sector/ Private Sector Task Force Report," unpublished report (Department of Library and Information Science, University of California, Los Angeles, August 2000).

22. Government Printing Office, *GPO/2001: Vision for a New Millennium* (Washington, D.C.: GPO, 1991), i, ii.

23. General Accounting Office, *Information Management: Electronic Dissemination of Government Publications*, GAO-01-428 (Washington, D.C.:General Accounting Office, March 2001), 24.

24. The predecessor to the *Sales Product Catalog* was the *Publications Reference File* (1976–1997), a microfiche catalog of all publications currently in stock for sale by the SuDocs.

URL SITE GUIDE

Appropriations Measures (Congress)
> http://www.house.gov/rules/apprpos_proc.htm

Bernan Press
> http://www.bernan.com

Biographical Directory of the United States Congress
> http://clerk.house.gov/histHigh/index.php

Budget Process
> http://www.house.gov/rules/bud_procres.htm

Congressional Budget Office
> http://www.cbo.gov/

Congressional Directory
Congressional Pictorial Directory
> http://www.access.gpo.gov/congress/107_pictorial/index.html

> http://www.access.gpo.gov/congress/cong016.html

Congressional Staff Directory
Congressional Quarterly
> http://www.csd.cq.com

Congressional Historical Facts
Office of the Clerk of the House
> http://clerkweb.house.gov/histrecs/history.htm

General Accounting Office
http://www.gao.gov/main.html

>History
>http://www.gao.gov/abou/history/splas.htm

>Reports
>http://www.gao.gov/audit.htm

>Government Leaders and Staff
>http://www.govstaff.com

>GPO Access
>http://www.access.gpo.gov/

Online Bookstore (GPO)
http://bookstore.gpo.gov/

Guide to Research Collections of Past House Members
http://clerk.house.gov/histHigh/Congressional_History/index.php

House of Representatives
http://www.house.gov

Library of Congress
http://www.loc.gov/

>Constitution of the United States of American: Analysis and Interpretation
>http://www.access.gpo.gov/congress/senate/constitution/index.html

>Global Legal Information Network
>http://lcweb2.loc.gov/law/GLINv1/glintro.htm

>History of Congress
>http://thomas.loc.gov/home/legbranch/history.html

>Information Sources for Legislative Research
>http://thomas.loc.gov/home/legbranch/otherleg.html

>Law Library Reading Room
>http://lcweb.loc.gov/rr/law/collections.html

>Science Reading Room
>http://lcweb.loc.gov/rr/scitech/
>http://lcweb.loc.gov/rr/scitech/catalogs.html

>>Science Tracer Bullets Online
>>http://lcweb2.loc.gov/sctb/

>THOMAS
>http://thomas.loc.gov

Office of Technology Assessment
http://www.wws.princeton.edu/~ota/

http://www.access.gpo.gov/ota/

Penny Hill Press
http://www.pennyhill.com/

http://www.pennyhill.com/aboutcrs.html

Senate
http://www.senate.gov

Explore the Senate's Past
http://www.senate.gov/learning/learn_history.html

Financial Disclosure Information

Campaign Donations
http://www.tray.com/fecinfo

Center for Responsive Politics
http://www.opensecrets.org/

Federal Election Commission
http://www.fec.gov

Office of the Clerk of the House
http://clerkweb.house.gov/pd/fds.htm

Chapter 5

The Presidency

Almost five decades ago, U.S. Supreme Court Associate Justice William O. Douglas, agreeing with a majority of his brethren about a limitation on the powers of the Chief Executive in the *Steel Seizure* case, offered a reminder to the American public:

> The great office of President is not a weak and powerless one. The President represents the people and is their spokesman in domestic and foreign affairs. The office is respected more than any other in the land. It gives a position of leadership that is unique. The power to formulate policies and mould opinion inheres in the Presidency and conditions our national life.[1]

This chapter reminds us that the president can use different fora in which to argue for, develop, execute, and justify policies. Presidential directives are known by various names, and some have prescribed forms and purposes. Executive orders and proclamations are probably two of the best known types, largely because of their long-standing use and publication. Others are less familiar, some because they are cloaked in official secrecy. There is also the oral presidential directive, the sense of which is captured in an announcement that records what the president has prescribed or instructed. In addition to directives, this chapter also covers presidential papers, presidential libraries, and presidential advisory committees and commissions.

EMERGENCY POWERS AND EXECUTIVE ORDERS

Emergency powers are those authorities and controls—deriving in varying degrees from the Constitution, the statutes, or a concept of executive prerogative—used to address an emergency. Although there are varying understandings of what constitutes an emergency, its characteristics generally are a sudden and unforeseen occurrence, endangerment of life and well-being, and requirement of an immediate response for which existing law may not always provide.

Federal law provides a variety of powers for the president to use in response to crises or emergency conditions threatening the nation. This authority is not limited to military or war situations. Some of these powers, deriving from the Constitution or statutory law, are continuously available to the president, with little or no qualification. Others—statutory delegations from Congress—exist on a standby basis and remain dormant until the president formally declares a national emergency pursuant to the National Emergencies Act of 1976, as amended (50 U.S.C. 1601–1651).

There are, however, limits on the president in his exercise of emergency powers. With the exception of the habeas corpus clause, the Constitution makes no allowance for the suspension of any of its provisions during a national emergency. Disputes over the constitutionality or legality of the exercise of emergency powers are judicially reviewable. Indeed, both the courts and Congress can restrain the executive's use of emergency powers, as can public opinion. Certainly Congress can modify, rescind, or render dormant its delegations of emergency authority. Furthermore, in 1976, when legislating the National Emergencies Act, it created a procedure for declaring and terminating a national emergency.

The president may issue executive orders or other directives in conjunction with, or in actually exercising, national emergency powers. Preparatory to exercising emergency powers and related authorities, the president may call upon the federal departments and agencies to engage in planning and preparedness activities. Much of this activity occurred during the Cold War regarding various governmental functions. In 1969, President Richard Nixon signed E.O. 11490, which consolidated the assignment of emergency preparedness functions in a single directive.[2] The most recent version of this order was signed by President Ronald Reagan in 1988. Executive Order 12656 sets out in considerable detail various assignments of planning and management responsibility for national preparedness in the event of any emergency, military or otherwise, threatening the national security of the United States. However, the delegations and provisions of authority described in the order are made on a standby basis. Section 102(b) of the directive states: "This Order does not constitute authority to implement the plans prepared pursuant to this Order. Plans so developed may be executed only in the event that authority for such execution is authorized by law." Such an authorization would occur primarily with a declaration of war by Congress or, to a lesser extent, with a declaration of national emergency by the president.

Executive Orders

Executive orders are one of the oldest types of presidential directive, an early model appearing in June 1789, when President George Washington directed the acting holdover officers of the Confederation government to prepare for him a report "to impress me with a full, precise, and distinct *general idea* of the affairs of the United States" handled by each official. Like most executive orders, this one was directed to, and governed actions by, executive officials and agencies. However, some executive orders, such as those concerning attacks on the United States and relying on the president's constitutional authority, may be of a more profound character. For example, President Franklin D. Roosevelt used an executive order (E.O. 9066) on February 19, 1942, to require the internment of American citizens of Japanese ancestry who were living in certain designated Pacific Coast defense areas.

The issuance of executive orders by presidents not only follows the practice of state governors but also relies on constitutional authority, such as the commander in chief role and the faithful execution of the laws clause, as well as statutory law. Under the new federal government, the Department of State initially was responsible for preserving presidential executive orders. Examples of early presidential directives having the characteristics of executive orders may be found in James D. Richardson's *A Compilation of Messages and Papers of the Presidents* (New York: Bureau of National Literature, 1897). In 1907, the Department of State began to assign identification numbers to both executive orders and proclamations, making a determined, but not totally successful, effort to include previously issued instruments of both types in this accounting.[3] The numbering of executive orders began with an October 20, 1862, instrument signed by President Abraham Lincoln that was denominated an "executive order." The Federal Register Act of 1935 effectively required that both executive orders and proclamations be published in the *Federal Register* (44 U.S.C. 1505). The first executive order so published was E.O. 7316 of March 13, 1936, concerning the enlargement of the Cape Romain migratory bird refuge in South Carolina. Beginning with this instrument, all subsequent presidential executive orders have been collected in periodic *Code of Federal Regulations* Title 3 compilations. Operative statutory authority concerning the issuance of executive orders is found primarily in chapter 15 of Title 44 of the *United States Code*. Regulations governing the preparation, presentation, filing, and publication of executive orders and proclamations are prescribed in E.O. 11030, as amended.

Figure 5.1 (page 94) shows the number of executive orders issued by President Franklin D. Roosevelt and subsequent office holders, as well as the scope of the series for each presidency.

National Emergency Orders

The experiences of two world wars and the subsequent Cold War instilled both great respect for, and a tradition of, planning and preparation for emergency conditions, resulting in designs for continuity of government, civil defense, resource conservation and prioritized use, and the assignment of preparedness responsibilities. During the past forty years, various executive orders have been issued, from time to time, regarding such matters.

Herbert Hoover
(1929–1933)
E.O.s 5075–6070
1,011 E.O.s issued

Franklin D. Roosevelt
(1933–1945)
E.O.s 6071–9537
3,728 E.O.s issued

Harry S. Truman
(1945–1953)
E.O.s 9538–10431
896 E.O.s issued

Dwight D. Eisenhower
(1953–1961)
E.O.s 10432–10913
486 E.O.s issued

John F. Kennedy
(1961–1963)
E.O.s 10914–11127
214 E.O.s issued

Lyndon B. Johnson
(1963–1969)
E.O.s 11128–11451
324 E.O.s issued

Richard M. Nixon
(1969–1974)
E.O.s 11452–11797
346 E.O.s issued

Gerald R. Ford
(1974–1977)
E.O.s 11798–11966
169 E.O.s issued

Jimmy Carter
(1977–1981)
E.O.s 11967–12286
320 E.O.s issued

Ronald Reagan
(1981–1989)
E.O.s 12287–12667
381 E.O.s issued

George Bush
(1989–1993)
E.O.s 12668–12833
166 E.O.s issued

William J. Clinton
(1993–2001)
E.O.s 12834–13197*
364 E.O.s issued

George W. Bush
(2001–Present)
E.O.s 13198– *

*Subject Index available.

Figure 5.1. Executive Orders. Produced by the Office of Federal Register, National Archives and Records Administration (http://www.access.gpo.gov/nara/index.html).

For example, E.O. 10997, signed by President John F. Kennedy on February 16, 1962, directed the secretary of the interior to "prepare national emergency plans and develop preparedness programs covering: (1) electric power, (2) petroleum and gas; (3) solid fuels; and (4) minerals." Such plans were to be "designed to provide a state of readiness in these resource areas with respect to all conditions of national emergency, including attack upon the United States." Among other features, they were to include "systems for the emergency application of priorities and allocations to the production and distribution" of such resources, as well as for the claiming of "materials, manpower, equipment, supplies, and services needed in support of assigned emergency responsibilities and other essential functions of the department." This directive indicated that it conferred no authority "to put into effect any emergency plan, procedure, policy, program, or course of action prepared or developed pursuant to this order. Such authority is reserved to the President." This order was explicitly revoked by E.O., 11490 of October 28, 1969.

NATIONAL SECURITY STATE

The founders and early practitioners of government inaugurated publication of the statutes and publication practices for the federal legislative, executive, and judicial branches. Largely perfected during the nineteenth century, they became a norm of government. With the rise of the administrative state in the twentieth century came a flood of new law that became fugitive because of the lack of an appropriate arrangement for systematic publications. This deficiency was corrected with the creation of the *Federal Register* and the *Code of Federal Regulations*. However, with the subsequent realization of the national security state at the end of World War II and the onset of the Cold War and its penchant for secrecy, publication of the law has become impaired not by circumstances of accident or inadequate means but rather as a consequence of concealment by design.

Presidential Directives

The National Security Act of 1947 (61 Stat. 495, 50 U.S.C. 401) sought to preserve and perpetuate the nation *by any and all means*. In 1951, the president signed an executive order giving almost every government agency broad discretionary authority to classify information "in order to protect the security of the United States."[4] The following year, a still secret presidential directive created the National Security Agency. Not officially acknowledged to exist until 1957, it remains one of the most reticent components of the national security Leviathan.[5]

The heart of the national security state, if for no other reason than its membership, is the National Security Council (NSC). After a modest beginning under President Truman, it gained importance during the Eisenhower administration, waned somewhat during the Kennedy administration, but regained its importance and has remained highly influential ever since. The written policy pronouncements of the president emanating from the Council increasingly appear to have assumed the character of secret law.

Shortly after its creation, the NSC began producing four types of policy papers: basic comprehensive policy statements on a broad variety of national security problems, together with pertinent political, economic, and military pursuit strategies; situation profiles of large geographic areas or specific countries; assessments of mobilization, arms control, atomic energy, and other functional matters; and organizational statements on the Council, foreign intelligence, and internal security structure and activities. The initial products in the series apparently were of the geographical type; the first comprehensive policy statement was completed and given Council approval in November 1948.[6]

The early NSC policy papers were initiated by the Council's members, executive secretary, and staff. Some ideas were also drawn from studies and reports prepared by the State-Army-Navy-Air Force Coordinating Committee, which was subsequently dissolved in 1949. The Department of State reportedly "was the most important single source of project requests, with the Defense Department a close second." Moreover, the early Council papers were drafted primarily by the Policy Planning Staff of the Department of State.[7] Whereas some of these papers came before the Council for information or served solely as a basis for discussion, those containing policy recommendations eventually reached the president. His signature indicated approval of the proposed policy.[8] Also, according to the first NSC executive secretary, if implementing legislation was required for the new policy, it was prepared by the appropriate department(s) and cleared in the usual way with the Bureau of the Budget before submission to Congress.[9] Nonetheless, there was some doubt about the adequacy of these instruments; critics contended they were neither sufficiently precise nor decisive to guide action and "too general for practical implementation."[10]

As a consequence of President Truman's NSC reorganization of July 1950, the procedure for policy paper preparation was somewhat tightened. Subsequent Council products were mostly concerned with regional policy, and these were initially drafted by the Department of State. When President Eisenhower took office, approximately 100 NSC papers were in effect as operative policy.[11]

During his tenure, President Eisenhower made greater use of the NSC than had his predecessor, and the NSC system became larger and more formal. These changes were reflected in the process of NSC policy paper preparation. Now, almost any part of the NSC system, from the president on down, might suggest topics for policy papers. In response, a preliminary staff study might be prepared within the NSC Planning Board, a new body composed of assistant secretary-level officials representing agencies having permanent or standing membership on the NSC. A first draft using the preliminary staff study would then be produced by the agency of primary interest, followed by various reviews, revisions, and, ultimately, presentation to the president. A new component of the NSC policy papers during this period was a "financial appendix" to indicate the fiscal implications of proposed policy.[12] The sequential numbering system for NSC papers begun by the Truman administration was continued by the Eisenhower administration. As a result, some 270 to 300 NSC policy papers were accounted for at the end of Eisenhower's second term. Many of them went through major revisions after their initial issuance. Indeed, in preparation for its successor, the Eisenhower administration updated almost every operative NSC paper, approving no less than eighteen revamped policies in its last month.[13]

Under the Kennedy administration, the NSC lost is prior superdepartmental status and became one more entity among many (e.g., special Cabinet committees and informal groups of officials) to assist and advise the president on national security matters. This change was reflected in the way in which NSC policy papers, now denominated National Security Action Memoranda (NSAM), were produced. Their generation began with a Cabinet official or a top presidential subordinate. This manager coordinated development of a draft position paper with other responsible individuals, often through the use of ad hoc interdepartmental groups. Fiscal considerations were integrated into the body of the document and no longer appeared in a separate "financial appendix." Discussion and debate continued all the way to and into the Oval Office. Once the president approved the recommendations of the position paper, his decision was recorded by the responsible agency or the NSC staff in a brief NSAM. President Johnson largely continued these arrangements, and approximately 375 NSAMs were produced during the Kennedy and Johnson administrations.

A few modifications occurred during the Nixon and Ford administrations. The appointment of Henry Kissinger as national security adviser introduced a presidential assistant of legendary power. He recruited a substantial and influential staff at the NSC. Together they largely initiated national security position papers, which were designated National Security Study Memoranda, and developed them through various interdepartmental groups composed of high level representatives from pertinent agencies. "At least 318 decision documents, resulting from these papers, were designated National Security Decision Memoranda (NSDM) and included such presidential decisions as establishing a policy to renounce the production of toxins except for defensive research and development purposes."[14]

President Carter renamed the NSAM the Presidential Review Memorandum, and he issued more than fifty-four decisions known as Presidential Directives.[15] The Reagan administration designated its instruments in the NSC series National Security Study Memoranda and National Security Decision Directives. The president issued "at least 298 directives."[16] Under the George H.W. Bush administration, the directives became National Security Directives, and President Clinton called them Presidential Decision Directives.

Although President George W. Bush and his national security advisers have provided little detail about his directives in this series, the first such instrument indicates that they are denominated National Security Presidential Directives (NSPDs) (see http://www.fas.org/irp/offdocs/nspd/nspd-1.htm). These may serve two purposes: decision and review.

Most of the directives produced up to 1960 have been declassified and are kept in the relevant presidential libraries administered by the National Archives and Records Administration (NARA), whereas most of those produced in subsequent years remain classified, "and details about them are largely unavailable for congressional or public scrutiny."[17] The National Security Council staff maintains those issued during the later years, and some, or summaries of them, are available from groups such as does the Federation of American Scientists in Washington, D.C. (see http://www.fas.org). The Bush Presidential Library (http://bushlibrary.tamu.edu) is unique in its listing of National Security Directives and National Security Reviews on its home page.

As the General Accounting Office (GAO) has noted, unlike executive orders, these directives "embody foreign and military policy-making guidance rather than specific instructions; are classified; are usually directed only to NSC and the most senior executive branch officials; and do not appear to be issued under statutory authority conferred by Congress."[18] However, these directives embody policy-making guidance, but some of them have provided specific instructions. For example, Presidential Decision Directive 63, issued by President Clinton, dealt with the fight against cyberterror. Among the tasks it recommended were the development of a plan to improve intelligence gathering and an expansion of international cooperation.

ADMINISTRATIVE ORDERS

The first administrative order, so denominated, was issued May 25, 1940. It established the Office for Emergency Management in the Executive Office of the President (see 3 C.F.R., 1938–1943 Comp., 1320). The directive appeared to be issued pursuant to, and as an extension of, an executive order (E.O. 8248) of September 8, 1939, which organized the Executive Office of the President and made generic reference to an office for emergency management that might be subsequently established in the event of a national emergency or the threat of a national emergency. The second administrative order, dated January 7, 1941, further defined the status and functions of the Office for Emergency Management and was also issued pursuant to E.O. 8248 (3 C.F.R. 1938–1943 Comp., 1320–21). Thus, the impression was left that administrative orders might be a subset of directives used to further detail policy primarily established by executive orders. However, this soon proved not to be the case.

The third administrative order, so designated, was a July 29, 1943, letter transferring certain functions of the Office for Emergency Management. The next two orders, issued April 13, 1945, concerned keeping flags at half-staff on all federal buildings and temporarily closed federal departments and agencies in conjunction with ceremonies on the occasion of President Franklin D. Roosevelt's death. Both were signed by Secretary of State Edward R. Stettinius Jr. A September 10, 1945, administrative order, signed by Secretary of War Henry L. Stimson, indicated how the term "World War II" was to be officially used. The next order, dated August 15, 1945, and signed by President Harry S. Truman, terminated the Office of Censorship and voluntary censorship of the domestic press and radio (3 C.F.R. 1943–1948 Comp., 1078–79).

These and subsequent instruments denominated as administrative orders took a variety of forms—delegations of authority, determinations, directives, findings, letters, memoranda, and orders—on a wide variety of administrative matters. In fact, some items appeared to overlap with other types of presidential directives. For example, some international trade instruments, sometimes in letter form, were considered to be administrative orders (3 C.F.R. 1964–1965 Comp., 372–73; (3 C.F.R. 1966–1970 Comp, 997–1005), as were designations of officials (3 C.F.R. 1966–1970 Comp., 1005). In 1972, certain instruments, identified as Presidential Determinations but appearing in Title 3 compilations of the *Code of Federal Regulations* (CFR) in the administrative orders category, began to have hyphenated identification numbers, the first figure indicating the year of issuance and the second marking the sequence of promulgation (3 C.F.R. 1971–1975 Comp., 1082). Presidential Determinations, as a particular type of administrative order, first appeared in the *Federal Register* and CFR in 1964 (3 C.F.R. 1964–1965 Comp., 372–74). Indications are that, during at least the past forty years, presidential directives published in the *Federal Register* in forms other than those of an executive order or proclamation have been denominated as administrative orders when reproduced in CFR Title 3 compilations.

CERTIFICATES

Apparently, only one Presidential Certificate, as such, was published in the *Federal Register* and subsequently included in a CFR Title 3 compilation. Issued March 27, 1940, pursuant to a farm crop production and harvesting loan statute of 1937 (50 Stat. 5), the instrument certified that four Washington counties were distressed emergency areas and, therefore, not subject to the loan limitations stated in the law (3 C.F.R. 1938–1943 Comp., 1322). Although there is evidence that presidents had issued statutorily authorized certificates prior to this time, no directives of this designation have appeared in subsequent CFR Title 3 compilations.[19]

DESIGNATIONS OF OFFICIALS

Since the establishment of the *Federal Register* and the CFR, presidential letters designating individuals to hold specified official positions in the government have been reproduced in these publications. The first, dated May 28, 1941, vested Secretary of the Interior Harold L. Ickes with the additional position and accompanying duties of Petroleum Coordinator for National Defense. The second established a new position, Coordinator of Information, and designated William J. Donovan, a private individual, to fill it (3 C.F.R. 1938–1943 Comp., 1323–25). Subsequent designations have been of both types: some an additional position for an individual already holding an official post, others an original appointment of a private person to an existing vacancy or newly created position. The president may unilaterally make designations where no Senate approval of the appointment is required and where he has the authority and resources to create new official positions to be filled by designees. Some designations are merely delegations of presidential authority to constitutional officers, such as Cabinet secretaries (3 C.F.R. 1938–1943 Comp., 1326; 3 C.F.R. 1943–1948 Comp., 1083). Two more recent designations, one in 1979 and another in 1982, were of a slightly different character: officials, by title, were designated to have authority to security classify information at the "Top Secret" level (3 C.F.R. 1979 Comp., 519; 3 C.F.R. 1983 Comp., 257–59).

GENERAL LICENSES

Indications are that only one presidential general license, as such, was published in the *Federal Register* and subsequently included in a CFR Title 3 compilation. Issued December 13, 1941, shortly after the Japanese attack on Pearl Harbor and congressional declarations of war on Japan and Germany (55 Stat. 795, 796), the general license signed by President Roosevelt authorized the conduct of certain export transactions otherwise prohibited during wartime by the Trading with the Enemy Act of 1917, as amended. It also delegated to the secretary of the treasury responsibility to regulate such transactions (3 C.F.R. 1938–1943 Comp., 1328). An emergency action taken to assist the prosecution of the war, the general license facilitated the shipment of material to U.S. allies for that effort. No directives of this designation have appeared in subsequent CFR Title 3 compilations.

INTERPRETATIONS

Only two presidential interpretations, denominated as such, have appeared in the *Federal Register* and CFR Title 3 compilations. The first, dated May 20, 1942, and signed by President Roosevelt, was a clarification and interpretation of E.O. 9128 of April 13, 1942, concerning functions of the Department of State and the Board of Economic Warfare (3 C.F.R. 1938–1943 Comp., 1329–30). The second, dated November 5, 1943, was a letter to Attorney General Francis Biddle from President Roosevelt. It concerned the construction of E.O. 9346 of May 27, 1943, regarding the insertion in government contracts of a provision obligating signatory contractors not to discriminate against any employee or applicant for employment on account of race, creed, color, or national origin (3 C.F.R. 1943–1948 Comp., 1084). Neither instrument was actually a presidential directive, but both did interpret previously issued directives. Furthermore, the president might arguably have asked the attorney general to prepare and issue these interpretations in his behalf, but apparently wished to offer his own viewpoint in these two instances.[20]

LETTERS ON TARIFFS AND INTERNATIONAL TRADE

Presidential letters on tariffs and international trade have appeared in the *Federal Register* and the CFR since the beginning of their publication. The earliest, dated March 20, 1936, and addressed to the secretary of the treasury, directs the continuation of duties on imported goods produced by certain specified countries (3 C.F.R. 1936–1938 Comp., 419). Indeed, the secretary of the treasury appears to be the recipient of all such published letters appearing in CFR Title 3 compilations through 1978. The last such letter to date appearing in these compilations was sent jointly to the Speaker of the House and the President Pro Tempore of the Senate on January 4, 1979. Presidential letters and memoranda on matters other than tariffs and international trade are sometimes denominated administrative orders and appear as such in CFR Title 3 compilations.

MILITARY ORDERS

CFR Title 3 compilations for the 1938–1943 and 1943–1948 periods contain the texts of twelve presidential directives denominated as military orders (3 C.F.R. 1936–1938 Comp., 419). The first of these was issued on July 5, 1939, and the last on October 18, 1948. Ten of them bear the signature of President Roosevelt; the other two were signed by President Truman. These directives appear to have been issued by the president in conjunction with the execution of his duties as commander in chief, and pertain to matters concerning administration of the armed forces and personnel. Indeed, half of them bear the commander in chief title below the president's signature. Moreover, although all make reference to "the authority vested in me as President of the United States and as Commander-in-Chief of the Army and Navy of the United States," two also cite a specific Article of War and six also cite explicit statutory authority for their issuance. No directives of this designation were subsequently produced in the *Federal Register* or CFR Title compilations until November 2001, when President George W. Bush issued a controversial military order on the detention, treatment, and trial, by military tribunals, of noncitizens alleged to be terrorists.[21]

PRESIDENTIAL ANNOUNCEMENTS

An oral presidential directive often is captured in an announcement that records what the president has prescribed or instructed. For example, President Richard Nixon established his Advisory Council on Executive Organization in this manner, with an April 5, 1969, announcement, as did President William Clinton when he inaugurated his National Performance Review task force on March 3, 1993.[22] By contrast, such temporary government reform study panels were mandated on various occasions during the first half of the twentieth century and during the Reagan administration with written charters expressed in statutes or executive orders. Such presidential announcements, as was the case in the examples cited, often are recorded in the *Weekly Compilation of Presidential Documents*. However, they do not appear in the *Federal Register* or in the *Public Papers of the Presidents of the United States* for Presidents Herbert Hoover, Truman, and the chief executives succeeding Truman.[23]

PRESIDENTIAL FINDINGS

Presidential findings, as such, initially appeared in the *Federal Register* and CFR Title 3 compilations as instruments determining that certain conditions of the Agricultural Trade Development and Assistance Act of 1954, as amended, had been satisfied and, therefore, sales of agricultural communities could proceed. Presidential findings of this type were reproduced in CFR Title 3 compilations as administrative orders (3 C.F.R. 1966–1970, 1006–8). In 1974, the reference to a presidential finding took on its current popular meaning when Congress adopted the so-called Hughes-Ryan amendment to the Foreign Assistance Act of that year. Set out in section 662 of the statute, it prohibited the expenditure of appropriated funds by, or on behalf of, the Central Intelligence Agency for intelligence activities "unless and until the President finds that each such operation is important to the national security of the United States and reports, in a timely fashion, a description and scope of such operation to the appropriate committees of Congress" (88 Stat. 1795, at 1804). The requirements of this provision subsequently went through a series of transformations, the vestiges of which were codified in the Intelligence Authorization Act, Fiscal Year 1991, but still require a written presidential finding satisfying certain conditions set forth in the statute for covert actions to occur (105 Stat. 429, at. 442). Such presidential findings, which are security classified, are to be "reported to the intelligence committees as soon as possible" after being approved "and before the initiation of the covert action authorized by the finding." Thus, these findings are not published in the *Federal Register* or reproduced in CFR Title 3 compilations.

REGULATIONS

CFR Title 3 compilations for the 1938–1943 and 1943–1948 periods contain the texts of nine administrative documents denominated as regulations. The first of these was issued on September 6, 1939, and the last on September 19, 1945. Eight of them bear the signature of President Roosevelt; another, signed by three commissioners of the U.S. Civil Service Commission, indicates that it was approved by President Truman. With the exception of one brief extension item and another relying on an executive order, all of these documents cite explicit statutory authority for their issuance. The Roosevelt items largely pertained to the allocation of defense materials to nations of Western Europe engaged in war with Germany. The regulations approved by Truman concerned within-grade salary advancements for federal employees. Although earlier examples of presidents issuing regulations can be found, no directives of this designation have appeared in subsequent CFR Title 3 compilations.[24] Current regulations governing the preparation, presentation, filing, and publication of executive orders and proclamations are prescribed in an executive order, E.O. 11030, as amended. Agency regulations appear in other titles of the CFR.

PROCLAMATIONS

Proclamations are one of the oldest types of presidential directive, the earliest appearing in October 1789 when President Washington declared Thursday, November 26, to be "a day of public thanksgiving."[25] Like most proclamations, it affected primarily the activities and interests of private individuals and, like many proclamations, it was at best hortatory. However, some proclamations, declaring emergency situations and invoking the president's constitutional authority as commander in chief or powers statutorily delegated to him by Congress to respond to exigencies, were of a more profound character. An early proclamation, promulgated by President Washington on August 7, 1794, exemplified this latter use of such instruments. Responding to rebellious activities in western Pennsylvania and Virginia protesting a federal excise tax on whiskey, the president called forth the militia and personally took command of them. This was done pursuant to statutory arrangements (1 Stat. 264–265).

The issuance of proclamations by the president followed a tradition established by British monarchs and practiced by royal governors in the North American colonies and by their elected successors after the Revolution.[26] Under the new federal government, the Department of State was responsible for preserving presidential proclamations. Numerous examples of the early proclamations may be found in Richardson's *A Compilation of the Messages and Papers of the Presidents*. In 1907, the Department of State began to assign identification numbers to both proclamations and executive orders, making a determined, but not totally successful, effort to include previously issued instruments of both types in this accounting.[27] The Federal Register Act of 1935 effectively required that both proclamations and executive orders be published in the *Federal Register* (44 U.S.C. 1505). The first proclamation so published was Proc. 2161 of March 19, 1936, concerning contributions to the American Red Cross for flood relief. Beginning with this instrument, all subsequent presidential proclamations have been reproduced in CFR Title 3 compilations. For the past twenty-five years, proclamations have been largely hortative, often being used to declare commemorative occasions. Regulations governing the preparation, presentation, filing, and publication of proclamations and executive orders are prescribed in E.O. 11030, as amended.

OTHER FORMS OF COMMUNICATION

A president communicates through various means, such as executive orders and national security directives, discussed above. This person also presents his message and policies—often for public consumption—through channels such as speeches, press conferences, weekly radio addresses, press releases, nominations to the courts and ambassadorships, treaties, and vetoes. It might be argued that presidential pardons are also a source of information policy. These pronouncements are available through sources such as the *Weekly Compilation of Presidential Documents* and the *Public Papers of the President*.

Nominations

Article II, section 2 of the Constitution gives the president the authority to nominate principal offers of the executive branch and the judiciary, but their appointment is subject to the advice and consent of the Senate. The legislative path for nominations consists of a series of steps in which the Executive Clerk of the Senate receives the presidential nomination and refers the name to the appropriate Senate committee. The appropriate committee issues a Senate Executive Report, most likely if there was a favorable vote on the nominee; only a simple majority of the plenary Senate is necessary for confirmation.

Senate Executive Reports, which are part of the Serial Set, are included in THOMAS, GPO Access, and CIS Congressional Universe. Other sources providing information on nominations are the Daily Digest of the *Congressional Record*, *Weekly Compilation of Presidential Documents*, *Public Papers of the President*, *CIS Index to U.S. Senate Executive Documents and Reports, 1818–1969* (1987), and the *Congressional Index* (CCH Incorporated).

Treaties and Agreements

Article II, section 2 of the Constitution also states that the president "shall have power by and with the advice and consent of the Senate to make treaties, provided two thirds of the Senators present concur." The coverage of foreign relations in Chapter 6 identifies and discusses the appropriate source material.

Presidential Reorganization Plans

Congress first authorized the president to propose plans for the reorganization of the executive departments and agencies in a 1939 statute (53 Stat. 561). The objective of such reconfigurations was to achieve efficiency and economy in administration. A presidential reorganization plan, submitted to Congress, became effective after sixty days unless both chambers of Congress adopted a concurrent resolution of disapproval. Such reorganization authority, renewed periodically a dozen times between 1945 and 1984, with slight variation, remained available to the president for nearly half a century. At different junctures, qualifications were placed on its exercise. For example, reorganization plans could not abolish or create an entire department or deal with more than one logically consistent subject matter. Also, the president was prohibited from submitting more than one plan within a thirty-day period and was required to include a clear statement on the projected economic savings expected to result from a reorganization.

Reorganization plans not disapproved by Congress were published in the *Federal Register* prior to being implemented and also in the *Statutes at Large* and the CFR (Title 3 for the year in which they became effective).

Modifications of the president's reorganization plan authority was made necessary in 1983 when the Supreme Court effectively invalidated continued congressional reliance on a concurrent resolution to disapprove a proposed plan.[28] Under the Reorganization Act Amendments of 1984, several significant changes were made in the law on reorganization plans. Any time during the period of sixty calendar days of continuous session of Congress following the submission of a reorganization plan, the president could make amendments or modifications to it. Within ninety calendar days of continuous session of Congress following the submission of a reorganization plan, both houses could adopt a joint resolution (which, unlike a concurrent resolution, becomes law with the president's signature) for a plan to be approved. This amendment, however, continued the president's reorganization plan authority only to the end of 1984, when it automatically expired (5 U.S.C. 901–912 [1988]). No president since then has requested its reauthorization.

PRESIDENTIAL PAPERS

Although the government of the United States is based on a written Constitution and laws, the management and preservation of the public records of the nation was generally neglected during the first century and a half of the existence of the Republic. Inattentiveness to the maintenance of official papers prevailed within both the infant bureaucracy and the White House. Although the secretary of state bore the responsibility for retaining copies of the most important government documents, lesser papers, without immediate administrative significance, disappeared in a clutter, disintegrated, became otherwise lost, or were destroyed by design.

Within this atmosphere, departing presidents had little choice with regard to the disposition of their records; there was no national archive to receive such papers and, for reasons of etiquette, politics, or both, there was reluctance to leave them behind. Thus, the early Chief Executives carried away their documents of office, entrusting them to their family, estate executors, and, often, to fate. After years and decades of the perils of private ownership, many collections of presidential records came to be established within the libraries of state and private universities, state historical societies, and the Library of Congress (LC). However, time levied a price on some caches of such documents before they came to rest in these institutions. For example, LC has possession of approximately 95 percent of President George Washington's papers, purchased from his heirs in 1834 and 1849 at a total cost of $45,000.

In various ways, fire has been the chief destroyer of retired presidential documents. President Martin Van Buren, for example, carefully selected papers from his administration and is thought to have burned the rest, leaving fewer than 7,000 items. Fewer than 1,000 of William Henry Harrison's papers have survived, many of them being destroyed in 1858 when his home in Ohio was consumed by flames.

Peculiarities surround the papers of some presidents. After leaving office, President Ulysses S. Grant reportedly returned certain of the letters he had received from political friends and associates to their writers. Most of Chester A. Arthur's papers "disappeared." The documents of Warren G. Harding's presidency vanished for a time and were thought to have been destroyed by his widow. The LC acquired some, but a quantity of them turned up in Marion, Ohio, where certain materials remain under seal, the most sensitive items to be released in 2014.

For over a century and a half, the papers of the president were regarded as his personal property to be taken with him when he left office. However, as the federal establishment began to grow, questions arose as to the propriety and wisdom of this practice. By the turn of the twentieth century, historians had become alarmed that papers were accidentally destroyed, lost, and sometimes only selectively released for scrutiny. Archivists lamented omissions in the record of the national government that the situation created. Not only might entire files be carried from the White House, but presidential correspondence might be retrieved from departmental files. As it applied to government records, the concept of presidential papers knew no bounds. This aspect of the practice became particularly acute in the aftermath of the creation of the Executive Office of the President in 1939. Franklin D. Roosevelt established a panoply of emergency and wartime agencies within this domain, all of which served the president in immediate and direct capacities and all of which, therefore, could be considered producers of "presidential papers." The potential loss of the documentary materials of these entities, however, presented both a records management problem and difficulty in administrative continuity.

Presidential Libraries

Addressing the situation described above, Franklin D. Roosevelt sought to return presidential papers to the public realm through a new type of institution, the presidential library. When he advanced the concept in 1938, two prototype libraries were already in existence. In 1914, the state of Ohio completed the Rutherford B. Hayes Memorial Library in Fremont, Ohio. Built in fulfillment of obligations to receive the former Chief Executive's papers and memorabilia, the library includes other historical material, such as some local and regional historical papers.

Herbert Hoover, Roosevelt's immediate predecessor, placed his presidential papers in the Hoover Library on War, Revolution, and Peace, located at Stanford University. In 1919, Hoover had pledged $50,000 to the university to establish an institution that would serve as a repository of largely original documents deriving from European propaganda and pamphleteering activities of World War I.[29] Built at a cost of $600,000 for the basic archival building, the resulting entity was later renamed the Hoover Institution on War, Revolution, and Peace. (Today, it is no longer attached to the university but maintains itself through donations and as a contract research organization. It continues to hold papers evolving from Hoover's public service since 1914. Certain of the presidential papers, however, were transferred to the Herbert Hoover Presidential Library at West Branch, Iowa, when that facility was completed and turned over to the Archivist of the United States in 1964.)

Franklin Roosevelt built upon these models and developed the concept of a publicly maintained presidential library. The idea apparently germinated in 1937. By December 1938, Roosevelt had organized an executive committee on the project. After an initial organizational meeting and gathering of that committee with the president on December 17, plans were made to organize a corporation to gather funds for the private construction of the library building. The Carnegie Corporation granted the executive committee $1,500 for its activities, and the first round of construction pledges totaled $450,000.

The declared purposes of the library construction corporation were to construct and equip a building or buildings on the grounds of the Roosevelt family home at Hyde Park, New York, or elsewhere, for either the corporation or the United States. This facility was to house and preserve such historical materials as Roosevelt might give, bequeath, or transfer to the corporation or to the United States, as well as any other acceptable historical materials. The corporation was to provide for the custody and maintenance of such buildings and historical materials, making the latter available to students, scholars, historians, teachers, and others until ownership and control should be taken over by the United States. It had power to solicit, accept, borrow, invest, and expend money and to transfer property to the United States, provided that adequate legislation was enacted for the acceptance of such property and for its permanent care and maintenance.[30]

Chartering legislation for the Roosevelt Presidential Library was enacted in 1939 (53 Stat. 1062). The Archivist of the United States, acting on behalf of the federal government, accepted the completed library edifice on July 4, 1940. The museum portion of the facility opened to the public approximately a year later; library materials were available for research use by the public in the spring of 1946.

The Policy Structure

Roosevelt's efforts to create a presidential library were both ad hoc and specific. Nonetheless, Harry S. Truman was no less attentive to history and the preservation of his presidential records. In 1950 a Missouri corporation was established to create a presidential library on Truman's behalf, following the model of his predecessor. Furthermore, in an unpublished January 17, 1953, letter to the Administrator of General Services (who had succeed the Archivist of the United States as the official recipient of publicly donated presidential records and archival facilities), Truman proposed to offer his White House papers for deposit in the national archival system pursuant to the somewhat awkward authority of the Federal Records Act (section 507(3), 64 Stat. 583, 588) or under future legislation in the event that the government accepted the proposed library.

While the Truman library corporation was endeavoring to raise funds for the construction of an archival edifice, Congress enacted the Presidential Libraries Act of 1955. Dwight D. Eisenhower approved the legislation—an amendment to the Federal Property and Administrative Services Act of 1949—in August (69 Stat. 695; 44 U.S.C. 2101, 2107–2108 (1976)). This law provided the statutory basis for all subsequent presidential libraries.

Under the terms of the Act, a former president was understood to have complete control over his official records, even to the point of his defining what constituted "presidential papers." These materials could be taken by the Chief Executive when he departed office. The Presidential Libraries Act established arrangements whereby a former president could, after privately constructing a depository edifice, deed both the building and such papers as he wished to house within it to the federal government. In accepting this property—buildings, land, records, and perhaps artifacts—the government agreed to abide by the terms of the deed or contract of bequest, which often meant that temporal restrictions were set on the public availability of some presidential materials. It was also understood that security classification and other limited common law restrictions, such as personal privacy, would be honored as well.

Pursuant to this authority, presidential libraries were subsequently created for former Presidents Truman, Hoover, Eisenhower, Lyndon B. Johnson, John F. Kennedy, Gerald R. Ford, and Jimmy Carter. However, new laws began to emerge, changing the arrangements for future presidential libraries. First, as a consequence of the Watergate incident and related matters, the official papers and records of President Richard Nixon were placed under federal custody by the Presidential Recordings and Materials Preservation Act of 1974 (88 Stat. 1695). The statute requires that these materials remain in Washington, D.C., where they are maintained under the supervision of the Archivist of the United States. Thus, Nixon could not take his presidential records and documents with him when he left office, nor could he place them in a presidential library outside the nation's capital.

In November 1978, the Presidential Records Act (92 Stat. 2523; 44 U.S.C. 2201–2207 (1982)) was enacted. This statute carefully defined "presidential records" and specified that all such material created on or after January 20, 1981, was subject to its provisions. The new law effectively made presidential records federal property that was to remain under the custody and control of the Archivist of the United States when each incumbent president left office. Carter was the last occupant of the Oval Office who could freely take away his records and papers.

At about this same time, there was a growing sentiment in Congress that would eventually result in another reform of presidential library law. Concern about the increasing cost of providing benefits to the nation's former presidents was beginning to build, legislatively manifesting itself initially in March 1980 in a proposal to adjust the federal largess bestowed upon former presidents and their families.[31] Presidential libraries, particularly their physical size and continued maintenance, were among the perquisites seen as contributing to the burden of the taxpayers.[32]

The Presidential Libraries Act of 1986 set certain reporting requirements, architectural and design conditions, and fiscal limitations regarding future presidential libraries, including requiring an operating endowment (100 Stat. 495; 44 U.S.C. 2101, 2112 [1988]). For example, prior to accepting any gift of land, a facility or equipment to create a presidential library, or making any physical or material change in an existing one, the Archivist must submit a written report to Congress providing certain details, as specified in the statute, about the transaction. However, portions of the endowment requirement for new libraries were specifically made applicable "to any President who takes the oath of office as President for the first time on or after January 20, 1985" (100 Stat. 498).

The George H. W. Bush Presidential Library is the first such facility to be subject to all of these recent reform requirements. In brief, this library, the Clinton Presidential Library, and all subsequent ones, must meet architectural and design standards prescribed by the Archivist of the United States pursuant to the 1986 Act.

The Library System

Through the National Archives and Records Administration, the government currently operates and maintains libraries for ten former presidents and will soon assume the responsibility for an eleventh such facility (for President Clinton). Federal experience with the first four libraries (Roosevelt, Truman, Hoover, and Eisenhower) established two patterns: The facility was located at what was considered to be the former president's hometown (birthplace or principal residence), and the library building(s), grounds, and holdings were deeded to the government.

Change in or exception to this practice occurred with the Johnson library, which was located on the campus of the University of Texas at Austin. Because the university could not legally deed its land to the federal government, another provision of the Presidential Libraries Act was relied upon to effect federal supervision of the facility. Rather than taking title to the presidential archival facility, the Archivist relied on his authority to

> make agreements, upon terms and conditions he considers proper, with a State, political subdivision, university, institution of higher learning, institute, or foundation to use as a Presidential archival depository land, buildings, and equipment of the State, subdivision, university, or other organizations, to be made available by it without transfer of title to the United States, and maintain, operate, and protect the depository as part of the national archives system.[33]

Pursuant to this authority, an agreement or memorandum of understanding was executed regarding the federal supervision of the Johnson library. This innovation was repeated in the case of the Ford and Bush libraries because their location on a university campus once again raised the land deed barrier.[34]

The Kennedy, Carter, Reagan, and Clinton presidential libraries, although deeded to the government, are located in major cities in close proximity to respective presidential hometowns. (The Richard M. Nixon Library in Yorba Linda, California, is a privately constructed and operated archival facility. It is not part of the National Archives' system; the provisions of the Presidential Recordings and Materials Preservation Act of 1974 still apply; and the actual presidential material held by NARA can be found at Archives II in College Park, Maryland.)

A complete list of the presidential libraries and the presidential materials projects, as well as links to their home pages, can be found at http://www.archives.gov/presidential_libraries/addresses/addresses.html. These sites tend to provide access to some collections (e.g., photographs) and services online, such as electronic access to the *Public Papers of the President*. Access to the collections of some presidents prior to the introduction of the modern presidential library system is available through the Library of Congress's American Memory (http://memory.loc.gov).

PRESIDENTIAL ADVISORY COMMITTEES AND COMMISSIONS

Advisory committees and commissions are created not only by the president but also by Congress for it and executive departments and agencies to use. The Federal Advisory Committee Act of 1972 (FACA), codified at 5 U.S.C. App., established a centralized management system and brought some order to the process of establishing and terminating advisory bodies. The General Services Administration (GSA), an independent agency, devised guidelines for implementation of FACA, and E.O. 12838 of February 10, 1993, placed a ceiling on the number of "discretionary advisory committees" (those created or under agency authority or authorized by Congress). Under FACA, GSA is responsible for ensuring that the sponsoring agencies follow the requirements of the Act and supporting GSA regulations.

The best source for information on the workings of FACA and advisory committees and commissions is the *Annual Report of the President on Federal Advisory Committees*, which GSA submits to the president. The annual *Encyclopedia of Governmental Advisory Organizations* (Farmington Hills, Mich.: Gale Group, 1985–) is the most comprehensive guide to permanent, continuing, terminated, and authorized advisory bodies reporting to the president, Congress, and executive departments and agencies.

SOURCES CENTRAL TO THE PRESIDENCY: A SUMMARY

This section discusses the *Federal Register*, *Code of Federal Regulations*, the *Weekly Compilation of Presidential Documents*, the *Public Papers of the President*, and the White House Web site. Clearly, these sources concentrate on the current president. For past individuals holding the office, the previously mentioned sources (except the current White House Web site) apply, as does the modern presidential library system (see http://www.archives.gov/index.html). For the earlier years, there are the holdings of the Library of Congress (see American Memory, http://memory.loc.gov) and *A Compilation of the Messages and Papers of the Presidents, 1789–1897 . . .* (53d Cong., 2d sess., H. Misc. Doc. 210), produced by James D. Richardson, a member of the House Committee on Printing and the chapter on "Presidential Papers" in Laurence F. Schmeckebier and Roy B. Eastin's *Government Publications and Their Use*.[35] The first 8,030 executive orders (1862–1938) are briefly profiled in one volume and indexed in another volume of *Presidential Executive Orders* (New York: Archives Publishing, 1944), prepared by the Historical Records Survey, under the editorship of Clifford L. Lord. Other useful titles are Greg Robinson, *By Order of the President: FDR and the Internment of Japanese America* (Cambridge: Harvard University Press, 2001); Kenneth R. Mayer, *With the Stroke of a Pen: Executive Orders and Presidential Power* (Princeton, N.J.: Princeton University Press, 2001); House Committee on the Judiciary, *Congressional Limitation of Executive Orders*, hearings, 106th Cong., 1st sess. (Washington, D.C.: GPO, 2000); House Committee on the Judiciary, *Executive Orders and Presidential Directives*, hearing, 107th Cong., 1st sess. (Washington, D.C.: GPO, 2001); and House Committee on Rules, *Executive Orders*, hearing, 106th Cong., 1st sess. (Washington, D.C.: GPO, 2000).

NARA has a Web page devoted to "Presidential Documents on NARA Web Sites" (http://www.archives.gov/research_room/getting_started/research_presidential_material). It covers executive orders, proclamations, and other presidential documents. JURIST: The Legal Education Network of the University of Pittsburgh School of Law is a Web site for "Presidential Pardons" (http://jurist.law.pitt.edu/pardons1.htm). The pardon, on the whole, is outside the regular checks and balances of the other branches. It gives exclusive, broad, and unfettered power to the president. Pardons are a form of clemency action that presidents since George Washington have exercised.

Federal Register

Begun in 1936, the *Federal Register* contains executive orders, presidential proclamations, and reorganization plans (presidential proposals submitted to both chambers of Congress to merge, abolish, or transfer functions of designated agencies of the executive branch below the rank of department). (Note that Title

5, *United States Code, Appendix*, collects the text of approved reorganization plans and gathers together all pertinent documents implementing them, any other presidential messages pertaining to them, historical and revision notes, and cross-references.) This source is now available through GPO Access and CIS's Congressional Universe.

Code of Federal Regulations

An annual issue of Title 3 typically contains executive orders and proclamations in separate numbered sequence, other presidential documents arranged by date, and regulations of the Executive Office of the President. Various tables and finding aids are also included, as is an index. Single volume compilations have been published for the 1936–1938, 1938–1943, 1943–1948, 1949–1953, 1954–1958, 1959–1963, 1964–1965, 1966–1970, and 1971–1975 periods. Annual CFR Title 3 volumes have been published for the subsequent years. Current full-text versions of many primary proclamations and executive orders, as amended, may be found in the periodically produced *Codification of Presidential Proclamations and Executive Orders,* prepared by NARA's Office of the Federal Register. The codification covers April 13, 1945, through January 20, 1989. The paper publication is out of print, but an electronic version (http://www.archives.gov/federal_register/code_of_federal_regulations/code_of_federal) contains a foreword, Proclamations and Executive Orders ("chapter titles link to document titles, which link to the text of documents"), Disposition Tables ("listing Proclamations and Executive Orders in numerical order, with links to all documents that appear in this publication"), and an index. The Web site also provides access to *Executive Orders Disposition Tables*, "beginning with E.O. 10432, January 24, 1953, including title, signature date, *Federal Register* citation, and detailed history of amendments and revocations." Like the *Federal Register*, the CFR is available through GPO Access and CIS's Congressional Universe.

Weekly Compilation of Presidential Documents

Begun on August 2, 1965, this source is a weekly (the previous week) record of various documents (executive orders, proclamations, addresses and remarks, communications to Congress, letters, messages, news conferences, reorganization plans, resignations, swearing-in ceremonies, retirements, and a checklist of White House Office press releases). It also cites laws approved by the president and lists nominations sent to the Senate. Since 1993, the *Weekly Compilation* has been available through GPO Access (http://www.acces.gpo.gov/nara/nara003.html).

Public Papers of the President

The annual series was initially began in 1957, covering the fifth year of the Eisenhower administration. Provision was made for retrospective collections, and subsequent volumes have covered the earlier years of the Eisenhower administration (1953–1956) as well as the Truman (1945–1952) and Hoover (1929–1933) administrations. Compilations for President Franklin Roosevelt and earlier chief executives have been published commercially. Kraus International has issued *The Cumulative Indexes to the Public Papers of the Presidents of the United States* (1977–1983). A CD-ROM product, *The Presidential Papers: Washington–Taft* (Provo, Utah: CDex Information Group, 1965), goes beyond, incorporating the Richardson series.

Prior to the 1977 volume, the *Public Papers* was an edited version of the *Weekly Compilation*. Beginning with the Carter administration, the 1977 volumes of the *Public Papers* were expanded to include virtually all materials published in the *Weekly Compilation*. However, beginning with 1989, executive orders and proclamations are not republished. A table, however, refers to the *Federal Register* and indicates where these documents were first published. Current volumes in this series arrange presidential materials in chronological order within each week. Text notes, footnotes, and cross-references are furnished by the editors for purposes of identification and clarity. The information is indexed by subject entries and by categories reflecting the type of presidential activity or document.

The *Public Papers* are available through GPO Access (http://www.access. gpo.gov/nara/pubpaps/srchpaps.html). The presidential libraries for Reagan and Bush, as well as the Presidential Materials Project for Clinton, provide these papers online. Other presidential libraries offer selected speeches and documents. Both the Carter and Johnson Presidential Libraries have the Daily Diary, the official log of the president's activities.

White House Web Site

The White House Web site (http://www.whitehouse.gov) covers the war on terrorism, "Today at the White House," major speeches of George W. Bush, presidential appointments, "News" (e.g., "Current News," "Press Briefings," "Proclamations," "Nominations," and "Radio Addresses"), and policies. There is also biographical information on the president, vice president, and first lady. The connection for "Your Government" provides a link to the agencies comprised in the Executive Office of the President and to executive departments and agencies. Among the other offerings are "Photos," "History & Tours" of the White House, and "Kids Only." It is important to remember that a president communicates through various agencies, including the Office of Management and Budget and the Office of Homeland Security, as well as Cabinet secretaries.

Other Sources

Executive orders and presidential proclamations also appear in CQ Washington Alert, Legi-Slate, WESTLAW, Congressional Universe, and GPO Access. The *Federal Register* and the *Code of Federal Regulations* are available from various commercial companies, such as Counterpoint Publishing, Inc. (Cambridge, Mass.). The *Congressional Record*, as well as the West Group's United States Code Congressional and Administrative News Advance Pamphlets, and the Advance Search pamphlets of LEXIS Law Publishing's United States Code Service also provide executive orders and proclamations.

Other sources that contain the text of reorganization plans include the *Congressional Record*, the Serial Set, Title 3 (*Code of Federal Regulations*), *Statutes at Large*, WESTLAW, LEXIS-NEXIS, and *Fedlaw EasySearch*, a CD-ROM product published by Oryx Press (Phoenix, Ariz.). The CD-ROM product also contains executive orders and proclamations.

CONCLUSION

This chapter emphasizes communication directly from the president or the White House. However, as Chapter 6 illustrates, statements and policies of the Chief Executive may come from the Executive Office of the President or another body within the executive branch.

The president's choice of an administrative policy instrument is his to make. If he is canceling or modifying a prior executive order, he needs to use an executive order to effect that change. If he is setting out policy de novo, he can use an executive order, national security directive, memorandum, or whatever. These policy memos are usually included in Title 3 of the *Code of Federal Regulations*, as, generally, "administrative orders" in the "Other Presidential Documents" section. Of course memoranda, unlike executive orders, do not have to meet the *Federal Register* publication requirement to become effective. An overarching consideration in choosing a policy instrument is its legal status and the president's authority to effect the policy at hand.

NOTES

1. Harold C. Relyea, "Preface," in *The Presidency and Information Policy*, ed. Harold C. Relyea (New York: Center for the Study of the Presidency, 1981), xix.

2. E.O. 11490, *Federal Register* 34 (October 30, 1969): 17567–99; subsequently amended by E.O. 11921, *Federal Register* 41 (June 15, 18976): 24294–336.

3. Laurence F. Schmeckebier and Roy B. Eastin, *Government Publications and Their Use* (Washington, D.C.: Brookings Institution, 1969), 341.

4. E.O. 10290, 3 *C.F.R.* (1949–1953 Comp., 790–97).

5. See James Bamford, *The Puzzle Palace* (Boston,: Houghton Mifflin, 1982).

6. Stanley L. Falk, "The National Security Council under Truman, Eisenhower, and Kennedy," *Political Science Quarterly* 79 (September 1964): 410.

7. Ibid., 409–10; Sidney W. Souers, "Policy Formulation for National Security," *American Political Science Review*,43 (June 1949): 539–540.

8. Falk, "National Security Council," 410–11.

9. Souers, "Policy Formulation for National Security," 541.

10. Walter Millis, Harvey C. Mansfield, and Harold Stein, *Arms and the State: Civil-Military Elements in National Policy* (New York: The Twentieth Century Fund, 1958), 182; Falk, "National Security Council," 410.

11. Robert Cutler, "The Development of the National Security Council," *Foreign Affairs*, 34 (April 1960): 449.

12. Falk, "National Security Council," 421–22; Cutler, "Development of the National Security Council," 450.

13. I. M. Destler, "The Presidency and National Organization," in *The National Security: Its Theory and Practice, 1945–1960*, ed. Norman A. Gaebner (New York: Oxford University Press, 1986), 239.

14. General Accounting Office, *National Security: The Use of Presidential Directives to Make and Implement U.S. Policy*, GAO/NSIAD-89-31 (Washington, D.C.: General Accounting Office, December 1988), 4.

15. Ibid.

16. Ibid., 5.

17. General Accounting Office, *National Security: The Use of Presidential Directives to Make and Implement U.S. Policy*, GAO/NSIAD-89-31 (Washington, D.C.: General Accounting Office, January 1992), 2.

18. Ibid., 1.

19. See, for example, Samuel I. Rosenman, comp., *The Public Papers and Addresses of Franklin D. Roosevelt*. Vol. 4: *The Court Disapproves, 1935* (New York: Random House, 1938), 113. The reference is to the certification of the proposed Constitution of the Philippine Islands.

20. The published legal interpretations of the attorneys general appear in periodical volumes of the *Official Opinions of the Attorney General of the United States* for the years 1789–1974 and in the succeeding *Opinions of the Office of Legal Counsel of the United States Department of Justice* for the years 1977 to date.

21. See *Federal Register* 66 (November 16, 2001): 57833–36.

22. See *Weekly Compilation of Presidential Documents* 5 (April 14, 1969): 530–31; *Weekly Compilation of Presidential Documents* 29 (March 8, 1993): 350–52.

23. See Warren R. Reid, "Public Papers of the Presidents," *American Archivist* 25 (October 1962): 435–39.

24. James D. Richardson's *A Compilation of the Messages and Papers of Presidents* (New York: Bureau of National Literature), for example, contains executive orders of June 10, 1921 (Alaskan railroad town sites), September 21, 1921 (budget preparation and submission), and April 4, 1924 (commercial research of government officials in foreign lands), as well as an undenominated instrument of November 8, 1921 (budget preparation and submission).

25. *Annals of Congress* 1 (September 25, 1789): 88, 914–15; *Annals of Congress* (September 26, 1790): 90; Richardson, *Compilation of the Messages and Papers*, vol. 1 (1897), 56.

26. See Hans Aufricht, "Presidential Proclamations and the British Tradition," *Journal of Politics* 5 (May 1943): 142–61.

27. Schmeckebier and Eastin, *Government Publications and Their Use*, 341.

28. See *INS v. Chadha*, 462 U.S. 919 (1983).

29. Paul Dickson, *Think Tanks* (New York: Atheneum, 1971), 303.

30. Waldo Gifford Leland, "The Creation of the Franklin D. Roosevelt Library: A Personal Narrative," *American Archivist* 18 (January 1955): 15–16.

31. Senate Committee on Governmental Affairs, *Former Presidents Facilities and Services Reform Act of 1986*, S. Rept. 99-349 (Washington, D.C.: GPO, 1986), 8–9.

32. See House Committee on Government Operations, *Presidential Libraries: Unexplored Funding Alternatives*, H. Rept. 97-732 (Washington, D.C.: GPO, 1982).

33. See 44 U.S.C. 2112(a) (1982); 44 U.S.C. 2112(a)(1)(B)(i) (1986).

34. A Ford museum is located in the former president's hometown of Grand Rapids, Michigan, but it is not a presidential library.

35. Schmeckebier and Eastin, *Government Publication and Their Use*, 330–47.

URL SITE GUIDE

American Memory
Library of Congress
> http://memory.loc.gov/

Code of Federal Regulations
> http://archives.gov/federal_register/code_of_federal_regulations/code_of_federal

> http://www.access.gpo.gov/nara/cfr/index.html

> http://www.acccess.gpo.gov/nara/about-cfr.html

Executive Orders
> http://www.archives.gov/federal_register/executive_orders/disposition_tabl

Federal Register
> http://www.access.gpo.gov/su_docs/aces/aces140.html

> http://www.access.gpo.gov/nara/index.html

Federation of American Scientists
> http://www.fas.org/

National Archives and Records Administration
> http://www.archives.gov/index.html

> Presidential Libraries
> > http://www.archives.gov/presidential_libraries/addresses/addresses.html

> Presidential Documents on NARA Web Sites
> > http://www.archives.gov/research_room/getting_started/research_
> > presidential_material

National Security Presidential Directives
President George W. Bush
    http://www.fas.org/irp/offdocs/nspd/nspd-1.htm

Presidential Pardons
JURIST
University of Pittsburgh
    http://jurist.law.pitt.edu/pardons.htm

Public Papers of the President
    http://www.access.gpo.gov/nara/pubpaps/srchpaps.html

Weekly Compilation of Presidential Documents
    http://www.access.gpo.gov/nara/nara003.html

White House
    http://www.whitehouse.gov

Chapter 6

Executive Branch

Information policy is far-reaching and encompasses areas such as national security, the management of information technology, agriculture, the economy, the environment, labor, the statistical gathering and reporting system, and telecommunications. Naturally, the coverage in this book and chapter is selective, but the resources discussed could be used to uncover other policies, address broader public policy issues, and search out the myriad publications and information that the government produces now as well as what it produced during the past 200 years. Furthermore, the resources addressed can be used to update the coverage provided in this chapter and book.

THE ADMINISTRATION

As explained in Article II, section 1 of the Constitution, "the executive Power shall be vested in a President of the United States of America." To exercise that power, the president draws on an organization of departments and agencies. The secretaries of the fourteen principal departments make up the traditional cabinet:

Agriculture

Commerce

Defense

Education

Energy

Health and Human Services

Housing and Urban Development

Interior

Justice

Labor

State

Transportation

Treasury

Veterans Affairs

In the administration of George W. Bush, cabinet rank also extends to the vice president; the president's chief of staff; the United States Trade Representative; and the directors of the Environmental Protection Agency, Office of Management and Budget, Office of National Drug Control Policy, and the Office of Homeland Security.

Instead of highlighting each of these cabinet entities and the other parts of the executive branch, this chapter highlights several themes: the Executive Office of the President; national security; scientific and technical information (STI); business, trade, and economic matters; telecommunications policy; and Indian affairs. For coverage of various components of the executive branch, consult *U.S. Government on the Web* (2001) and the *U.S. Government Manual* (see later in this chapter).

With the advent of the Internet, the executive branch is making more use of the Web to interact with the public. Now, they—as does Congress—use Webcasts of meetings and news conferences, e-mail messages (even some departmental libraries accept e-mail queries from the public), and the release of photographs and satellite imagery. The Jimmy Carter Library and Museum, for instance, "holds approximately 500,000 still photographs; 834 of these photos are accessible on the Internet . . ." (see http://www.jimmycarterlibrary.org/documents/index.phtml). The Franklin D. Roosevelt Library and Museum has "thousands of on-line copyright free photos" representing the president and first lady, the "Great Depression & New Deal," and "World War II" (http://www.fdrlibrary.marist.edu/photos. html). At this site it is also possible to order a print of a photograph.

EXECUTIVE OFFICE OF THE PRESIDENT

The Executive Office of the President (EOP) consists of a group of agencies "created, at least in theory, to assist the president immediately with advice, administration, coordination, and other kinds of support. . . . Some existed before this enclave was established in 1939; many were created by succeeding presidents; others were wished upon them by Congress. Some have endured; others have vanished quickly."[1] *The Executive Office of the President*, edited by Harold C. Relyea, provides an excellent historical overview of the enclave, including its precursors and prototypes, and the agencies and personnel comprised in the Executive Office of the President (EOP).[2] Relyea notes that:

> Among the more enduring constructs of the Executive Office are the White House Office and the Office of Management and Budget (formerly the Bureau of the Budget), which were among the initial EOP structures. The Council of Economic Advisers, established in 1946, and the National Security

Council, created in 1947, also appear to hold permanent status. Both the Office of the Special Representative for Trade Negotiations and the Council on Environmental Quality have endured for over two decades. It also seems unlikely that the President's administrative support staff unit, known as the Office of Administration, will soon be eliminated. If such did happen, its function would most likely have to be assumed by the White House Office, which would increase both its personnel and budget. Indeed, this unit was created, in part, in response to, and to avoid, subsequent criticism that the White House staff was too large and too costly.[3]

Office of Management and Budget

The Office of Management and Budget (OMB) influences

the flow of information and statistical data through four interrelated means. The first involves its philosophy of, and role in, information collection. The second relates to its well-known budgetary responsibilities. The third involves the forms approval process, through which forms used by agencies to collect information must pass through before they can be used. Finally, OMB basically controls the Information Collection Budget, which regulates the amount of time it takes a respondent to complete a form of the federal government.[4]

Among its various roles and responsibilities, OMB forges the president's budget and provides financial and grants management for the executive branch. It also provides procurement policy, statements of administration policy, and information and regulatory policy for the branch. At its Web site (http://www.whitehouse.gov/omb), OMB covers each of these activities, as well as some information provided to Congress. The various budget documents that the president submits, as well as OMB circulars, bulletins, and memoranda, are found at this site.

The Council of Economic Advisers

The Council of Economic Advisers (CEA) duties and functions are to

- Assist and advise the president in the preparation of the *Economic Report*;

- Gather timely and authoritative information concerning economic developments and economic trends, both current and prospective, to analyze and interpret such information for the purpose of determining whether such developments and trends are interfering, or are likely to interfere, with the achievement of such policy, and to compile and submit to the president studies relating to such developments and trends;

- Appraise the various programs and activities of the federal government for the purpose of determining the extent to which such programs and activities are contributing, and the extent to which they are not contributing, to the achievement of such policy; and to make recommendations to the president with respect thereto;

- Develop and recommend to the president national economic policies to foster and promote free competitive enterprise, avoid economic fluctuations, or diminish the effects thereof, and to maintain employment, production, and purchasing power; and

- Make and furnish such studies, reports thereon, and recommendations with respect to matters of federal economic policy and legislation as the president may request. (http://www.whitehouse.gov/cea)

A key publication of the Council is the annual *Economic Report of the President*, the latest of which appears at the CEA's Web site; past editions are available through GPO Access (http://w3.access.gpo.gov/eop). This source provides economic analyses and trends.

Council on Environmental Quality

The Council on Environmental Quality (CEQ), which was established as part of the National Environmental Policy Act of 1969, and received additional responsibilities under the Environmental Quality Improvement Act of 1970,

> coordinates federal environmental efforts and works closely with agencies and other White House offices in the development of environmental policies and initiatives. . . . In addition, CEQ reports annually to the President on the state of the environment; oversees federal agency implementation of the environmental impact assessment process; and acts as a referee when agencies disagree over the adequacy of such assessments. (http://www.whitehouse.gov/ceq)

CEQ produces an annual report and some other publications.

Office of the United States Trade Representative

The U.S. Trade Representative (USTR) is the nation's "chief trade negotiator and the principal trade policy advisor to the President. In this role, the USTR and the agency's staff are responsible for developing and implementing trade policies which promote world trade growth and create new opportunities for American businesses, workers and agricultural produces" (http://www.ustr.gov/about-ustr/index.shtml). The agency's Web site covers the Trade Representative and the agency's history, role, key officials, and so on. It also addresses "Hot Topics," and provides resources and coverage of the World Trade Organization, "Trade & Development," "Trade & Enforcement," "World Regions," and other topics. There is a section devoted to "Sectors:" "Agriculture," "E-commerce," "Industry & Telecommunications," "Intellectual Property," "Investment," "Services," "Telecommunications," and "Textiles." The site map (http:www.ustr. gov/sitemap.shtml) is exceedingly helpful. It explains "How to Navigate This Site" and provides links and explanations of "Commonly Requested Topics" (e.g., "Agreements" and "Dispute Settlement").

Office of Science and Technology Policy

Created in 1976, the Office of Science and Technology Policy (OSTP) provides the president with policy advice and coordination of the nation's science and technology investment. OSTP has not always assumed its expected role, one of "advancing fundamental science, education and scientific, literacy, investment in applied research, and international cooperation" (http://www. ostp.gov/html/OSTP_insideostp.html). At any rate, access to its publications is available through the Government Printing Office's *Catalog of United States Government Publications*; *FedWorld,* the database of the National Technical Information Service; and the agency's Web site. That site maintains "Information Archives."

The Office of Homeland Security

Created in the aftermath of the terrorist attacks of September 11, the Office of Homeland Security coordinates "national strategy to strengthen protections against terrorist threats or attacks in the United States." Its home page (http://www.whitehouse.gov/homeland) offers "tips to protect against terrorism," briefings, and information. It also identifies some of the actions taken by the administration to protect the homeland.

NATIONAL SECURITY

National security is a broad and often nebulous policy term that, at a minimum, embraces both national defense and foreign affairs. The new national security perspective found its way into government in the aftermath of World War II and with the onset of the Cold War. Testifying in 1945 before the Senate Committee on Military Affairs on legislation concerning the consolidation of the armed forces under a new department management structure, Secretary of the Navy James Forrestal stressed that he was using the term national security "consistently and continuously" in his remarks rather than the more traditional national defense phrase.[5] Explaining that "it has been a fetish of mine that the question of national security is not merely a question of the Army and the Navy," he said:

We have tried to take into account our whole potential for war, our mines, industry, manpower, research, and all the activities that go into normal civilian life. I do not think you can deal with this only by the War and Navy Departments. This has to be a truly global effort.
That is the way we approached it, not from a limited area, but tried to bring in every element of our Government.[6]

Forrestal subsequently laid out before the committee "a list of eight requirements against which to measure any plan for national security," as follows:

(1) Organized means for the integration of foreign and military policy.

(2) Organizations in being for directing industrial mobilization and for reconciling industrial mobilization with natural resources.

 That means in particular that you don't create military demands beyond your capacity to fill them or that will do injury to other great and urgent demands. And that question of balance, in my view, is one of the most important considerations in war.

(3) A more efficient organization for the translation of strategic requirements into requirements for materiel and personnel.

(4) Provision for the coordination of military and other war budgets.

(5) Adequate means for the elimination of waste and duplication in and between the military departments.

(6) An efficient coordinated intelligence organization serving all Government departments and agencies.

(7) An organizational means for fostering scientific research and development within the military departments and among civilian organizations.

(8) Full opportunity for each branch of the military services to develop for its specialized task.[7]

Most of these requirements were met with the National Security Act of 1947 (61 Stat. 495), which established an independent air force under a new administrative department, unified the three armed services and their administrative departments under a National Military Establishment supervised by a Secretary of Defense, and created the Central Intelligence Agency, the National Security Council, and the National Security Resources Board (61 Stat. 495). The statute marked the institutionalization of the national security concept and the beginning of the national security state. It did not, however, define the term.

Nonetheless, the national security concept was seen as having adaptive value. In June 1949, Sidney W. Souers, executive secretary of the recently created National Security Council, described the concept as "a point of view rather than a distinct area of government responsibility."[8]

Throughout the Cold War era, presidents established various policies and practices relying on the national security concept and their point of view regarding its meaning and scope. What evolved, civil liberties attorney John Shattuck observed in 1983, was a

> national security framework within which postwar presidents have sought 'the freedom to pursue [their] planned course of action.' To make up for their lack of constitutional authority to act so freely, every president since Truman has relied on two doctrines to justify executive initiatives to protect national security: inherent presidential power and post-hoc congressional ratification.[9]

Shattuck concluded that the president's national security powers have become "powers to act in peacetime as if the country were at war." But since at least 1945, he noted, "we have lived in a twilight zone in which the distinctions between war and peace are so blurred, and the instability of the world so constant that presidents have lacked any objective guideposts for the exercise of their national security powers."[10] Thus, the nation experienced a number of national security misadventures, not the least of which were the Bay of Pigs debacle, the Vietnam tragedy, events surrounding the Watergate incident, and perhaps the Iran-Contra affair.[11]

The Military and the Media During Wartime

During the time of war, a question logically arises:

> What is the "plan for media coverage of U.S. military action to ensure that at least a small pool is activated at the time of deployment, and to assist, not manage journalists in the collection and reporting of news [?"] . . . Despite . . . [the existence of a plan], the message conveyed by the actions of the White House and military command in the Persian Gulf War [as well as during the operations in Grenada and Panama] is that the military continues to make it difficult for the media to engage in independent coverage of combat.[12]

In 1992, Steven L. Katz, the counsel for the Senate Committee on Government Affairs, wrote about the

> enormous gap between decision makers in the Pentagon, other military officials including the Joint Chiefs of Staff, and representatives of the press. While these cultural attributes are unlikely to change, the military and the media must overcome such traits and beliefs to ensure that there exists a mutual objective: informing the American public with timely, accurate, independent, and thorough reporting in a manner consistent with preserving military security during wartime.[13]

A 1,546-page hearing transcript of the Senate Committee on Governmental Affairs, entitled *Pentagon Rules on Media Access to the Persian Gulf War,*[14] discussed the tension between the military and the press covering a military engagement. The military-press relationship discussed in this document, as well as a special issue of *Government Information Quarterly,*[15] identified the rules for covering military operations. The press had the greatest latitude during the Vietnam War. Subsequent conflicts have seen the military apply much more rigid restrictions, as discussed in those hearings.

Department of Defense Web Site

DefenseLINK, the home page of the Department of Defense (DoD) (http://www.defenselink.mil), provides access to news, images, publications, current developments, the departmental organizational structure, and information about DoD. There is a site map, frequently asked questions, a subject search, and a list of publicly-available Web sites. There is also a clear explanation of the DoD's policy toward the release of information, privacy, and the use of cookies for monitoring Web traffic, as well as coverage of the Freedom of Information Act (see "DoD Webmasters Policies and Guidelines," http://www.defenselink. mil/webmasters).

Other Web Sites

Corona, "the nation's first photo reconnaissance satellite system," operated from August 1960 to May 1972. Declassified in February 1995, the program provides documents and imagery. At present, these resources are under review and are being processed for transfer to the National Archives and Records Administration (see http://www.nro.gov/corona.html).

Founded in 1985, the National Security Archive, which is located at George Washington University's Gelman Library (Washington, D.C.), "has become the world's largest non government library of declassified documents." The Archive makes these documents accessible to researchers and the public, and seeks to develop "comprehensive collections of documents on specific topics" (e.g., The Iran-Contra Affair, 1983–1988; the Cuban Missile Crisis, 1962; and the Berlin Crisis, 1958–1962) (http://www.gwu.edu/~nsarchiv/nsa/the_archive.html). Twelve of the Archives microfiche collections are available on the Web as part of the Digital National Security Archive (http://nsarchive.chadwyck.com). Furthermore, the National Security Archive Electronic Briefing Books "provide online access to critical declassified records on specific issues, including U.S. national security, foreign policy, and more" (see http://www.gwu.edu/~nsarchiv/ NSAEBB).

Other sites are the following:

- Project on Government Secrecy of the Federation of American Scientists (http://www.fas.org/sgp), which seeks "to challenge excessive government secrecy and to promote public oversight." In addition to providing key documents and policies, there are newsletters, namely *Secrecy & Government Bulletin* and *Secrecy & Security News*.

- Nationalsecurity.org (http://www.nationalsecurity.org), which The Heritage Foundation devotes "to disseminating information and policy analyses regarding U.S. national security issues. This site is meant to function as a clearinghouse for reporters, researchers, and concerned Americans interested in gaining access to publications and links on a wide spectrum, of national security issues."

- National Security of the American Civil Liberties Union (http://www.aclu.org/issues/security/hmns.html), which covers legislation and other policy developments.

- *National Security Studies Quarterly* (http://ssp.georgetown.edu/nssq), which is produced by Georgetown University's Center for Peace and Security Studies.

FOREIGN AFFAIRS AND INFORMATION ON OTHER COUNTRIES

Foreign affairs and dealing with other countries are not the sole providence of the secretary of state and the Department of State. Naturally, the president and vice president, national security advisor, National Security Council, Department of Agriculture, Department of Commerce, and other actors might be involved, depending on the issue or situation. Presidential nominations of key personnel in the State Department and ambassadors abroad serve as a reminder that international relations is not the sole province of the president and the executive branch. The Senate, and both chambers (and respective committees) play a consulting and, at times, partner role, but they can also block administration policy.

Types of information related to international relations that users typically seek are

- The text of treaties (current and retrospective),

- A listing of treaties still in effect,

- Current activities of the State Department,

- Personnel serving in embassies,

- Declassified diplomatic correspondence,

- Nominations and hearings for ambassadors, and

- Viewpoints on issues and policies from other countries.

Adelaide R. Hasse's *Index to United States Documents Relating to Foreign Affairs, 1828–1861*, 3 vols. (Washington, D.C.: Carnegie Institution of Washington, 1914; reprinted by Kraus, 1965) covers sources such as the *Congressional Globe*, Serial Set, and House and Senate Journals. (To locate Serial Set numbers, review Chapter 2, the accompanying CD-ROM, and the charts in the front of the *Checklist of United States Public Documents*.)

Other information can be found in congressional appropriations reports and hearings, as well as the floor debates recorded in the *Congressional Record*. Of course, some information might be sensitive, classified, and withheld from public scrutiny.

Treaties (Current/Retrospective and Those in Force)

Charles Bevans compiled *Treaties and Other International Agreements of the United States of America*, which covers the years 1776–1949. The *Statutes at Large*, prior to 1950, included the text of treaties. More recently, there is *United States Treaties and Other International Agreements*, which covers the years since 1952. A periodical, the *Department of State Bulletin*, was published from 1939 to January 1978, when it was replaced by the *United States Department of State Dispatch*. Both include treaties and the U.S. position on key issues.

Treaties in Force is an annual record of all treaties and agreements in force as of January 1 (for that year). Having ascertained that a treaty is currently in effect, the information seeker could turn to one of the above sources for the actual treaty:

Bevans, *Statutes at Large*, and *Department of State Bulletin*, prior to 1950;

Department of State Bulletin, for 1950–1951; and

United States Treaties and Other International Agreements, for 1952 to the present.

Current State Department Activities/Personnel Serving in Embassies

The Web site (http://www.state.gov) presents the State Department's (and administration's) position on issues, as well as information useful to Americans traveling abroad. It also provides access to information on some personnel of foreign embassies—those in nonsensitive positions. Countries are briefly highlighted in the "Country Background Notes."

Declassified Diplomatic Correspondence

Secret provisions of past treaties and the U.S. position on the negotiation of a treaty, as well as other declassified material, may be found in the *Foreign Relations of the United States* (see Chapter 7) and on the State Department's Web site. For example, the *Foreign Relations of the United States* contains the diplomatic exchange between Germany and the United States over the sinking of the *Lusitania* prior to American entry into World War I, coverage of U.S. military operations and diplomatic actions in Nicaragua during the 1920s, the fall of China to communist forces in the late 1940s, and the origins of the Vietnam War.

Nominations and Hearings for Ambassadors

Relevant source material emanates from the White House and the Senate Foreign Relations Committee. The White House Web site (http://www. whitehouse.gov) identifies nominations, as do the *Weekly Compilation of Presidential Documents* and the *Public Papers of the President*, both of which are produced by the National Archives and Records Administration and published by the Government Printing Office (GPO). Both publications are also available through GPO Access. For coverage of hearings, it would be necessary to visit the committee's Web site (http://foreign.senate.gov/menu.html) or an index, such as the *Catalog of United States Government Publications* or one of its predecessors (see Chapter 2).

Other Country Sources

The Library of Congress maintains "Country Studies," an online version of the country profiles provided by the Country Studies/Area Handbook Program sponsored by the Department of Army. The series has never been comprehensive but rather focuses on lesser-known "areas of the world or regions in which U.S. forces might be deployed."

> [T]he Country Studies Series presents a description and analysis of the historical setting and the social, economic, political, and national security systems and institutions of countries throughout the world and examines the interrelationships of those systems and the ways they are shaped by cultural factors.

> The books represent the analysis of the authors and should not be construed as an expression of an official United States Government position, policy, or decision. The authors have sought to adhere to accepted standards of scholarly objectivity. (http://lcweb2.loc.gov/frd/cs/cshome.html)

Hardcopy editions of the books in the series, except for the regional study on Macau, are available from GPO's Bookstore program (see GPO Access, http://bookstore.gpo.gov).

The Web site of the Central Intelligence Agency (CIA) (http://www. odci.gov) provides publications such as the *World Factbook*, which contains factual information on countries, a listing of the heads of state in other countries, and citations to other publications. In 1996, *Emergence of the Intelligence Establishment, 1945–1950*, was released. It is the first volume devoted entirely to creation of the foreign intelligence community, including the establishment of the Central Intelligence Agency (CIA).

Both the Foreign Broadcast Information Service (FBIS) and the Joint Publications Research Service (JPRS), subagencies of the CIA, provided English translations of various media in foreign countries worldwide. FBIS focused mainly on current news gathered from newspapers, radio, television, and periodicals. JPRS reports were translations of unclassified foreign documents, scholarly works, research reports, and journal articles considered to be important source material for research in the social sciences and, especially, in the sciences and technology.

The *FBIS Daily Reports* were issued in print from 1941 to mid-1996. For much of that period they were issued in eight parts, covering all the regions of the world. The printed reports were available for a fee through NTIS and on microfiche through GPO's depository library program. As of September 1996, the *FBIS Daily Reports* ceased publication.

Various indexing tools exist to find specific materials. The *FBIS Daily Reports Index* on CD-ROM (1982–1996) is a consolidated search tool for reports issued during that time period. Paper indexes for each FBIS world region also exist. Both indexes were published by the Readex Corporation.

The *JPRS Reports* were issued from 1957 through 1996. A large number of these reports were concerned with some phase of Soviet or other communist country activity. Until 1984, the reports were issued by a single series number. From 1984, they were arranged by subseries (e.g., Worldwide Reports: Law of the Sea; China Reports: Political, Sociological, and Military Affairs). Indexing to *JPRS Reports* was provided by the commercial *Transdex Index* from 1974 to 1996. The *Monthly Catalog of United States Government Publications* and other miscellaneous indexes provide coverage from 1958 through mid-1975. For a description of these other indexing sources, see http://www.lib.umd.edu/ MICROFORMS/uspub_research.html).

In 1996, *FBIS* and *JPRS Reports* merged into *World News Connection*, an online news service available via the Web through NTIS subscription (see http://wnc.fedworld.gov). The content, with coverage from 1994 to date, is still provided by FBIS, which continues to exist as a government entity. Generally, the information is available within twenty-four to seventy-two hours from the time of original publication or broadcast.

USATrade, a Web service of the U.S. Commercial Service (http://usatrade.gov/ website/website.nsf), presents information about exporting and the services of the agency. There are directories, market research data and reports, and other services. STAT- USA/Internet, an electronic fee-based service of the Department of Commerce, provides business and economic information, such as the National Trade Data Bank; the Economic Bulletin Board, a comprehensive source for government-sponsored economic releases and business leads; GLOBUS (Global Business Procurement Opportunities); and Bureau of Economic Analysis economic information, including news releases and data files.

TECHNICAL REPORT LITERATURE

As Thomas E. Pinelli, Rebecca O. Barclay, and John M. Kennedy have written, the focus of federal science and technology has shifted from military superiority during the Cold War to "the belief that federally-funded science and technology plays a major role in the economy and the competitiveness of the United States in a global economy."[16] After the terrorist attacks of September 11, another shift began to occur: use of research funding to help combat terrorism.

The United States has produced scientific and technical information (STI) for more than two hundred years. Many of these products have had limited distribution, to a specific agency and perhaps its contractors and grantees. Further, there have been various information transfer mechanisms. Over the years, a number of policies have shaped STI policy. Examples include the Stevenson-Wydler Technology Innovation Act of 1980 (PL 96-480), the Japanese Technical Literature Act of 1986 (PL 99-382), the American Technology Preeminence Act of 1991 (PL 102-245), the National Science and Technology Policy, Organization and Priorities Act of 1976 (PL 94-212), and the Information Technology Management Reform Act of 1996 (PL 104-106).

Writing in 1988, Gary R. Purcell described the technical report as "the primary publication type used for the dissemination of vast quantities of information derived from federally-funded research and development projects. The report is also the primary publication type that major industrial firms use for the internal reporting of the results of proprietary research and development activities."[17] Further, it "is a form of publication intended for the rapid dissemination of information. It is most commonly used to report progress on, and the final results of, scientific investigation."[18]

In a 1989 staff paper, the then Office of Technology Assessment referred to the federal government as "the largest single source of scientific and technical information . . . in the world," and noted that "scientific advancement and technological innovation depend on the open exchange of STI." Further, it advocated a "stronger executive branch commitment and leadership" for STI in the Executive Office of the President, especially from the Office of Science and Technology Policy and the Office of Management and Budget.[19] One of the questions that the paper raised was: "How can the federal government improve public access to its resources of STI?"[20] Although the paper mentioned, but did not focus on, NTIS, this agency has long played a role, but not an exclusive one, in the collection, dissemination, and preservation of STI.

National Technical Information Service

The National Technical Information Service (NTIS), an agency of the Department of Commerce, evolved from the Office of the Publication Board (PB) in 1945 to collect and declassify World War II technical data for dissemination to industry and the government. It now collects, organizes, announces, markets, sells, and preserves technical knowledge, information, and data, especially government-sponsored research and development reports. These resources, produced by federal, state, and local governments and their contractors, both foreign and domestic, include data files, computer programs, and government-owned patent applications. Together, these resources are of value to business and industry, state and local governments, other federal agencies, and the general public as the United States becomes even more competitive in the global economy.

The NTIS also provides fee-based services for federal agencies, including brokerage services (e.g., billing and collecting for other agencies that charge for products and services), distribution services (e.g., disseminating other agencies' products or operating the Web site of the Internal Revenue Service), and Web services (e.g., FedWorld: http://www.fedworld.gov). Agency transfer of research to NTIS is generally governed by 15 U.S.C. 3704b-2, and this statute is implemented by 15 C.F.R. 1180. Nonetheless, agencies often have not supplied the results of federally funded research and development activities. Title 15, *United States Code*, sections 1151–1171, also direct the clearinghouse to be largely self-supporting. Salaries, marketing, postage, and other operating costs must be recouped from sales income, not from appropriations; some developmental programs are excluded.

The NTIS distributes publications and other source materials that are unclassified and of unlimited distribution for the Department of Energy (Office of Science and Technical Information), National Aeronautics and Space Administration (NASA), and Department of Defense's Defense Technical Information Center (DTIC). Part of the DoD scientific and technical information program, DTIC provides access to, and the transfer of, scientific and technical information for departmental personnel and contractors, and other government agency personnel and their contractors.

During the Reagan and Clinton administrations, there were attempts to eliminate NTIS. In the first instance, the Republican administration wanted to privatize NTIS, removing some of its resources to the private sector. In the other instance, William M. Daley, then commerce secretary, recommended NTIS's closing in August 1999. He believed that there was no need for an agency to sell government information resources when agencies were posting them on their Web sites for free. As he announced, "these changes in the information marketplace have made obsolete the need for NTIS to serve as a clearinghouse and, thus have in turn made it increasingly difficult for NTIS to maintain its operation on a self-sustaining basis, as established by Congress." Further, "NTIS sales have dramatically declined over the last six years with the advent of the personal computer and increased use of the Internet. In fact, NTIS' core clearinghouse business has not operated at a profit since FY 1993."[21] At the same time, the secretary downsized the clearinghouse.

In May 2001 the General Accounting Office (GAO) noted that "the increasing availability of scientific, technical, and engineering information on the Web is raising fundamental policy questions about the future direction of NTIS."[22] According to GAO, the clearinghouse held about 2.46 million reports, a number of which were published in the 1980s or earlier and were duplicated in the holdings of other repositories.[23] More recent publications might also be available through the Web site of the issuing agency.[24]

One information policy analyst, Robert Gellman, supports the demise of the agency. He believes that "the Internet is eliminating the role of information intermediaries like NTIS," and that the agency is in violation of both the Paperwork Reduction Act, which "prohibits royalties for government information and restrictions on its reuse and mandates marginal-cost pricing," and the Freedom of Information Act, which limits fees for government information.[25] A basic unanswered question is: "Is there a need for a central repository to disseminate STI?" The previously mentioned GAO report responds:

> Answering this question requires knowing (1) the extent to which agencies could be relied upon to provide permanent public access to publications and (2) in the absence of a central repository, what type of bibliographic information and control over government publications are needed to ensure that reports can be identified and located indefinitely.[26]

The GAO also raised another question: "What obligations should a central repository have to retain all reports indefinitely?" It estimated "that only 1 percent of the NTIS reports over 12 years old has sold since 1995." The conclusion drawn was that

> it may be useful to consider whether all scientific, technical, and engineering information should be retained permanently. How long to retain such information, however, would have to be based on demand patterns for older documents and on the costs and benefits of retaining documents of various age strata. This decision should also be based on a policy determination about permanent access and the need to maintain a central repository, as opposed to reliance on other repositories such as libraries.[27]

Two important conclusions from the GAO investigation are that

- Permanent public availability of and access to government information are critical parts of the overall strategy to meet the public information needs of the public and need to be strengthened; and

- NTIS is the only fail-safe source to make research results available when they are no longer available from the originating agency.[28]

Other Distributors of Federal Technical Report Literature

Other technical report sources include NASA, the Educational Resources Information Center (ERIC) of the Department of Education, the Office of Scientific and Technical Information (OSTI) of the Department of Energy (DOE), the Defense Technical Information Center of the Department of Defense, GPO, the National Science Foundation, the Environmental Protection Agency, and the Departments of Agriculture and Health and Human Services (e.g., National Library of Medicine).

The OSTI, in partnership with GPO, offers PubSCIENCE, "a modernization of Nuclear Science Abstracts and the Energy Science and Technology Database" (http://pubsci.osti.gov/about.html). It provides access to peer-reviewed journal literature in the physical sciences and other energy-related disciplines. There is also DOE Information Bridge ("an open source to full text and bibliographic records of Energy (DOE) research and development reports in physics, chemistry, materials, biology sciences, energy technologies, engineering, computer and information science," http://www.osti.gov/bridge); a database for full-text DOE report literature; the PrePrint Network for preprints in science and technology (http://www.osti.gov/preprint); the EnergyFiles Virtual Library Collection of Energy Science and Technology (see http://www.osti.gov/EnergyFiles); and the *Energy Citations Database (1948–Present)*, which "contains bibliographic records from energy and energy-related scientific and technical information from . . . DOE . . . and its predecessor agencies, the Energy Research & Development Administration (ERDA) and the Atomic Energy Commission (AEC). The Database provides access to DOE publicly available citations from 1948 through the present, with continued growth through regular updates" (http://www.osti. gov/energycitations).

The National Library of Medicine provides access to health information and resources on its home page (http://www.nlm.nih.gov). Among its Web offerings are references to and abstracts from biomedical journals, information about clinical research studies, a directory of health organizations, a digital archive of life science journal literature (PubMed Central), sources of cancer information, coverage of bioethics, a history of medicine, and so forth (see http://www.nlm.nih.gov/hinfo.html). There is also coverage of telemedicine (http://www.nlm.nih.gov/research/telemedinit.html).

TELECOMMUNICATIONS POLICY

The 1934 Communications Act (PL 73-416, 48 Stat. 1064) gave the president and the Federal Communications Commission (FCC) responsibility for managing uses in the United States of the radio frequency spectrum. The president delegated authority to the Department of Commerce's National Telecommunications and Information Administration (NTIA). The Telecommunications Act of 1996 (PL 104-104, 110 Stat. 56), which is to "promote competition and reduce regulation in order to secure lower prices and higher quality services for American telecommunications consumers and encourage the rapid deployment of new telecommunications technologies" (Section 1), shifted numerous regulatory rulemaking responsibilities to the FCC.

For information on telecommunications policy consult the *Code of Federal Regulations* (Title 47 on "Telecommunication"), NTIA (http://www.ntia.docgov), FCC (http://www.fcc.gov), and GPO Access (http://bookstore.gpo.gov/regulatory/telecom.html). Another handy tool is GPO's Subject Bibliography 298 on "Telecommunications" (http://bookstore.gpo.gov/sb/sb-296.html). This bibliography identifies other public laws, reports, compilations, and statistics. The FCC Web site covers the 1996 Telecommunications Act, and the *New York Times*, *The Washington Post*, and the *Wall Street Journal* provide recent news, developments, and proposed mergers, involving telecommunications, cable, and satellite providers.

Broadband Internet Access

Broadband Internet access gives individuals the ability to send and receive data at speeds much faster than conventional "dial up" Internet access over existing telephone lines. The private sector is deploying nationwide new broadband technologies (cable, modem, digital subscriber line (DSL), satellite, and fixed wireless Internet). Concerns in Congress have arisen that, while the number of new broadband subscribers continues to grow, the rate of broadband deployment in urban and high income areas appears to be outpacing deployment in rural and low-income areas, thereby creating a potential "digital divide" in broadband access. The Telecommunications Act authorizes FCC to intervene in the telecommunications market if it determines that broadband is not being deployed to all Americans in a "reasonable and timely fashion."

At issue is what, if anything, should be done at the federal level to ensure that broadband deployment is timely, that industry competes on a level playing field, and that service is provided to all sectors of American society. At present, the debate in Congress centers on the following approaches: (1) easing certain legal restrictions and requirements (imposed by the Telecommunications Act) on incumbent telephone companies that provide high-speed data (broadband) access, (2) compelling cable companies to provide "open access" to competing Internet Service Providers (ISPs), and (3) providing federal financial assistance for broadband deployment in rural and economically disadvantaged areas.

BUSINESS, TRADE, ECONOMIC, AND MONETARY MATTERS

The *Commerce Business Daily* (*CBD*), published by the Department of Commerce, is the means by which government agencies notify the public of proposed procurements, contract awards, sources sought, surplus property sales, and other related notices. The Web version is known as *CBD Net* (see http://cbdnet.access.gpo.gov). However, it merits mention that notices appearing in the electronic version do not satisfy the requirements of the Federal Acquisition Rule (FAR Part 5) until they appear in *CBD*'s paper copy. Prior to conducting a search of *CBDNet*, it is advisable to consult the "Reader's Guide" for an explanation of commonly used abbreviations and general exceptions to inclusion in *CBD* (see http://cbdnet.access.gpo.gov/read-gd.html).

The *Catalog of Federal Domestic Assistance* covers assistance programs and eligibility requirements. Entries are classified by type of assistance (e.g., loans, scholarships and fellowships, and exchange programs). The *Catalog* can be searched via the Web (see http://www.cfda.gov). In addition, NTIS provides access to resources related to business, trade, and economics (see http://www.ntis.gov).

Another resource is the Federal Trade Commission, which enforces different federal antitrust and consumer protection laws. Its Web site (http://www.ftc.gov) provides "Business Guidance"; access to its regional offices; publications; and coverage of "Consumer Protection," "Economic Issues" (evaluations of the economic impact of the Commission's actions), "Formal Actions, Opinions & Activities," and so forth.

Some other options include the Bureau of Export Administration (BXA) and other agencies within the Department of Commerce (DoC). The Bureau covers export administration regulations; trade sanctions; commercial encryption export controls; and topics such as "Export Enforcement," "Computers," "Chemical Weapons," and "Compliance" (see http://www.bxa.doc.gov). The site map nicely breaks down the coverage (http://www.bxa.doc.gov/SiteMap.html).

Another example within DoC is the Office of Technology Policy (OTP), which develops and advocates "national policies and initiatives that use technology to build America's economic strength. Working in partnership with the private sector to achieve this objective, OTP's goals also include the creation of high-wage jobs and improvements in our quality of life" (http://www.ta.doc.gov). The International Trade Administration provides international trade assistance and information, including trade statistics, market research, export documentation, and so forth (see http://www.ita.doc.gov). The National Institute of Standards and Technology (NIST) provides technology, measurements, and standards that "help U.S. industry invent and manufacture superior products reliably, ensure a fair marketplace for consumers and businesses, and promote acceptance of U.S. products in foreign markets." NIST provides "the support needed to promote innovation, enhance product and service quality, and reduce costs in these and other important areas" (http://www.nist.gov).

The U.S. Trade and Development Agency (TDA), an independent agency, "assists in the creation of jobs for Americans by helping U.S. companies pursue overseas business opportunities." The agency's home page (http://www.tda.gov) provides its annual report, coverage of regions and sectors, related links, and other useful information, such as a summary of the types of activities that TDA funds.

The Small Business Administration (SBA), another independent agency, has a well-laid out Web site (http://www.sba.gov). There is a most helpful site map that leads information seekers quickly to the type of information sought and lists of business resources (http://www.sbaonline.sba/gov/hotlist). Pro-Net "is an electronic gateway of procurement information—for and about small businesses" (http://pro-net.sba.gov/index2.html).

The mission of the Securities and Exchange Commission (SEC) is to "maintain the integrity of the securities markets." Its Web site (http://www.sec.gov) provides access to EDGAR for disclosure documents that public companies file. One feature is a fifteen-page introduction to the agency and what it does.

The Overseas Private Investment Corporation assists private investment abroad by providing political risk insurance and loan help to U.S. businesses in more than 1,409 emerging markets and developing nations (http://www.opic.gov).

Turning to monetary policy, the Federal Reserve System (FED) plays an important role in overseeing the economy. The System consists of a Board of Governors and twelve district banks. For convenient access to each of the FED's components, as well as for new releases, publications, speeches, services, economic education, and economic data (e.g., discount rates, statistical releases, and a presentation on "What's a dollar worth?"), see http://minneapolisfed.org/info/sys/collection.html.

Another key entity is the Department of the Treasury, which

> is organized into two major components: the Departmental offices and the operating bureaus. The Departmental Offices are primarily responsible for the formulation of policy and management of the Department as a whole, while the operating bureaus carry out the specific operations assigned to the Department. . . . [B]ureaus make up 98% of the Treasury work force. The basic functions of the Department . . . include:

- Managing federal finances;

- Collecting taxes, duties and monies paid to and due to the United States and paying all bills of the United States;

- Producing all postage stamps, currency and coinage;

- Managing government accounts and the public debt;

- Supervising national banks and thrift institutions;

- Advising on domestic and international financial, monetary, economic, trade and tax policy;

- Enforcing federal finance and tax laws;

- Investigating and prosecuting tax evaders, counterfeiters, forgers, smugglers, illicit spirits distillers, and gun law violators; and

- Protecting the president, Vice president, their families, candidates for those offices, foreign missions resident in Washington and visiting foreign dignitaries. (http://www.ustreas.gov/opc/opc0042.html)

The Department's Web site (http://www.ustreas.gov) provides access to both offices and bureaus (see http://www.ustreas.gov/offices/index.html or http://www.ustreas.gov/bureaus/index.html). Some of the most frequently requested types of information resources are available at http://www.ustreas.gov/information.html.

INDIAN AFFAIRS

Historically, information about Native Americans could be found in the Serial Set (e.g., 07 and 08 of the American State Papers), the annual report of the Department of War, and historical and current indexes (see Chapter 2). Laurence F. Schmeckebier, in *The Office of Indian Affairs: Its History, Activities and Organization*, covers Indian Affairs from times prior to the formation of the union to the creation of the Office of Indian Affairs in the Department of the Interior and the activities of that office into the 1920s. He discusses three periods of the Indian policy of the government: (1) The Treaty Period (up to 1871), (2) the Reservation Period (1871–1887), and the Allotment and Citizenship Period (1887 to the time of the publication of his work). He notes that "the history of the Office of Indian Affairs is practically the history of the Indian policy of the United States."[29] In discussing the policy, he explains that he did not attempt "to give an account of the dealings with the separate tribes, except as illustrations of the general course pursued."[30] In the appendices, he covers topics such as statistics, publications, laws, and financial statements.

Indian Affairs: Laws and Treaties (Washington, D.C.: GPO,1904), compiled and edited by Charles J. Kappler, is a seven-volume collection of U.S. treaties, laws, and executive orders pertaining to Indian tribes. A subsequent edition covers 1904–1941 (GPO, 1975), and Oklahoma State University has a digital version at http://digital.librry.okstate.edu/kappler.

"A Century of Lawmaking for a New Nation. U.S. Congressional Documents and Debates" (http://lcweb2.loc.gov/ammem/amlaw/) covers the "Continental Congress and Constitutional Convention," "Journals of Congress," "Statutes and Documents," and "Debates of Congress." Among the "Statutes and Documents" are selected documents from the Serial Set, some of which cover "correspondence on the emigration of Indians, 1831–33." "A Century of Lawmaking for a New Nation" also has some "special presentations and related collections," one of which is "Indian Land Cessions in the United States, 1784 to 1894" (it includes maps).

Under the title "Indian Affairs," *The Catalog of United States Government Publications* (see Chapter 3) identifies the following committee print:

History, jurisdiction, and summary of legislative activities of the United States Senate, Committee on Indian Affairs during the One Hundred Fourth Congress, 1995–1996. 1998. United States. Y4.IN2/11/:S. PRT. 105–47

The Superintendent of Documents retrieval number for access to this print in a depository library is Y4.IN2/11/:S. PRT. 105-47. The *Catalog's* record also discloses that the Item Number is 100-B-05. To retrieve this publication, GPO Access will lead us to the nearest library likely to hold this publication (see http://www.access.gpo.gov/cgi-bin/locate; http://www.access.gpo.gov/su_docs/locators/findlibs/index.html).

Other sources on Native Americans and tribes include the following:

- Advisory Council on Historic Preservation, which covers the Tribal Historic Preservation Officers, deals with national historical preservation programs. Federally recognized Native American tribes can assume more formal responsibility for the preservation of significant historic properties on their lands (see http://www.achp.gov/thpo.html).

- Indian Arts and Crafts Board (Department of the Interior) promotes "the economic development of American Indians and Alaska Natives through the expansion of the Indian Arts and crafts market. A top priority of the Board is the implementation and enforcement of the Indian Arts and Crafts Act of 1990, a truth-in-advertising law that provides criminal and civil penalties for marketing products as 'Indian-made' when such products are not made by Indians, as defined by the Act. . . . The Board's other activities include providing professional business advice, information on the Act and related marketing issues, fundraising assistance, and promotional opportunities to Native American artists, craftspeople, and cultural organizations" (http://www.doj.gov/iacb/enter.html).

- Administration for Native Americans (Administration for Children and Families within the Department of Health and Human Services) "promotes the goal of social and economic self-sufficiency and "is the only federal agency serving all Native Americans" (http://www.acf.dhhs.gov/programs/ana).

- Office of Tribal Justice (Department of Justice) "was established to provide a single point of contact within the Justice Department for meeting the broad and complex federal responsibilities owed to Indian tribes" (http://www.usdoj.gov/otj/index.html).

- Indian Health Service (IHS) (Department of Health and Human Services) (http://www.ihs.gov) "is responsible for providing federal health services to American Indians and Alaska Natives."

- Bureau of Indian Affairs (Department of the Interior) (http://www.doi.gov/bia/information/navam.htm) provides access to other Native American Web sites, as well as other resources, including collections of relevant "Treaties, Laws and Executive Orders" and FedLaw—Native Americans (with links to the *United States Code*) (http://www.doi.gov/bia/information/treaties.htm). However, at this time Bureau sites are shut down due to litigation (see pages 382–83).

- Office of Indian Education Programs (Bureau of Indian Affairs) has as its mission " to provide quality opportunities from early childhood through life in accordance with Tribe's needs for cultural and economic well-being in keeping with the wide diversity of Indian Tribes and Alaska Native villages" (http://www.oiep.bia.edu).

- National Indian Gaming Commission, which was created in 1998, is an independent regulatory agency whose mission centers on the regulation of gaming activities on Indian lands (see http://www.nigc.gov).

The home page for the Department of the Interior, when functioning, directs those searching for departmental resources to check the heading "American Indians" or "DOI Board of Indian Appeals." "American Indians" leads to departmental, other government, and other Web sites on American Indians and Alaska Natives (see http://www.doi.gov/oait/links.htm).

On the legislative side is the Committee on Indian Affairs (http://indian.senate.gov/nscominfo.htm), which the Senate re-established in 1977. Note that the home page provides a brief history of the committee.

THE *UNITED STATES GOVERNMENT MANUAL*

The *United States Government Manual* is one of the most important sources for identifying federal agencies, including those in all three branches of government:

> A typical agency description includes a list of principal officials, a summary statement of the agency's purpose and role in the federal government, a brief history of the agency, including its legislative or executive authority, a description of its programs and activities, and a "Sources of Information" section, This last section provides information on consumer activities, contracts and grants, employment, publications, and many other areas of public interest. (http://www.access.gpo.gov/su_docs/help/hints/manual.html)

Since the 1995/1996 edition, it has been searchable online (http://www.access. gpo.gov/nara/nara001.html). "Online Recent Changes," provides updates of personnel changes for the current edition.

NONGOVERNMENT SOURCES

This section of the chapter highlights some commercial sources, as well as a product produced by a depository library, that complement the previous discussions.

Treaties and International Agreements Online

Oceana Publications, Inc., has an online service for treaties and international agreements that libraries can purchase on annual subscription and "individuals, law firms and corporations can purchase research time." Available at http://www.oceanalaw.com/, the service provides more than 12,000 treaties that can be searched by subject, country, treaty name, location signed, whether or not in force, termination date, and so forth. The publisher also offers *Consolidated Treaties and International Agreements*, an annual two-volume set of current U.S. treaties and agreements.

Uncle Sam—Who's Who in the Federal Government

The Government Publications Department, Regional Depository Library, University of Memphis, has produced *Uncle Sam—Who's Who in the Federal Government* (http://www.lib.memphis.edu/gpo/whos3.htm), which identifies and provides biographical information for the president and vice president, Cabinet secretaries, the congressional leadership, chairs of congressional committees, "Administrators of Selected Federal Agencies," "U.S. Ambassadors," the "Joint Chiefs of Staff," and Supreme Court justices. There is also a "Who Was Who" section.

Agency Histories

In the late 1950s, John L. Andriot began publishing guides to major U.S. government series and to federal statistics. One of these guides, *Guide to U.S. Government Publications*, is regularly updated and lists series issued to depository libraries in SuDocs class sequence. Now issued by Donna Andriot, each entry provides a brief note on the agency's creation and history. It is possible to trace an agency's shifting within a department's organizational structure (or across departments) over time. For example, the Children's Bureau and Women's Bureau have shifted. Andriot notes the locations for each entity for specific years.

A Historical Guide to the U.S. Government (Oxford University Press, 1998), edited by George Thomas Kurain, provides background information on a number of government agencies and discusses key concepts related to government information policy and the management of government operations.

CONCLUSION

As this chapter demonstrates, the executive branch—consisting of Cabinet departments, the Executive Office of the President, and assorted independent entities—produces resources related to the humanities, social sciences (including public administration), engineering, the behavioral and physical sciences, and medicine. Some of this information is aimed at specialized audiences, whereas other material is intended for the general public. However, as the section on national security illustrates, it is not just the information resources that information seekers should know. They should also be aware of the policy context and the fact that this context evolves over time and from administration to administration.

NOTES

1. *The Executive Office of the President: A Historical, Biographical, and Bibliographical Guide*, ed. Harold C. Relyea (Westport, Conn.: Greenwood Press, 1997), 3.

2. Ibid.

3. Ibid., 25.

4. Arthur L. Morin, "Regulating the Flow of Data: OMB and the Control of Government Information," *Public Administration Review* 54, no. 5 (September/October 1994): 435.

5. Senate Committee on Military Affairs, *Department of Armed Forces, Department of Military Security*, 79th Cong., 1st sess., hearings (Washington, D.C.: GPO, 1945), 99.

6. Ibid., 8–9.

7. Ibid., 578–79.

8. Sidney W. Souers, "Policy Formulation for National Security," *American Political Science Review* 43 (June 1949): 535.

9. John Shattuck, "National Security a Decade after Watergate," *Democracy* 3 (Winter 1983): 61–62.

10. Ibid.

11. To this list, some would also add the more recent intervention of the United States armed forces in the Persian Gulf; see, for example, Michael J. Glennon, "The Gulf War and the Constitution," *Foreign Affairs* 70 (Spring 1991): 84–101.

12. Steven L. Katz, "Ground Zero: The Information War in the Persian Gulf," *Government Information Quarterly* 9 (1992): 177–78.

13. Ibid., 405.

14. Senate Committee on Governmental Affairs, *Pentagon Rules on Media Access to the Persian Gulf War,* hearing, S. Hrg. 102-178 (Washington, D.C.: GPO, 1991).

15. See Steven L. Katz (guest editor), "Sand Trap: The Military and the Media during the Persian Gulf War, *Government Information Quarterly* 9 (1992): 375–493.

16. Thomas E. Pinelli, Rebecca O. Barclay, and John M. Kennedy, "U.S. Scientific and Technical Information Policy," in *Federal Information Policies in the 1990s,* ed. Peter Hernon, Charles R. McClure, and Harold C. Relyea (Norwood, N.J.: Ablex, 1996), 218.

17. Gary R. Purcell, "Technical Report Literature," in *Public Access to Government Information: Issues, Trends, and Strategies*, 2d ed., ed. Peter Hernon and Charles R. McClure (Norwood, N.J.: Ablex,1988), 207.

18. Ibid., 210.

19. "Federal Scientific and Technical Information in an Electronic Age: Opportunities and Challenges," unpublished OTA Staff Paper (Washington, D.C.: Office of Technology Assessment, Communication and Information Technologies Program, 1989), 1.

20. Ibid., 2.

21. Department of Commerce, "Commerce Secretary William M. Daley Announces Intention to Close National Technical Information Service," press release, August 12, 1999, 1.

22. General Accounting Office, *Information Management: Dissemination of Technical Reports*, GAO-01-490 (Washington, D.C.: General Accounting Office, May 2001), 3.

23. Ibid., 8, 15.

24. Ibid., 15.

25. Robert Gellman, "NTIS Is An Information Policy Disaster," *Government Computer News* (October 21, 1996): 29.

26. General Accounting Office, *Information Management*, 24.

27. Ibid.

28. Ibid.

29. Laurence F. Schmeckebier, *The Office of Indian Affairs: Its History, Activities and Organization* (Baltimore, Md.: The Johns Hopkins Press, 1927), 1.

30. Ibid.

URL SITE GUIDE

A Century of Lawmaking for a New Nation
http://lcweb2.loc.gov/ammem/amlaw/

Bookstores (GPO)
http://bookstore.gpo.gov/

> Telecommunications
> http://bookstore.gpo.gov/regulatory/telecom.html
> http://bookstore.gpo.gov/sb/sb-296.html

Bureau of Export Administration
Department of Commerce
http://www.bxa.doc.gov/

Catalog of Federal Domestic Assistance
http://www.cfda.gov/

Central Intelligence Agency
http://www.odci.gov/

Commerce Business Daily
http://cbdnet.access.gpo.gov

Corona
http://www.nro.gov/corona.html

Council of Economic Advisers
http://www.whitehouse.gov/cea/

> Economic Report of the President
> http://w3.access.gpo.gov/eop/

Council on Environmental Quality
http://www.whitehouse.gov/ceq/

Country Studies
Library of Congress
http://lcweb2.loc.gov/frd/cs/cshome.html

DefenseLINK
Department of Defense
http://www.defenselink.mil/

> DoD Webmasters Policies and Guidelines
> http://www.defenselink.mil/webmasters/

Department of State
http://www.state.gov/

Department of the Treasury
http://www.ustreas.gov/

Frequently Requested Types of Information
http://www.ustreas.gov/information.html

Office and Bureaus
http://www.ustreas.gov/offices/index.html

Federal Communications Commission
http://www.fcc.gov

Federal Reserve System
http://minneapolisfed.org/info/sys/collection.html

Federal Trade Commission
http://www.ftc.gov/

Government Printing Office (for Location of Depository Libraries)
http://www.access.gpo.gov/cgi-bin/locate

http://www.access.gpo.gov/su_docs/locators/findlibs/index.html

International Trade Administration
Department of Commerce
http://www.ita.doc.gov/

JPRS
http://www.lib.umd.edu/MICROFORMS/uspub_research.html

National Institute of Standards and Technology
Department of Commerce
http://www.nist.gov/

National Library of Medicine
http;//www.nlm.nih.gov/

Assorted Information
http://www.nlm.nih.gov/hinfo.html

Telemedicine
http://www.nlm.nih.gov/research/telemedint.html

National Technical Information Service
http://www.ntis.gov/

FedWorld
http://www.fedworld,gov/

World News Connection
http://wnc.fedworld.gov/

National Telecommunications and Information Administration
http://www.ntia.doc.gov/

Office of Homeland Security
http://www.whitehouse.gov/homeland/

Office of Management and Budget
http://www.whitehouse.gov/omb/

Office of Science and Technology Policy
http://www.ostp.gov/

Office of Technology Policy
Department of Commerce
http://www.ta.doc.gov

Office of the United States Trade Representative
http://www.ustr.gov/

Overseas Private Investment Corporation
http://www.opic.gov

Project on Government Security
Federation of American Scientists
http://www.fas.org/sgp/

Securities and Exchange Commission
http://www.sec.gov/

Senate Foreign Relations Committee
http://foreign.senate.gov/menu.html

Small Business Administration
http://www.sba.gov/

>Pro-Net
>http://pro-net.sba.gov/index2.html

STAT-USA
http://www.stat-usa.gov/

Treaties and International Agreements
Oceana Publications, Inc.
http://www.oceanalaw.com/

Uncle Sam—Who's Who in the Federal Government
University of Memphis Library
http://www.lib.memphis.edu/gpo/whos3.htm

United States Government Manual
http://www.access.gpo.gov/nara/nara001.html

U.S. Trade and Development Agency
http://www.tda.gov/

USA Trade
http://usatrade.gov/website/website.nsf

White House
http://www.whitehouse.gov

Holdings

Franklin D. Roosevelt Library and Museum
http://www.fdrlibrary.marist.edu/photos.html

Jimmy Carter Library and Museum
http://www.jimmycarterlibrary.org/documents/index.phtml

Indians and Indian Tribes

Administration for Native Americans
http://www.acf.dhhs.gov/programs/ana

Advisory Council on Historic Preservation
http://www.achp.gov/thpo.html

Bureau of Indian Affairs
http://www.doi.gov/bia/information/navam.htm

http://www.doi.gov/bia/information/treaties.htm

Office of Indian Education Programs
http://www.oiep.bia.edu/

Committee on Indian Affairs
U.S. Senate
http://indian.senate.gov/nscominfo.htm

Department of the Interior
http://www.doi.gov/oait/links.htm

Indian Arts and Crafts Board
http://www.doi.gov/iacb/enter.html

Indian Health Service
http://www/ihs.gov/

Kappler Report
http://digital.library.okstate.edu/kappler

National Indian Gaming Commission
http://www.nigc.gov/

Office of Tribal Justice
http://www.usdoj.gov/otj/index.html

National Security

American Civil Liberties Union
http://www.aclu.org/issues/security/hmns.html

Digital National Security Archive
http://nsarchive.chadwyck.com/

Electronic Briefing Books
http://www.gwu.edu/~nsarchiv/NSAEBB/

National Security Archive
http://www.gwu.edu/~nsarchiv/nsa/the_archive.html

Nationalsecurity.org
http://www.nationalsecurity.org/

National Security Studies Quarterly
Georgetown University
http://ssp.georgetown.edu/nssq/nssg/index.html

Partnerships

DOE Information Bridge
http://www.osti.gov/bridge/

Energy Citations Database
http;//www.osti.gov/energycitations/

EnergyFiles Virtual Library Collection of Energy Science and Technology
http://www.osti.gov/EnergyFiles

PrePrint Network
http://www.osti.gov/preprint

PubSCIENCE
http://pubsci.osti.gov/

 **Chapter 7**

Freedom of Information Act and Declassified Records

The executive branch attempts to ensure secrecy by its security classification of records, its exercising of executive privilege (this may not always be successful), its exemption of information from disclosure under the Freedom of Information Act (FOIA), or holding closed meetings of collegially headed agencies. The key question is whether such actions are legally permissible. Numerous reports and studies have shown, for example, that over-classification is widespread and that much government information is still withheld from public scrutiny.

GOVERNMENT SECRECY

In 1991, the National Archives and Records Administration (NARA) discovered that the oldest military documents in its files that had been reviewed and still remained classified were dated April 15, 1917. One document, designated WCD-9944-X-1, concerned U.S. troop movements in Europe during the First World War. "Although this document was subsequently released after a lengthy Freedom of Information Act proceeding, several others from the very same day remain secret."[1]

The protection of government information vital to the defense and security of the nation has long been a matter of federal policy and practice. Several arrangements have been developed in this regard, including encryption, document registry, and security classification. The last of these is the practice of designating information officially secret in accordance with policy criteria and, usually, at one of three levels of sensitivity: Top Secret, Secret, or Confidential. There are also a series of caveats at each of these levels that seek to limit distribution.[2] Consequently, information may be available to authorized individuals, that is, those who have been granted a security clearance for the level of information sensitivity involved and who have a "need to know" or, in other words, require access to perform their duties. In the case of the Department of Defense, the National

Technical Information Service provides only those publications deemed "unclassified" and "unlimited" in distribution to the public.

As the history of security classification policy indicates, armed forces regulations long prescribed policy and practices for official secrecy. In 1857, however, the president was statutorily empowered

> to prescribe such regulations, and make and issue such orders and instructions, not inconsistent with the Constitution or any law of the United States, in relation to the duties of all diplomatic and consular offices, the transaction of their business . . . , the safekeeping of the archives, the public property in the hands of all such officers [and] the communication of information . . . from time to time, as he may think conducive to the public interest.[3]

With the arrival of the twentieth century, Congress enacted criminal punishments for the improper disclosure of national defense secrets in 1911 (36 Stat. 1084) and again in 1917 (40 Stat. 217). It was also in 1917 that both the Commissioner of Patents (40 Stat. 394) and the president (40 Stat. 411 at 422) were statutorily authorized to make secret those patent applications which, if disclosed, might be "detrimental to the public safety or defense, or may assist the enemy or endanger the successful prosecution of the war."

In 1946 (60 Stat. 755 at 766) and in 1954 (68 Stat. 919 at 940), Congress legislated the required protection of certain atomic energy information, denominated *Restricted Data*, from the moment of its creation. Generally speaking, such data were understood to have military or weapons production value. Because such information is "born secret," an affirmative determination of the government is necessary for it to be removed from its privileged status.

In 1947 (61 Stat. 495 at 498) and again in 1949 (63 Stat. 208 at 211), Congress required the Director of Central Intelligence to protect "intelligence sources and methods from unauthorized disclosure."

Security Classification

Security classification principles and procedures were initially expressed in regulations of the armed forces, the first such directive creating a prototype security classification system appearing in early 1912. Security classification policy assumed a presidential character in 1940. The reasons for this late development are not entirely clear, but it probably was prompted by desires to clarify the authority of civilian personnel in the national defense community to create official secrets, to establish a broader basis for protecting military information in view of growing global hostilities, and to better manage a discretionary power of increasing importance to the entire executive branch.

Relying on a 1938 statute concerning the security of armed forces installations and equipment and "information relative thereto" (52 Stat. 3), Franklin D. Roosevelt issued the first presidential security classification directive (E.O.

8381) in March 1940. However, the legislative history of the statute that the president relied on to issue his order provided no indication that Congress anticipated that such a security classification arrangement would be created.

Executive orders became the most visible element in the larger process of developing classification policies and practices. E.O. 10104, adding a fourth level of classified information, aligned U.S. information security categories with those of our allies in 1950. A 1951 directive (E.O. 10290) completely overhauled the security classification program. Information was now classified in the interest of "national security," and classification authority was extended to non-military agencies that presumably had a role in "national security" policy.

Criticism of the 1951 order prompted President Dwight D. Eisenhower to issue a replacement order (10501) in November 1953. This directive and later amendments to it, as well as E.O. 11652 of March 8, 1972, and E.O. 12065 of June 28, 1978, successively narrowed the bases and limited discretion for assigning official secrecy to agency records.

Shortly after President Ronald Reagan issued E.O. 12356 on April 2, 1982, it was criticized for reversing the limiting trend set by prior security classification orders of the previous thirty years by expanding the categories of classifiable information, mandating that information falling within these categories be classified, making reclassification authority available, admonishing classifiers to err on the side of classification, and eliminating arrangements for automatic declassification.

With the democratization of many Eastern European countries, the demise of the Soviet Union, and the end of the Cold War, President Clinton ordered a sweeping review of the rules on security classification in general and of E.O. 12356 in particular with a view to reform.[4]

Many began to suspect that the security classification program could be improved when the Department of Defense (DoD) Security Review Commission, chaired by retired General Richard G. Stilwell, declared late in 1985 that there were "no verifiable figures as to the amount of classified material produced in DoD and in [the] defense industry each year." Nonetheless, it was concluded that "too much information appears to be classified and much at higher levels than is warranted."[5]

The cost of the security classification program became clearer when the General Accounting Office (GAO) reported in October 1993 that it was "able to identify governmentwide costs directly applicable to national security information totaling over $350 million for 1992." After breaking this figure down—it included only $6 million for declassification work—the report added that "the U.S. government also spends additional billions of dollars annually to safeguard information, personnel, and property."[6] By 1995, other accounts of the "hefty" costs of classification-related activities were reported and provided additional evidence of the need to further overhaul security classification.[7]

Finally, on April 17, 1995, President Clinton signed E.O. 12958, which requires the automatic declassification of most classified information that is twenty-five or more years older and provides for automatic declassification of most new documents after ten years. Facing resistance to declassification from some quarters of Congress and a few recalcitrant agencies, President Clinton issued E.O. 13142 (November 19, 1999), extending the deadline for automatic declassification of twenty-five-year-old documents by eighteen to thirty-six months. Under the 1995 Executive Order (12958), most documents that were at least twenty-five years old were supposed to be declassified by April 2000. That deadline was thus extended until October 2001 in most cases, and until April 2003 for records that are replete with intelligence sources or methods or that require multi-agency review.

SECURITY CLASSIFICATION REVIEW

In 1997, the Commission on Protecting and Reducing Government Secrecy, which was popularly known as the Moynihan Commission, transmitted its final report to the president and the congressional leadership.[8] In an appendix, the report identified six prior "major reviews" of what it termed "the U.S. secrecy system." The first of these reviews concluded in 1956; the most recent such assessment occurred in 1994. Findings and recommendations were proffered in each case.[9] These "major reviews" were the major studies of official secrecy that were most similar to the Commission's study.[10]

The Commission unanimously offered sixteen recommendations, some of which were to "statutorily establish the basic principles of security classification and declassification programs"; "implement within one year a single set of security standards for special access programs"; "base classification decisions, including the establishment of special action programs, on a range of factors in addition to damage to the national security, such as the cost of protection, vulnerability, threat, risk, value of the information, and public benefit from release"; "restructure agencies' records management programs and systematic declassification programs to maximize access to records that are likely to be the subject of significant public interest"; "take certain specific actions to enhance the proficiency of classifiers and improve their accountability by requiring additional information on the rationale for classification, by improving classification guidance, and by strengthening training and evaluation programs"; "assign responsibility for classification and declassification policy development and oversight to a single executive branch body, designated by the President and independent of the agencies that classify"; and "statutorily mandate a central office—a National Declassification Center—at an existing agency to coordinate federal declassification policy and activities." To date, these recommendations have not been enacted.

EXAMPLES OF DECLASSIFIED DOCUMENTS

During Word War II and the Cold War, the Department of Defense (and its predecessor, the Department of War) and other national security agencies conducted or sponsored extensive radiological, chemical, and biological research programs. The exact numbers may never be known. Nonetheless, some participants suffered immediate, acute injuries, and some died. In other cases adverse health problems were not discovered until decades later.[11]

Stories in the press have documented instances in which the Federal Bureau of Investigation (FBI) monitored groups and individuals, and/or the public supplied the agency with information on individuals and the FBI then started files on them. Examples include John Steinbeck, Albert Einstein, John Lennon, Carl Sandburg, William Faulkner, Tennessee Williams, and Marilyn Monroe. Furthermore, the FBI conducted counterintelligence visits to libraries to identify potential spics and to determine what resources they were using.[12] Reportedly, during World War II scientists in Cambridge, Massachusetts, had bats from the Carlsbad Caverns in New Mexico shipped by railroad car to them. They experimented with bombs that could be attached to the animals so that bats could be released in Nazi Germany. Apparently, the scientists could not produce bombs sufficiently light in weight to permit the bats to fly with them! The experiment was declassified, but information about the bombs was not.[13]

THE FREEDOM OF INFORMATION ACT

The Freedom of Information Act (5 U.S.C. 552), enacted in 1966 and amended at various times (1974, 1976, 1986, and 1996), establishes a statutory right to know about the activities and operations of the federal executive branch. The law provides any person (individual or corporate, regardless of nationality) with access to identifiable, existing records of departments and agencies without having to demonstrate a need or even a reason for such a request. The burden of proof for withholding material sought by the public is placed on the government.

Although the statute specifies nine categories of information that may be protected from disclosure, these exemptions do not require agencies to withhold records but merely permit access restrictions. Allowance is made in the law for the exemption of

- Information properly classified for national defense or foreign policy purposes as secret under criteria established by an executive order;

- Information relating solely to agency internal personnel rules and practices;

- Data specifically excepted from disclosure by a statute that either requires that matters be withheld in a non-discretionary manner or establishes particular criteria for withholding or refers to particular types of matters to be withheld;

- Trade secrets and commercial or financial information obtained from a person and privileged or confidential;

- Inter- or intra-agency memoranda or letters that would not be available by law except to any agency in litigation;

- Personal, medical, and similar files the disclosure of which would constitute an unwarranted invasion of personal privacy;

- Certain kinds of investigative records compiled for law enforcement purposes;

- Certain information relating to the regulation of financial institutions; and

- Geological and geophysical information and data, including maps, concerning wells.

The FOIA provides that disputes over the availability of agency records may be settled ultimately in court.

Presidential Records

Presidential and vice presidential records are outside the scope of the FOIA. When an incumbent president departs from office, his official records, regardless of form or format, are removed from the White House by staff of the National Archives and Records Administration (NARA). Thereafter, these records are under the control of the Archivist, as they are the property of the federal government. Placed in temporary archival storage, the materials begin undergoing processing by NARA professionals and subsequently are scheduled for release for public inspection. The former president may set limits, for a period not to exceed twelve years after his departure from office, on access to his records in accordance with statutorily specified restriction categories (44 U.S.C. 2204) similar to those in the FOIA (5 U.S.C. 552(b)(1)-(9)). After twelve years, these limitations are no longer applicable, and only the exemptions of the FOIA may be relied upon to protect undisclosed records. These procedures were embellished in 1989 when President Ronald Reagan, a few days before he left office, issued a little noticed directive, E.O. 12677, requiring the Archivist to notify the incumbent and the former presidents of his intention to release to the public records of those former presidents and provide an opportunity for them to review the disclosure. The directive indicated that, as a result of their reviews, the former or the incumbent president might exert a claim of executive privilege to prohibit the Archivist from releasing records scheduled for public disclosure.

Additional clarification came on November 1, 2001, when President Bush signed Executive Order 13223, "Further Implementation of the Presidential Records Act," which declared that the Archivist of the United States will "administer Presidential records under section 2204(c) of title 44 in the following manner":

(a) At an appropriate time after the Archivist receives a request for access to Presidential records under section 2204(c)(1), the Archivist shall provide notice to the former president and the incumbent President and, as soon as practicable, shall provide the former president and the incumbent President, copies of any records that the former President and the incumbent President request to review.

(b) After receiving the records he requests, the former President shall review those records as expeditiously as possible, and for no longer than 90 days for requests that are not unduly burdensome. The Archivist shall not permit access to the records by a requester during this period of review or when requested by the former President to extent the time for review.

(c) After review of the records in question, or of any other potentially privileged records reviewed by the former President, the former President shall indicate to the Archivist whether the former President requests withholding of or authorizes access to any privileged records.

(d) Concurrent with or after the former President's review of the records the incumbent President or his designee may also review the records, in question, or may utilize whatever other procedures the incumbent President deems appropriate to decide whether to concur in the former President's decision to request withholding of or authorize access to the records.

Section six of the executive order "does not expand or limit the rights of a court, House of Congress, or authorized committee or subcommittee of Congress to obtain access to the records of a former President pursuant to section 2205(2)(A) or section 2205(2)(C)."

Section eight adds further clarification to the twelve-year period for withholding privileged records by explaining that, during this time,

after the conclusion of a Presidency during which section 2204(a) and section 2204(b) of title 44 apply, a former President or the incumbent President may request withholding of any privileged records not already protected from disclosure under section 2204. If the former president or the incumbent President so requests, the Archivist shall not permit access to any such privileged records unless and until the incumbent President agree to authorize access to the records or until so ordered by a final and nonappealable court order.

Section eleven applies to vice presidential records (44 U.S.C. 2207). It notes that the executive order applies to "any such records that are subject to any constitutionally based privilege that the former Vice President may be entitled to invoke."[14] Consequently, anyone seeking presidential and vice presidential records must establish a "demonstrated, specific need" for those records. Such a requirement generated some negative reaction.[15]

Federal Register

To aid the public in retrieving public information, the FOIA requires publication in the *Federal Register* of

(a) descriptions of . . . [each agency's] central and field organization and the established places at which the employees (and in the case of a uniformed service, the members) from whom, and the methods whereby, the public may obtain information, make submittals or requests, or obtain decisions;

(b) statements of the general course and method by which its functions are channeled and determined, including the nature and requirements of all formal and informal procedures available;

(c) rules of procedure, descriptions of forms available or the places at which forms may be obtained, and instructions as to the scope and contents of all papers, reports, or examinations;

(d) substantive rules of general applicability adopted as authorized by law, and statements of general policy or interpretations of general applicability formulated and adopted by the agency; and

(e) each amendment, revision, or repeal of the foregoing.[16]

Submitting a FOIA Request

In practical terms, making a request involves three activities. First, the requester identifies the agency that may have responsive records. Second, he or she reasonably describes the records sought. And, finally, after marking the envelope to indicate a FOIA request, the requester's letter should include his or her telephone number in case the agency needs to make contact. More detailed information on invoking the Act can be found at the FOIA Web pages for each executive branch department and agency (see *U.S. Government on the Web*, 292–293), the Act itself (http://www.archives.gov/research_room/foia_reading_room/foia_ reading_room), or citizen guides on using the FOIA (e.g., http://frwebgate. access.gpo.gov/cgi-bin/getdoc.cgi?dbname=106_cong_reports&docid=). Note that the home page for the Department of Justice (DoJ) has a section devoted to FOIA that contains information on "making a FOIA request," a reference guide that documents the procedures for making a request to DoJ, and links to "Other Federal Agencies' FOIA Web Sites" (http://www.usdoj.gov/sitemap/index. html). This URL also identifies frequently requested DoJ records and explains that agencies may place their FOIA information on their home page under an icon for a public reading room.

The Charging of Fees

Agencies responding to FOIA requests are permitted by the statute to charge fees for certain activities—document search, duplication, and review—depending on the type of requester (a commercial user; an educational or noncommercial scientific institution, whose purpose is scholarly or scientific research; a news media representative; or the general public). However, requested records may be furnished by an agency without any charge or at a reduced cost, according to the law, "if disclosure of the information is in the public interest because it is likely to contribute significantly to public understanding of the operations or activities of the government and is not primarily in the commercial interest of the requester." Both the Office of Management and Budget (OMB) and the Department of Justice coordinate FOIA policy and activities within the executive branch, and therefore, the previously-mentioned DoJ Web presentation on the FOIA provides relevant information.

FOIA Use

The General Accounting Office (GAO) noted that, in fiscal year 1999, twenty-five agencies "processed about 1.9 million FOIA requests, providing records in full for 82%; 23 agencies reported that 1.6 million requests were processed with median times of 20 days or fewer, while 140,000 were processed with medians over 20 days." According to GAO, "various factors determine the workflow, fees, and time needed to process a FOIA request, such as amount and type of information requested and where in the organization the responsive records would likely be found," and "completeness of the request."[17] (For additional information about the use of, and compliance with, the Act, see the annual reports of government entities; see http://www.usdoj.gov/sitemap/index.html).

Categories of Requesters

Members of the public and public interest groups might seek information in an effort to hold the executive branch accountable. Other requesters might be scholars, reporters, and corporations. David H. Price, an anthropologist, notes that the FOIA "is a largely untapped resource for . . . social scientists," and encourages them to make greater use of it. He also shares his experiences in invoking the Act.[18]

Electronic FOIA Amendments

The FOIA was amended in 1996 by the Electronic Freedom of Information Amendments (E-FOIA). Among its modifications, E-FOIA confirmed that the FOIA applied to electronic records, required that material be provided in the form or format sought by the requester, and mandated the creation of so-called electronic reading rooms that the public can access online to examine important and high-visibility agency records. Each executive department and agency is supposed to have an electronic reading room on the Web; however, some have lagged behind others in creating such a site, there is variation in the amount and type of information provided, and some sites are easier than others to locate.

Key Sources

As already noted, an important Web site is that of the Department of Justice. Various reports and policy instruments from the attorney general, as well as the *FOIA Update*, a newsletter that existed from 1979 to 2000, and *FOIA Post*, its replacement, can be found at DoJ's Office of Information and Privacy (http://www.usdoj.gov/04/foia/readingrooms/oip.htm).

OMB also issues relevant policy instruments and has a Freedom of Information Act Web page (http://www.whitehouse.gov/omb/foia/). It explains how to submit a FOIA request to OMB and what goes in the written request.

Another important agency is the Information Security Oversight Office (ISOO), an administrative component of NARA. ISOO's director is appointed by the Archivist of the United States but receives policy and program guidance from the Assistant to the President for National Security Affairs. The director's position was established under Executive Order 12958, "Classified National Security Information," and the duties and responsibilities arise from that order and E.O. 12829, "National Industrial Security Program." Both orders are available at ISOO's home page (http://www.archives.gov/isoo/index.html). This site also explains ISOO's mission, goals, and functions. A key resource of the Office is its annual report to the president, which, since 1993, have been placed on the Web (http://www.archives.gov/isoo/annual_reports/annual_reports.html).

Another excellent resource is the "Project on Government Secrecy," maintained by the Federation of American Scientists (http://www.fas.org). The Project also provides links to ISOO documents (see http://www.fas.org/sgp/isoo/index.html) and "Other Government Secrecy Related Web Sites." The Federation produces an important newsletter called "Secrecy & Government Bulletin," which it also provides at the Web site.

Arvin S. Quist, Classification Officer, Oak Ridge Gaseous Diffusion Plant, Oak Ridge National Laboratory, has produced a projected four-volume set, *Security Classification of Information*. The first volume covers *Introduction, History, and Adverse Impacts* (prepared by the Oak Ridge Gaseous Diffusion Plant for the Department of Energy under contract DE-AC05-84OR21400, September 1989). The Department of Energy, Office of Declassification, has produced *Drawing Back the Curtain of Secrecy: Restricted Data Declassification Policy 1946 to the Present*, which "provides historical perspective on the sequence of declassification actions performed by the Department of Energy and its predecessor agencies. It is meant to convey the amount and types of information declassified over the years."[19]

James T. O'Reilly's two-volume *Federal Information Disclosure*, third edition (Eagan, Minn.: West Group, 2002) is a legal treatise on various government information laws; and the House Permanent Select Committee on Intelligence, *Compilation of Intelligence Laws and Related Laws and Executive Orders of Interest to the National Intelligence Community*, committee print, 104th Cong., 1st sess. (Washington, D.C.: GPO, 1995), covers the FOIA and other government information laws and directives.

NARA'S ELECTRONIC READING ROOM

The NARA reading room (http://www.archives.gov/research_room/foia_reading_room/electronic_reading_room.html) "contains information routinely available to the public as well as documents frequently requested under the Freedom of Information Act." Examples of collections here are Holocaust-era Assets, the Nixon White House Tapes, the Cold-War Era, Unidentified Flying Objects, and the JFK Assassination Records Collection Database. The President John F. Kennedy Assassination Records Collection Act (PL 102–526) requires all material relating to the assassination to be deposited with NARA. In December 1992, NARA established the collection, which initially consisted only of material already in NARA's custody. As agencies complete their internal reviews and transfer newly opened records to NARA, the collection will increase in size and completeness. The Act also mandated the creation of an electronic index to the records in the collection. That index is available through the Web (http://www.archives.gov/iwg/about_iwg/about_iwg.html).

Another example of NARA's holdings is "The Nazi War Crimes and Japanese Imperial Government Records" (see http://www.archives.gov/research_room/jfk/index.html). NARA's Center for Legislative Archives "is the repository, reference center, and outreach facility for the historically valuable records of the U.S. Congress" (see http://www.archives.gov/records_of_congress/contact_cla.html).

INTELLIGENCE COMMUNITY

The agencies that make up this community have Web sites (see http://www.odci.gov/ic/icagen2.htm for general access to them). According to E.O. 12333, the intelligence community consists of the Central Intelligence Agency; the National Security Agency; the Defense Intelligence Agency; the offices within the Department of Defense for the collection of specialized national foreign intelligence through reconnaissance programs; the State Department's Bureau of Intelligence and Research; the intelligence elements of the Army, Navy, Air Force, and Marine Corps, the Federal Bureau of Investigation, the Department of the Treasury; and the Department of Energy; and the staff elements of the Director of Central Intelligence. Web sites for these agencies and organizations may be sparse in information content.

Secrecy might apply to the actions and activities of these agencies, but the name of an agency might even be kept from public disclosure. For example, in September 1992, the name of the National Reconnaissance Office (NRO), which operates the U.S. satellite surveillance program, was declassified after having been in existence for thirty-two years. The Pentagon then tried to block the release of any information about that office from becoming public.[20]

The agencies of the intelligence community have what is called the nation's "black budget." Their funds are concealed in secret appendixes to appropriations legislation. The previously mentioned *Secrecy & Government Bulletin* has devoted extensive coverage to the black budget and the disclosure of the intelligence budget. Following September 11, the intelligence budget has been substantially increased and the overall budget is classified.

The Central Intelligence Agency, as discussed in *U.S. Government on the Web*, has a site rich in content. There is, for instance, a listing of unclassified maps available through the National Technical Information Service; the *World Factbook*, which provides facts and statistics on more than 250 countries; the *Handbook of Economic Statistics* and the *Handbook of International Statistics*; and a Directory of Officials series covering a number of countries.

FOREIGN RELATIONS SERIES

The series entitled *Foreign Relations of the United States* (FRUS), which is produced by the State Department's Office of the Historian, began in 1861 and includes more than 350 individual volumes to date. FRUS contains declassified records that provide insights into diplomatic activity related to foreign policy developments, crises, and incidents. "A staff of approximately 20 historians and editors at the Office of the Historian . . . compile and prepare the volumes for publication. This staff is assisted by an Advisory Committee on Historical Diplomatic Documentation. Agencies whose documents are included in a volume participate in a declassification review" (http://www.state.gov/www/about_state/history/hac,html). The agencies from which the records are obtained include presidential libraries, the "Departments of State and Defense, National Security Council, Central Intelligence Agency, Agency for International Development, and other foreign affairs agencies as well as the private papers of individuals involved in formulating U.S. foreign policy" (http://www.state.gov/r/pa/ho/frus).

The series is now out through the Johnson administration, with the "volumes on the Nixon administration . . . now being researched, annotated, and prepared for publication" (http://www.state.gov/r/pa/ho/frus). The volume of material to review at the various sites, restrictive declassification policies, a time-consuming appeals process, and so forth mean that the process of preparing the set for any administration is slow. Given the amount of relevant material produced by any administration, the series must be highly selective in topics and records included. Yet there are some declassified records for diplomatic activities surrounding the Vietnam War (through the Johnson administration), the years leading up to World War II (both Japan and Germany), the Yalta and other World War II conferences, the sinking of ships by German U-boats prior to American entry into World War I, U.S. involvement in Latin America in the 1920s and 1930s, and other armed conflicts and treaty negotiations.

Hardbound copies are available through the sales program of the Superintendent of Documents, Government Printing Office (http://bookstore.gpo.gov), and recent volumes are also available online (via the State Department).

PRESIDENTIAL LIBRARIES

These libraries, discussed in Chapter 5, may provide some source material that has been declassified and converted to a digital form. For example, the Roosevelt Library (http://www.fdrlibrary.marist.edu/safe.html) offers the President's Secretary's File (PSF), which is divided into five series: the Safe Files (some documents kept locked in the president's White House safe), the Confidential Files, the Diplomatic Files (those pertaining to U.S.-Vatican relations during World War II , dealing with Anglo-American relations, and dealing with U.S.-German relations during the 1930s and 1940s), the Departmental Files, and the Subject Files. The Safe Files, dating from 1933 to 1945, consist of formerly national security classified material, mainly from the World War II period. These files include correspondence, reports, and memoranda on topics such as the Manhattan Project (development of the atomic bomb); the Atlantic Charter and the United Nations; the War, Navy, Treasury and State Departments; countries such as Germany, Japan, Italy, Russia, and China; and individuals such as General George Marshall and Harry Hopkins.

The Johnson Presidential Library has an oral history collection that includes the secret records that the president made of a number of his telephone calls and meetings. These complement the FRUS coverage of the Vietnam War.

POLICY EXCEPTIONS

A wide assortment of laws and practices govern the withholding and release of government records and other documentation (see Table 7.1, page 162, for examples). Of course, there are exceptions to the general patterns discussed in this chapter. Presidents might declassify information that would rally public support to their policies or discredit the opposition (e.g., early release of records about the Yalta conference). Congress, the press, and an upset public might also force the declassification and/or disclosure (leaking) of information. Some government documents are undoubtedly sensitive, but their sensitivity might stem less from national security considerations than from the fact that their information content could be embarrassing to an agency or certain officials. These officials might attempt a cover up and the destruction of records.

Table 7.1. Examples of Laws Controlling the Release of Government Information

Bureau of the Census	Release of individual census records transferred and preserved at the National Archives is prohibited for seventy-two years (then the average life span). Based on a special arrangement between the Archivist of the United States and the Bureau in 1952.
Central Intelligence Agency	Withholds information about its organization, functions, names, official title, salaries, or numbers of personnel employed (50 U.S.C. 403g). The CIA Director prevents unauthorized disclosure of intelligence sources and methods (50 U.S.C. 403d) and requires agency personnel to sign prepublication agreements. They must also submit, for censorship review, any of their writings about the agency and its activities, real or presumed.
Internal Revenue Service	26 U.S.C. 6103 and 7213 protect income tax returns. However, the courts are divided about whether tax returns become publicly available if the agency deletes identification of individual taxpayers.
National Security Agency	Keeps secret information about its functions and activities, as well as the names, titles, salaries, and number of persons employed. (50 U.S.C. 402)
Nuclear Regulatory Commission	Restrictions placed by the Atomic Energy Act. (42 U.S.C. 2014y)
Secret Service	Withholds information on presidential security for fifty years. If past practices still relate to that security, documents might be withheld even longer.
President	The Presidential Records Act of 1978 (92 Stat 2523, 44 U.S.C. 2204) makes presidential papers available to the public, with specific exemptions, within twelve years after the conclusion of the president's final term of office. Thus, for a president serving two terms, the oldest records are released in twenty years.

Legislative Branch

Requests for access to unpublished congressional papers and documents, although sometimes complied with by both chambers, involve the rights of privilege of both bodies. That privilege is rooted in the Constitution, principally the speech or debate clause. Proposals to extend the FOIA to Congress have to be assessed in light of that privilege. Note that congressional papers, such as communications with constituents, may not be protected by speech or debate clause immunity. Nevertheless, there may be policy reasons for maintaining the confidentiality of such papers. For example, preserving the confidentiality of communications from and to constituents may encourage citizens to express their views frankly to their elected representatives.

The lack of complete access to all material produced is not confined to the executive branch. Secrecy also pertains to the other branches of government. When circumstances warrant it, Congress holds closed proceedings and discusses sensitive issues dealing with trials for removal of an impeached president from office, national security, or foreign policy. Congressional committees may receive briefings, examine protected information, and collect testimony in secret. Such information, then, does not appear in the *Congressional Record* or transcripts of hearings released to the public.

The papers of members of Congress remain their personal property. They may donate them to a library or archive, or they may destroy or otherwise dispose of the papers that they accumulated in their role as a public figure. They may also place special restrictions on the use of papers that they deposit in a library or archive.

The House of Representatives has adopted a thirty-year standard for safeguarding institutional records not previously made public. Both unpublished records and records that have been printed and circulated are sent to the Clerk of the House, who, in turn, transfers them to NARA. Even for records older than the standards and in the custody of NARA, the Clerk of the House must grant permission for their use. The records remain the property of the House, and the National Archives serves as agent for the Clerk. Any committee, however, might circumvent the thirty-year requirement and grant an exception.

In December 1980, the Senate adopted a twenty-year rule covering the availability of most of its records. Individual committees can extend or lessen the time period as they deem appropriate. The Senate forwards to NARA for immediate use its noncurrent treaty files, legislative records, petitions, and executive communications.

Judicial Branch

The records of the judiciary are not covered by formal statutory provisions. In accordance with Rule 6e of the Federal Rules of Criminal Procedure, materials relating to grand jury proceedings are closed. By order of the court, certain other documents may be unavailable. The papers of a judge are personal and do not constitute government information. The papers of Thurgood Marshall were deposited with the Library of Congress and, upon his death, were opened as specified in the deed of deposit. Their availability was condemned by a number of jurists, who argued that they indicated how the current Supreme Court operated and reflected the personalities of those judges.

The records of the federal district courts and courts of appeals are deposited with NARA or the Federal Records Center that serves the geographical area in which the court is located. Records of the Supreme Court are housed at NARA and are generally open to the public.

SOURCES FROM THE PRIVATE AND NONPROFIT SECTORS

As a result of E.O. 11652, signed by President Richard Nixon in 1962, a large number of post-World War II documents have become declassified. Carrollton Press, Inc. (Washington, D.C.) began to acquire, index, abstract, film, and make them publicly available.

The National Security Archive is an independent, nongovernmental research institute and library located at George Washington University, Washington, D.C. The Archive was founded in 1985 by journalists and scholars who had obtained documents from the government under FOIA and sought to establish a centralized repository for these materials. Its holdings include "more than 2 million pages of accessioned materials in over 200 separate collections," and it seeks to make these collections available to scholars and the public.

The Archive collects and publishes declassified documents acquired through FOIA. It also indexes and publishes many of these documents in books, microform, and electronic formats. The Archive has produced a series of microform collections on U.S. foreign policy, as well as a CD-ROM index to the entire series, co-published by Chadwyck-Healy, Inc. The subject areas of these collections range from the Cuban Missile crisis to the Iran-Contra affair to the U.S. intelligence community. A full list of these collections can be found at its Web site, http://www.gwu.edu/~nsarchiv/nsa.

The Archive also publishes books for more general use, including *White House E-Mail: The Top Secret Computer Messages the Reagan-Bush White House Tried to Destroy,* and *South Africa and the United States: The Declassified History.* For a complete list of publications, check the Web site.

Since 1982, Primary Source Media, a division of the Gale Group, has offered the *Declassified Documents Reference System (DDRS),* a microfiche collection of selected declassified documents released by presidential libraries, the White House, and selected agencies (the Central Intelligence Agency, the Federal Bureau of Investigation, and the State Department). *DDRS* is available, by subscription, in a Web version and on CD-ROM (see http://www.ddrs. psmedia.com).

CONCLUSION

Freedom of information is a dynamic concept in government information policy and practice. When the term came into use in the United States more than fifty years ago, its context and substance were synonymous with freedom of the press.[21] Its meaning later shifted, focusing more on public accessibility of unpublished government records and legal barriers to such availability.[22] Then, in a policymaking forum—a hearing by a House subcommittee—an even more precise concept was formulated.[23] That model was further refined in the congressional legislative process and became law in 1966: the FOIA.

It was not a universally welcomed proposal and, therefore, because political accommodations had to be reached for its statutory enactment, it was not well formulated. This was understood at the time of its creation.[24] More important, experience with the new Act soon demonstrated that it did not work very effectively. Consequently, it was amended. The statute also underwent administrative interpretation by executive branch entities and legal explication by the federal courts, with some provisions receiving a high judicial gloss.[25] The sometimes conflicting policy pronouncements resulting from these competing efforts have contributed to the dynamic character of the concept of freedom of information.

More than a century ago, as a graduate student, Woodrow Wilson, later to be the twenty-eighth president, wrote *Congressional Government*, the first major analysis of the federal legislature. There he offered a somewhat startling observation: "The informing function of Congress should be preferred even to its legislative function." In operational terms, what he had in mind regarding the "informing function" was what is now called oversight. "Unless Congress have and use every means of acquainting itself with the acts and the disposition of the administrative agents of the government," he wrote, "the country must be helpless to learn how it is being served."[26] Although new freedom of information arrangements since the time of his observations have enhanced the ability of the country "to learn how it is being served" by administrative agents, congressional oversight still contributes significantly to the effective operation of government.

NOTES

1. Steven Aftergood, "Swimming in Secrets," *Government Information Insider* 3 (September/October 1993): 7.

2. See Stephen Budiansky, Keeping Research under Wraps," *U.S. News & World Report* (March 22, 1993): 48–50.

3. 11 Stat. 52, at 60.

4. Tim Weiner, "President Moves to Release Classified U.S. Documents," *New York Times,* May 5, 1993, A18.

5. Department of Defense, Department of Defense Security Review Commission, *Keeping the Nation's Secrets* (Washington, D.C.: GPO, 1985), 48–49.

6. General Accounting Office, *Classified Information: Costs of Protection Are Integrated with Other Security Costs*, GAO/NSIAD-94-55 (Washington, D.C.: General Accounting Office, October 1993), 1.

7. "Classification Costs Reported," *Secrecy & Government Bulletin* 60 (July 1996): 2.

8. Commission on Protecting and Reducing Government Secrecy, *Report of the Commission on Protecting and Reducing Government Secrecy* (Washington, D.C.: GPO, 1997).

9. Ibid., G-1–G-2.

10. For a discussion of these reviews, see Harold C. Relyea, "Security Classification Reviews and the Search for Reform," *Government Information Quarterly* 16 (1999): 5–27.

11. See U.S. Advisory Commission on Human Radiation Experiments, *Final Report of . . .* (Washington, D.C.: GPO, 1995).

12. See Congress. House. Committee on the Judiciary. Subcommittee on Civil and Constitutional Rights, *FBI Counterintelligence Visits to Libraries*, hearings (Washington, D.C.: GPO, 1989).

13. Joe Michael Feist, "II. Bats Away!," *American Heritage* (April 1982): 93–94.

14. See "Executive Order 13233: Further Implementation of the Presidential Records Act," *Federal Register* 66 (214) (November 5, 2001): 56025–29.

15. See, for instance, Richard Reeves, "Writing History to Executive Order," *New York Times,* November 16, 2001, A 23.

16. 5 U.S.C. 552(a)(1).

17. General Accounting Office, *Information Management: Progress in Implementing the 1996 Electronic Freedom of Information Act Amendments*, GAO-01-378 (Washington, D.C.: General Accounting Office, March 2001), 12.

18. David H. Price, "Anthropological Research and the Freedom of Information Act," *Cultural Anthropology Methods* 9 (February 1997): 12–15.

19. Department of Energy, Office of Declassification, has produced *Drawing Back the Curtain of Secrecy: Restricted Data Declassification Policy 1946 to the Present* (January 1, 1995).

20. See "Get Smarter: Demystifying the NRO," *Secrecy & Government Bulletin* 39 (August–September 1994): 1.

21. Herbert Brucker, *Freedom of Information* (New York: Macmillan, 1949); and Kent Cooper, *The Right to Know* (New York: Farrar, Straus, and Cudahay, 1956).

22. Harold L. Cross, *The People's Right to Know* (Morningside Heights, N.Y.: Columbia University Press, 1956); and James Russell Wiggins, *Freedom or Secrecy* (New York: Oxford University Press, 1964).

23. House Committee on Government Operations, *Availability of Information from Federal Departments and Agencies*, part 3, hearings, 84th Cong., 2d sess. (Washington, D.C.: GPO, 1956), 495–96.

24. Kenneth Culp Davis, "The Information Act: A Preliminary Analysis," University of *Chicago Law Review* 34 (Summer 1967): 761–816.

25. See Patrick J. Carome and Thomas M. Susman, "American Bar Association Symposium on FOIA, 25th Anniversary," *Government Information Quarterly* 9 (1992): 223–65.

26. Woodrow Wilson, *Congressional Government* (Cleveland, Ohio: Meridian Books, 1956), 198.

URL SITE GUIDE

Central Intelligence Agency
http://www.odci.gov/

Citizens Guide to Use of FOIA/Privacy Act
http://frwebgate.access.gpo.gov/cgi-bin/getdoc.cgi?dbname=106_
cong_reports&docid=

Declassified Documents Reference System
Primary Source Media
http://www.ddrs.psmedia.com

FOIA Page
Office of Management and Budget
http://www.whitehouse.gov/omb/foia/index.html

FOIA Web Sites
Department of Justice
http://www.usdoj.gov/sitemap/index.html

Office of Information and Privacy
http://www.usdoj.gov/04/foia/readingrooms/oip.htm

FOIA Post
http://www.usdoj.gov/04/foia/readingrooms/oip.htm

Foreign Relations Series
Department of State
http://www.state.gov/www/about_state/history/hac.html

http://www.state.gov/r/pa/ho/frus/

Intelligence Community
http://www.odci.gov/ic/icagen2.htm

National Archives and Records Administration
http://www.archives.gov/index.html

Center for Legislative Archives
http://www.archives.gov/records_of_congress/contact_cla.html

Electronic Reading Room
http://www.archives.gov/research_room/foia_reading_room/
electronic_reading_room.html

Nazi War Crimes and Japanese Imperial Government Records
http://www.archives.gov/research_room/jfk/index.html

>   JFK Collection
>   http://www.archives.gov/iwg/about_iwg/about_iwg.html

>   FOIA
>   http://www.archives.gov/research_room/foia_reading_room/foia_
>   reading_room

Information Security Oversight Office
http://www.archives.gov/isoo/index.html

>   Annual Reports
>   http://www.archives.gov/isoo/annual_reports/annual_reports.html

National Security Archive
http://www.gwu.edu/~nsarchiv/nsa/

Online Bookstore
Superintendent of Documents
Government Printing Office
http://bookstore.gpo.gov/

President's Secretary's File
Roosevelt Presidential Library
http://www.fdrlibraruy.marist.edu/safe.html

Project on Government Secrecy
Federation of American Scientists
http://www.fas.org/

>   ISOO Documents
>   http://www.fas.org/sgp/isoo/index.html

Chapter 8

Paperwork Reduction: Government Information Management Issues

Replacing the Federal Reports Act of 1942, the Paperwork Reduction Act of 1980 (PRA) was enacted largely to relieve the public of the mounting information collection and reporting requirements of the federal government. It also promoted coordinated information management activities on a governmentwide basis by the director of the Office of Management and Budget (OMB) and prescribed information management responsibilities for the executive agencies. The management focus of the PRA was sharpened with 1986 amendments that refined the concept of "information resources management" (IRM), defined as "the planning, budgeting, organizing, directing, training, promoting, controlling, and management activities associated with the burden, collection, creation, use, and dissemination of information by agencies, and includes the management of information and related resources such as automatic data processing equipment." This key term and its subset concepts received further definition and explanation in the PRA of 1995, making IRM a tool for managing the contribution of information activities to program performance and for managing related resources, such as personnel, equipment, funds, and technology.

PAPERWORK BURDEN

Since its inception in 1789, the federal government has required paperwork for a variety of reasons, not the least of which are direction, accountability, and service delivery. The Constitution mandates one of the largest paperwork requirements, the decennial census.[1] The first Congress set the initial paperwork obligation in the eleventh law it adopted, an act of September 1, 1789, concerning the documentation of marine vessels (1 Stat. 55).

The burdensome nature of paperwork became much more acute with the rise of the federal administrative state in the early years of the twentieth century. The adoption of the Sixteenth Amendment to the Constitution in February 1913 authorized Congress to impose taxes on incomes, from whatever source derived, without apportionment among the states and without regard to any census or enumeration. The War Revenue Act of October 1917 made the income tax the chief source of revenue during the participation of the United States in World War I and introduced the American citizenry to the travails of tax reporting (see 40 Stat. 300).

Simultaneous with these developments was an increase in federal regulatory and compliance agencies with new reporting and recordkeeping requirements for financial, health and safety, and business activities. An autonomous Department of Labor was established in 1913 (37 Stat. 736), along with the Federal Reserve System (38 Stat. 251). The Federal Trade Commission was created in the following year (38 Stat. 717). The entry of the United States into World War I in 1917 prompted a multiplicity of new regulatory entities to deal with transportation, shipping, trade, manufacturing, and food and fuel production.

In the years following the end of World War I, the provision of new personal benefits to the public added to federal reporting and recordkeeping requirements. First came veterans' programs and the establishment of the Veterans Administration in 1930. Next was the arrival of the New Deal in 1933, with the subsequent provision of a variety of old age security, unemployment, disability, and welfare benefits. The New Deal also engendered a variety of new financial, banking, industrial, farming, communications, housing, and public works regulatory programs. Finally, the outbreak of war in Europe in 1939 and the entry of the United States into World War II in 1941 brought a variety of new reporting and recordkeeping requirements for virtually all sectors of the nation and its citizens.

Federal Reports Act of 1942

Federal officials were not unaware of the growing reporting and recordkeeping burden being generated by new regulatory and personal benefits programs. At the highest level, President Franklin D. Roosevelt indicated, in a May 16, 1938, letter to the Central Statistical Board, his concern "over the large number of statistical reports which Federal agencies are requiring from business and industry." Informing the board of his "desire to know the extent of such reports and how far there is duplication among them," he tasked the panel "to report to me on the statistical work of the Federal agencies, with recommendations looking toward consolidations and changes which are consistent with efficiency and economy, both to the Government and to private industry."[2]

In response, the board indicated that, for the fiscal year ending June 30, 1938, the executive agencies had collected over 135 million returns from individuals and businesses, but concluded that most of this information was needed by the government and that, while such reporting should be coordinated, it should remain decentralized.[3] Although this reply apparently ended the matter for the president, there were those in Congress who remained sensitive to the paperwork issue. Among them was the Senate Special Committee to Study the Problems of American Small Business, which developed the draft Federal Reports Act of 1941, which ultimately resulted in the Federal Reports Act of 1942 (FRA) (56 Stat. 1078; 44 U.S.C. 3501–3520 (1982)). The president signed it into law on December 24, 1942.

Implementing the FRA, the Bureau of the Budget (BOB) required each agency seeking information from at least ten persons to submit the proposed questionnaire along with an explanation of its administration and a full justification for its use, including an estimate of the time required for completion of the instrument. In 1942, the BOB director also had inaugurated the Advisory Council on Federal Reports, composed of representatives from leading national business organizations, who met quarterly to consider broad questions concerning federal reporting requirements. However, when representatives from agencies seeking information subsequently began to meet with council members to discuss collections, the situation came under criticism and congressional investigation, and reform legislation—the Federal Advisory Committee Act of 1972 (FACA)—was enacted (86 Stat. 770). The council was reconstituted as the Business Advisory Council on Federal Reports, an industry trade group, rather than as an advisory committee under FACA.

Some agencies were critical of the length of time the BOB review process occasionally required before collections could be undertaken. Regulatory agencies complained that the Office of Management and Budget (OMB), which replaced the BOB in 1970, refused to allow them to collect information from regulated industries and thus infringed upon their statutory duties. In 1973, Congress responded by exempting the independent regulatory agencies from OMB review (86 Sat. 576).

Congressional unhappiness with OMB had also been prompted by a 1972 report by the Senate Select Committee on Small Business, which concluded that there was "an indifference of OMB officials towards their basic responsibilities. . . . Since only a relative handful (between one and five percent) of forms [were] disapproved, [the] committee [could] only conclude that hundreds of unnecessary or duplicative forms [were] being imposed on the public."[4] The committee also believed that OMB, "not knowing the problems of small business respondents," could not "effectively adapt 'data requests to respondent's records'"; had "shown a consistent lack of initiative in rigorously pursuing the directives of the Federal Reports Act;" and had refused "to adequately staff or properly equip, with data processing tools, its Statistical Policy Division," the office that was responsible for administering the FRA. Ultimately, the committee recommended that GAO be given the FRA responsibilities then vested in OMB.[5] The congressional response to this and similar criticism of OMB regarding reporting and recordkeeping burdens was the creation of the Commission on Federal Paperwork in 1974.

Commission on Federal Paperwork

A national study panel, the Commission on Federal Paperwork, was statutorily mandated to study, report findings, and make recommendations concerning the adequacy of laws, regulations, and procedures to ensure that the federal government was obtaining needed information from the private sector with minimal burden, duplication, and cost (see 88 Stat. 1789). By the time the commission concluded its work in September 1977, it had issued thirty-six reports and had offered 770 recommendations.[6] The commission called for new legislation, replacing the FRA, "to regulate the collection, management, and use of Government-held information as well as its disclosure." It also urged the establishment of an executive office to, among other functions, "coordinate information management responsibilities . . . and to monitor agency compliance with information laws."[7]

The commission's organic statute specified that, upon the submission of the panel's final report, OMB was to coordinate and formulate executive branch views concerning the commission's recommendations, begin implementing those recommendations in which the executive concurred, and propose legislation needed to carry out those recommendations in which the executive concurred (see 88 Stat. 1790). A September 1979 OMB progress report, the third such required semiannual report, indicated that more than 50 percent of the commission's recommendations pertaining to the executive branch (269 of 520) had been implemented.[8] Six months later, however, a GAO assessment criticized OMB for overstating the progress that had been made in implementing the commission's recommendations. The GAO urged Congress to enact legislation requiring OMB to "establish a legislative program for those recommendations still pending and create an Office of Federal Information Policy within OMB."[9]

The Paperwork Reduction Act of 1980

On December 11, 1980, President Jimmy Carter signed the Paperwork Reduction Act (PRA) into law (94 Stat. 2812; 44 U.S.C. 3501–3520 (1982)). Capitalizing on OMB's FRA experience and its role in management improvement and regulatory reform under the Carter administration, the PRA made OMB the principal policymaker and overseer of government paperwork activities. The statute established a new Office of Information and Regulatory Affairs (OIRA) within OMB, to which the director of OMB was to delegate his paperwork functions (44 U.S.C. 3503 (1982)). These functions included:

- Reviewing and approving information collection requests proposed by agencies;

- Determining whether the collection of information by an agency is necessary for the proper performance of its functions;

- Ensuring that all procedural requirements for collecting information were fulfilled;

- Designating a collection agency to obtain information for two or more agencies;

- Setting goals for reduction of the burdens of federal information collection requests;

- Overseeing action on the recommendations of the Commission on Federal Paperwork; and

- Designing and operating the Federal Information Locator System.[10]

The PRA also assigned information management responsibilities to the director of OMB. Indeed, the statute's title was somewhat misleading. The director was broadly mandated to "develop and implement Federal information policies, principles, standards, and guidelines" and to "provide direction and oversee the review and approval of information collection requests, the reduction of the paperwork burden, [and] Federal statistical activities, records management activities, privacy of records, interagency sharing of information, and acquisition and use of automatic data processing telecommunications, and other technology for managing information resources."[11]

Among the "general information policy functions" enumerated for the director were

- Developing and implementing uniform and consistent information resources management policies and overseeing the development of information management principles, standards, and guidelines and promoting their use;

- Initiating and reviewing proposals for changes in legislation, regulations, and agency procedures to improve information practices, and informing the president and the Congress of the progress made therein;

- Coordinating, through the review of budget proposals and otherwise, agency information practices;

- Promoting, through the use of the Federal Information Locator System, the review of budget proposals and other methods, as well as greater sharing of information by agencies;

- Evaluating agency information management practices to determine their adequacy and efficiency, as well as their compliance with the policies, principles, standards, and guidelines promulgated by the director; and

- Overseeing planning for, and conduct of research with respect to, federal collection, processing, storage, transmission, and use of information.[12]

Additional functions were specified for "statistical policy and coordination," "records management," personal privacy protection, and "Federal automatic data processing and telecommunications." All of the executive agencies were assigned responsibilities as well, largely for ensuring the elimination of duplicative and unnecessary collection of information. The statute required each agency head to designate a senior official, who was to report directly to the agency head, to carry out the agency's PRA responsibilities (see 44 U.S.C. 3506).

The remaining provisions of the new law specified the details of the information collection clearance process, including the use of a hearing or a statement submission arrangement (see 44 U.S.C. 3507–3508); the designation of a central collection agency to obtain information for two or more agencies (44 U.S.C. 3509); the directing of information sharing by agencies (see 44 U.S.C. 3510); the establishment and operation of a Federal Information Locator System to "serve as the authoritative register of all information collection requests" (see 44 U.S.C. 3511); a selective "review, at least once every three years, [of] the information management activities of each agency to ascertain their adequacy and efficiency" (see 44 U.S.C. 3513); and keeping "Congress and its committees fully and currently informed of the major activities under" the PRA and reporting annually to both houses in such detail as specified in the statute (see 44 U.S.C. 3514).

The Paperwork Reduction Reauthorization Act of 1986

As originally enacted, the PRA authorized appropriations for OIRA through the fiscal year ending September 30, 1983. Implementation difficulties gave Congress a basis for amending the statute while reauthorizing OIRA funding.[13] The text of the measure (S. 2887) to reauthorize and amend the PRA was included, as Title VIII, in the continuing resolution making appropriations for FY1987 (see 100 Stat. 3341-335).

The PRA amendments, among other modifications, refined "information resources management," as used in the statute; made future heads of OIRA presidential appointees subject to Senate approval; revised the statistical policy and coordination functions of the OMB director; established a chief statistician position; created a new Information Technology Fund to be administered by GSA; slightly modified the Federal Information Locator System; set new paperwork reduction goals of 15 percent for fiscal years 1987–1989; and authorized appropriations of $5.5 million for each of the fiscal years 1987, 1988, and 1989. The authorization indicated that such appropriations were to be used by OIRA to carry out only the functions prescribed by the PRA, as amended (see 100 Stat. 3341-340).

In the months following the reauthorization of the PRA, OIRA review of agency regulatory actions continued to engender congressional ire. Late in the 101st Congress, in the face of strong opposition from the Bush administration, efforts were made to move legislation (H.R. 3695/S. 1742) reauthorizing the PRA while limiting OIRA's control over the regulatory review process. Initially, in March 1990, House managers negotiated with OMB to legislate a simple three-year reauthorization for OIRA if OMB would accept, separate from the legislation, an administrative agreement limiting OMB's regulatory power, to become effective when the reauthorization was enacted into law. Although the House managers thought they had administration consent to this arrangement, the White House withdrew its support in early April, just as the reauthorization measure was about to be taken to the House floor.

The Senate bill, unlike its House counterpart, contained many restrictions on OIRA, and when it was scheduled for consideration by the Committee on Governmental Affairs in early April, Republican members of the panel, who opposed the OIRA limitations, boycotted the meeting. Later, in early June, after some accommodations had been reached, the committee approved the bill on a 14–0 vote.

Further negotiation with the Bush administration produced another compromise during the last week of the 101st Congress. Administration officials agreed to restrain OMB's exercise of its regulatory power if Congress would forego writing limits on OIRA's review of agency regulatory actions into law. Senate committee leaders indicated they would bring a stripped-down version of their bill to the floor.

In light of this deal, House managers brought their bill to the floor, and, on October 23, it was adopted on a voice vote. The next day, OMB released a statement indicating that the Bush administration strongly endorsed the Senate reauthorization measure, but several Republican senators reportedly placed anonymous holds on the legislation and it failed to receive consideration prior to the October 28 adjournment.

With the inauguration of the Clinton administration, the PRA reauthorization bill approved by the Senate was drafted as a complete revision of the act due to the number of changes it effected. Some technical modifications, such as word substitutions, the deletion of obsolete provisions, and section reorganizations, were included. Appropriations for OIRA were authorized for eight years at $8 million each year. The 1986 goal of an annual 5 percent reduction in public paperwork burdens was continued. One of the most controversial portions of the bill overturned a Supreme Court ruling that the PRA allowed OMB to review information collection intended for government use but did not extend to regulations intended to force businesses to produce information for a third party, such as the public or its employees.[14] Agencies were required to develop a paperwork clearance process to review and solicit public comment on proposed information collection prior to submission for OMB review. The OMB was required to disclose publicly communications it received regarding information collection and to review the status of any collection upon public request. The OMB was also tasked with developing governmentwide policies and guidelines for information dissemination and promoting public access to information maintained by federal agencies. Counterpart responsibilities were prescribed for the executive agencies to ensure that the public had timely and equitable access to public information, to solicit public input on their information dissemination activities, and to prohibit restrictions on the dissemination or re-dissemination of public information. The bill emphasized efficient and effective use of new technologies and reliance on a diversity of public and private sources to promote the dissemination of government information, particularly in electronic formats. Finally, agency heads were charged with responsibility to carry out IRM activities to improve agency productivity, efficiency, and effectiveness, and new IRM accountability arrangements were also established.

The Paperwork Reduction Act of 1995

Although the House and Senate majority parties in the 103rd Congress shifted to minority status in the 104th Congress as a consequence of the 1994 elections, important groundwork for PRA reauthorization legislation had been laid with the bipartisan, compromise Senate bill of the prior Congress. The Clinton administration restrained OIRA's review of agency regulatory actions and saw the PRA as an important part of its efforts at improving customer service.[15] Bipartisan support for reducing the paperwork burden on the public remained strong in both houses of Congress. The Paperwork Reduction Act of 1995 (109 Stat 163; 44 U.S.C. 3501–3520 (1997 Supp. III)) was signed into law by President Clinton on May 22, 1995.

The legislation was drafted as a complete revision of the act. Some technical modifications, such as word substitutions, the deletion of obsolete provisions, and section reorganizations, were included. The administrator of OIRA was made a presidential appointee subject to Senate confirmation. Appropriations for OIRA were authorized for six years at $8 million each year. A paperwork reduction goal of 10 percent was set for the first two authorization years and 5 percent thereafter. The purview of the act was extended to educational and nonprofit institutions, federal contractors, and tribal governments. The authority and functions of OIRA were revised, specifying information dissemination and related agency oversight responsibilities. The OMB was required to conduct pilot projects to test alternative policies and procedures, as well as to develop a governmentwide strategic information resources management plan. The OMB director was tasked with establishing an Interagency Council on Statistical Policy.

The federal agencies were required to establish a process, independent of program responsibility, to evaluate proposed collections of information, manage information resources to reduce information collection burdens on the public, and ensure that the public had timely and equitable access to information products and services. Except where specifically authorized by statute, the agencies were prohibited from establishing exclusive, restricted, or other distribution arrangements that interfered with timely and equitable public availability of public information; restricting or regulating the use, resale, or re-dissemination of public information by the public; charging fees or royalties for resale or re-dissemination of public information; or establishing user fees that exceeded the cost of dissemination. Actions that the agencies must take with respect to information technology were specified, and the Federal Information Locator System was replaced with an agency-based electronic Government Information Locator Service to identify the major information systems, holdings, and dissemination products of each agency.

INFORMATION TECHNOLOGY MANAGEMENT REFORM ACT

The PRA of 1995 was modified the following year with the adoption of new procurement reform and information technology management legislation. President Clinton signed the Information Technology Management Reform Act (110 Stat. 186) in February 1996. Division D of the statute, concerning "Federal Acquisition Reform," was denominated the Federal Acquisition Reform Act of 1996 (110 Stat. 642). Division E, concerning "Information Technology Management Reform," was known as the Information Technology Management Reform Act of 1996 (110 Stat. 679). The two divisions were subsequently denominated the Clinger-Cohen Act (110 Stat. 3009-393).

The Clinger-Cohen Act contains several provisions that either amend or gloss provisions of the PRA of 1995 as set out in chapter 35 of Title 44 of the *United States Code.*[16] Among the amendments was one establishing a chief information officer (CIO) in each agency, replacing the designated senior official mandated by the PRA at 44 U.S.C. 3506. The duties and qualifications of the CIO were prescribed in the Clinger-Cohen Act. Another amendment redefined "information technology" as used in the PRA.

Other Clinger-Cohen Act provisions glossed the responsibilities prescribed in the PRA. The capital planning and investment control duties assigned to the OMB director by the Clinger-Cohen Act were to be performed, according to that statute, "in fulfilling the responsibilities under section 3504(h)" of the PRA. Similarly, the director was to "encourage the use of performance-based and results-based management in fulfilling the responsibilities assigned under section 3504(h)" of the PRA. The Clinger-Cohen Act required agency heads, "[i]n fulfilling the responsibilities assigned under section 3506(h)" of the PRA, to "design and implement . . . a process for maximizing the value and assessing and managing the risks of the information technology acquisitions of the . . . agency" and to perform certain prescribed duties. Also, agency heads were to "identify in the strategic information resources management plan required under section 3506(b)(2) . . . [of the PRA] any major information technology acquisition program, or any phase or increment of such a program, that has significantly deviated from the cost, performance, or schedule goals established for the program."[17]

GOVERNMENT PAPERWORK ELIMINATION ACT

More recent amendments to the PRA were enacted in 1998 as the Government Paperwork Elimination Act (GPEA). In the 105th Congress, the language of the noncontroversial Senate bill (S. 2107) was attached, as Title 17, to the Omnibus Consolidated and Emergency Supplemental Appropriations Act, 1999, which cleared both houses of Congress and was signed into law by President Clinton on October 21, 1998 (112 Stat. 2681-749). As enacted, GPEA makes the director of OMB responsible for providing governmentwide direction and oversight regarding "the acquisition and use of information technology, including alternative information technologies that provide for electronic submission, maintenance, or disclosure of information as a substitute for paper and for the use and acceptance of electronic signatures."[18] In fulfilling this responsibility, the director, in consultation with the National Telecommunications and Information Administration (NTIA) of the Department of Commerce, was tasked with developing, in accordance with prescribed requirements, procedures for the use and acceptance of electronic signatures by the executive departments and agencies. A five-year deadline was prescribed for the agencies to implement these procedures.

The director of OMB was also tasked by GPEA to "develop procedures to permit private employers to store and file electronically with Executive agencies forms containing information pertaining to the employees of such employers."[19] In addition, the director, in cooperation with NTIA, is to conduct an ongoing study of the use of electronic signatures under the GPEA, with attention to paperwork reduction and electronic commerce, individual privacy, and the security and authenticity of transactions. The results of this study are to be reported periodically to Congress.

Finally, electronic records submitted or maintained in accordance with GPEA procedures, "or electronic signatures or other forms of electronic authentication used in accordance with such procedures, shall not be denied legal effect, validity, or enforceability because such records are in electronic form." The act further specifies: "Except as provided by law, information collected in the provision of electronic signature services for communications with an executive agency . . . shall only be used or disclosed by persons who obtain, collect, or maintain such information as a business or government practice, for the purpose of facilitating such communications, or with the prior affirmative consent of the person about whom the information pertains."[20]

GOVERNMENT INFORMATION SECURITY AMENDMENTS

The most recent provisions appended to the PRA of 1997 are the requirements of legislation initially introduced in mid-November 1999 by Senator Fred Thompson (R-Tenn.), chairman of the Committee on Governmental Affairs, with Senator Joseph Lieberman (D-Conn.), the committee's ranking minority member. The report accompanying the bill when it was reported from committee in April 2000 proffered the following description:

> The Government Information Security Act would provide a comprehensive framework for establishing and ensuring the effectiveness of controls over information resources that support Federal operations and assets. It is modeled

on the "best practices" of leading organizations in the area of information security. It does this by strengthening responsibilities and procedures and coordinating information policy to ensure better control and oversight of systems. It also recognizes the highly networked nature of the current Federal computing environment and provides for government-wide management and oversight of the related information security risks including coordination of security efforts between civilian, national security and law enforcement communities.[21]

The PRA, according to the committee report, would be amended in four general areas:

- *Agency responsibilities:* Agency heads would be responsible for developing and implementing security policies. This responsibility would be delegable to the agency's chief information officer or comparable official. Each agency would be responsible for developing and implementing an agencywide security program that must include risk assessment considering internal and external threats; risk-based policies; security awareness training for personnel; periodic reviews of the effectiveness of security policies including remedies to address deficiencies; and procedures for detecting, reporting, and responding to security incidents. Further, each agency would be required to identify specific actions—including budget, staffing, and training resources—necessary to implement the security program and include this as part of its Government Performance and Results Act performance plan.

- *Director of OMB responsibilities:* The agency plans must be affirmatively approved by the director of OMB, who also would be responsible for establishing governmentwide policies for the management of programs that support the cost-effective security of federal information systems by promoting security as an integral part of each agency's business operations. Other responsibilities of the director would include overseeing and coordinating agency implementation of security policies and coordinating with the National Institute for Standards and Technology on the development of standards and guidelines for security controls for federal systems. Such standards would be voluntary and consensus-based and developed in consultation with industry. To enforce agency accountability, the director would be authorized to take budgetary action with respect to an agency's information resources management allocations. The OMB director may delegate these responsibilities only down to the deputy director for management.

- *Annual audit:* Based on the General Accounting Office's audit findings, S. 1993 adds a new requirement that each agency must annually undergo an independent evaluation of its information security program and practices to be conducted either by the agency's inspector general (IG), the General Accounting Office (GAO) or an independent external auditor. The GAO then will review these evaluations and report annually to Congress regarding the adequacy of agency information programs and practices.

- *National security systems:* S. 1993 would require that the same management framework be applied to all systems including national security systems. However, to ensure that national security concerns are adequately addressed and that the appropriate individuals have oversight over national security and other classified information, the bill, as amended, would vest responsibility for approving the security plan for these systems in the secretary of defense and the director of central intelligence, rather than the director of OMB. In addition, for these systems, the secretary of defense or the director of central intelligence shall designate who conducts the evaluation of these systems with the IG conducting an audit of the evaluation. Finally, the bill also allows the defense and intelligence agencies to develop their own procedures for detecting, reporting, and responding to security incidents.[22]

During mid-June Senate floor consideration of the Defense Authorization bill for FY2001, the proposal was attached to that legislation, remained in the final version approved by the Senate on July 13, and in the subsequent conference committee version of the legislation, which cleared Congress on October 12 and was signed by the president on October 30 (PL 106-398).

GOVERNMENT INFORMATION MANAGEMENT ISSUES

Replacing the ineffective Federal Reports Act of 1942, the Paperwork Reduction Act of 1980 was enacted largely to relieve the public from the mounting information collection and reporting requirements of the federal government. It also promoted coordinated information management activities on a governmentwide basis under the leadership of the OMB director and prescribed information management responsibilities for the executive agencies. The management focus of the PRA was sharpened with the 1986 amendments, which refined the concept of IRM, defined as "the planning, budgeting, organizing, directing, training, promoting, controlling, and management activities associated with the burden, collection, creation, use, and dissemination of information by agencies, and includes the management of information and related resources such as automatic data processing equipment."[23] This key term and its subset concepts received further definition and explanation in the PRA of 1995 (109 Stat. 165-166), making IRM a tool for managing the contribution of information activities to program performance and for managing related resources, such as personnel, equipment, funds, and technology.[24] The PRA authorized OIRA appropriations through FY2001 (see 44 U.S.C. 3520). The reauthorization of these appropriations provides an opportunity for upgrading the PRA by addressing government information management issues arising from the changing technological environment.[25] The rest of this chapter discusses some of these issues.

Administrative Management

Since the adoption of the original PRA (1980), there has existed within OMB an Office of Information and Regulatory Affairs, which, through its administrator, currently assists the director of OMB with

- Advice on federal information resources management policy;

- Overseeing "the use of information resources to improve the efficiency and effectiveness of governmental operations to serve agency missions, including burden reduction and service delivery to the public;" and

- Developing, coordinating, and overseeing "the implementation of Federal information resources management policies, principles, standards, and guidelines," and providing direction and overseeing "the review and approval of the collection of information and the reduction of the information collection burden; agency dissemination of and public access to information; statistical activities; records management activities; privacy, confidentiality, security, disclosure, and sharing of information; and the acquisition and use of information technology."[26]

The Clinger-Cohen Act mandated chief information officers (CIOs) within the principal executive departments and several of the larger independent agencies.[27] These CIOs are statutorily responsible for

(1) Providing advice and other assistance to the head of the executive agency and other senior management personnel of the executive agency to ensure that information technology is acquired and information resources are managed for the executive agency in a manner that implements the policies and procedures of [the Clinger-Cohen Act], consistent with chapter 35 of title 44, *United States Code*, and the priorities established by the head of the executive agency

(2) Developing, maintaining, and facilitating the implementation of a sound and integrated information technology architecture for the executive agency; and

(3) Promoting the effective and efficient design and operation of all major information resources management processes for the executive agency, including improvements to work processes of the executive agencies.[28]

A few months before the Clinger-Cohen Act was signed into law, President Clinton issued E.O. 13011 of July 16, 1996, which, among other provisions, established a Chief Information Officers Council to function "as the principal interagency forum to improve agency practices on such matters as the design, modernization, use, sharing, and performance of agency information resources." Among the responsibilities assigned to the council by the president's directive are the following:

(1) Develop recommendations for overall Federal information technology management policy, procedures, and standards;

(2) Share experiences, ideas, and promising practices, including work process redesign and the development of performance measures, to improve the management of information resources;

(3) Identify opportunities, make recommendations for, and sponsor cooperation in using information resources;

(4) Assess and address the hiring, training, classification, and professional development needs of the Federal Government with respect to information resources management;

(5) Make recommendations and provide advice to appropriate executive agencies and organizations, including advice to OMB on the government-wide strategic plan required by the Paperwork Reduction Act of 1995; and

(6) Seek the views of the Chief Financial Officers Council, Government Information Technology Services Board, Information Technology Resources Board, Federal Procurement Council, industry, academia, and State and local governments on matters of concern to the Council as appropriate.[29]

Chaired by the OMB deputy director for management, the council is composed of the CIOs and deputy CIOs of twenty-eight designated departments and agencies; two representatives from other agencies; and six other specified officials, including the administrator of OIRA. The original Senate bill (S. 946) underlying the Clinger-Cohen Act provided for such a council, chaired by the director of OMB, with a chief information officer of the United States—an immediate deputy to the director of OMB—serving as the executive director of the panel.

Considering PRA reauthorization as an opportunity for streamlining the existing administrative management arrangements for information resources and providing a more sound basis for operation, several issues arise.

Mandate and Mission of the CIO Council

Is the council's organic authority adequate, or should it be statutorily mandated, as contemplated in the Senate bill underlying the Clinger-Cohen Act? What should be the mission and role of the council relative to the mission and role of OIRA? Although the panel could be expected to be tasked with advisory, coordination, informational, and educational missions, should it be precluded from issuing any policies, principles, standards, or guidelines, which, more properly, might be offered to OMB as recommendations and, if accepted, issued as OMB instruments? Might the budget and personnel summary of the council be included in the president's budget as a line item as a matter of accountability?

Leadership of the Council

Although there appears to be a degree of agreement that leadership of the council should be vested in some senior OMB official, should it be the director, as was proposed in the Senate bill underlying the Clinger-Cohen Act; the deputy director for management, as established by E.O. 13011; or, given the many other responsibilities of these officials, the administrator of OIRA or a chief information officer of the United States?

Chief Information Officer of the United States

The original Senate bill underlying the Clinger-Cohen Act provided for a chief information officer of the United States (CIOUS), who would be appointed by the president with Senate approval and would serve as an immediate deputy to the director of OMB. As portrayed in the Senate bill, this official would head the new Office of the Chief Information Officer of the United States within OMB; perform the functions of the director of OMB prescribed in chapter 35 of Title 44, *United States Code*; perform certain information technology procurement duties prescribed in the Senate bill; and serve as the executive director of the proposed Federal Information Council (the prototype of the CIO Council). Texas Governor George W. Bush endorsed the CIOUS idea in June 2000 during his campaign for the Republican presidential nomination. Subsequently, in the early weeks of his administration, President Bush vacated his endorsement of a CIOUS. Would existing administrative management arrangements for information resources be improved, with regard to efficiency and economy of operation, by establishing such a chief information officer of the United States?[30]

Government Information Security

References to "automatic data processing and telecommunications technologies" in the PRA of 1980 were a recognition of government use of computer processing and the resulting creation, use, and storage of government information in electronic forms and formats. However, in defining these terms, the statute excluded applications involving intelligence, cryptologic, and military command and control activities—traditional areas of protected national security information. Thus, information security, in the national security context, was excluded from the scope of the PRA and seemingly was not yet a concern in any other context, such as homeland security.

A few years later, when adopting the Computer Security Act of 1987, Congress declared "that improving the security and privacy of sensitive information in Federal computer systems is in the public interest, and hereby creates a means for establishing minimum acceptable security practices for such systems, without limiting the scope of security measures already planned or in use."[31] Thus, still steering clear of protected national security information, the statute mandated the National Bureau of Standards (later renamed the National Institute of Standards and Technology) of the Department of Commerce to develop "standards, guidelines, and associated methods and techniques for computer systems . . . to control loss and unauthorized modification or disclosure of sensitive information in such systems and to prevent computer-related fraud and misuse."[32]

When legislating the PRA of 1995, Congress indicated that one of the purposes of the statute was to "ensure that the creation, collection, maintenance, use, dissemination, and disposition of information by or for the Federal Government is consistent with applicable laws, including laws relating to . . . privacy and confidentiality, including section 552a of title 5 [the Privacy Act]; security of information, including the Computer Security Act of 1987 (PL 100-235); and access to information, including section 552 of title 5 [the Freedom of Information Act]."[33] Privacy and security responsibilities were assigned to the director of OMB, including overseeing and coordinating agency compliance with the three aforementioned laws (see 44 U.S.C. 3504(g)), and also to the agencies, including the assumption of responsibility and accountability for compliance with the same three laws (see 44 U.S.C. 3506(g)).

The government information security amendments to the PRA enacted through the defense reauthorization act for FY2001 are expected to strengthen security practices. Viewed incrementally, what next steps might be taken, and might they be pursued through the PRA reauthorization? Recent criticism by GAO and others would seem to suggest that the situation could benefit from further reform.[34] Relying on GAO's evaluations, Representative Stephen Horn (R-Calif.), chairman of the House Subcommittee on Government Management, Information, and Technology, issued a report card on federal computer security at a September 11, 2000, hearing, giving more than a quarter of the twenty-four major executive agencies a failing grade of F and an overall executive branch grade of D-.[35] A year later, Horn gave the government an overall grade of F, with only three of twenty-four agencies receiving a grade of C or B.[36]

Web Site Management

Executive agencies have relied on, and otherwise interpreted, a variety of authorities for the creation and management of their Web sites. Prominent among these are the Federal Records Act, the Freedom of Information Act, the

Privacy Act, the Paperwork Reduction Act, the Computer Security Act, and, most recently, the Clinger-Cohen Act. However, adaptation and interpretation of these statutes have sometimes resulted in what one guiding document calls "vexing legal and policy concerns." The document, initially prepared by the World Wide Web Federal Consortium in 1995 and subsequently revised, provides guidelines and best practices for the development, maintenance, and enhancement of executive agency Web sites. Relevant statutes and regulations are identified; a checklist of home page creation standards is provided; and a few questions and answers, prepared by OIRA concerning "vexing legal and policy concerns," are offered.[37]

In mid-April 1997, OIRA drafted five principles concerning federal agency use of the World Wide Web. "While proper use of the Web has great advantages for an agency," the draft memo commented, "it also introduces a number of challenges in applying existing law and regulation to new ways of conducting agency business":

> Agencies should apply the following principles when planning and operating Web-based services. While these principles interrelate, the first deals primarily with strategy and planning, the second with service delivery, the third with information access and dissemination, the fourth with collecting information from the public, and the fifth concerns the management of Federal Records.
>
> 1. When planning for new Web applications, or reviewing existing ones, agencies should set clear strategic goals with performance measurements that demonstrate value; account for and maximize efficient use of agency resources; prepare for consistent service, maintenance and product delivery; and provide for the security of agency information and systems.
>
> 2. Agencies should use the Web as a supplemental service delivery tool to attend to the needs of all Americans—including the financially disadvantaged, those with disabilities, and those without reasonable access to advanced technologies; establish partnerships with other agencies and organizations to enhance customer service; deliver services in timely and equitable terms without neglecting traditional delivery methods.
>
> 3. Agencies should strive for accuracy, relevance, timeliness and completeness of agency information made available electronically; when practicable, provide cost-free access, but, if required, limit fees to the direct cost of dissemination and avoid improperly restrictive access practices; communicate regularly with the public through the *Federal Register* and other means in shaping and altering information services and products; support the Government Information Locator Service (see 44 U.S.C. 3511); and make information dissemination products available to Federal Depository Libraries.
>
> 4. Agencies should collect from the public only that information necessary for the performance of official functions; solicit public comment and customer feedback on information collections consistent with law; respect

and guard the public's personal privacy and ensure the security of their information; and promote customer confidence through public notice in the *Federal Register* describing those circumstances when the agency collects and uses (e.g., for system performance measurements or security) electronic mail and Internet Protocol addresses, user statistics and activity logs, and similar data produced as a result of electronic interaction with the agency.

5. Agencies should create, use, preserve and dispose of electronically published records in a manner consistent with the management of the individual underlying records, recognizing that in most instances compilations of existing records are not considered by the National Archives and Records Administration as new and distinct records. Agencies should use, preserve, and dispose of information generated through interactive Web sites (e.g., those delivering services or collecting information via on-line application forms and surveys) in a manner consistent with National Archives and Records Administration guidance for electronic mail and other electronic records.[38]

Neither these principles, nor any comprehensive Web site management guidance, has been issued by OMB for agency compliance. The OMB director did issue a June 2, 1999, memorandum to the heads of executive departments and agencies directing the posting of clear privacy policies on federal Web sites and providing guidance for this action.[39] Such policies "must clearly and concisely inform visitors to the site what information the agency collects about individuals, why the agency collects it, and how the agency will use it." Also, they "must be clearly labeled and easily accessed when someone visits a web site," according to the memorandum. Agencies were reminded that, pursuant to the Privacy Act, they must protect an individual's right to privacy when they collect personal information.

A June 22, 2000, followup memorandum was issued by OMB after press disclosures that the National Drug Control Policy Office, an agency within the Executive Office of the President, was secretly tracking visitors to its Web site through the use of computer software known as "cookies."[40] Addressing this revelation, it stated:

Particular privacy concerns may be raised when uses of web technology can track the activities of users over time and across different web sites. These concerns are especially great where individuals who have come to government web sites do not have clear and conspicuous notice of any such tracking activities. "Cookies"—small bits of software that are placed on a web user's hard drive—are a principal example of current web technology that can be used in this way. The guidance issued on June 2, 1999, provided that agencies could only use "cookies" or other automatic means of collecting information if they gave clear notice of those activities.

Because of the unique laws and traditions abut government access to citizens' personal information, the presumption should be that "cookies" will not be used at Federal web sites. Under this new Federal policy, "cookies" should not be used at Federal web sites, or by contractors when operating web sites on behalf of agencies, unless, in addition to clear and conspicuous notice, the following conditions are met: a compelling need to gather the data on the site; appropriate and publicly disclosed privacy safeguards for handling of information derived from "cookies"; and personal approval by the head of the agency. In addition, it is Federal policy that all Federal web sites and contractors when operating on behalf of agencies shall comply with the standards set forth in the Children's Online Privacy Protection Act of 1998 with respect to the collection of personal information online at web sites directed to children.[41]

In September, GAO, reporting on a survey of online privacy protections at federal Web sites, found that twenty-three of seventy agencies had disclosed personal information gathered from their Web sites to third parties, mostly other agencies. At least four agencies were discovered to be sharing such information with private entities: trade organizations, bilateral development banks, product manufacturers, distributors, and retailers. The offending agencies were not identified by GAO. Responding to these findings, some privacy advocates called for updating the Privacy Act, while others urged better oversight and enforcement of that statute.[42]

When completing action on the FY2001 appropriations legislation for the Department of Transportation and related agencies, House and Senate conferees included a Web site privacy provision. Section 501 of the conference committee version of the bill (H.R. 4475) prohibited agencies funded by Title V of the legislation (1) to collect, review, or create any aggregate list, derived by any means, that includes the collection of any personally identifiable information relating to an individual's access to, or use of, any federal government Internet site of the agency; or (2) to enter into any agreement with a third party, including another government agency, to collect, review, or obtain any aggregate list, derived by any means, that includes the collection of any personally identifiable information relating to an individual's access to or use of any nongovernmental Internet site. These limitations do not apply to (1) any record of aggregate data that does not identify particular persons; (2) any voluntary submission of personally identifiable information; (3) any action taken for law enforcement, regulatory, or supervisory purposes, in accordance with applicable law; and (4) any action that is a system security action taken by the operator of an Internet site and is necessarily incidental to the rendition of the Internet site services or to the protection of the rights or property of the provider of the Internet site.[43]

The first limitation may be viewed as a response to the June 2000 press revelation that the National Drug Control Policy Office was secretly tracking visitors to its Web site. The second limitation may be regarded as a response to the September GAO report indicating that twenty-three agencies had disclosed personal information gathered from their Web sites to third parties. President

Clinton signed the transportation appropriation bill into law on October 23, 2000 (PL 106-346).

Two days before the president's action, press disclosures revealed that a GAO followup study contended that thirteen federal agencies had ignored the OMB June 22 memorandum prohibiting the tracking of visitors to government Web sites. An appended letter from the OMB deputy director for management defended agency use of so-called session cookies, which, the letter said, facilitate transactions at the Web site and are not banned by OMB. Session cookies last only as long as one is visiting the Web site. Clearly prohibited are "persistent cookies," which may track Web habits for long periods of time, and the dissemination of a person's information to a private company. GAO found seven agencies engaging in one or both of these activities.[44]

In mid-April 2001, Senator Thompson released the preliminary findings of agency IGs who were required by a provision of the Treasury-Postal title of the Consolidated Appropriations Act of 2001 to report on how their agencies collect and review personal information on their Web sites (PL 106-554, sec. 646). Reports on sixteen agencies found sixty-four Web sites making use of "persistent cookies."[45] Shortly thereafter, a GAO senior attorney criticized OMB's contradictory guidelines about federal agency use of "cookies." The OMB, it was observed, had encouraged agencies to comply with the fair information practice principles of the Federal Trade Commission, which are not statutorily mandated, and also adhere to the requirements of the Privacy Act.[46] As discussed in the next chapter, the treasury appropriations bill for fiscal year 2001 prohibits the use of agency funds

> (1) to collect, review, or create any aggregate list, derived from any means, that includes the collection of any personally identifiable information relating to an individual's access to or use of any Federal Government Internet site of the agency; or (2) to enter into any agreement with a third party . . . to collect, review, or obtain any aggregate list, derived from any means, that includes the collection of any personally identifiable information relating to an individual's access to or use of any nongovernmental Internet site.[47]

Conferees retained provisions from the House-passed version of the FY2002 treasury appropriations bill (section 638 of H. R. 2590) continuing, in modified and expanded form, a limitation on federal agency monitoring of personal information during use of the Internet. The initial version of the prohibition appeared in the transportation appropriations bill (section 501) funding some treasury appropriations accounts for FY2001 (PL 106-346). Some confusion existed concerning the section's application to all executive agencies or only those funded by the treasury appropriations bill. The new language approved by the conferees eliminated this confusion, saying, none of the funds "made available in this or any other Act may be used by any Federal agency" for the following purposes:

(1) to collect, review, or create any aggregate list, derived from any means, that includes the collection of any personally identifiable information relating to an individual's access to or use of any Federal Government Internet site of the agency; or

(2) to enter into any agreement with a third party (including another government agency) to collect, review, or obtain any aggregate list, derived from any means, that includes the collection of any personally identifiable information relating to an individual's access to or use of any nongovernmental Internet site.[48]

Specified exceptions to these limitations include

(1) any record of aggregate data that does not identify particular persons;

(2) any voluntary submission of personally identifiable information;

(3) any action taken for law enforcement, regulatory, or supervisory purposes, in accordance with applicable law; or

(4) any action described in subsection . . . (1) that is a system security action taken by the operator of an Internet site and is necessarily incidental to the rendition of the Internet site services or to the protection of the rights or property of the provider of the Internet site.[49]

In the aftermath of these controversies, issues remain concerning the conditions to be satisfied in the event certain kinds of "cookies" are used, if all or certain agencies are to be subject to the prescribed "cookies" use policy, and OMB's contradictory guidelines. Provisions regarding these matters might be appended to the PRA during the reauthorization process.

Furthermore, proposals concerning other, somewhat larger, issues, like the responsibilities of the director of OMB and the agencies regarding Web site management, may emerge as part of the PRA reauthorization process. These provisions could involve some of the concepts discussed in the following sections.

Web Site Accounting

In the interests of promoting efficient and economical use of agency resources, facilitating OMB oversight, and ensuring that agency information practices do not exceed statutory limitations (see, e.g., 5 U.S.C. 3107), proposals could require agencies to register with, or otherwise report to, the director of OMB all existing Web sites they maintain and subsequently create. Beyond this requirement, agencies might be obligated to obtain OMB approval of new Web sites they propose to create.

Web Site Management Guidelines

The director of OMB might be authorized to issue explicit Web site management guidelines for agency compliance. Such guidelines might be required to specify basic expectations concerning Web site accessibility to the public, content, organization and layout, and information security and personal privacy. In brief, the step toward governmentwide Web site management taken by OMB in 1999 with its guidance on Web site privacy may be judged worthy of expansion.[50]

Web Site Archives

A Web site management matter of special concern to some data users is the length of time documents or data are available on a Web site and their subsequent retrieval from archival status through the Web site. The Web site management guidelines of the director of OMB might be required to address this issue, or the agencies might be required to comply with standards specified in their Web site management responsibilities. Retrieval of Web site documents or data from archival status through the Web site may be regarded as information provision consistent with the 1996 amendments to the Freedom of Information Act (see 110 Stat. 3408; 5 U.S.C. 552).

E-mail Management

As the April 1997 OIRA draft principles for federal agency use of the World Wide Web suggest, electronic mail or e-mail management was as much of a concern as Web site management. Both areas raise concerns about information security and personal privacy. Some aspects of e-mail management are subject to governmentwide direction by the Archivist of the United States pursuant to the records management responsibilities assigned to that position by Title 44 of the *United States Code* (see chapters 21, 22, 25, 27, 29, 31, and 33). However, the PRA establishes a degree of overlapping responsibility between the Archivist and the director of OMB, particularly in the context of the latter's responsibility for information resources management policy, information dissemination, records management, privacy and security, and information technology.[51] Reauthorization proposals may address the issues this situation raises.

Guidance on E-mail Use

Although the Archivist exercises records management responsibilities for e-mail once it has been created, reauthorization proposals may task the director of OMB with providing guidance on the use of e-mail by federal agencies and their officers and employees. For example, to what extent may e-mail of a personal nature be generated and transmitted from a government workstation by a federal employee? May a federal worker provide his or her government e-mail address to receive communications not related to his or her official duties?[52]

Both of these issues might be addressed through appropriate reauthorization legislation provisions amending the PRA. Also, the volume of e-mail is of concern. It was recently reported that, in the private sector, office employees are devoting nearly an hour of each work day to sifting through e-mail messages, more than a third of which are unnecessary communications sent by co-workers and employers.[53]

Public Information Dissemination

As the 106th Congress moved toward final adjournment, the National Commission on Libraries and Information Science (NCLIS) issued a November 27, 2000, discussion draft of *A Comprehensive Assessment of Public Information Dissemination*.[54] The assessment had initially been requested by Senator John McCain (R-Ariz.), the chairman of the Senate Committee on Commerce, Science, and Transportation, in mid-June as a followup on assistance the commission had provided to his committee regarding the future of the National Technical Information Service (NTIS) of the Department of Commerce.[55] In his letter to NCLIS, Senator McCain recalled testimony received by his committee "on the need for a formal study on the proposed organizational changes to . . . [NTIS] and overall government information dissemination policy." In making his request for "a review of the reforms necessary for the federal government's information dissemination practices," he asked that the study "include assessments of the need for"

- Proposing new or revised laws, rules, regulations, missions, and policies;

- Modernizing organization structures and functions so as to reflect greater emphasis on electronic information planning, management, and control capabilities, and the need to consolidate, streamline, and simplify missions and functions to avoid or minimize unnecessary overlap and duplication;

- Revoking [the] NTIS [financial] self-sufficiency requirement; and

- Strengthening other key components of the overall federal information dissemination infrastructure.[56]

A month later, in a mid-July letter, Senator Lieberman joined Senator McCain's request, and suggested two additions to the NCLIS study: "[I]nclude . . . any relevant sections of the Paperwork Reduction Act that may need revision, because [the Governmental Affairs] Committee will be considering the law's reauthorization next Congress," and "consider the viability of maintaining NTIS as a centralized fully electronic repository of federal scientific and technical information, accessible via the Internet and equipped with search and retrieval capabilities."[57]

The November 27 discussion draft begins with a working definition of "public information as information created, compiled and/or maintained by the federal government. We assert," the report continues, "that public information is information owned by the people, held in trust by their government, and should be available to the people except where restricted by law." These restrictions, it was stated, are "stipulated in various statutes such as the Freedom of Information Act, the Privacy Act, national security legislation, and a few other laws."[58]

The definition included the information holdings of all three branches of the federal government, and, while recognizing that restrictions on the public availability of some types of information existed, tended to regard these restrictions as being only statutorily prescribed and few in number. Such a view neglects the nonstatutory authority of congressional bodies, the president, and federal judges to limit information availability. It also appears to be uninformed regarding the numerous instances when Congress has legislated provisions protecting information from disclosure. The Commission on Federal Paperwork reported in July 1977 that it had identified "approximately 200 statutes concerning confidentiality [of information], about 90 of which relate to the disclosure of business or commercial data."[59] A 1984 survey conducted by the American Society of Access Professionals identified 135 statutory provisions cited by a total of forty federal executive agencies during 1975–1982 in conjunction with the Freedom of Information Act exemption recognizing statutory protection of various kinds of information.[60] Also, in addition to the Privacy Act, there are at least two dozen additional statutory provisions restricting the disclosure of personally identifiable information by executive agencies.

The report offers numerous findings, conclusions, and recommendations, and some statements of findings appear to be expressed in terms of a recommendation. Major recommendations proffered by the report include the following:

- Formally recognizing and affirming the concept that public information is a strategic national resource, with the president issuing a directive to the heads of executive departments and agencies designating government "knowledge holdings" as a strategic national asset and emphasizing the importance of agency proactive initiatives in making their information resources accessible to all Americans;

- Creating, as a new independent executive agency, a Public Information Resources Administration to provide overall policy leadership, management, oversight, and accountability for public information resources, with both new relevant authorities and responsibilities and transfers of existing relevant authorities and responsibilities from extant government entities;

- Transferring the NTIS to the new Public Information Resources Administration once it is established;

- Requiring an Information Dissemination Budget line item at the individual agency level and establishing an overall Information Dissemination Budget line item in the president's budget that aggregates individual agency requirements with those of the new Public Information Resources Administration;

- Enacting the draft Public Information Resources Reform Act of 2001 to provide a new statutory foundation for the formal establishment of government's "knowledge holdings" as a strategic national asset;

- Establishing a new Congressional Information Resources Office, incorporating the Government Printing Office, to execute programs necessary to support legislative branch public information resources management responsibilities;

- Establishing a new Judicial Information Resources Office within the Administrative Office of the U.S. Courts to execute programs necessary to support judicial branch public information resources management responsibilities;

- Supporting NTIS information collection, editing, and related tasks with appropriated funds; and

- Updating NTIS revenue sources to include appropriated funds, sales income, and reimbursements from other agencies for services provided.[61]

In general, the report seeks formal recognition and affirmation of the concept that public information is a strategic national resource, although many would contend that this objective has already been met with the Paperwork Reduction Act of 1995. Many of its findings and recommendations promote proactive agency information dissemination activities and practices. These efforts, as the commission was warned, "could result in a misuse of agency resources to promote the agency and generate propaganda," a caution the report dismisses as "unreasonable fears."[62] Nevertheless, long-standing congressional displeasure with zealous information activities was benchmarked almost a century ago with the Gillett Act prohibition on using appropriated funds to pay a publicity expert, unless specifically provided for that purpose (see 5 U.S.C. 3107).

CONCLUSION

Chapter 1 discussed information policy and how it is organized around the information life cycle. The policies addressed in this chapter cover that life cycle and enable government entities to "rely on Web sites as a means of disseminating information, providing access to agency services, and providing the forms, resources, and information necessary for citizens to interact with their government." These Web sites "also provide a means by which agencies conduct day-to-day business and archive basic agency information related to the conduct of business."[63] Bruce Smith, Bruce T. Fraser, and Charles R. McClure of Florida State University note that

[a]s federal agencies move to the Web environment for business, the federal government continues to amend and create new policy instruments for the conduct of that business. Any written law, guidelines, regulation, or other official statement that describes how information will be collected, managed, protected, accessed, disseminated, and used can be considered an information policy instrument. This definition also includes presidential executive orders; Office of Management and Budget (OMB) circulars, bulletins, and memorandum; and internal agency documentation.[64]

Clearly, information policy focusing on the management of federal resources undergoes periodic review and, when necessary, revision. Yet to date, because the materials included on agency Web sites have not been labeled as records (see Chapter 1), agencies enjoy latitude in making decisions about the retention of nonrecords removed from their Web sites. As those researchers at Florida State University conclude, "key issues yet to be resolved concern the appropriate policies for managing federal Web sites such that electronic information and documents are timely, accurate, official, acceptable in courts of law, and accessible for historical purposes."[65]

NOTES

1. Article I, section 2 prescribes that "The actual Enumeration shall be made within three Years after the Meeting of the Congress of the United States, and within every subsequent Term of ten Years, in such Manner as they shall by Law direct." The first such statute was an act of March 1, 1790 (1 Stat. 101).

2. Commission on Federal Paperwork, *History of Paperwork Reform Efforts: A Report of the Commission on Federal Paperwork* (Washington, D.C.: GPO, July 29, 1977), 15.

3. Ibid.

4. Senate Select Committee on Small Business, *The Federal Paperwork Burden*, 93rd Cong., 1st sess., S. Rept. 93-125 (Washington, D.C.: GPO, 1973), 25–26.

5. Ibid., 30, 34, 60, and 63.

6. See Commission on Federal Paperwork, *Final Summary Report, A Report of the Commission on Federal Paperwork* (Washington, D.C.: GPO, October 3, 1977).

7. Ibid., 52.

8. Office of Management and Budget, *Paperwork and Red Tape: New Perspectives; New Directions* (Washington, D.C.: GPO, September 1979), 5.

9. General Accounting Office, *Program to Follow-Up Federal Paperwork Commission Recommendations Is in Trouble*, GGD-80-36 (Washington, D.C.: General Accounting Office, March 14, 1980), i–iv.

10. 44 U.S.C. 3504(c).

11. 44 U.S.C. 3504(a).

12. 44 U.S.C. 3504(b).

13. See General Accounting Office, *Implementing the Paperwork Reduction Act: Some Progress, but Many Problems Remain*, GAO/GGD-83-35 (Washington, D.C.: General Accounting Office, April 20, 1983); General Accounting Office, *More Guidance and Controls Needed over Federal Recordkeeping Requirements Imposed on the Public*, GAO/GGD-83-42 (Washington, D.C.: General Accounting Office, April 1983); Department of Justice, Office of the Assistant Attorney General, Office of Legal Counsel, "Re: Paperwork Reduction Act of 1980," unpublished document (1982).

14. See *Dole* v. *United Steelworkers of America*, 494 U.S. 26 (1990).

15. See Office of the Vice President, *From Red Tape to Results, Creating a Government That Works Better & Costs Less: Improving Customer Service* (Accompanying Report of the National Performance Review) (Washington, D.C.: GPO, September 1993), 19–22.

16. The Clinger-Cohen Act (110 Stat. 680) also repealed a section of the Federal Property and Administrative Services Act popularly known as the Brooks Act (40 U.S.C. 759), which authorized the administrator of general services to coordinate and provide for the procurement, maintenance, and utilization of automatic data processing equipment.

17. Information Technology Management Reform Act of 1996 (110 Stat. 186), §§ 3506(h) and 3506(b)(2).

18. 44 U.S.C. 3504(a)(1)(B)(vi), as amended.

19. 112 Stat. 2681-750.

20. 112 Stat. 2681-751.

21. Senate Committee on Governmental Affairs, *Government Information Security Act of 1999* (report to accompany S. 1993), 106th Cong., 2d sess., S. Rept. 106-259 (Washington, D.C.: GPO, 2000), 1–2.

22. Ibid., 2–3.

23. 100 Stat. 3341-336.

24. See David Plocher, "The Paperwork Reduction Act of 1995: A Second Chance for Information Resources Management," *Government Information Quarterly* 13 (1996): 35–50.

25. Concerning the information collection or paperwork burden aspect of PRA administration, see General Accounting Office, *Paperwork Reduction Act: Burden Increases at IRS and Other Agencies*, GAO Testimony GAO/T-GGD-00-114 (Washington, D.C.: General Accounting Office, April 12, 2000); General Accounting Office, *Paperwork Reduction Act: Burden Estimates Continue to Increase*, GAO Testimony GAO-01-648T (Washington, D.C.: General Accounting Office, April 24, 2001).

26. 44 U.S.C. 3503(b)–3504(a)(1).

27. 110 Stat. 684; section 5125 of the statute amended 44 U.S.C. 3506 to establish CIOs in the departments and agencies mandated by 31 U.S.C. 901(b) to have chief financial officers.

28. 110 Stat. 685.

29. 3 C.F.R., 1996 Comp., 204.

30. Establishing a position of chief information officer for the federal government was among the policy recommendations offered in Robert D. Atkinson and Jacob Ulevich, *Digital Government: The Next Step to Reengineering the Federal Government* (Washington, D.C.: Progressive Policy Institute, Technology and New Economy Project, March 2000), 13, available at http://www.dlcppi.org (accessed May 17, 2002). Texas Governor George W. Bush, the anticipated Republican presidential nominee, endorsed the federal CIO position in a June 9, 2000, government reform speech in Philadelphia, PA. Bills creating such a position were offered in the House by Representatives Jim Turner (D-Tex.; H.R. 4670) and Tom Davis (R-Va.; H.R. 5024), and both measures were referred to the Committee on Government Reform. See House Committee on Government Reform, *Establishing a Federal CIO: Information Technology Management and Assurance within the Federal Government*, hearing, 106th Cong., 2d sess., Sept. 12, 2000 (Washington, D.C.:GPO, 2000); General Accounting Office, *Executive Guide: Maximizing the Success of Chief Information Officers*, GAO/AIMD-00-83 (Washington, D.C.: General Accounting Office, March 2000).

31. 101 Stat. 1724.

32. 101 Stat. 1725.

33. 44 U.S.C. 3501(8).

34. See General Accounting Office, *Federal Information Security: Actions Needed to Address Widespread Weaknesses*, GAO Testimony GAO/T-AIMD-00-135 (Washington, D.C.: General Accounting Office, March 29, 2000); General Accounting Office, *Information Security: Serious and Widespread Weaknesses Persist at Federal Agencies*, GAO/AIMD-00-295 (Washington, D.C.: General Accounting Office, September 2000).

35. House Committee on Government Reform, Subcommittee on Government Management, Information, and Technology, *Computer Security: How Vulnerable Are Federal Computers?*, hearing, 106th Cong., 2d sess., Sept. 11, 2000 (Washington, D.C.: GPO, 2000).

36. William Jackson, "Government Gets a Collective F for Its IT Security," *Government Computer News* (November 19, 2001): 12.

37. Available at http://www.dtic.mil/staff/cthomps/guidelines/summary (accessed May 17, 2002).

38. Office of Management and Budget, Office of Information and Regulatory Affairs, Memorandum for Agency Chief Information Officers, "Principles for Federal Agency Use of the World-Wide Web," from Sally Katzen, unpublished preliminary draft (April 14, 1997).

39. This memorandum is available from the OMB Web site under the heading "Information Policy and Technology." Note that the site for the Clinton administration is now available at http://www.clinton.archives.gov/.

40. See John F. Harris and John Schwartz, "Anti-Drug Web Site Tracks Visitors," *Washington Post,* June 22, 2000, A23; Lance Gay, "White House Uses Drug-Message Site to Track Inquiries," *Washington Times,* June 21, 2000, A3.

41. This memorandum is available from the OMB Web site at http://www.whitehouse.gov/OMB/inforeg/index.htm under the heading "Information Policy and Technology;" for a critique of the OMB memorandum, see Walter R. Houser, "OMB Cookie Memo Crumbles under Its Own Weight," *Government Computer News* 19 (July

24, 2000): 21, and "As It's Written, OMB Policy on Cookies Is Half-baked," *Government Computer News* 19 (November 6, 2000): 27.

42. Lance Gay, "GAO Finds Agencies Sharing Data of On-line Visitors," *Washington Times,* September 8, 2000, A3; General Accounting Office, *Internet Privacy: Agencies' Efforts to Implement OMB's Privacy Policy,* GAO/GGD-00-191 (Washington, D.C.: General Accounting Office, September 2000).

43. See *Congressional Record* (daily edition) 146 (October 5, 2000): H8935–36, H8980.

44. Associated Press, "U.S. Agencies Ignore Ban, Track Visitors to Web Sites," *Washington Times,* October 22, 2000, C3; D. Ian Hopper, "Agencies Track Online Visitors Despite Rules," *Washington Post,* October 22, 2000, A13; D. Ian Hopper, "Renewed Ban on U.S. Web 'Cookies'," *Washington Post,* October 24, 2000, A25; General Accounting Office, *Internet Privacy: Federal Agency Use of Cookies,* GAO-01-147R (Washington, D.C.: General Accounting Office, October 20, 2000).

45. Associated Press, "Federal Web Sites Can Track Visitors," *Washington Times,* April 17, 2001, A8; Senator Thompson's release of the preliminary findings can be found at http://www.senate.gov/~gov_affairs/041601a_press.htm.

46. Drew Clark, "Conflicting Guidelines on Web 'Cookies' Spur Confusion," *GovExec.com Daily Briefing,* April 24, 2001, available at http://www.govexec.com/.

47. H.R. 2590, PL 106-346.

48. H.R. 2590, FY2002 Treasury appropriations bill (2001).

49. Ibid.

50. For existing privacy guidance, see Office of Management and Budget, Memorandum for the Heads of Executive Departments and Agencies, "Privacy Policies on Federal Web Sites," from Jacob J. Lew, Director, M-99-18 (Washington, D.C., June 2, 1999), available at http://www.whitehouse.gov/omb/memoranda/m99-18.

51. See 44. U.S.C. 3504(b), 3504(d), 3504(f), 3504(g), and 3504(h).

52. Concerning current agency practices, findings, and technology applications, see Heather Harreld, "And Forgive Us Our Trespasses," *Federal Computer Week* 15 (February 5, 2001): 28–29, 32.

53. Tim Lemke, "Workers Wasting Hours on E-mail," *Washington Times,* April. 24, 2001, B7, B9.

54. The report and related documents are available at the NCLIS Web site, http://www.nclis.gov/govt/assess/assess.html.

55. In mid-August 1999, the Secretary of Commerce announced his intention to close the NTIS and transfer its holdings to the Library of Congress. Self-supporting through the public sale of scientific and technical reports sponsored by federal agencies, the NTIS, according to the secretary, was experiencing rapidly declining revenues due to the free availability of its salable information via the Internet

56. See the NCLIS Web site, http://www.nclis.gov.

57. Ibid.

58. National Commission on Libraries and Information Science, *A Comprehensive Assessment of Public Information Dissemination; First Draft* (Washington, D.C.: GPO, November 27, 2000), 6.

59. Commission on Federal Paperwork, *Confidentiality and Privacy: A Report of the Commission on Federal Paperwork* (Washington, D.C.: GPO, July 29, 1977), 26.

60. American Society of Access Professionals, *The (b)(3) Project: Citations by Federal Agencies (1975–1982)* (Washington, D.C.: American Society of Access Professionals, 1984); the FOIA exemption may be found at 5 U.S.C. 552(b)(3).

61. Commission on Federal Paperwork, *History of Paperwork Reform Efforts.*

62. NCLIS, *Comprehensive Assessment of Public Information Dissemination*, 33.

63. Bruce Smith, Bruce T. Fraser, and Charles R. McClure, "Federal Information Policy and Access to Web-based Federal Information," *Journal of Academic Librarianship* 26 (July 2000): 274.

64. Ibid.

65. Ibid., 279.

Chapter 9

Personal Privacy Protection: The Legislative Response

An expectation of personal privacy seemingly has long prevailed in American culture and society. Some may regard personal privacy as one of the "Blessings of Liberty" mentioned in the preamble of the Constitution. Others might trace its roots to the "right of the people to be secure in their persons, houses, papers, and effects" given expression in the Fourth Amendment of that document. Although there may be some ambiguity about the facets of personal privacy, the American people, particularly during the latter half of the twentieth century, have increasingly turned to Congress to respond to their concerns regarding perceived threats to, or the loss of, personal privacy. These responses, which have significantly contributed to the policy development of the personal privacy concept, are reviewed here, and current personal privacy issues receiving legislative treatment are identified and discussed.

AN EVOLVING VALUE

The concept of privacy has probably long been a value of humankind. As a sentiment—the wish not to be intruded upon—it very likely predates recorded history and was experienced before it was given a name. In the thinking of the influential seventeenth-century British philosopher John Locke, privacy was one of the presocietal or "natural rights" that was preserved when individuals, by social contract, agreed to form a society. Furthermore, when society, by a second social contract, agreed to form a government, privacy was one of the rights the government was expected to preserve and protect. When a Bill of Rights was appended to the American version of Locke's second contract, it gave constitutional recognition to privacy expectations in the First Amendment, including the right not to have to speak, privacy of opinion, freedom of association, and the right of anonymous or pseudonymous expression; the Third Amendment, prohibiting the quartering of troops in private homes during peacetime without the owner's consent; the Fourth Amendment, guaranteeing personal security against unwarranted searches and seizures; and the Fifth Amendment, specifying the privilege against self-incrimination.[1] In a landmark 1965 decision, the U.S. Supreme Court viewed these and the Ninth Amendment as being the sources of a penumbral right of privacy.[2]

In his seminal study of privacy, attorney Alan F. Westin has written that American society, prior to the Civil War, "had a thorough and effective set of rules with which to protect individual and group privacy from the means of compulsory disclosure and physical surveillance known in that era."[3] Toward the end of the nineteenth century, new technology—the telephone, the microphone and dictograph recorder, and improved cameras—presented major new challenges to privacy protection. Consequently, understandings of privacy became a bit desperate. Judge Thomas Cooley, in his influential treatise on torts, described privacy as the inalienable and natural "right to be let alone."[4] This view was given more popular expression by Samuel D. Warren and Louis D. Brandeis in their now-famous 1890 *Harvard Law Review* article on the right to privacy.[5] However, as a British study committee observed in 1972, this perspective "turns out on closer examination to go so far beyond any right which the individual living in an organized society could reasonably claim, that it would be useless as a basis for the granting of legal protection. Any law which proclaimed this as a general right . . . would have to qualify the right in so many ways that the generality of the concept would be destroyed."[6]

New technology would continue to threaten and weaken personal privacy. In 1956, sociologist Edward A. Shils described privacy as "the voluntary withholding of information reinforced by a willing indifference."[7] By that time, however, it had become quite apparent to many that it was increasingly difficult and, in some cases, probably impossible to voluntarily withhold personal information any longer because there were elements of society that had obviously forsaken a willing indifference to such desires.

A few years later, Congress began to probe a variety of privacy issues. For example, in 1965, one subcommittee of the Senate Committee on the Judiciary began omnibus hearings on the invasion of privacy by federal agencies,[8] while a companion subcommittee examined psychological testing procedures and the rights of federal employees.[9] The following year, this latter panel explored the privacy rights of federal civil servants.[10] Another subcommittee began major hearings in 1967 concerning privacy protection by prohibiting wire interception and eavesdropping.[11] It also scrutinized computer privacy in that same year.[12] In 1969, Senate subcommittee attention was given to privacy, the census, and federal questionnaires.[13] In 1971, omnibus hearings were held on federal databanks, computers, and the Bill of Rights.[14]

In the House, the Committee on Government Operations (now Government Reform) chartered a Special Subcommittee on Invasion of Privacy in 1965.[15] It launched a general inquiry that year, then focused on the computer and invasion of privacy the following year, and was a major critic of a proposed national databank under discussion in the 1960s.[16] In 1968, a subcommittee of the House Committee on Post Office and Civil Service examined privacy and the rights of federal employees.[17] That same year, a special subcommittee explored the practices of commercial credit bureaus and their privacy implications.[18] In 1972, a subcommittee of the House Committee on the Judiciary held hearings on the security and privacy of criminal arrest records.[19]

In 1968, at the urging of Alan F. Westin, the Russell Sage Foundation funded the Project on Computer Databanks of the Computer Science and Engineering Board, National Academy of Sciences. This undertaking, directed by Westin, examined the use of computers by government and private organizations for collecting, processing, and exchanging information about individuals; the effect of such computer use on the way organizations use records to make judgments about the rights, benefits, and opportunities of individuals; and the impact of computerized records systems on privacy and due process rules. In the final report, published in 1972, the Project found that "computer usage has not created the revolutionary new powers of data surveillance predicted by some commentators"; that some important increases in the efficiency of organizational recordkeeping resulted from computerization; and that, "even where these increases in efficiency are taking place, organizational policies which affect individual rights are still generally following the precomputer patterns in each field of record-keeping."[20]

The report, however, was not satisfied with a pattern of organizations merely adapting their computerized systems of recordkeeping to the existing civil liberties rules in their particular fields. Thus, it recommended that compulsory data collection be limited "so that matters that ought not to be considered in making decisions about individuals do not become part of the formal records at all;" that individuals be given greater rights of access to records maintained about them; and that "new rules for data sharing and confidentiality . . . be fashioned."[21]

Early in 1972, Secretary of Health, Education, and Welfare (HEW) Elliot L. Richardson established the Secretary's Advisory Committee on Automated Personal Data Systems. Headed by Willis H. Ware of the Rand Corporation, the panel was asked to analyze and make recommendations about four areas of interest:

- Harmful consequences that may result from using automated personal data systems;

- Safeguards that might protect against potentially harmful consequences that may result from using automated personal data systems;

- Measures that might afford redress for any such harmful consequences; and

- Policy and practice relating to the issuance and use of individuals' Social Security numbers.[22]

In its final report, issued in July 1973, the advisory committee recommended "the enactment of legislation establishing a Code of Fair Information Practice for all automated personal data systems." Such a code, in the view of the panel, should "define 'fair information practice' as adherence to specified safeguard requirements"; "prohibit violation of any safeguard requirements as an 'unfair information practice' "; "provide that an unfair information practice be subject to both civil and criminal penalties"; "provide for injunctions to prevent violations of any safeguard requirement"; "give individuals the right to bring suits for unfair information practices to recover actual, liquidated, and punitive damages, in individual or class actions"; and "also provide for recovery of reasonable attorneys' fees and other costs of litigation incurred by individuals who bring successful lawsuits."[23]

LEGISLATING PRIVACY PROTECTION

During the past three decades, Congress has legislated privacy protections in various policy areas and has initiated two broad privacy studies with a view to producing both findings and policy recommendations. Major developments resulting from these initiatives are summarized in the following sections.

Fair Credit Reporting Act

Before the HEW Secretary's Advisory Committee on Automated Personal Data Systems issued its July 1973 final report recommending a Code of Fair Information Practice, Congress experimented with such a set of ground rules when it made an initial effort at legislating a new kind of privacy protection with the Fair Credit Reporting Act of 1970 (86 Stat. 1128; 15 U.S.C. 1681 et seq.). This statute regulates the collection and dissemination of personal information by consumer reporting agencies and persons, including corporations, that regularly procure or cause to be prepared investigative consumer reports on any individual for use by a third party. Among its provisions, the new law authorized the subject of a consumer report to request of the preparer agency details concerning the nature and scope of all information in its files regarding that individual, the identity of the sources of the information, and the name of any recipient of the information. In addition, the report subject might seek to correct or otherwise amend the preparer agency's information by providing supplemental data.

Crime Control Act

When legislating the Crime Control Act of 1973, Congress prohibited state agencies receiving law enforcement assistance funds pursuant to the statute and federal personnel from making unauthorized disclosures of personally identifiable criminal history research or statistical information. It also permitted "an individual who believes that criminal history information concerning him contained in an automated system is inaccurate, incomplete, or maintained in violation of this [law] . . . to review such information and to obtain a copy of it for the purpose of challenge or correction."[24]

Privacy Act

With the Privacy Act of 1974, Congress addressed several aspects of privacy protection (88 Stat. 1896; 5 U.S.C. 552a). First, it sustained some traditional major privacy principles. For example, an agency shall "maintain no record describing how any individual exercises rights guaranteed by the First Amendment unless expressly authorized by statute or by the individual about whom the record is maintained or unless pertinent to and within the scope of an authorized law enforcement activity."[25]

Second the Privacy Act provides an individual who is a citizen of the United States, or an alien lawfully admitted for permanent residence, with access and emendation arrangements for records maintained on him or her by most, but not all, federal agencies. General exemptions in this regard are provided for systems of records maintained by the Central Intelligence Agency and federal criminal law enforcement agencies.

Third, the statute embodies a number of principles of fair information practice recommended by the HEW Secretary's Advisory Committee on Automated Personal Data Systems. For example, it sets certain conditions concerning the disclosure of personally identifiable information; prescribes requirements for the accounting of certain disclosures of such information; requires agencies to "collect information to the greatest extent practicable directly from the subject individual when the information may result in adverse determinations about an individual's rights, benefits, and privileges under Federal programs";[26] requires agencies to specify their authority and purposes for collecting personally identifiable information from an individual; requires agencies to "maintain all records which are used by the agency in making any determination about any individual with such accuracy, relevance, timeliness, and completeness as is reasonably necessary to assure fairness to the individual in the determination"; and provides civil and criminal enforcement arrangements.

Privacy Study Commission

The Privacy Act also mandated the Privacy Protection Study Commission, a temporary, seven-member panel tasked to "make a study of the data banks, automated data processing programs, and information systems of governmental, regional, and private organizations, in order to determine the standards and procedures in force for the protection of personal information."[27] The commission was to "recommend to the President and the Congress the extent, if any, to which the requirements and principles of [the Privacy Act] should be applied to the information practices of [such] organizations by legislation, administrative action, or voluntary adoption of such requirements and principles, and report on such other legislative recommendations as it may determine to be necessary to protect the privacy of individuals while meeting the legitimate needs of government and society for information."[28]

The commission began operations in early June 1975 under the leadership of chairman David F. Linowes, a University of Illinois political economist, educator, and corporate executive, and vice chairman Willis H. Ware, the Rand Corporation research scientist who had headed the HEW Secretary's Advisory Committee on Automated Personal Data Systems.[29] Two years later, in July 1977, the final report of the panel, offering 162 recommendations, was submitted to the president and Congress.[30] In general, the commission urged the establishment of a permanent, independent entity within the federal government to monitor, investigate, evaluate, advise, and offer policy recommendations concerning personal privacy matters; better regulation of the use of mailing lists for commercial purposes; adherence to principles of fair information practice by employers; limited government access to personal records held by a private sector recordkeeper through adherence to recognized legal processes; and improved privacy protection for educational records. The panel also recommended the adoption of legislation to apply principles of fair information practice, such as those found in the Privacy Act, to personal information collected and managed by the consumer credit, banking, insurance, and medical care sectors of the U.S. economy.

Congressional response to the commission's report was largely positive, some 200 bills incorporating its recommendations being introduced. However, a concerted effort to enact legislation applying principles of fair information practice to personal information collected and managed by the insurance and medical care industries was stalemated into the final days of the 96th Congress. The opposition was sufficient to discourage a return to such legislative efforts for several years.

President Carter appointed a cabinet committee to study the commission's recommendations and received additional evaluations and supplemental recommendations from an interagency task force, resulting in a package of national privacy policy proposals that was sent to Congress on April 2, 1979.[31] While these developments were underway, the Carter administration worked with Congress to produce the Right to Financial Privacy Act of 1978, discussed below. Congress largely deferred action on the president's 1979 package of privacy proposals until 1981, but this effort became moot with President Carter's failure to win a second term in 1980.

Federal Paperwork Commission

In 1974, Congress also established a temporary Commission on Federal Paperwork, giving it a broad mandate to consider a variety of aspects of the collection, processing, dissemination, and management of federal information, including "the ways in which policies and practices relating to the maintenance of confidentiality of information impact upon Federal information activities."[32] One of its reports was devoted to confidentiality and privacy. Issued July 29, 1977, it offered twelve recommendations.[33]

A recommended new organization to centralize and coordinate existing information management functions within the executive branch, and proposed limits on the use of statistical information or disclosing it in identifiable form without the consent of the data subject, were realized in the Paperwork Reduction Act of 1980. The statute established a new Office of Information and Regulatory Affairs within the Office of Management and Budget (OMB) to assist the OMB director with the governmentwide information coordination and guidance functions assigned to that office by the act.

Indicating that one of the purposes of the Paperwork Reduction Act was "to ensure that the collection, maintenance, use and dissemination of information by the Federal Government is consistent with applicable laws relating to confidentiality, including . . . the Privacy Act,"[34] the statute assigned the OMB director the following privacy functions: "(1) developing and implementing policies, principles, standards, and guidelines on information disclosure and confidentiality, and on safeguarding the security of information collected or maintained by or on behalf of agencies; (2) providing agencies with advice and guidance about information security, restriction, exchange, and disclosure; and (3) monitoring compliance with [the Privacy Act] and related information management laws."[35] These privacy functions would be expanded, and privacy responsibilities would be specified for the federal agencies, in a 1995 recodification of the act (109 Stat. 163; 44 U.S.C. 3501 et seq.). In 1988, amendments governing computer matches of personal information by government agencies, discussed below, were enacted (102 Stat. 2507).

Family Educational Rights and Privacy Act

Another privacy statute enacted by the 93rd Congress in 1974 was the Family Educational Rights and Privacy Act (FERPA), also known as the Buckley Amendment in reference to its sponsor, Senator James L. Buckley (R-N.Y.), who offered the proposal as a floor amendment to the General Education Provisions Act during Senate consideration of the Education Amendments of 1974 (88 Stat. 571; 20 U.S.C. 1232g). As originally approved, the FERPA gave the parents of minor children and students over eighteen years of age the right to inspect, correct, amend, and control the disclosure of information in the education records of educational agencies or institutions receiving federal funds. It also obliged these institutions to inform parents and students of their rights and to establish policies and procedures for the exercise of such rights.

In its 1977 final report, the Privacy Protection Study Commission assessed the provisions and implementation of the FERPA and offered several recommendations for clarifying and strengthening the statute.[36] Prior to 1994, Congress amended the FERPA with technical modifications on a few occasions; substantive amendments were effected, primarily, with the Improving America's Schools Act of 1994 (108 Stat. 3924) and, less so, with the Higher Education Amendments of 1998 (112 Stat. 1835). These included provisions explicitly prohibiting the allocation of federal funds to any state educational agency or institution "that has a policy of denying, or effectively prevents, the parents of students the right to inspect and review the education records maintained by the State . . . on their children;" permitting access to student records by "State and local officials or authorities to whom such information is specifically allowed to be reported or disclosed pursuant to State statute . . . if the allowed reporting or disclosure concerns the juvenile justice system"; permitting the disclosure of student records to "the entity or person designated in a Federal grand jury subpoena" or in other subpoenas issued "for a law enforcement purpose"; prohibiting an educational agency or institution from releasing students records, "for a period of not less than five years," to a third party that violated the FERPA requirements governing access to such records; and clarifying that nothing in FERPA prohibits an educational agency or institution from placing relevant disciplinary information in a student's records or revealing that information to teachers or other school officials "who have legitimate educational interests in the behavior of the student."[37] According to one estimate, "these amendments [were] apparently intended to expand the coverage of FERPA, strengthen incentives to comply with the Act, eliminate schools' and institutions' dilemmas about restricting access to records that are subpoenaed, and prevent the Act from interfering with educational professionals' need to know about students' behavior."[38]

Privacy Protection Act

Congress enacted the Privacy Protection Act of 1980 to protect a First Amendment right of privacy threatened by police searches. The statute was prompted by a Supreme Court ruling involving a Stanford University newspaper complaint. On April 12, 1971, four local police officers, armed with a search warrant, conducted a no-notice, surprise search of the offices of the *Stanford Daily*, a student newspaper published at Stanford University. They were seeking unpublished photographs that they believed would assist them in identifying the assailants of fellow officers injured at a recent demonstration before the Stanford University Hospital. The officers, after thoroughly exploring the newspaper offices, failed to find the photographs. Subsequently, both they and the local district attorney were sued, pursuant to 42 U.S.C. 1983, by staff members of the student newspaper alleging violations of their civil rights and contending that a subpoena, rather than a search warrant, should have been used. Both the federal trial and appellate courts agreed with the plaintiffs that the Fourth and Fourteenth Amendments barred issuing warrants to search for materials held by nonsuspect third parties when no probable cause was shown that a subpoena, which can be challenged in court before being enforced, would be impractical. However, on May 31, 1978, the U.S. Supreme Court, in a 5–3 decision, ruled that the Constitution did not bar police officers from obtaining warrants and then making unannounced searches of newspaper offices for evidence, even though neither the newspaper nor its reporters were suspected of criminal activity.[39]

Sorting out the ramifications of the court's decision, Congress responded with the Privacy Protection Act of 1980, which prohibits federal, state, and local law enforcement officers from using warrants to search and seize "work products" of news and other organizations engaged in First Amendment activities, except in specified circumstances; defines "work products" as materials prepared for communicating information to the public, including mental impressions, conclusions, opinions, or theories of the person who prepared the material; prohibits federal, state, and local law enforcement officers from seizing "documentary materials" from persons engaged in First Amendment activities, except in specified circumstances; defines "documentary materials" as materials upon which information is recorded, including written or printed materials, photographs, films, negatives, and video and audio tapes; provides a civil cause of action for damages for any person aggrieved by a search for, or seizure of, materials in violation of the statute; requires the attorney general to issue guidelines for the procedures to be employed by federal officers in searching for evidence held by a person not suspected of a crime; and allows administrative sanctions against any Department of Justice officer or employee who violates such guidelines, but prohibits a private individual from filing a lawsuit regarding such a violation (see 94 Stat. 1879; 42 U.S.C. 2000 et seq.).

Cable Communications Policy Act

The day before its final adjournment, the 98th Congress approved the Cable Communications Policy Act of 1984, culminating a four-year effort to balance the rights of the industry against those of the cities that granted franchises (see 98 Stat. 2779). Section 631 of the statute requires cable services to provide subscribers with an initial and, thereafter, an annual, written statement concerning the services' collection, use, and management of personally identifiable information with respect to subscribers. Information required to be included in this statement is specified in the section. A cable subscriber has a right of access to all personally identifiable information regarding himself or herself that is collected and maintained by a cable service, and may correct any error in such information. A cable service may use the cable system to collect personally identifiable information in order to obtain information necessary to render a cable or other service provided by the cable operator to the subscriber or to detect unauthorized reception of cable communications. With very limited exceptions, a cable service is prohibited from disclosing personally identifiable information concerning any subscriber without his or her prior consent. Any person aggrieved by any act of a cable service in violation of section 631 may bring a civil action, and the court may award actual damages, punitive damages, and litigation costs and attorneys' fees reasonably incurred.

Electronic Communications Privacy Act

In October 1986, Congress cleared legislation providing privacy protection to communications transmitted with new forms of technology. The Electronic Communications Privacy Act of 1986 (ECPA) extends existing privacy guarantees for conventional telephones to cellular telephones operated by high-frequency radio waves, transmissions by private satellite, paging devices, and electronic mail messages transmitted by, and stored in, computers (see 100 Stat. 1848).

Title I of the statute amends the federal criminal code to extend the prohibition against the unauthorized interception of wire and oral communications to include, with some exceptions, specific types of electronic communications and the communications of any provider of wire or electronic communication services. Providers of an electronic communication service, with specified exceptions, are prohibited from knowingly divulging the contents of any communication carried on that service. Any person whose wire, oral, or electronic communication is intercepted, disclosed, or intentionally used in violation of chapter 119 of the federal criminal code may bring a civil action to recover damages, but must do so not later than two years after the date upon which the alleged violation was discovered. The title also specifies additional crimes for which the interception of wire, oral, or electronic communication can be authorized to facilitate the investigation of such crimes. It provides additional requirements for applications, court orders, and the implementation of court orders for the interception of such communications. Certain intelligence activities approved by the attorney general are not to be affected by the communications interception provisions of chapters 119 and 121 of the federal criminal code, and allowance is made for a court-authorized mobile tracking device to be used outside the jurisdiction of the authorizing court. The warning of a person that he or she is the subject of electronic surveillance is made a criminal offense, and a final provision allows the attorney general to initiate a civil action to obtain an injunction to prevent felony level violations of the ECPA.

Title II, concerning stored wire and electronic communications and transactional records access, makes it a criminal offense to access, without authorization, a facility through which an electronic communication service is provided, or to exceed an authorized access to such a facility. It also prohibits the provider of an electronic communication service or remote computing service, except under certain circumstances, from divulging the contents of any communication stored, carried, or maintained by such service. The title specifies procedural requirements for a government entity to obtain access to electronic communications in electronic storage, including court-ordered creation of back-up copies of the contents of such communications. Provision is made for any subscriber or customer of a communication service who is aggrieved by a willful or intentional violation of the title (which is chapter 121 of the federal criminal code) to initiate a civil action to recover appropriate relief. Finally, the director of the Federal Bureau of Investigation (FBI) is granted access to telephone or communication service information and records relevant to any authorized foreign counterintelligence investigation. No officer, employee, or agent of a wire or electronic communication service provider may disclose to any person that the FBI has sought or obtained such access to telephone or communication service information.

Title III of the statute addresses the use of pen registers and trap and trace devices. A pen register is a device that records or decodes numbers dialed or otherwise transmitted by telephone; a trap and trace device captures an incoming electronic or other impulse and can identify the number from which the call was made. The title prohibits the installation or use of a pen register or a trap and trace device without a court order pursuant to the ECPA or the Foreign Intelligence Surveillance Act of 1978, and imposes criminal penalties for violations of this prohibition.[40] Government attorneys and state law enforcement officers are authorized to apply for a court order allowing the installation and use of a pen register or a trap and trace device; a certification by the applicant that information likely to be obtained by such an installation is relevant to an ongoing criminal investigation is required for the issuance of such an order. Furthermore, providers of a wire or electronic communication service, landlords, custodians, and other persons are required to furnish all information, facilities, and technical assistance necessary to accomplish the installation of a pen register or a trap and trace device if such assistance is ordered by the court. Anyone providing such assistance shall be compensated for any reasonable expenses incurred, and no cause of action shall lie in any court against anyone providing such assistance. The attorney general must report annually to Congress on the number of applications made by law enforcement agencies of the Department of Justice for pen register and trap and trace device orders.

Computer Security Act

Recognizing the increasing use of computers by federal agencies and the vulnerability of computer-stored information, including personal information, to unauthorized access, Congress enacted the Computer Security Act of 1987 (101 Stat. 1724). The statute requires each federal agency to develop security plans for its computer systems containing sensitive information. Such plans are subject to review by the National Institute of Standards and Technology (NIST) of the Department of Commerce, and a summary, together with overall budget plans for information technology, is filed with OMB. NIST is authorized to set security standards for all federal computer systems except those containing intelligence, cryptologic, or certain military information, or information specifically authorized under criteria established by an executive order or statute to be kept secret in the interest of national defense or foreign policy. The statute also mandates a Computer Systems Security and Privacy Advisory Board within the Department of Commerce, which, among other duties, is to identify emerging managerial, technical, administrative, and physical safeguard issues relative to computer systems security and privacy and advise NIST and the Secretary of Commerce on security and privacy issues pertaining to federal computer systems. Each federal agency is directed to provide all employees involved with the management, use, or operation of its computer systems with mandatory periodic training in computer security awareness and accepted computer security practice.

Computer Matching and Privacy Protection Act

Congress amended the Privacy Act in 1988 to regulate the use of computer matching conducted by federal agencies or making use of federal records subject to the statute. The amendments were denominated the Computer Matching and Privacy Protection Act of 1988 (102 Stat. 2507). A controversial matter for more than ten years, computer matching—the computerized comparison of records for the purpose of establishing or verifying eligibility for a federal benefit program or for recouping payments or delinquent debts under such programs—had begun in 1977 at the Department of Health and Human Services. The effort, dubbed Project Match, compared welfare rolls in selected jurisdictions with federal payroll records in the same areas. The controversy surrounding this and similar computerized matches pitted privacy protection advocates, who alleged that personally identifiable data were being used for purposes other than those prompting their collection, against those using the technique to ferret out fraud, abuse, and the overpayment of federal benefits. As the practice subsequently became more widespread, controversy over its use grew.

The amendments regulate the use of computer matching by federal agencies involving personally identifiable records maintained in a system of records subject to the Privacy Act. Matches performed for statistical, research, law enforcement, tax, and certain other purposes are not subject to such regulation. For matches to occur, a written matching agreement, effectively creating a matching program, must be prepared specifying such details, as explicitly required by the amendments, as the purpose and legal authority for the program; the justification for the program and the anticipated results, including a specific estimate of any savings; a description of the records being matched; procedures for providing individualized notice, at the time of application, to applicants for and recipients of financial assistance or payments under federal benefits programs and to applicants for and holders of positions as federal personnel that any information they provide may be subject to verification through the matching program; procedures for verifying information produced in the matching program; and procedures for the retention, security, and timely destruction of the records matched and for the security of the results of the matching program. Copies of such matching agreements are transmitted to congressional oversight committees and are available to the public upon request. Executive oversight of, and guidance for, matching programs is vested in the director of OMB. Notice of the establishment or revision of a matching program must be published in the *Federal Register* thirty days in advance of implementation.

The amendments also require every agency conducting or participating in a matching program to establish a "Data Integrity Board," composed of senior agency officials, to oversee and coordinate program operations, including the execution of certain specified review, approval, and reporting responsibilities. Agencies are prohibited from reducing, suspending, or terminating financial assistance to an individual without first verifying the accuracy of computerized data used in the matching program and without first giving the individual thirty days to contest the action.

Video Privacy Protection Act

Another 1988 privacy statute was enacted in response to an incident that occurred during the 1987 fight over the unsuccessful nomination of Robert H. Bork to the Supreme Court. During the Bork confirmation hearings, a reporter obtained and published a list of the videotapes the Bork family had rented, prompting an outcry from members of Congress in both political parties who felt Bork's privacy had been invaded. A legislative response was enacted the following year. The Video Privacy Protection Act of 1988 prohibits videotape service providers from disclosing their customers' names, addresses, and specific videotapes rented or purchased, except in specifically defined circumstances (see 102 Stat. 3195; 18 U.S.C. 2710 note). Such exceptions include disclosure to the customer; to any person with the informed, written consent of the customer given at the time the disclosure was sought; to a law enforcement agency pursuant to a warrant, grand jury subpoena, or court order; or (name and address only) to a direct marketing business, as long as the customer has an opportunity to reject such a disclosure. Any person aggrieved by any action of a person in violation of the statute may bring a civil action, the court being authorized to award actual damages, punitive damages, and litigation costs and attorneys' fees reasonably incurred. Such a lawsuit must be initiated within two years of the discovery of the alleged violation.

Driver's Privacy Protection Act

Enacted as Title XXX of the Omnibus Violent Crime Control and Law Enforcement Act of 1994, the Driver's Privacy Protection Act (DPPA) prohibits a state department of motor vehicles, and any officer, employee, or contractor of such an entity, from knowingly disclosing or otherwise making available to any person "personal information about any individual obtained by the department in connection with a motor vehicle record" without the driver's consent.[41] Explicit exceptions to this rule include "matters of motor vehicle or driver safety and theft, motor vehicle emissions, motor vehicle product alterations, recalls, or advisories, performance monitoring of motor vehicles and dealers by motor vehicle manufacturers, and removal of non-owner records from the original owner records of motor vehicle manufacturers to carry out the purposes" of certain enumerated statutes. A criminal fine may be levied against any person who knowingly violates the statute, and a civil penalty of not more than $5,000 may be imposed by the attorney general against a state department of motor vehicles for each day of substantial noncompliance. A civil action may be brought against a person who knowingly violates the DPPA by the driver whose privacy was compromised by the violation.

On January 12, 2000, the Supreme Court unanimously ruled that the DPPA is a valid exercise of the constitutional authority of Congress to regulate commerce, and does not violate the Tenth Amendment.[42] The drivers' information that the statute governs was seen as being used by insurers, marketers, and others engaged in interstate commerce to contact drivers with customized solicitations, making this information "an article of commerce" subject to congressional regulation. Relying on a 1988 ruling, the Court found that the DPPA does not "commandeer" states into enforcing federal law applicable to private entities.[43] The statute regulates state activities directly rather than seeking to control the manner in which states regulate private parties. Also, the DPPA was seen as generally applicable, regulating both the states as initial suppliers and private parties that resell drivers' information: "the universe of entities that participate as suppliers to the market for motor vehicles."[44]

Telecommunications Act

Enacted in response to significant structural and marketing changes occurring within the telecommunications industry, the Telecommunications Act of 1996 is a major rewrite of national telecommunications policy, establishing a single, comprehensive regulatory framework that will capture the benefits of competition while ensuring that the users and suppliers of a developing and diversified information industry will be protected from exploitative practices and abuse (see 110 Stat. 56). Among the provisions of the statute, section 702 specifies that, except as required by law or with the approval of the customer, a telecommunications carrier receiving or obtaining customer proprietary network information by virtue of its provision of a telecommunications service can only use, disclose, or permit access to individually identifiable customer proprietary network information in providing the telecommunications service from which such information derives or services necessary to, or used in, the provision of such telecommunications service, including the publishing of directories. Upon affirmative written request of the customer, a telecommunications carrier must disclose that customer's proprietary network information to any person designated by the customer, including the customer himself or herself. Customer proprietary network information, according to the statute, is information that relates to the quantity, technical configuration, type, destination, and amount of use of a telecommunications service subscribed to by any customer of a telecommunications carrier, and that is made available to the carrier by the customer solely by virtue of the carrier-customer relationship, and includes, as well, information contained in the bills pertaining to telephone exchange service or telephone toll service received by a customer of a carrier, but does not include subscriber list information.

Health Insurance Portability and Accountability Act

Compared with the Clinton administration's famous, but failed, 1994 plan to overhaul the entire health care system, the Health Insurance Portability and Accountability Act of 1996 (HIPAA) was miniature in scope (110 Stat. 1936). The statute sought to guarantee the portability of health insurance coverage for individuals who had health insurance benefits. It also created a pilot program for medical savings accounts, increased the deductibility of health insurance for the self-employed, and provided tax breaks to increase the use of long-term care insurance.

Of particular interest for privacy protection are provisions of the statute's administrative simplification subtitle instructing the secretary of Health and Human Services (HHS) to develop standards to support electronic data interchange for a variety of administrative and financial health care transactions. Specifically, HIPAA requires the secretary to issue regulations to establish standard electronic formats for billing and other common transactions, including the use of uniform data codes for reporting diagnoses, referrals, authorizations, and medical procedures; mandates the development of unique identifiers (i.e., identification numbers) for patients, employers, health plans, and health care providers; and requires the secretary to issue security standards, including an electronic signature standard, to safeguard confidential health information against unauthorized access, disclosure, and misuse.

Beyond these obligations, the subtitle prescribes a timetable for Congress and the secretary to develop comprehensive medical records privacy standards that would define the circumstances under which the uses and disclosures of such information required a patient's authorization, and gives patients the right to access and amend their personally identifiable health information. The secretary was required to report to Congress by August 1997 on ways to protect the privacy of personally identifiable health information; Congress was given two years after receiving that report to enact health records privacy legislation; and, if it failed to do so, the secretary was instructed to issue health privacy regulations by February 21, 2000 (see 110 Stat. 2021; 42 U.S.C. 1320d). As discussed below, the secretary presented her recommendations to Congress on September 11, 1997, and, because Congress did not enact legislation guided by those recommendations, she issued proposed health records privacy regulations on November 3, 1999. The newly installed Bush administration initially delayed final issuance of the regulations, but then decided to proceed with implementation.[45]

Several health records privacy bills were introduced during 1999, but lawmakers were unable to meet the HIPAA-imposed deadline for enacting comprehensive health privacy legislation. With the failure of Congress to meet its self-imposed deadline, HHS issued final privacy regulations in 2001 and Secretary Tommy G. Thompson announced that the department would immediately begin the process of implementing the patient privacy rule and of issuing guidelines on how the rule should be implemented "to clarify some of the confusion regarding the impact the rule might have on health care delivery and access" and also "consider any necessary modifications that will ensure the quality of care does not suffer inadvertently from this rule."[46]

The privacy rule gives patients the right to inspect and amend their medical records and restricts access to and disclosure of individually identifiable health information. Health care providers must obtain a patient's general consent to use or disclose their medical information for treatment, payment, and other health care operations. In addition, both health plans and providers must obtain a patient's specific authorization to use and disclose information for nonroutine and most non-health care purposes. The rule specifies certain national priority activities for which health information may be disclosed without a patient's authorization.

Hospitals, health insurers, and pharmaceutical companies claim the rule will compromise patient care by placing unacceptable restrictions on access to health information and be extremely costly to implement. They are especially critical of the rule's general consent provision and the requirement that, with the exception of treatment-related disclosures, providers and health plans use or disclose no more than the minimum amount of information necessary to accomplish the intended purpose. Industry groups have also criticized the rule for requiring providers and plans to enter into contracts with their business associates to ensure that these groups, which are not directly covered under HIPAA, adhere to the same privacy protections. Clearly, issues related to health information privacy, standards, and security continue, but little legislative action has been taken by the 107th Congress.

Children's Online Privacy Protection Act

Although the Clinton administration and many members of Congress preferred to rely on industry self-regulation for realizing Internet privacy protection, frustration with the industry's slow response regarding minors led to the enactment of the Children's Online Privacy Protection Act of 1998 (COPPA) as part of the Omnibus Consolidated and Emergency Supplemental Appropriations Act, 1999 (112 Stat. 2681-728; 15 U.S.C. 6501–6506). The statute requires the operator of a commercial Web site or online service targeted at children under the age of thirteen to provide clear notice of information collection and use practices; to obtain verifiable parental consent prior to collecting, using, and disseminating personal information about children under thirteen; and to provide parents access to their children's personal information and the option to prevent its further use. On October 20, 1999, the Federal Trade Commission issued a final rule to implement COPPA (64 *Federal Register* 59888–59915 (November 3, 1999)). The statute authorizes the commission to bring enforcement actions and impose civil penalties for violations of the rule in the same manner as for its other rules. At the end of the first year of COPPA implementation, most Web sites geared for children reportedly failed to follow the statute's requirements,[47] but the law also prompted a reduction of Web site services available to children under the age of thirteen.[48] The FTC announced that three online companies had agreed to pay $100,000 in fines to settle charges that they had collected personal information from children without their parent's permission.[49]

Gramm-Leach-Bliley Act

Enacted in November 1999, the Financial Services Modernization Act, popularly known as the Gramm-Leach-Bliley Act, constitutes a historic overhaul of federal laws governing the financial services industry (PL 106-102,113 Stat. 1338). Repealing laws restricting cross-ownership among banks, brokerages, and insurers, the statute establishes a new regulatory framework for maintaining the safety and stability of the financial services industry and requires a number of regulatory agencies to develop new regulations for its implementation. Named for its principal congressional champions—Senator Phil Gramm (R-Tex.), Representative James A. Leach (R-Iowa), and Representative Tom Bliley (R-Va.)—the statute requires relevant federal regulatory agencies to issue rules obligating financial institutions to establish standards to ensure the security and confidentiality of customer records; prohibits financial institutions from disclosing nonpublic personal information to unaffiliated third parties without providing customers with the opportunity to decline such disclosures; prohibits financial institutions from disclosing customer account numbers to unaffiliated third parties for use in telemarketing, direct mail marketing, and e-mail marketing; requires financial institutions to disclose, when a customer relationship is initially established and annually thereafter, their privacy policies, including their polices regarding the sharing of information with affiliates and unaffiliated third parties; and mandates a study of the information sharing practices among financial institutions and their affiliates to be conducted by the secretary of the treasury, relevant regulatory agencies, and the Federal Trade Commission (FTC). Regulatory agency rules implementing these privacy protections became effective on November 12, 2000. Although a May 2001 GAO report indicated that assessment of the statute's privacy provisions was premature,[50] the FTC conducted a sting operation in April that revealed violations of the act's identity theft protections,[51] and criticism of financial institution's required privacy policy notices to consumers as being too confusing and obscure were beginning to appear in the press.[52]

Safe Harbor Privacy Principles

The European Union's (EU) *Directive on the Protection of Individuals with Regard to the Processing of Personal Data and the Free Movement of Such Data*, which went into effect in October 1998, requires all fifteen EU member states to make their national privacy laws consistent with the directive. The EU can limit the flow of data among countries not having comparable protections for personally identifiable data, thereby preventing EU organizations from transferring personal data to countries in which the EU does not deem legal protections for personal data to be "adequate." In contrast, the U.S. approach to privacy differs from that of the European Community, and it relies on a sectoral approach, based on a combination of legislation, regulation, and self-regulation. Because of these differences in approach, U.S. companies feared that the EU directive might impede the flow of information from EU states if the United States were deemed to have inadequate privacy protection in critical areas such as medical information.

To prevent the interruption of data transfers, the Department of Commerce negotiated the "safe harbor" framework with the EU, and, on July 21, 2000, the Department issued a set of Safe Harbor Privacy Principles to enable U.S. companies receiving personal data transfers from EU countries to meet the "adequacy" requirements of the EU's directive (see 65 *Federal Register* 45665–45686 (July 24, 2000)). The Safe Harbor Privacy Principles ensure that data flows between the EU and the United States are not interrupted. Organizations receiving personal data transfers from the EU and complying with the principles should be considered to meet the "adequacy" requirements of the directive.

Although any organization that receives data from the EU must comply with the directive, joining "safe harbor" is voluntary. Participation is open to any U.S. organization that is subject to regulation by the FCC, which enforces a variety of consumer protection laws, including those related to unfair and deceptive practices, and to U.S. air carriers and ticket agents that are subject to regulation by the Department of Transportation. Organizations that do not fall under the jurisdiction of either agency are not eligible for "safe harbors." Notably, this includes U.S. financial firms and telecommunications carriers. In particular, the EU does not consider that either the Fair Credit Reporting Act (P. L. 91-508, 15 U.S.C. 1681 et seq.) or the Financial Services Modernization Act provide adequate privacy protection. As a result, negotiations continue between the United States and Europe to achieve an agreement covering the financial sector.

Children's Internet Protection Act

Included as Title XVII of the Consolidated Appropriations Act, 2001, the Children's Internet Protection Act began as separate legislation sponsored by several members in both houses of Congress (PL 106-554). As enacted, the statute requires schools and libraries that receive "E-rate" discounts, or reduced charges, for Internet access to certify to the Federal Communications Commission that they are using filters to block child pornography and obscene, hard-core pornography sites. Other material, "inappropriate for minors," such as soft-core pornography, may be blocked as well. Opponents of the proposal have contended that it is an unfunded mandate, a federal intrusion into family and local community matters, and a violation of First Amendment guarantees.[53] The anticipated legal challenge to the new law by civil liberties and library organizations occurred in March 2001when a lawsuit was filed in federal district court in Philadelphia.[54]

SOME PRIVACY ISSUES BEFORE CONGRESS

During the twentieth century, comprehensive reviews of personal privacy issues were undertaken by the Privacy Protection Study Commission and, to a lesser extent, the Commission on Federal Paperwork, both panels reporting in 1977. These commissions recommended the creation of a permanent federal agency to address, exclusively or in balanced measure, personal privacy matters. Some realization of this proposal occurred with the establishment of the Office of Information and Regulatory Affairs within OMB, which, critics allege, has shown only limited interest in privacy since its creation in 1980.[55]

In a climate of opinion supportive of government downsizing, the creation of a new federal privacy review agency is considered not likely to occur. Indeed, the chartering of such an entity has not been legislatively proposed in Congress for almost a decade.[56]

Alternatively, an existing agency might be tasked with performing studies and evaluations that would collectively result in a comprehensive review of personal privacy issues. This approach, however, presents problems of finding a host agency having a sufficiently broad and compatible mandate to support the desired studies and evaluations, ensuring that the host agency has adequate resources to perform the desired studies and evaluations, and ensuring that the host agency would not relegate its new privacy responsibilities to a low level of priority.

Another, perhaps less cumbersome, alternative would be a temporary privacy study body. Producing a comprehensive review of personal privacy issues would be the only mission of the entity, and all of its resources would be devoted to that mission. The operating arrangements and products of the Privacy Protection Study Commission provide precedential models for a new entity, and the resulting final report might offer findings and recommendations that could have currency for a few years, allowing the development of implementing proposals and related legislative strategies compatible with the agendas of relevant congressional committees of jurisdiction.

In the 106th Congress, three bills were introduced to establish a temporary study commission to examine personal privacy issues. One of these, offered in the House on March 21, 2000, by Representative Asa Hutchinson (R-Ark.) as the Privacy Commission Act (H.R. 4049), would have created a seventeen-member Commission for the Comprehensive Study of Privacy Protection to "conduct a study of issues relating to protection of individual privacy and the appropriate balance to be achieved between protecting individual privacy and allowing appropriate uses of information." The final report of the panel would have been submitted to the president and Congress not later than eighteen months after the appointment of all of the members of the commission. Referred to the Committee on Government Reform, the bill was considered at May 15–16, 2000, hearings before the Subcommittee on Government Management, Information, and Technology.[57] However, an attempt to approve the bill on the House floor on October 2, 2000, under a suspension of the rules failed.

Medical Records

Current efforts to legislate privacy protection for medical records are, in many regards, a renewal of the failed 1980 attempt to act on the recommendations of the Privacy Protection Study Commission. A laboriously crafted compromise on medical records legislation collapsed in the final days of the 98th Congress because sponsors could not reconcile the conflicting demands of civil libertarians, psychiatrists, and the intelligence and law enforcement communities. The proposal basically would have applied the principles of the Code of Fair Information Practice, developed by the HEW Secretary's Advisory Committee on Automated Personal Data Systems in 1973, to the patient records of medical and health institutions, not to those kept by private physicians.

Several developments have prompted the recent return to legislating medical records privacy. Growth in the application of information technologies to all aspects of health care and structural changes in health care delivery and payment systems have not only offered significant opportunities for providing improved health care at contained costs but also increased the threats to patient privacy and medical records confidentiality. Examples include the use of electronic medical records for maintaining clinical information and the use of telemedicine to provide remote access to physicians, medical equipment, and diagnostic facilities by underserved communities. A 1997 study by the National Research Council reported that "the health care industry spent an estimated $10 billion to $15 billion on information technology in 1996."[58]

Major organizational changes in the health care industry also have provided an impetus for expanding the use of information technology. There is a greater need to integrate information provided by participating institutions that are part of managed care systems, as compared to fee-for-service providers. Managed care organizations collect vast amounts of data on the costs, processes, and outcomes associated with various diseases, conditions, and treatments. In this new environment, data must be coordinated from patient services delivered in different settings, such as hospitals, clinics, pharmacies, and physicians' offices, so that care and payment can be provided efficiently. The result has been a growing number of secondary and tertiary users of personal health information.

Rapidly increasing requirements for the collection, integration, analysis, and storage of health information have resulted in the creation of large scale databases, the capability to link data from distributed databases, and the ability for more people in dispersed locations to access data. A variety of mechanisms, both technological and organizational, may be employed to ensure that unauthorized access does not occur and that sufficient audit trails are maintained for proper accountability. Technical measures can be employed to limit access to authorized users for specifically designated purposes. Encryption, the use of smart cards or other unique identifiers for authenticating users, access control software, firewalls to prevent external attacks, and physical security and disaster recovery procedures have all become important elements in creating a technologically secure environment. Computerization has also made it possible to develop approaches for making data anonymous so that individuals cannot be identified. Management practices, including the establishment of strong privacy policies, education and training, and implementing effective sanctions for abuses can contribute substantially to maintaining confidentiality of medical records.

The implementation of the EU Data Privacy Directive in October 1998 (described previously) provided further impetus for congressional action in the 106th Congress. Article 25 of the directive requires EU member states to enact laws that prohibit the transfer of personal data to non-EU countries that lack an "adequate level of protection." Determinations of adequacy are to be made by the European Commission. If a finding of inadequacy is made, EU member states must block transfers of personal data to that third country. The United States views, with concern, the prohibition on the transfer of data from EU member countries to third countries that do not provide adequate privacy protection. Following two years of discussions with the Europeans, the Department of Commerce issued a set of "safe harbor" principles to enable U.S. companies to meet the "adequacy" requirements of the EU directive.

Online Communication

During the past decade, as greater numbers of Americans have explored the Internet, privacy concerns have grown regarding the collection, use, and storage of personal information by Web site operators. The Clinton administration and many members of Congress preferred to rely on industry self-regulation for realizing privacy protection, but frustration with industry's slow response regarding minors led to the enactment of the Children's Online Privacy Protection Act of 1998, which is described previously (112 Stat. 2681-728; 15 U.S.C. 6501–6506). During the 106th Congress, legislation was offered to address several issues regarding Internet privacy. These included, among others, the responsibilities of Web site operators who collect, use, and store personal information; the extent to which the activities and operations of "individual reference services" or "look-up services" result in personal privacy invasion; online profiling to determine what Web sites are visited by a particular user and the development of a profile of the user's preferences and interests; and the extent to which the personal information storage and transmittal practices of Web site operators contribute to identity theft, in which one individual assumes the identity of another using personal information.[59]

When press disclosures in July 2000 revealed the existence of Carnivore, a new FBI e-mail surveillance system, Congress took immediate action. The Subcommittee on the Constitution of the House Committee on the Judiciary held a July 24 oversight hearing on Fourth Amendment issues raised by the Carnivore program, receiving testimony from Federal Bureau of Investigation (FBI) and Department of Justice officials as well as concerned legal experts and representatives of civil liberties organizations. In early August, the attorney general announced that an independent review of the Carnivore program and its implications for personal privacy would be conducted, but declined, contrary to the request of twenty-eight members of Congress, to suspend the program during the interim period before study results were reported.[60] The Senate Committee on the Judiciary reviewed the Carnivore program at a September 6 hearing. In late November 2000, a preliminary draft of the Carnivore study, conducted by the Illinois Institute of Technology Research Institute, found the Internet wiretap program to be a sound law enforcement tool but recommended some modifications to protect people's routine e-mail and other communications from unlawful interception.[61] Some critics contended that those conducting the study were biased in favor of the new technology, while others argued that bias resulted not only from the selection of the reviewers but also from the ground rules for the study.[62]

At an October 3, 2000, Senate Committee on Commerce hearing on proposed legislation to protect the privacy of Internet users (S. 809, S. 2606, and S. 2928), representatives from America Online, Inc., and Hewlett-Packard Company voiced support for a bipartisan proposal introduced by Senator John McCain (R-Ariz.), the committee chair, and Senator John F. Kerry (D-Mass.), among others. The measure (S. 2928) would have required Web sites to give online visitors conspicuous notice of their privacy policies, as well as the choice to opt out of efforts to collect data about visitors. Enforcement authority was vested in the Federal Trade Commission. Consumer advocates, however, regarded the bill as too weak.

In the aftermath of the September 11 terrorist attacks, debate over the issue of law enforcement monitoring of electronic mail and Web use has intensified, with some advocating increased tools for law enforcement to track down terrorists and others cautioning that fundamental tents of democracy, such as privacy, should not be endangered in that pursuit. Language in the House-passed Department of Justice authorization bill (H.R. 2215) requires the Department to report to Congress on its use of Internet monitoring software such as Carnivore (now called DCS 1000), but Congress has also passed, and the president signed into law, anti-terrorism legislation (H.R. 3162, PL 107-56) that would make it easier for law enforcement to monitor Internet activities. The parallel debate over Web site information policies concerns whether industry self-regulation or legislation is the best approach to protecting consumer privacy. In particular, consumers appear concerned about the extent to which Web site operators collect personally identifiable information (PII) and share those data with third parties without their knowledge. Clearly, this is an issue that has generated numerous pieces of legislation in the 107th Congress.

CONCLUSION

An expectation of personal privacy seemingly has long prevailed in American culture and society. The Bill of Rights gave constitutional recognition to privacy expectations in the First Amendment, including the right not to have to speak, privacy of opinion, freedom of association, and the right of anonymous or pseudonymous expression; the Third Amendment, prohibiting the quartering of troops in private home during peacetime without the owner's consent; the Fourth Amendment, guaranteeing personal security against unwarranted searches and seizures; and the Fifth Amendment, specifying the privilege against self-incrimination. Although there may be some ambiguity about personal privacy, the American people, particularly during the latter half of the twentieth century, have increasingly turned to Congress to respond to their concerns regarding perceived threats to, or the loss of, personal privacy. These responses, which have significantly contributed to the policy development of the personal privacy concept, include developments regarding a comprehensive privacy review, Privacy Act amendments, banking and financial transactions, medical records, online communication, and electronic commerce. Clearly, renewed interest is growing in creating a study commission to conduct a comprehensive assessment of privacy policy and practice in both the public and private sectors and to make recommendations for better protecting the privacy of individuals.[63]

NOTES

1. Alan F. Westin, *Privacy and Freedom* (New York: Atheneum, 1970), 330–33.

2. *Griswold* v. *Connecticut*, 381 U.S. 479 (1965); see R. H. Clark, "Constitutional Sources of the Penumbral Right to Privacy," *Villanova Law Review* 19 (June 1974): 833–84.

3. Westin, *Privacy and Freedom*, 337–38.

4. Thomas M. Cooley, *A Treatise on the Law of Torts, or the Wrongs Which Arise Independent of Contract* (Chicago: Callaghan, 1888), 29.

5. Samuel D. Warren and Louis D. Brandeis, "The Right to Privacy," *Harvard Law Review* 4 (December 15, 1890): 193–220.

6. United Kingdom, Committee on Privacy, *Report of the Committee on Privacy* (London: Her Majesty's Stationery Office, 1972), 10.

7. Edward A. Shils, *The Torment of Secrecy* (New York: Free Press, 1956), 26.

8. See Senate Committee on the Judiciary, Subcommittee on Administrative Practice and Procedure, *Invasions of Privacy*, hearings (Washington, D.C.: GPO, 1965–1967), six parts.

9. See Senate Committee on the Judiciary, Subcommittee on Constitutional Rights, *Psychological Tests and Constitutional Rights*, hearings (Washington, D.C.: GPO, 1966).

10. See Senate Committee on the Judiciary, Subcommittee on Constitutional Rights, *Privacy and the Rights of Federal Employees*, hearings (Washington, D.C.: GPO, 1966).

11. See Senate Committee on the Judiciary, Subcommittee on Administrative Practice and Procedure, *Right of Privacy Act of 1967*, hearings (Washington, D.C.: GPO, 1967), six parts.

12. See Senate Committee on the Judiciary, Subcommittee on Administrative Practice and Procedure, *Computer Privacy*, hearings (Washington, D.C.: GPO, 1967–1968), two parts.

13. See Senate Committee on the Judiciary, Subcommittee on Constitutional Rights, *Privacy, the Census and Federal Questionnaires*, hearings (Washington, D.C.: GPO, 1969).

14. See Senate Committee on the Judiciary, Subcommittee on Constitutional Rights, *Federal Data Banks, Computers and the Bill of Rights*, hearings (Washington, D.C.: GPO, 1971), two parts.

15. See Morris S. Ogul, *Congress Oversees the Bureaucracy* (Pittsburgh: University of Pittsburgh Press, 1976), 92–128.

16. See House Committee on Government Operations, *Privacy and the National Data Bank Concept*, H. Rept. 1842 (Washington, D.C.: GPO, 1968).

17. See House Committee on Post Office and Civil Service, *Privacy and the Rights of Federal Employees*, hearings (Washington, D.C.: GPO, 1968).

18. See House Committee on Government Operations, *Commercial Credit Bureaus*, hearings (Washington, D.C.: GPO, 1968).

19. See House Committee on the Judiciary, *Security and Privacy of Criminal Arrest Records*, hearings (Washington, D.C.: GPO, 1972).

20. National Academy of Sciences, Computer Science and Engineering Board, Project on Computer Databanks, *Databanks in a Free Society, Report of the Project on Computer Databanks* (New York: Quadrangle Books, 1972), 341.

21. Ibid., 348–49.

22. Department of Health, Education, and Welfare, Secretary's Advisory Committee on Automated Personal Data Systems, *Records, Computers, and the Rights of Citizens* (Washington, D.C., July 1973), ix.

23. Ibid., xxiii, 50.

24. 87 Stat. 197, 215–16; 42 U.S.C. 3789g.

25. 5 U.S.C. 552a(e)(7).

26. 88 Stat. 1896.

27. 88 Stat. 906.

28. 88 Stat. 1906.

29. See David F. Linowes, "The U.S. Privacy Protection Commission," *American Behavioral Scientist* 26 (May–June 1983): 577–90.

30. Privacy Protection Study Commission, *Personal Privacy in an Information Society* (Washington, D.C.: GPO, 1977).

31. See General Services Administration, National Archives and Records Service, Office of the Federal Register, *Public Papers of the Presidents of the United States: Jimmy Carter, 1979* (Washington, D.C.: GPO, 1980), 581–87.

32. 88 Stat. 1789.

33. Commission on Federal Paperwork, *Confidentiality and Privacy: A Report of the Commission on Federal Paperwork* (Washington, D.C.: GPO, 1977), 139–75.

34. 94 Stat. 2816.

35. Ibid.

36. Privacy Protection Study Commission, *Personal Privacy in an Information Society*, 393–444.

37. 108 Stat. 3924 and 112 Stat. 1835.

38. Congressional Research Service, unpublished report.

39. *Zurcher* v. *Stanford Daily*, 436 U.S. 547 (1978).

40. The latter statute may be found at 50 U.S.C. 1801 et seq.

41. 108 Stat. 2099; 18 U.S.C. 2721 note.

42. *Reno* v. *Condon*, 120 S. Ct. 666; 68 USLW 4037 (January 12, 2000).

43. See *South Carolina v. Baker*, 485 U.S. 505 (1988).

44. Ibid.

45. See Robert O'Harrow Jr., "Protecting Patient Data," *Washington Post,* March 23, 2001, E1, E4; Kristina Stefanova, Privacy Rules Revisited," *Washington Times,* March 29, 2001, B8, B9; Associated Press, "Bush Moves to Protect Patient Privacy," *Washington Times,* April 13, 2001, B9, B10.

46. See "Statement by HHS Secretary Tommy G, Thompson Regarding the Patient Privacy Rule" (Washington, D.C.: Department of Health and Human Services, April 12, 2002), http://www.hhs.gov/news/press/2001/pres/20010412.html.

47. Associated Press, "Children's Web Sites Ignore Privacy Rules," *Washington Times,* March 29, 2001, B9.

48. Associated Press, "Law to Protect Children from Internet Intrusion Curtailing Their Usage," *Washington Times,* April 14, 2001, C12.

49. William Glanz, "Web Sites Fined over Privacy of Children," *Washington Times,* April 20, 2001, B8; Robert O'Harrow Jr., "3 Web Firms to Pay Fines for Collecting Data on Children," *Washington Post,* April 20, 2001, E3.

50. General Accounting Office, *Financial Privacy: Too Soon to Assess the Privacy Provisions in the Gramm-Leach-Bliley Act of 1999*, GAO-01-617 (Washington, D.C.: General Accounting Office, May 2001).

51. Robert O'Harrow Jr., "Three Charged with Selling Confidential Data in FTC Sting," *Washington Post,* April 19, 2001, E3.

52. Eileen Alt Powell, "Banks' Privacy Policies Hidden among Mail Inserts," *Washington Post,* April 26, 2001, B9, B10; John Schwartz, "Privacy Policy Notices Are Called Too Common and Too Confusing," *New York Times,* May 7, 2001, A1, A12.

53. Cheryl Wetzstein, "New Measure Takes Aim at Obscene Sites on Web," *Washington Times,* December 24, 2000, C2.

54. Associated Press, "Libraries Lodge Legal Challenge to Internet Filters," *Washington Times,* March 20, 2001, B6, B10; Robert O'Harrow Jr., "Curbs on Web Access Face Attack," *Washington Post,* March 20, 2001, A4; Cheryl Wetzstein, "ACLU, Library Group Sue to Stop Child Internet Protection Act," *Washington Times,* March 21, 2001, A3

55. See Robert M. Gellman, "Fragmented, Incomplete, and Discontinuous: The Failure of Federal Privacy Regulatory Proposals and Institutions," *Software Law Journal* 6 (April 1993): 199–238.

56. See, however, Robert Gellman, "Taming the Privacy Monster: A Proposal for a Non-Regulatory Privacy Agency," *Government Information Quarterly* 17 (2000): 235–41.

57. House Committee on Government Reform, *H.R. 4049, to Establish the Commission for the Comprehensive Study of Privacy Protection*, hearings (Washington, D.C.: GPO, 2001); see also House Committee on Government Reform, *The Privacy Commission: A Complete Examination of Privacy Protection*, hearing (Washington, D.C.: GPO, 2001).

58. National Research Council, Computer Science and Telecommunications Board, *For the Record: Protecting Electronic Health Information* (Washington, D.C.: National Academy Press, 1997), 2.

59. Identity theft is punishable under the Identity Theft and Assumption Deterrence Act of 1998 (112 Stat. 3007).

60. Elisabeth Frater, "Law Enforcement: The Carnivore Question," *National Journal* 32 (September 2, 2000): 2722–23.

61. The final version of the evaluation, "Independent Technical Review of the Carnivore System: Final Report," issued December 8, 2000, can be found at the Department of Justice Web site, http://www.usdoj.gov/jmd/publications/carniv_final.pdf.

62. David A. Vise and Dan Eggen, "Study: FBI Tool Needs Honing," *Washington Post,* November 22, 2000, A2.

63. Evidence of this in the 107th Congress is the Privacy Commission Act (H.R. 4049 and H.R. 583), as well as S. 851.

Chapter 10

Administrative Law and Regulatory Agencies

Executive branch agencies translate public laws into detailed and precise rules and regulations for implementing those statutes assigned to them. These administrative pronouncements have the force and effect of law; that is, they are "designed to implement, interpret, or prescribe law or policy or to describe the procedure of practice requirements of an agency."[1] Because the process of developing these regulations is called *rulemaking*, a regulation is sometimes referred to as a *rule*.

As stipulated in their enabling statutes, which establish new programs and amend and extend their duties and responsibilities, agencies can issue regulations, most of which are issued informally under the notice-and-comment procedure of the Administrative Procedure Act (APA) of 1946 (PL 79-404, 60 Stat. 237). At 5 U.S.C. 701–710, the APA subjects agency actions to judicial review except where a statute precludes such review or "where agency action is committed to agency discretion by law." Less commonly, some agencies (Federal Trade Commission, the Consumer Product Safety Commission, and the Occupational Safety and Health Administration) add elements of adjudicatory proceedings (e.g., cross-examination and rebuttal witnesses) to the notice-and-comment requirements when promulgating regulations. Rarely do agencies conduct their rulemaking in a formal adjudicatory proceeding.

Regulations might be divided into economic and social regulations. The former type

> generally cover sectors of the American economy such as electricity, natural gas, communications, transportation, aviation, agriculture and banking. These regulations usually take the form of overt barriers to entry or exit, licensing and tariffing laws, and price and wage controls. Most economic regulations were created around the time of the New Deal.[2]

The latter type include those statutes or rules that are intended to protect citizen or worker health and safety, accomplish environmental and other aesthetic goals, or promote civil rights objectives. Most social regulations were conceived in the late 1960's or early 1970s,"[3] and they provide substantial benefits, but also impose significant costs.

The present-day regulatory state

> is enormous. . . . [S]ome 55 federal regulatory agencies and more than 130,000 staff develop, implement and enforce a myriad of regulations, with more than 2,000 new rules issued every year. According to Professor Thomas Hopkins of the Rochester Institute of Technology, regulations now cost more than $721 billion. The costs of "social" regulations alone, particularly environmental regulation, has almost tripled over the last twenty years from about $80 billion in 1977 to more than $267 billion in 2000.[4]

For the past thirty years, "the significant increase . . . in the number and scope of federal regulations and regulatory programs dealing with health, safety, and the environment has stimulated the reform effort. These 'social' regulations and regulatory programs, while providing substantial benefits, also impose significant costs."[5]

REGULATORY REFORM

As Rogelio Garcia of the Congressional Research Service explains,

> Achieving a proper balance between costs, both in terms of dollars and of government intrusiveness, and benefits is at the heart of the debate over regulatory reform. Part of the problem, however, is the lack of consensus over the actual costs and benefits of regulations, and how best to attain such data. The difficulty is compounded by the fact that cost-benefit analysis—the best tool for assessing available data—relies on subjective assumptions, incomplete data, and other uncertainties.[6]

He notes that

> Proponents of comprehensive reform contend that many federal regulations are too costly and intrusive. They argue that the public and private resources needed to address problems in health, safety, and environmental areas are limited; that those resources must be allocated more efficiently to address the greatest needs of society in the most cost-effective manner, so that the costs of regulations do not exceed the benefits. Finally, they contend that the existing system tends to be overtly risk conscious, and question what they perceive as the lack of stringent analytical guidelines in the methodology used to assess risk hazards as well as costs and benefits when developing regulations.

These perceived shortcomings, they argue, result in unnecessary, costly, and intrusive rules that impeded economic growth and development.

Opponents of comprehensive change believe that some of the reform efforts focus too much on costs and not enough on benefits. They argue that such efforts would hinder the ability of regulatory agencies to safeguard the public's health and safety, and to protect the environment. Given the uncertainty regarding some of the risks involved, they contend it is necessary to retain a relatively effective process that has helped to clean the environment and avoid unforeseen consequences. They assert that the existing methodology is adequate to evaluate costs and benefits and that the proposed reforms would prevent or unnecessarily delay needed regulations and impose additional costs on the agencies.

Several factors make it difficult to resolve existing differences regarding the need for regulatory reform. First, the contending parties often disagree about the need for a particular regulation. Second, the data necessary for effective use of risk assessment, cost-benefit, and cost-effectiveness analyses—tools required for sound rulemaking—often are ambivalent and incomplete. Finally, the above tools depend largely on assumptions and other subjective factors, thereby exposing them to bias and manipulation.[7]

The President

In 1981, President Ronald Reagan issued Executive Order (E.O.) 12291, which, for the first time, required federal agencies to prepare a cost-benefit analysis when developing regulations and to submit those regulations to the Office of Management and Budget (OMB) for review and clearance. In 1985, the president issued E.O. 12498 in an effort to improve the coordination of regulatory activities and the management of the regulatory process. Agencies were directed to prepare an annual agenda containing all contemplated or planned regulatory actions for the coming year. Except for emergency situations, they were prohibited from taking any regulatory actions that had not been included in that agenda, unless OMB approved those actions.

In 1989, concern about continuing cost increases related to compliance with regulations led President George H. W. Bush to establish the President's Council on Competitiveness. Chaired by Vice President Dan Quayle, the Council, which was made up of high-level officials but staffed from the vice president's office, replaced the Reagan-era Task Force on Regulatory Relief chaired by then-Vice President Bush. Operating in secrecy, the Council had "a stranglehold in the regulatory agency rulemaking process."[8] The Council focused on reducing the cost of new and existing regulations, as well as the number of regulations.[9] "The general consensus of those who studied the council was that its failure to disclose the basis for its selection of rules for review or its communications with those outside government during the course of review threatened its legitimacy."[10]

President William Clinton abolished the Council, and, on September 30, 1993, he issued E.O. 12866, which revoked E.O. 12291 and E.O. 12498, but which incorporated, in slightly modified form, the cost-benefit analysis and the coordinated review and clearance provisions of the earlier orders. Clinton's order also offered a "statement of regulatory philosophy and principles":

> Federal agencies should promulgate only such regulations as are required by law, are necessary to interpret the law, or are made necessary by compelling public need, such as material failures of private markets to protect or improve the health and safety of the public, the environment, or the well-being of the American people. In deciding whether and how to regulate, agencies should assess all costs and benefits of available regulatory alternatives, including he alternative of not regulating. Costs and benefits shall be understood to include both quantifiable measures (to the fullest extent that these can be usefully estimated) and qualitative measures of costs and benefits that are difficult to quantify, but nevertheless essential to consider. Further, in choosing among alternative regulatory approaches, agencies should select those approaches that maximize net benefits . . . , unless a statute requires another regulatory approach.[11]

Within OMB, the Office of Information and Regulatory Affairs (OIRA), mandated by the Paperwork Reduction Act of 1980, was charged with conducting the review. (However, to date, OIRA has focused on regulatory matters while neglecting the information management responsibilities stipulated under that statute and other legislation.[12])

Although Presidents Reagan and Bush were receptive to complaints about cost, President Clinton took a cost-benefit approach. He also charged the National Performance Review (NPR), a task force headed by Vice President Al Gore, to improve the regulatory process. On March 4, 1995, President Clinton instructed agencies to review their existing regulations and to eliminate or revise those that were outdated. In April 1996, he directed agency heads to use their enforcement discretion to waive the penalty, in whole or in part, for a regulatory violation that was corrected within a reasonable time, or when the amount waived was used to correct the violation.

Upon assuming the presidency, George W. Bush directed that no new or proposed regulations be published until they could be reviewed and cleared. He also required that those regulations sent to the Office of the Federal Register at the end of the Clinton administration that had not been published be returned to the issuing agency for review and possible approval, and that the effective date of those regulations that had been published, but had not yet taken effect, be postponed for sixty days. Regulations issued by independent regulatory boards and commissions were exempted from the moratorium, as were regulations issued in response to a health or safety emergency or a legislative or judicial deadline. As a result, numerous stories appeared in the press that centered around the

Environmental Protection Agency and the Department of the Interior about reconsideration of regulations relating to the amount of mercury permissible in drinking water and the national parks.

Congress

Congress has passed legislation deregulating various sectors of the economy. It has abolished economic regulations that affect industries such as banking, telecommunications, and transportation. As a consequence, agencies such as the Civil Aeronautics Board and the Interstate Commerce Commission were terminated. Although Congress has not passed comprehensive regulatory reform legislation, it has addressed the matter on a partial basis through acts such as the following:

- The Paperwork Reduction Act of 1980 (444 U.S.C. 3501–3520) resulted, in part, from the belief that the growth in regulations imposed significant paperwork burdens on individuals, businesses, and organizations. The 1995 Paperwork Reduction Act (PL 104-13, 109 Stat. 163-85) required a 10 percent reduction in paperwork for fiscal years 1996 and 1997, and a 5 percent reduction in each of the following four years.

- The Regulatory Flexibility Act of 1980 (5 U.S.C. 601–602), since amended, directed agencies to prepare analyses that showed how their regulations affected businesses, organizations, subnational government, and so forth. Agencies were encouraged to tailor their regulations to be less burdensome on their groups. The Act also required agencies to publish semiannual regulatory agendas describing regulatory actions in the process of development.

- The Unfunded Mandates Reform Act of 1995 (PL 104-4, 109 Stat. 48, 2 U.S.C. 602 et seq.) requires agencies, except for independent regulatory boards and commissions, to prepare a cost-benefit analysis when developing a major regulation.

- The Truth in Regulating Act of 2000 (PL 106-312, 114 Stat. 1248–1250) requires the General Accounting Office (GAO) to evaluate the cost-benefit analysis prepared by agencies when they develop a regulation.

- The Small Business Regulatory Enforcement Fairness Act (SBREFA) (PL 104-121, 110 Stat. 847, 857–874) provides for regulatory relief in five subtitles. For example, subtitle D (110 Stat. 864) amends the Regulatory Flexibility Act by allowing judicial review of an agency's regulatory flexibility analysis. Agencies must also send a proposed rule and copy of an initial regulatory flexibility analysis, or a determination that such analysis is not required, to the Small Business Administration for comment. Furthermore, a review panel is to consider the impact on small businesses of regulations issued by the Occupational Safety and Health Administration and the Environmental Protection Agency.

The Congressional Review Act, which is subtitle E, section 251, of SBREFA (5 U.S.C. 801–808), stipulates that major and nonmajor rules must be submitted to both chambers of Congress before either can take effect. A major rule is one that has resulted in, or is likely to result in, an annual effect on the economy of at least $100 million; a major increase in costs or prices for consumers, individual industries, government agencies, or geographic regions; or significant adverse effects on competition, employment, investment, productivity, innovation, or the ability of U.S.-based enterprises to compete with foreign-based enterprises in domestic and export markets. Major rules are not effective until sixty days after publication in the *Federal Register* or submission to Congress and GAO, whichever is later. A rule is broadly defined as "the whole or part of an agency statement of general applicability and future effect designated to implement, or prescribe law or policy."[13]

Although 5 U.S.C. 801 et seq. is silent about GAO's role relating to nonmajor rules, the agency's Office of the General Counsel established a database that compiles information about the fifteen to twenty rules GAO receives on average each day. The database captures the title, issuing agency, type of rule, Regulation Identification Number, proposed effective date, date published in the *Federal Register*, congressional review trigger date, and any joint resolutions of disapproval that may be enacted. The database is available at http://www.gao.gov.

In 1995, the House of Representatives unilaterally established a Corrections Calendar (H. Res. 168), which would expedite the repeal of rules and regulations deemed excessive or "dumb." Bills reported favorably from committee may be placed on the Corrections Calendar on the second and fourth Tuesday of each month. A three-fifths vote is required to pass corrections legislation.

The laws noted in this section, and the efforts to modify the regulatory process, have tended to focus on the following areas:

- Use of cost-benefit analysis and cost-effectiveness analysis when developing regulations, especially regulations likely to impose costs of $100 million or more a year;

- Use of risk assessment analysis to determine the probability of certain hazards occurring and their adverse effects;[14]

- Use of a regulatory budget (which is used to get agencies to set regulatory priorities) to provide an overview of regulatory costs and set a cap on those costs;

- Subjecting new regulations to review and possible disapproval by Congress;

- Widening the scope of judicial review of regulatory actions;

- Imposing a moratorium on new regulations while agencies review their existing regulations to determine if they should be revised or abolished;

- Reducing and streamlining the paperwork required by regulations;

- Establishing a fair procedure for compensation of property owners when all or some of their property is "taken" by a regulatory action;

- Establishing a sunset mechanism whereby regulations or regulatory programs are terminated unless Congress or the agency determines otherwise; and

- Restricting mandates imposed on state and local government unless federal funds are provided to offset the costs of those mandates.[15]

OFFICE OF MANAGEMENT AND BUDGET

As the previous section notes, Congress has given OMB's OIRA the authority to review economically significant regulations and oversee the plans that agencies prepare for the review of existing regulations.[16] The OMB communicates within the executive branch about rulemaking and other policy issues through circulars, which comprise instructions or information that have a continuing effect of at least two years on executive departments and agencies.

The OMB is planning to expand the amount of information available online regarding its role in analyzing and passing on those regulations proposed by federal agencies. Among other items, it will post lists of regulations under review, copies of letters sent between OIRA and agencies, copies of correspondence with outside groups, and information regarding meetings with these groups. The OMB anticipates the creation of a computerized tracking system to manage the regulation review process.

A provision of the Omnibus Appropriations Act for FY 1999 (PL 105-277), popularly known as the Shelby amendment, directed OMB to revise Circular A-110 to make data from federally funded research governed by the circular available to the public through the Freedom of Information Act (FOIA). The provision also authorizes user fees. The OMB published proposed revisions to A-110 in February and August 1999, and issued the final revision on September 30, 1999; it took effect on November 8.

To balance the need for public access while protecting the research process, OMB limits the kinds of data that will be publicly accessible. It excludes personal and business-related confidential data and limits applicability to federally funded data produced under an award that has been published or cited by a federal agency and used in developing an agency action that has the force and effect of law. Needless to say, the provision is controversial. Some argue, for instance, that the public has the right to review scientific data underlying research funded by government taxpayers, and others believe that OMB has narrowed the scope of public access to research data more than Congress intended. Others maintain that the FOIA is an inappropriate vehicle to allow wider public access; that researchers will have to spend additional time and money putting data into a form required by the government, thereby interfering with ongoing research; and that private sector cooperation and funding for government/university/industry partnerships will be jeopardized.

On another front, section 515(a) of the Treasury and General Government Appropriations Act for Fiscal Year 2001 (PL 106-554) directed OMB to "provide policy and procedural guidance to Federal agencies for ensuring and maximizing the quality, objectivity, utility, and integrity of information (including statistical information) disseminated by Federal agencies in fulfillment of the purposes and provides of . . . the Paperwork Reduction Act." In response, on October 1, 2001, OMB issued "Guidelines for Ensuring and Maximizing the Quality, Objectivity, Utility, and Integrity of Information Disseminated by Federal Agencies" (see http://www.whitehouse.gov/omb/fedreg/text/final_information_quality_guidelines. html). The guidelines represent an attempt to deal with quality in the dissemination of government information since the advent of the Internet.[17] The OMB views quality as "an encompassing term comprising utility, objectivity, and integrity," and defines each of these terms. For example, *utility* refers to the usefulness of the information to the intended users; *objectivity* "involves a focus on ensuring accurate, reliable, and unbiased information;" and *integrity* "refers to the security of information—protection of the information from unauthorized access or revision, to ensure that the information is not compromised through corruption or falsification."[18]

Section 515 directs agencies subject to the Paperwork Reduction Act to issue information quality guidelines "no later than one year after the date of issuance of the OMB guidelines"; "establish administrative mechanisms allowing affected persons to seek and obtain correction of information maintained and disseminated by the agency that does not comply with these OMB guidelines"; and "report to . . . OMB the number and nature of complaints received by the agency regarding agency compliance with these OMB guidelines . . . and how such complaints were resolved."[19]

The guidelines are also controversial because they might diminish the amount of information that the government disseminates as "accurate." Accuracy is not always an easy concept to demonstrate. As some insist, it may well require replication and evidence of the reproducibility of the results of a study.[20]

ONLINE RULEMAKING

Executive departments and agencies may place on their Web sites those laws, regulations, and perhaps executive orders that deal with subjects under their jurisdiction. They might do so in a highlighted section of the site called "laws & regulations," "regulations," or "docket." Examples of agencies doing so are the Environmental Protection Agency (see http://www.epa.gov/epahome/rules.html. Food Safety and Inspection Service of the Department of Agriculture (http://www.fsis.usda.gov/OPPDE/rdad/Rulemaking.htm), Securities and Exchange Commission (http://www.sec.gov/rules/concept.shtml; http://www.sec.gov/rules.shtml), and the Department of the Interior (http://www.doi.gov/nrl/RegWeb/RuleHome.html).

Both the Department of Health and Human Services (HHS) and the Department of Transportation go a step further and are in the process of developing electronic rulemaking—using the Internet to receive and display public comments obtained through the rulemaking process. "Of particular importance in the rulemaking context is that the Web greatly facilitates both two-way communication and many kinds of forums or discussions. As a matter of public participation, it effectively opens up the docket room to the public during as well as after the public comment period. As a matter of internal management, . . . [it] greatly simplifies and expedites responding to public comment."[21] Electronic technology can "make a huge difference to rulemaking . . . [in three areas]":

- In the internal development of both proposed and final rules, agency staff or other departmental staff can be linked to drafts so that each can not only make suggestions but see the suggestions of others and understand the rationale and approach. . . .

- In the public comment stage, the public can not only post comments on a proposed rule, but also review the comments of others. Interactive dialog (with or without government staff actively involved) can be used to hone issue identification, improve suggestions for change, or even reach consensus.

- In the internal development of final rules, all public comments on particular sections can be electronically available to all reviewing staff, already organized by section and issue. Changes responsive to particular comments, and responses to other comments, can be generated with the pertinent responses, and no others, at staff finger tips.[22]

In the case of HHS, it has joined with the Logistics Management Institute to test "the use of the Internet in development of regulations." Electronic rulemaking includes:

- Preparation and staff review of draft regulatory actions;

- Publication of proposed rules and supporting documents;

- Collection, electronic posting, and analysis of public comments on proposed rules;

- Creating a forum in which comments are shared with the public during the rulemaking period and public discussions and responses are shared;

- Electronic scanning of paper comments and posting to the central forum;

- Organizing comments by rule topic and issue;

- Responding to comments;

- Modification of the proposals based on public comment; and

- Issuance of final regulation.

This effort includes

> The creation of an information service on regulatory reform and management through which key documents are posted for downloading and comment, or disseminated by ListServ or other technology to users. Subjects to be covered include electronic rule-making, regulations management, cost-effective imaging, and regulatory analysis. Products from the pilot projects will include a manual, recommend software, and pre-formatted web documents and systems allowing ready adoption in future rulemaking. (http://globe.lmi.org/erm)

Information on the development of online rulemaking and this Web site can be found at http://globe.lmi.org/erm/pubs.htm, which contains a "library" that provides background documentation as well as links to related sites.

The Department of Transportation has a Docket Management System (DMS) for electronic submissions. Both registered and unregistered users can submit documents and comments (see http://dmses.dot.gov/submit). Additional information about the DMS Web is available at http://dms.dot.gov and http://dms.dot.gov/reports.

EMERGENCY RULEMAKING

The APA clarified the public's role in the rulemaking process. Under normal circumstances, agencies publish "proposed rules" so that interested parties can respond either in writing or in person at administrative hearings. However, this procedure may be waived under extraordinary circumstances, such as a health threat to the population. For example, the newly created Department of Transportation position of undersecretary for security has responsibility for protecting the nation's skies, airports, highways, trains, businesses, ports, and waterways. The undersecretary has broad regulatory powers, including the issuance, rescinding, and revision of regulations to carry out the functions of the Transportation Security Administration. If it is determined that a regulation or security directive must be issued quickly to protect transportation security, the undersecretary can do so, thereby bypassing the notice-and-comment phase. In such instances, there is no review within the Department of Transportation or by OMB, or placement in the *Federal Register*.

PUBLICATIONS

The major publications for transmitting rules and regulations to the public are the *Federal Register* and the *Code of Federal Regulations* (CFR). There is also the *Regulatory Program of the U.S. Government*, an annual publication that E.O. 12498 mandated. It presents the significant regulatory actions planned for the regulatory year (April 1–March 31) by federal agencies (independent regulatory agencies are exempt) and approved by OMB. It describes specific agency actions, provides an overview of each agency's regulatory plans for the year, gives the schedule for implementation of the actions listed, and identifies agency contact people.

Background

Political scientist Cornelius M. Kerwin discusses the history of rulemaking prior to 1935, when there was no central system for announcing and providing access to those rules and regulations that the executive branch promulgated. Access to those documents was through the reporting system used by individual agencies because no central system was in place. Kerwin notes that, in its first sessions, Congress enacted laws that gave the president "the authority to issue rules that would govern those who traded with Indian tribes."[23] Congress later gave the executive branch the power to write rules related to trade and commerce. Rulemaking, however, remained limited until the late nineteenth century, when Congress "turned its attention to domestic issues and problems and sought solutions." Rulemaking expanded during the Progressive Era and, with the New Deal, it became "a major governmental function."[24] From the 1880s through the 1930s, the Interstate Commerce Commission, the Federal Reserve System, and Federal Trade Commission, to name a few examples, were created, and Congress gave powers to agencies to regulate the purity of milk, stockyards, and meat packing houses; manage public lands; protect wildlife; and so forth.

Title 5 of the *United States Code* (U.S.C.), especially in sections 553, 556, and 557, covers rulemaking. Section 553, for instance, governs "notice-and-comment," which means (1) publication of proposed rulemaking, (2) opportunity for public participation, and (3) publication of a final rule when specified by the agency but not less than thirty days before its effective date. The *Federal Register* covers agency statements of organization, procedural rules, and the public notices mandated for agency rulemaking.[25] There are omissions among the publications included in the *Federal Register*. For instance, the courts have mandated refinements in the rulemaking procedures of many agencies, some executive orders have instituted procedural requirements, and deregulation and the presence of the World Wide Web have enabled agencies to pursue other methods for promulgating administrative law.

Federal Register

Informal notice-and-comment rulemaking requires that an agency publish a notice of proposed rulemaking in the *Federal Register;* afford all interested persons an opportunity to participate in the proceeding through the submission of written comments or, at the discretion of the agency, by oral presentations; and, when consideration of the relevant matter presented is completed, incorporate in the final rule a detailed, comprehensive statement of its basis and purpose. A final rule must be published in the *Federal Register* "not less than 30 days before its effective date."[26] In brief, the *Federal Register*, which began publication March 14, 1936, provides presidential directives such as executive orders and proclamations and notices of proposed and recently adopted rules and regulations, the semiannual regulatory agenda (short descriptions of proposed regulatory actions in the coming year), announcements of meetings, the availability of grants, research proposals, information collection activities under review by OMB, announcements of agency hearings, proposed changes to agency records systems, and reorganization plans for the executive branch. Under an agency heading, documents are arranged by type of action (e.g., final rule, proposed rule, and notice of meeting). Proposed rules and regulations offer a time period for interested parties to make a rebuttal. For example, a proposed regulation designated ketchup as a vegetable in the school lunch program, and the public had the opportunity to register its concurrence or opposition. However, the public commentary is not binding on the agency, which can choose to accept or reject it.

Each paper-copy issue contains a "List of Sections Affected" (LSA) highlighting those rules and regulations affected by its contents (as well as those for the month). There is a quarterly cumulated index that enables users to search quickly through the year to identify proposed and actual changes.

Since 1994, the *Federal Register* has been available through GPO Access; the 1994 database, however, "contains no fields or section identifiers" (http://www.access.gpo.gov/su_docs/aces/aces140.html). As of March 1, 1996, Sunshine Act meetings were included among the Notices section of the *Federal Register*. It is possible to browse the table of contents of the current issue and to browse those of back issues (1998–). Also online are (1) a History of Line Item Veto Notices (until the Supreme Court declared such vetoes unconstitutional in 1998) and (2) Unified Agenda (Semiannual Regulatory Agenda):

> Executive Order 12866 (58 FR 51735) and the Regulatory Flexibility Act (5 U.S.C. 602) require that agencies publish semiannual regulatory agendas describing regulatory actions they are developing or have recently completed. The agendas are published in the *Federal Register*, usually during April and October each year, as part of the Unified Agenda of Federal Regulatory and Regulatory Actions.

> In the table of contents for the *Federal Register* issue, the agendas are listed by the issuing agency under the Proposed Rule section . . .. Each agenda begins with a preamble. Many include a table of contents. (http://www.access. gpo.gov/su_docs/aces/aces1406.html)

It is possible to limit a search of the *Federal Register* to contents and preliminary pages, final rules and regulations, proposed rules, notices, presidential documents, Sunshine Act meetings (as of March 1, 1996, these meetings are included in the Notices section), reader aids, or corrections.

Code of Federal Regulations

The *Code of Federal Regulations* (CFR), the codification of the general and permanent rules published in the *Federal Register*, is divided into fifty titles, or broad subject areas. Title 3 covers the president and the text of presidential directives, as specified in Chapter 5. Some other titles include 10 (Energy), 11 (Federal Elections), 21 (Food and Drugs), 22 (Foreign Relations), 25 (Indians), 28 (Judicial Administration), 32 (National Defense), 34 (Education), 40 (Protection of Environment), 45 (Public Welfare), 47 (Telecommunications), and 49 (Transportation). The titles are revised as follows:

Title 1–16 (as of January 1);

Title 17–27 (as of April 1);

Title 28–41 (as of July 1); and

Title 42–50 (as of October 1).

The titles are divided into chapters. Each chapter is the name of a government agency that administers that subject area. Therefore, the regulations of a department may be in several titles depending on the scope of its authority. The chapters are subdivided into parts and sections. The *Federal Register* is keyed to the CFR's titles and sections.

The CFR is also available through GPO Access, as is the "List of CFR Sections Affected" (see http://www.access.gpo.gov/nara/cfr/cfr-table-search.html).

Privacy Notices

Both the CFR and *Federal Register* provide Privacy Act notices. Furthermore, GPO Access has Privacy Act Issuances, an annual compilation that describes those agency records maintained on individuals. In accordance with the Privacy Act of 1974 (see Chapter 9), accompanying regulations assist individuals who request information about their records.

A Tutorial

The Office of Federal Register, National Archives and Records Administration, offers an online tutorial (http://www.archives.gov/federal_register/tutorial/about_tutorial.html)that can be downloaded. The topics covered include

- The regulatory process, focusing on the role of the public;

- The relationship between the *Federal Register* and CFR;

- A "Guided Tour" of a typical edition of the *Federal Register* and a volume of the CFR;

- Using the *Federal Register*/CFR finding aids; and

- Using OFR/NARA publications on the World Wide Web.

There is also a PDF (portable document format) file, "Federal Register: What It Is and How to Use It."

Shepard's CFR Citations

In *Shepard's Code of Federal Regulations Citations*, the CFR is the *cited* source and the *citing* sources include court cases (the Supreme Court and lower federal courts, as well as state courts) and some legal periodicals. Symbols indicate whether the citing source included the date of the cited CFR regulation. A triangle symbol informs the reader that the editor supplied the correct date, and an asterisk shows that the citing source properly included the date.

EXAMPLES

To find an up-to-date list of endangered species turn to the *Code of Federal Regulations,* as follows :

- Consult the Index and Finding Aids volume, which has a general subject index. (Some CFR titles have their own indexes.) We discover that chapter I, Title 50, of the CFR covers the U.S. Fish and Wildlife Service, Department of the Interior, and that section 17.11 provides a table of endangered and threatened species.

- We find that table in Title 50, but, from the above discussion, we know that the Title is revised every October. Thus, the list may have changed since Title 50 was last published.

- To update the list, we move from the CFR to the *Federal Register* and its quarterly indexes. We look in the section, "LSA—List of CFR Affected," for Chapter I of Title 50 and then for section 17.11. If that section is mentioned, there might be a reference to "table amended" or "table corrected" and the page number in the *Federal Register* where there is coverage of the amended or corrected table.

- Before terminating our search, we may need to move beyond the quarterly indexes to the *Federal Register* for a month or until a quarterly index has been published. Among the "CFR Parts Affected during [month]," we look for the section on 50 CFR and mention of our section in the recently adopted or "proposed" rules. Again, a page number would be provided.

- Finally, "CFR Parts Affected in This Issue" completes the updating information.

Now that both the CFR and *Federal Register* are online, we can conduct a search of both. At http://www.access.gpo.gov/nara/cfr/cfr-table-search.html, there are options such as

- About the CFR online;

- Search the entire set of CFR databases by keyword (current data);

- Retrieve CFR sections by citation (current and/or historical data);

- Search or browse your choice of CFR titles and/or volumes (current and/or historical data);

- LSA (List of CFR Sections Affected) (current and/or historical data); and

- Search the *Federal Register* for related documents (current and/or historical).

There is an annual *Federal Register Index* (1994–2001) and a cumulative index for the current year at http://www.archives.gov/federal_register/the_federal_register/indexes.html.

Because agencies may either not include rules and regulations in the *Federal Register* or may do so selectively, we might proceed to the Web site of the agency—the Fish and Wildlife Service—to see if it offers rules and regulations online. Furthermore, it is useful to check Web sites because proposed rules are likely to appear sooner in an online format than they do in a paper copy. It also takes additional time for the print publication to be shipped to a depository library and placed on the shelf. Looseleaf services, and the Web sites, of associations and other groups may make available rules and regulations applicable to a given subject.

The Nuclear Regulatory Commission (NRC) establishes "regulations on the safe use of nuclear materials at nuclear power plants, uranium mills, fuel facilities, waste repositories, and transportation systems. NRC also regulates other uses of nuclear materials, such as nuclear medicine programs at hospitals, academic activities, research work, and industrial applications."[27] The NRC regards the *Federal Register* as "the official vehicle to inform the public about its rulemaking. . . . NRC publishes . . . [here] its proposed and final rules, advance notices of proposed rulemaking, petitions for rulemaking, policy statements, semiannual agendas of regulations, memorandum of understanding, and announcements of meetings on rulemaking actions."[28]

Further,

- NRC's final rules are codified in the *Code of Federal Regulations* in 10 CFR Chapter I (Parts 0–199). Chapter I of 10 CFR is revised annually as of January 1 and is available in a softbound, two-volume addition from the . . . GPO. . . . The NRC maintains a version of 10 CFR Chapter I on the Internet that is updated weekly.

- The NRC publishes a compilation of its codified regulations and related documents in the *NRC Rules and Regulations*, a four-volume looseleaf set that is updated monthly.

- In an effort to further public access to and participation in its rulemaking activities, the NRC has developed a Web site entitled "RuleForum." [http://ruleforum.illnl.gov] This site contains rulemakings that have been published by the NRC in the *Federal Register* and petitions for rulemakings that have been received and docketed by the NRC.

Through this Web site, the public is made aware of and may officially comment on these petitions and proposed rules electronically. Proposed rules and petitions are placed on the web site when the comment period opens and are removed shortly after the comment period expires. Background files on proposed rules and petitions are available for viewing or downloading from file libraries.

. . . Additionally, all final rules published in the *Federal Register* are maintained on the Web site for 90 days.[29]

The Bureau of Export Administration, Department of Commerce, places its regulations in CFR and any published changes in the *Federal Register*. A Web site maintained by the Government Printing Office (http://w3.access.gpo.gov/bis/ear/ear_data.html) provides all of the "regulations, including the Commerce Control List, the Commerce Country Chart, and the Denied Persons List." Changes to the Web site are made within forty-eight to seventy-two hours. The site also has a table with all of the *Federal Register* notices that revise the text of regulations since the complete revision date of March 25, 1996. In addition, the National Technical Information Service (NTIS) has the Export Administration Regulation (EAR) Marketplace Web site (http://bxa.fedworld.gov) that also provides the EAR database. The NTIS database has a Prohibited Parties Page that includes four searchable and downloadable lists of prohibited parties (The Entry List, Denied Persons List, Debarred Party List, and the Specially Designated Nationals List). The site also includes a table with all *Federal Register* notices that revise the text of the EAR since its complete revision in March 1996. The NTIS even has a looseleaf/paper version of the EAR.

REGULATORY AGENCIES

The agencies that issue regulations can be divided into two groups: (1) those subject to the president's direction and control and (2) those relatively independent of such direction and control. The second category encompasses independent regulatory agencies, such as the Federal Reserve System, Federal Trade Commission, Federal Communications Commission, National Labor Relations Board, Federal Energy Regulatory Commission, and Consumer Product

Safety Commission (see 44 U.S.C. 3502(5) for a list of these agencies). These agencies have quasi-judicial authority and may also publish decisions, reports, orders, advisory opinions, and so forth on their home pages. GPO Access (http://www.access.gpo.gov/su_docs/admin.html) provides resources for the Federal Labor Relations Authority (1998–), GAO's Comptroller General (October 1995–), Merit Systems Protection Board (1994–), National Labor Relations Board, National Mediation Board, and the Office of Compliance. The latter was established to implement and enforce the 1995 Congressional Accountability Act (P L 104-197, 110 Stat. 2415).

The renderings of these agencies are subject to review by the courts, and the publications of regulatory agencies also appear in the collection of the National Technical Information Service and the Government Printing Office's *Catalog of United States Government Publications*, commercial looseleaf services, online services (e.g., LEXIS-NEXIS and WESTLAW), and so forth. Some compilations or series of decisions rendered by agencies and published in official government documents are available to depository libraries. Examples include *Agriculture Decisions*, issued semiannually; the biweekly *FCC Record* (1986–), which contains the earlier Federal Communications Commission *Reports*, 1st and 2d series; and the bound volumes of the *Decisions of the Federal Trade Commission*.

OTHER PRODUCTS

The Center for Regulatory Effectiveness (CRE), established in 1996 after the passage of the Congressional Review Act, provides "Congress with independent analyses of agency regulations. From this initial organizing concept, CRE has grown into a nationally recognized clearinghouse for methods to improve the federal regulatory process" (http://www.thecre.com). The CRE has "two paramount goals: to ensure that the public has access to data and information used to develop federal regulation, and to ensure that information which federal agencies disseminate to the public is of the highest quality. CRE also serves as a regulatory watchdog" (http://www.thecre.com). The home page, The CRE.com (http://www.thecre.com), covers issues, services, and hyperlinks. An example of issues is a link to "emerging regulatory issues" and of a service is the "CRE report card."

The American Bar Association has the ABA Administrative Procedure Database (http://www.law.fsu.edu/library/admin/admin2.html), which provides selective coverage of agency "decisionmaking." Furthermore, a number of law schools have relevant materials on their home pages. For example, the University of Virginia School of Law has a nineteen-page resource guide entitled "Federal Administrative Decisions & Other Actions" (http://www.law.virginia.edu/admindec), which covers the executive branch, independent agencies, regulatory agencies, and congressional agencies (e.g., General Accounting Office and the Government Printing Office). Public policy specialist Henry H. Perritt Jr., dean of Chicago-Kent College of Law, has a syllabus for teaching a course on administrative law on his Web site (see http://www.kentlaw.edu/academics/courses/admin-perritt/Ad98sy12.htm). The regional depository library at the University of Memphis has a four-page resource guide, "Uncle Sam—Administrative Law (http://www.lib.memphis.edu/gpo/admin.htm). The University of Michigan Documents Center has an eleven-page guide to "Laws and Regulations" (http://www.lib.umich.edu/govdocs/fedlaws.html).

The *Federal Register* and the CFR are available through WESTLAW, LEXIS-NEXIS, Legi-Slate, CIS's Congressional Universe, and CQ Washington Alert. The Bureau of National Affairs, Inc. (Washington, D.C.) has an *Environment Library* on CD-ROM, which includes the *Federal Register* and the CFR, and CIS Congressional Universe offers a *Federal Register*. Counterpoint Publishing (Cambridge, Mass.) offers the *Federal Register* as a weekly CD-ROM product and the CFR as a monthly product. Other publishers of both products may be found through *CD-ROMs in Print* (Farmington Hills, Mich.: Gale Group).

Finally, given the focus of part of this chapter on OMB and OIRA, it merits mention that OMB Watch is a nonprofit research, educational, and advocacy organization that monitors OMB and executive branch activities affecting public interest and community groups. OMB Watch maintains a Web site (http://www.ombwatch.org).

ACCESS TO RULES AND REGULATIONS IN THE LEGISLATIVE AND JUDICIAL BRANCHES

Legislative agencies may issue regulations directly or through publication in the *Federal Register*. In the latter case, notice and comment may or may not be involved, but there is inclusion in the CFR. For example, regulations of the Copyright Office of the Library of Congress (LC) are included in Title 37 of the CFR; other general LC regulations are placed in Title 36. Rules, regulations, and standing orders of both chambers of Congress appear in the *Congressional Record*, as do the rules adopted by the committees. Rules also appear on committee Web sites.

The courts also issue regulations, which, depending on the court, appear in Titles 26 and 32 of the CFR or may be issued pursuant to statute by circuits as rules of criminal and civil procedure or by the Supreme Court. Some judicial agencies also issue regulations and rules, which are usually published directly, not in the *Federal Register* or CFR. Again, the Web sites for the courts (see Chapter 11) are likely to include these rules and regulations. Further, the federal judiciary maintains a Web site on "Federal Rulemaking," which covers "federal rules of practice, procedure, and evidence. The site provides access to the national and local rules currently in effect in the federal courts, as well as background information on the federal rules and the rulemaking process" (http://www.uscourts.gov/rules).

CONCLUSION

As Kerwin argues, "rulemaking is a significant government function that has, since the start of the republic, come to play an increasingly pivotal role in the definition of American public policy and law."[30] Rulemaking, as expressed in the APA, enables the public to receive information about a law or agency policy, participate in the formulation of that law and policy, and hold the agency accountable in applying that law or policy. Publication in the *Federal Register* or on the Web advances these functions and gives the public input into the process. At the same time, Congress and the federal judiciary are also involved in shaping rulemaking and making it function more efficiently and effectively.[31] Needless to say, political preferences and philosophies influence (and do affect) rulemaking, and, as Kerwin points out, "judges are not without legal and political philosophies . . ., and when they review the handiwork of rulemakers, they do so through the prism of these beliefs."[32] Rulemaking is integral to government information policies and resources and does not stand on the outer fringes of those policies and resources.

NOTES

1. E.O. 12866, section 3(d).

2. Regulation.org, "What Is Regulation?," 1, available at http://www.regulation.org/whatisreg.html.

3. Ibid.

4. Ibid., 1–2.

5. Rogelio Garcia, "Federal Regulatory Reform: An Overview" (Washington, D.C.: Congressional Research Service, 2000), 1, available at http://cnie.org/NLE/CRSreports/Risk/rsk-3.cfm. Parts of this chapter draw upon this excellent introduction.

6. Ibid.

7. Ibid., 3.

8. Christine Triano and Gary D. Bass, "The New Game in Town: Regulation, Secrecy, and the Quayle Council on Competitiveness," *Government Information Quarterly* 9 (1992): 108.

9. The papers of the Council are housed at the Bush Presidential Library.

10. Cornelius M. Kerwin, *Rulemaking: How Government Agencies Write Law and Make Policy* (Washington, D.C.: CQ Press, 1994), 248.

11. E.O. 12866, section 1(a).

12. For a discussion of information resources management, see Office of Management and Budget, Circular A-130: "The Management of Federal Information Resources," *Federal Register* 50 (December 24, 1985): 52730–51, and the subsequent revisions of the Circular. The latest is identified in Chapter 1 and reprinted on the accompanying CD-ROM.

13. 5 U.S.C. 801–808.

14. Risk analysis is the systematic evaluation of the probability of certain hazards occurring and their adverse effects.

15. Gary L. Galemore, "Federal Regulatory Reform: An Overview," Issue Brief (Congressional Research Service) (November 1, 2001). Unpublished paper. We wish to acknowledge Mr. Galemore for providing part of the policy context for this chapter.

16. Kerwin, *Rulemaking,* 245–250, discusses OMB's relationship with the agencies.

17. The focus on governmentwide dissemination can be found in the Paperwork Reduction Act of 1995, OMB Circular A-130, "Management of Federal Information Resources," and OMB Circular A-110, "Uniform Administrative Requirements for Grants and Agreements with Institutions of Higher Education, Hospitals, and Other Non-Profit Organizations."

18. Office of Management and Budget, *Guidelines for Ensuring and Maximizing the Quality, Objectivity, Utility, and Integrity of Information Dissemination by Federal Agencies* (Washington, D.C.: Office of Management and Budget, 2001); available at http://www.whitehouse.gov/omb/fedreg/text/final_information_quality_guidelines.html.

19. Ibid.

20. See Karen Robb, "Verification Rule Could Stifle Information Flow," *Federal Times* (August 20, 2001).

21. Walton Francis, Senior Advisor, Office of the Assistant secretary for Planning and Evaluation, Department of Health and Human Services, "Electronic Rulemaking: Outline of Opportunities and Issues (May 25, 1997), 1, available at http://globe.lmi.org/erm/docs/erm525.htm.

22. Ibid., 1–2.

23. Kerwin, *Rulemaking*, 8–10.

24. Ibid.

25. For a list of public laws setting out the requirements for the publication of rulemaking in the *Federal Register*, see http://www.archives.gov/federal_register/public_laws/publication_laws.html.

26. Interested persons can petition for issuance, amendment, or repeal of a rule (5 U.S.C. 553).

27. Nuclear Regulatory Commission, "Rulemaking," 1, available at http://www.nrc.gov/NRC/rule.html.

28. Ibid., 1–2.

29. Ibid.

30. Kerwin, *Rulemaking*, 35.

31. See Ibid., 217–20, for a discussion of how Congress ensures "the accountability of those who write the rules." It is important to note that "Congress does use appropriations bills to send substantive and procedural messages to agencies" (220).

32. Ibid., 250.

URL SITE GUIDE

ABA Administrative Procedure Database
American Bar Association
> http://www.law.fsu.edu/library/admin/admin2.html

Code of Federal Regulations
GPO Access
> http://www.access.gpo.gov/nara/cfr/cfr-table-search.html

CRE.com
Center for Regulatory Effectiveness
> http://www.thecre.com/

Course Syllabus
Home Page (Henry H. Perritt, Jr.)
> http://www.kentlaw.edu/academics/courses/admin-perritt/Ad98sy12.htm

Federal Register
> http://www.access.gpo.gov/su_docs/aces/aces140.html

> Annual Indexes
>> http://www.archives.gov/federal_register/the_federal_register/indexes.html

> Tutorial
>> http://www.archives.gov/federal_register/tutorial/about_tutorial.html

Federal Administrative Decisions & Other Actions
University of Virginia School of Law
> http://www.law.virginia.edu/admindec

General Accounting Office
> http://www.gao.gov/

Environmental Protection Agency
> http://www.epa.gov/

> Rulemaking
>> http://www.epa.gov/epahome/rules.html

Export Administration Regulation Marketplace
National Technical Information Service
> http://bxa.fedworld.gov/

GPO Access
> http://www.access.gpo.gov/

> Regulatory Bodies
>> http://www.access.gpo.gov/su_docs/admin.html

Judicial Branch
> http://www.uscourts.gov/

> Federal Rulemaking
>> http://www.uscourts.gov/rules/

Laws and Regulations
University of Michigan
Documents Center
http://www.lib.umich.edu/govdocs/fedlaws.html

Laws That Affect Federal Register Publication
http://www.archives.gov/federal_register/public_laws/publication_laws.html

National Archives and Records Administration
http://www.archives.gov/index.html

Tutorial (FR and CFR)
http://www.archives.gov/federal_register/tutorial/about_tutorial.html

Office of Management and Budget
http://www.whitehouse.gov/omb/

Guidelines on Quality of Information Disseminated
http://www.whitehouse.gov/omb/fedreg/text/final_
information_quality_guidelines.html

OMB Watch
http://www.ombwatch.org/

Regulatory Agencies
GPO Access
http://www.access.gpo.gov/su_docs/admin.html

RuleForum
http://ruleforum.llnl.gov/

Uncle Sam—Administrative Law
University of Memphis Library
http://www.lib.memphis.edu/gpo/admin.htm

Rules/Regulations

Bureau of Export Administration
http://w3.access.gpo.gov/bis/ear/ear_data.html

Department of Health and Human Services
http://globe.lmi.org/erm/

http://globe.lmi.org/erm/pubs.htm

Department of the Interior
http://www.doi.gov/nrl/RegWeb/RuleHome.html

Department of Transportation
http://dmses.dot.gov/submit/

http://dms.dot.gov/reports/

http://dms.dot.gov/

Food Safety and Inspection Service
Department of Agriculture
http://www.fsis.usda.gov/OPPDE/rdad/Rulemaking.htm

Securities and Exchange Commission
http://www.sec.gov/rules/concept.shtml

http://www.sec.gov/rules.shtml

Chapter 11

Judicial Branch

The judicial branch forms a pyramid, with the more than ninety U.S. district, or trial, courts at the bottom; the appellate courts (eleven regional ones, a twelfth circuit for the District of Columbia, and the Court of Appeals for the Federal Circuit) in the middle; and the highest court—the Supreme Court—at the apex of the pyramid. In addition, from time to time, Congress has established special courts to deal with particular types of cases. Among these are the Court of Federal Claims, the United States Tax Court, the Court of International Trade, the Court of Veterans Appeals, and the United States Court of Appeals for the Armed Forces. The latter court, which was created in 1951 as the U.S. Court of Military Appeals (and, in 1994, given its current name) addresses questions of law arising from trials by court martial in the armed services in which the death sentence is imposed, and it has worldwide jurisdiction in cases certified for review by the Judge Advocate General or cases in which the accused, facing a severe sentence, petitions the Court and shows good cause for further review.

For a graphic depiction of the federal court system, see http://www. uscourts.gov/outreach/structure.jpg. That depiction also notes "federal administrative agencies and boards" that exist "outside the judicial branch." This is a reference to the fact that some executive branch entities, including some independent agencies, with quasi-judicial authority, render decisions, but the federal courts (district or courts of appeal) may review them.

As discussed in Chapter 7 of *U.S. Government on the Web*, most of the courts have home pages that, for instance, provide information about the court, decisions or opinions, dockets, rules, publications, case handling guides, and visiting the court. Administrative bodies provide support services for the courts. The Federal Judiciary HomePage (http://www.uscourts.gov), maintained by the Administrative Office of the United States Courts, provides links to the Supreme Court, as well as district (and, at the trial level, bankruptcy courts) and appellate courts (see http://www.uscourts.gov/links.html). The "Library" serves "as a clearinghouse for information from and about the Judicial Branch" (http://www. uscourts.gov/library.html) and includes publications, forms, statistical reports, and responses to frequently asked questions.

The Judicial Conference of the United States makes "policy with regard to the administration of the United States courts." More precisely, it

> makes a comprehensive survey of the conditions of business in the courts of the United States; prepare[s] plans for the assignment of judges to or from courts of appeals or district courts, where necessary; submit[s] suggestions to the various courts in the interest of promoting uniformity of management procedures and the expeditious conduct of court business; exercise[s] authority provided in 28 U.S.C. 372 (c) for the review of circuit council conduct and disability orders filed under that section; and . . . [carries] on a continuous study of the operation and effect of the general rules of practice and procedure in use within the federal courts, as prescribed by the Supreme Court pursuant to law. (http://www.uscourts.gov)

In addition, the Judicial Conference "supervises the Director of the Administrative Office of the United States Courts" and "acts in a variety of specific areas dealing with the administration of the courts" (http://www.uscourts.gov/judconf.html).

The Federal Judicial Center (http://www.fjc.gov), which "is the education and research agency for the Federal Courts," offers publications (e.g., "reports, manuals, monographs and other material"), historical sources (e.g., biographies of federal judges since 1789, histories of individual courts, "Topics in Judicial History," and landmark legislation), and current activities ("resources for managing capital cases, class action notice page, and recent publications").[1] In addition to presenting these sites, Chapter 7 of *U.S. Government on the Web* identifies the home page for related Web sites, such as those of some law schools, the Global Legal Information Network of the Library of Congress (LC) (http://lcweb2.loc.gov/law/GLINv1/GLIN.html), and some societies, as well as free, fee-based, and subscription services.

The purpose of this chapter is to provide an overview that complements the discussion in *U.S. Government on the Web* and to limit the discussion to information policy issues, focusing on the transition of the courts to e-government and sources at the federal level. There is no discussion of the courts at the subnational level, nor is there much discussion of the legal publishing industry that exists outside the federal court system. (For discussions of these topics, see legal reference and bibliographic tools.[2])

HISTORICAL COVERAGE

To the extent that the early federal courts purchased printing, discretionary funds were used for this purpose. Initially, however, there probably was not a great need for printing by the trial and lower appellate courts, because not many opinions or decisions were authored by judges, and handwritten copies of records largely proved to be adequate. As the quantity of judgments began to grow and accumulate and interest in these decisions increased, private reporters responded to the situation. As noted in Chapter 1, during the nineteenth century more than 200 separate case reporters, most covering only a single court, published decisions from various federal courts other than the Supreme Court. This reporting was not systematic; in some instances, the private reporters presented varying texts of the same decision, and there were problems in locating the reports for many courts anywhere but in their own locales or the largest law libraries.

Private enterprise subsequently sought to improve case law publication. In 1880 West began publishing the *Federal Reporter* series, systematically reproducing the written (not all) decisions of the federal trial and appellate courts. Collecting the decisions of the various early reporters, the West Publishing Company reorganized this material and, between 1894 and 1897, produced a thirty-volume set, entitled *Federal Cases*, containing all available lower federal court case law up to 1882. In 1932 West inaugurated the *Federal Supplement* series of trial court opinions and reserved the *Federal Reporter* for appellate court opinions. Another series, *Federal Rules Decisions*, was begun by West in 1940. It selectively reproduces a limited number of lower federal court decisions concerning procedural matters. Subsequently, a number of specialized reporting series have been commercially produced. Single copies of lower federal court decisions are available from the issuing court in typescript or printed versions called slip opinions.

The publication of Supreme Court decisions began in 1790 as a private venture when the Court's opinions were reproduced by Alexander J. Dallas, a noted Pennsylvania attorney, in four comprehensive volumes (the first of these, however, contained only decisions from several Pennsylvania courts). He discontinued this endeavor when the Court left Philadelphia for Washington, D.C., but, at the end of the 1804 term, William Cranch, then chief justice of the circuit court of the District of Columbia, took up the publication task for the 1801–1815 era. In March 1817, a statute authorized the Court to appoint and compensate a reporter for printing and publishing its decisions, with a specified number of copies being supplied, "without any expense to the United States," to "certain designated Federal officials."[3] Subsequent reporters appointed under this arrangement included Henry Wheaton (1817–1827), Richard Peters Jr. (1828–1843), Benjamin Howard (1843–1861), Jeremiah Black (1861–1863), and John Williams Wallace (1864–1875). With the decisions of the 1874 term, the so-called nominative reporter system was discontinued. It was not until 1922 that contemporary practice was established. The Supreme Court reporter was divested of all interest in the reports; the Government Printing Office (GPO) was given responsibility for securing the Court's printing, including publication of the *United States Reports* (as the published opinion series is titled); and the Superintendent of Documents was authorized to sell published opinions to the public.[4]

Interest in early Supreme Court decisions was sufficiently strong that commercial publishers were attracted to marketing these opinions. Among the more renowned ventures were (Richard) *Peter's Condensed Reports* and (Benjamin) *Curtis' Reports of Decisions*, both of which were recompilations of the Court's major rulings. The West Publishing Company launched *West's Supreme Court Reporter,* which began with decisions from the 1882 term. Following the turn of the century, commercial publishers produced additional reportorial series with research features and a multiplicity of specialized collections of Court decisions.

Publication of the decisions of the federal specialized courts has long been a government responsibility, largely realized through GPO. For example, decisions of the Court of Claims were printed as a special series of congressional documents from the court's creation in 1855 until 1863.[5] With the creation of GPO in 1860, the Superintendent of Public Printing was authorized to secure printing for all three branches, including, specifically, the Court of Claims.[6] Consequently, beginning in 1863, decisions of the Court of Claims were produced by GPO as a distinctive series. Similarly, decisions of the Customs Court, created in 1890, were initially published in semiannual volumes produced by the Treasury Department. Relocated briefly in the Justice Department in 1930, the Customs Court was statutorily transferred to the Administrative Office of the United States Courts in 1939 and, until its absorption into the Court of Appeals for the Federal Circuit in 1892, its decisions were published by GPO as a distinctive series.[7]

A number of works, including, for instance, Lawrence M. Friedman's *A History of American Law* (initially published by Simon & Schuster in 1973) provide historical coverage (see pp. 282–85). *The Oxford Companion to the Supreme Court of the United States* (Oxford University Press, 1992), edited by Kermit L. Hall, James W. Ely Jr., Joel B. Grossman, and William M. Wiecek, covers topics such as "Reports, Supreme Court" (pp. 727–28) and "Reporting of Opinions" (pp. 728–29).

POLICY CONTEXT

Associate Justice Stephen Breyer once observed that:

> . . . the Constitution considered as a whole, creates a framework for a certain kind of government. Its general objectives can be described abstractly as including (1) democratic self-government, (2) dispersion of power (avoiding concentration of too much power in too few hands), (3) individual dignity (through protection of individual liberties), (4) equality before the law (through equal protection of the law), and (5) the rule of law itself.

> . . . the Court, while always respecting language, tradition, and precedent, nonetheless has emphasized different general constitutional objectives at different periods in its history. Thus one can characterize the early nineteenth century as a period during which the Court helped to establish the authority of

the federal government, including the federal judiciary. During the late nineteenth and early twentieth centuries, the Court under-emphasized the Constitution's efforts to secure participation by black citizens in representative government—efforts related to the participatory "active" liberty of the ancients. At the same time, it over-emphasized protection of property rights, such as an individual's freedom to contract without government interference, to the point where President Franklin Roosevelt commented that the Court's *Lochner*-era decisions had created a legal "no-man's land" that neither state nor federal regulatory authority had the power to enter.

The New Deal Court and the Warren Court in part re-emphasized "active liberty." The former did so by dismantling various *Lochner*-era distinctions, thereby expanding the scope of democratic self-government. The latter did so by interpreting the Civil War Amendments in light of their purposes and to mean what they say, thereby helping Africa-Americans become members of the Nation's community of self-governing citizens—a community that the Court expanded further in its "one person, one vote" decisions.

More recently, in my view, the Court has again under-emphasized the importance of the citizen's active liberty. I will argue for a contemporary re-emphasis that better combines "the liberty of the ancients" with that "freedom of governmental restraint" that Constant called "modern."[8]

Jane E. Kirtley, a professor, lawyer, and former media reporter, looking at the most recent period and access issues, has observed that the public now scrutinizes the judicial branch "to an unprecedented extent." Yet, that branch of government "remains a uniquely arcane and impenetrable world with language and procedures that are often forbidding to the layperson."[9]

E-GOVERNMENT

The federal judiciary rapidly expanded its presence on the Web in the late 1990s. More courts provide access to resources (e.g., opinions) and make a concerted effort to disseminate those resources broadly. The diversity of these resources has also expanded and the Web sites are more stable: fewer dead links and less shifting of contents to new URLs.[10] Furthermore, the judiciary sees an instructional role for its Web sites by providing resources useful to teachers and their students.

With the unfolding of Project Hermes, the Supreme Court began the electronic dissemination of its opinions. In summer 2001, the Judicial Conference of the United States Committee on Automation and Technology, as part of a concern about privacy and security issues related to the provision of electronic public access to court case files, recommended that courts limit the case information they place on the Web. In September, the Judicial Conference, which is the principal policymaking body for the federal court system, reviewed the recommendations and decided to post documents relating to civil cases online but not to do the same for criminal case files, which contain the names and addresses of law enforcement officials and crime witnesses. Federal court files are available online for a fee of seven cents per page. A "model appropriate use policy" banned court employees from using their office computers to access file-sharing services, such as Napster, or to create, download, view, store, copy, or transmit sexually explicit materials or those related to gambling or illegal weapons.[11]

The courts offer different electronic services and resources that are discussed in the annual *Directory of Electronic Public Access Services to Automated Information in the United States Federal Courts* (http://pacer.psc. uscourts.gov/pubaccess.html). This directory describes Public Access to Court Electronic Records (PACER), an electronic public access service of the Administrative Office of the United States Courts that allows users to obtain case and docket information from the district, bankruptcy, and appellate courts, and from the *U.S. Party/Case Index*, a national index for these courts that allows searchers to find out whether a party is involved in federal litigation almost anywhere in the nation (see http://pacer.uspci.uscourts.gov; http://pacer.psc.uscourts.gov/ pacerdesc.html). Another tool is *The Third Branch*, a monthly newsletter of the Administrative Office of the U.S. Courts, produced since 1995 and providing articles on the works of the courts (http://www.uscourts.gov/ttb/index.html).

SUPREME COURT

The Supreme Court comprises the chief justice of the United States and such number of associate justices as Congress determines. By an Act of June 25, 1948 (28 U.S.C. 1), Congress set the number of associate justices at eight. The president nominates each justice and the Senate engages in advice and consent. Justices then hold the position "during good Behaviour" (Article III, section 1); there is no term limit. Article III, section 2 specifies the areas to which judicial power extends, and, according to 28 U.S.C. 2071 et seq., Congress has conferred on the Supreme Court the power to prescribe rules of procedure to be followed by the lower courts. The Court's term begins on the first Monday in October and lasts until the first Monday in October of the next year.

Opinions

The opinions of the Supreme Court are publicly disseminated

by means of four printed publications and two computerized services. Prior to the issuance of (1) bound volumes of the U.S. Reports, the Court's official decisions appear in three temporary printed forms: (2) bench opinions (which are transmitted electronically to subscribers over the Court's Project Hermes service); (3) slip opinions (which are posted . . . [electronically]; and (4) preliminary prints. (http://www.supremecourtus/opinions/info_opinions.html)

"In addition to all of the opinions issued during a particular period," a bound volume of the *United States Reports*

> may contain a roster of Justices and Court officers during that period; an allotment of Justices by Federal Circuit; announcements of Justices' investitures and retirements; memorial proceedings for deceased Justices; a cumulative table of cases reported; orders in cases decided in summary fashion; reprints of amendments to the Supreme Court's Rules and the various sets of Federal Rules of Procedure; a topical index; and a statistical table summarizing case activity for the past three Court Terms. (http://www.supremecourtus/opinions/info_opinions.html)

The Court's opinion Web page provides additional clarification of bench opinions, slip opinions, preliminary prints, and bound volumes:

> • **Bench Opinions**: On days that opinions are announced by the Court from the bench, the text of each opinion is made available immediately to the public and the press in a printed form called a "bench opinion." The bench opinion pamphlet for each case consists of the majority or plurality opinion, any concurring or dissenting opinions written by the Justices, and a prefatory syllabus prepared by the Reporter's office that provides a synopsis of the decision. Bench opinions are printed at the Court in 5 ½ x 8 ½ . . . [inch] self-cover pamphlets. They are made available to the public by the Court's Public Information Office. The text of each bench opinion is also disseminated electronically via Project Hermes, one of the Court's two opinion dissemination systems (this Website is the other). The Hermes system is basically a file server linked by modem to paying subscribers, who include universities, news media, publishing companies, and other private organizations. A number of these organizations provide on-line access to the bench opinions, either directly or via the Internet, within hours after they are released by the Court. Hermes subscribers who redisseminate bench opinions to the general public are identified in the file entitled *"Where to Obtain Supreme Court Opinions"* . . . [see below].

> **Caution**: In case of discrepancies between the print and electronic versions of a bench opinion, the print version controls. Moreover, bench opinions are replaced, generally within hours, by slip opinion pamphlets and, in case of discrepancies between the bench and slip opinions, the slip opinion controls.

> • **Slip Opinions**: Several days after an opinion is announced by the Court, it is printed in a 6 x 9 . . . [inch] self-cover pamphlet called a "slip opinion." Each slip opinion consists of the majority or plurality, any concurring or dissenting opinions, and the syllabus. It may contain corrections not appearing in the bench opinion. Slip opinion page proofs are sent to a commercial printing company under contract with the GPO, and the company prints the slip opinions in accordance with the Court's specifications. The slip opinion pamphlets are distributed free of charge, while supplies last, by the Court's Public

Information Office. They are also sold by the Office of the Superintendent of Document at GPO regional bookstores. The text of each slip opinion is also disseminated electronically via posting on this Website, usually within hours after the opinion is announced. The number of slip opinions published each term has varied over the years from as few as 75 to as many as 150.

Caution: In case of discrepancies between the print and electronic versions of a slip opinion, the print version controls. Moreover, individual slip opinions are cumulated and replaced within months by preliminary print pamphlets and, in case of discrepancies between the slip opinion and preliminary print version of a case, the preliminary print controls.

• **Preliminary Prints**: The preliminary prints of the *U.S. Reports* constitute the third generation of opinion publication and dissemination. These are brown, soft-cover "advance pamphlets" that contain, in addition to the opinions themselves, all of the announcements, tables, indexes, and other features that make up the *U.S. Reports*. The contents of two, or in some instances three, preliminary prints will eventually be combined into a single bound volume. Thus, the title of each preliminary print includes a part number, e.g., Preliminary print, Volume 530, Part 1. Prior to publication, all of the materials that go into a preliminary print undergo an extensive editing and indexing process, and permanent page numbers are assigned that will carry over into the bound volume. Copies of the page proofs to be published in a preliminary print are sent to a commercial printing company under contract with the GPO, and that company prints the pamphlets in accordance with the Court's specifications. Official versions of preliminary prints are made available to the public by the Office of Superintendent of Documents at the GPO, and can be purchased either through annual subscription or over the counter at GPO regional bookstores. The number of preliminary prints published for each term varies from as few as 8 to as many as 12 separate issues, depending on the number of opinions issued during the term. "Sliplists"[12] identifying cases to appear in upcoming preliminary prints, as well as Counsel Listing[13] for those cases, are posted on this website.

Caution: Individual preliminary prints are cumulated and replaced about a year later by bound volumes, and, in case of discrepancies between the preliminary print and bound volume versions of a case, the bound volume controls.

• **Bound Volumes**: The fourth and final generation of opinion publication is the casebound set of law books entitled *United States Reports*. The opinions and other materials contained in the preliminary prints are published in this series of books. Prior to publication, all of the opinions and other materials that make up each volume undergo a final editing and indexing process. The materials are then sent to a commercial printing company under contract with the GPO, and that company prints and binds the books in accordance with the Court's specifications. The official bound volumes are sold by the Superintendent of Documents at the GPO, and can be purchased over the counter at GPO regional bookstores. The number of bound volumes published each Term varies from as few as three to as many as five, depending on the number of opinions issued during the Term. Electronic versions of bound volumes issued for October Term 1991 and subsequent years will be posted on this Website after the printed volumes have been issued.

Caution: In case of discrepancies between the print and electronic versions of these bound volume materials, the print version controls. In addition, GPO Access includes, as a convenience to users, a database of unofficial versions of bound volume opinions issued between 1937 and 1975.[14] This database was created by the Air Force and is made available as a finding aid only. Because neither GPO nor the Court has performed costly validation processes, the authenticity or completeness of the data cannot be verified. Only the bound volumes of the *United States Reports* contain the final, official text of the opinion of the Supreme Court (http://www.supremecourtus/opinions/info_opinions.html).

At http://www.supremecourtus.gov/opinions/01slipopinion.html, the Court offers additional discussion of slip opinions.

Each year the staff of the Supreme Court compiles a list of Supreme Court opinion publishers. That list identifies official publishers of print and electronic opinions and unofficial publishers of print, microform, and electronic (online, CD-ROM, and fax) opinions (see http://www.supremecourtus.gov/opinions/opinions.html).

Orders

The vast majority of cases filed in the Supreme Court are disposed of summarily by unsigned orders. Such an order will, for example, deny a petition for certiorari without comment. Regularly scheduled lists of orders are issued on each Monday that the Court sits, but "miscellaneous" orders may be issued in individual cases at any time. Scheduled order lists are posted . . . on the day of their issuance, while miscellaneous orders are posted on the day of issuance or the next day (http://www.supremecourtus.gov/orders/01ordersofthecourt.html).

Journal

The *Journal of the Supreme Court of the United States*

contains the official minutes of the Court. It is published chronologically for each day the Court issues orders or opinions. The Journal reflects the disposition of each case, names the court whose judgment is under review, lists the cases argued that day and the attorneys who presented oral argument, contains miscellaneous announcements by the Chief Justice from the Bench, and sets forth the names of attorneys admitted to the Bar of the Supreme Court. It does not contain the opinions of the Court, which are published in the *United States Reports*. (http://www.supremecourtus.gov/orders/journal.html)

Electronic files of the *Journal* date from October 1993.

Court Rules

The Court's rules, as revised on January 11, 1999, are available at http://www.supremecourtus.gov/ctrules/ctrules.html. This page also identifies citations for previous revisions of the rules. The rules cover topics such as court jurisdiction, the admission of attorneys to the bar, and making motions to a justice.

Docket

"The automated docket system is the Court's case tracking system. It contains information about cases, both pending and decided" (http://www. supremecourtus.gov/docket/docket,html). It is possible to search for cases by using the Supreme Court docket number at http://www.supremecourtus.gov/ docket/docket.html.

Case Citation Finder

Found at the Supreme Court Web site, the Case Citation Finder "sets forth the official citations, in the form recommended by the Reporter of Decisions, for every signed, *per curiam*,[15] and in-chambers opinions published (or soon to be published) in the *United States Reports*" (http://www.supremecourtus.gov/ opinions/casefinder.html). The citations are divided into eight court terms, dating from 1790, and there is guidance on how to conduct a search (see http:// www.supremcourtus.gov/opinions/casefinder.html).

Other

"Public Information" (http://www.supremecourtus.gov/publicinfo/publicinfo. html) includes press releases, speeches by some justices, media advisories, and so forth. Another item is "Related Websites," which, among other options, includes the National Association of Attorneys General, the Office of the Solicitor General, and the Supreme Court Historical Society (http://www.supremecourtus.gov/ websites/websites.html).

"Oral Arguments" (http://www.supremecourtus.gov/oral_arguments/oral_ arguments.html) covers the Court's schedule, argument calendars, day call, hearing list, argument transcripts, "Where to Find Briefs," and so forth. Another page, "About the Supreme Court" (http://www.supremecourtus.gov/about/ about.html), provides PDF documents on the history of the Court, biographies of the justices, "Members of the Supreme Court (1789 to Present)," information on the Supreme Court building, and so forth.

OTHER FEDERAL COURTS

There are ninety-four federal judicial districts, including a minimum of one district per state and the District of Columbia and Puerto Rico. These districts have trial or district courts. The Virgin Islands, Guam, and the Northern Mariana Islands also have district courts. "Federal courts have exclusive jurisdiction over bankruptcy cases":

> [Such] cases cannot be filed in state court. Each of the . . . federal judicial districts handles bankruptcy matters. The primary purposes of the law of bankruptcy are: (1) to give an honest debtor a 'fresh start' in life by relieving the debtor of most debts, and (2) to repay creditors in an orderly manner to the extent that the debtor has property available for payment. (http://www. uscourts.gov/bankruptcycourts.html)

Two special trial courts have national jurisdiction over certain kinds of cases. First, the Court of International Trade "addresses cases involving international trade and customs issues." Next, the United States Court of Federal Claims has jurisdiction over "most claims for money damages against the United States, disputes over federal contracts, unlawful 'takings' of private property by the federal government, and a variety of other claims against the United States" (http://www.uscourts.gov/districtcourts.html).

The judicial districts are organized into twelve regional circuits, each of which has a court of appeals that hears appeals from the district courts located within their circuit as well as appeals from decisions of federal administrative agencies. The Court of Appeals for the Federal Circuit "has nationwide jurisdiction to hear cases in specialized cases, such as those involving patent laws and cases decided by the Court of International Trade and the Court of Federal Claims" (http://www.uscourts.gov/courtsofappeals.html). As previously noted, the Web sites for all of these courts are available at http://www.uscourts.gov/links.html (or see Chapter 7 of *U.S. Government on the Web*).

Researcher Robert A. Mead has noted that, "in the 1970s, the federal courts of appeals enacted limited publication rules that allowed the circuits to determine which judicial opinions should be released for publication."[16] In the pre-Internet age, unpublished opinions "were essentially undiscoverable, unless the opinion was somehow newsworthy or the researcher gleaned information from an attorney familiar with the case." With the Internet and electronic databases, " 'unpublished' opinions are published electronically, in more or less the same manner as other decisions of the federal courts of appeals."[17] However, "unpublished" opinions may not be cited or relied upon in briefs or argument.

OTHER SOURCES

An excellent starting point for Web sites that specialize in legal information is the Library of Congress page on "U.S. Judicial Branch Resources." Among the resources are:

- *The Constitution of the United States of America, Analysis and Interpretation*, which "provides annotations to cases bearing on Constitutional law decided by the Supreme Court";

- *The Constitution and Annotations*, with links to full text Supreme Court opinions from 1906 to July 1, 1996;

- Other useful Constitution-related sites;

- The *United States Code*;

- U.S. Code Classification tables (in Public Law, title, and section order);

- The Public Laws Index;

- Popular Names Tables ("a listing of commonly used names for laws, e.g., 'Brady Law' ");

- State statutes;

- Regulations (*Federal Register*, *Code of Federal Regulations*, and Unified Agenda, which "summarizes the rules and proposed rules that each federal agency expects to issue during the following six months");

- Judicial opinions (for Supreme Court, Circuit Courts of Appeal, and state courts);

- Court rules (Federal Rules of Civil Procedure, Federal Rules of Evidence, and Supreme Court rules);

- Comptroller General decisions;

- Selected "Executive Branch Material (e.g., for executive orders);

- Law journals; and

- Law-related Internet sites. (http://lcweb.loc.gov/global/judiciary.html)

The Library of Congress Law Library also offers the "United States Judiciary: The Federal Court System and Decisions" (http://www.loc.gov/law/guide/usjudic.html), which provides:

- Overviews: "About the Supreme Court;" "History of the Federal Judiciary;" and "Understanding the Federal Courts," which "discusses the relationship between the U.S. federal court system and the various states";

- Access to Supreme Court decisions from a variety of Web sites;

- Access to the sites of the U.S. Court of Appeals and the district courts;

- Access to the sites of courts of "special jurisdiction": U.S. Court of Appeals for Armed Forces, U.S. Court of Appeals for Veterans Claims, U.S. Court of Federal Claims, U.S. Court of International Trade, and U.S. Tax Court;

- Federal Court Procedure: Federal Rules of Appellate Procedure, Federal Rules of Civil Procedure, Federal Rules of Criminal Procedure, and Federal Rules of Evidence; and

- Miscellaneous: links to court Web sites, the U.S. Federal Courts Finder of Emory University School of Law ("provides a map and text links to online collections of decisions of the courts of the U.S. federal system"), and so forth. (http:/www.loc.gov/law/guide/usjudic.html)

GPO Access provides some judicial resources (i.e., the case of *State of New York, ex. rel. Eliot Spitzer, et al. v. Microsoft Corporation*, Supreme Court Decisions, and a list of Judicial Branch Web Sites) and access to those judicial branch Web sites hosted on GPO Access (see http://www.access.gpo.gov/su_docs/judicial.html).

The General Services Administration provides FedLaw for quick access to a variety of legal resources from other government Web sites, including access to the *United States Code*, GAO decisions, laws and regulations, "Arbitration and Mediation" ("federal laws; arbitration and mediation rules; alternate dispute resolution"), general research and reference ("legal and business research sites; finding people, places, and things"), professional associations and organizations, "How-to legal-related Sites" ("tips for lawyers and about writing"), privacy policy, and so forth (http://www.legal.gsa.gov).

Bernan (Lanham, Md., http://www.berman.com) has published a *Biographical Directory of the Federal Judiciary, 1779–2000*, which lists judges and justices by administration and provides an index of important cases and of judges by degree-granting university or law school.

Naturally, Lexis and Westlaw are excellent providers of a wide assortment of resources on the judiciary, and both have fee-based Web sites. The former (http://www.lexis.com/research) includes a variety of products and services, citation format assistance, citations services, and database searching. Westlaw (http://www.westlaw.com/), which is a product of West Group, also offers full-text coverage of legal documents from the federal judiciary.

FindLaw (http://www.findlaw.com/) provides links to legal resources, government Web sites, and legal services. There is a bookstore and access to the Supreme Court Center, which identifies those lawyers who practice before the Court and their area of legal practice.

CONCLUSION

Anyone new to legal bibliography and research should consult the URL listed in the chapter's first endnote, which explains the role of and lists finding aids produced by the government and the not-for-profit and commercial sectors. Core materials useful in researching legal issues include dictionaries, encyclopedias, directories, indexes, handbooks, and so forth. For example, Shepard's Citations traces a reference in a later authority (*citing* a source such as case or statute) to an earlier authority (*cited* source). The concept is similar to citation indexes, such as the *Social Sciences Citation Index*. Using Shepard's, one can determine the history of a cited source (e.g., whether a higher court reversed a decision or a statute was repealed) and how other courts and secondary sources (e.g., law review articles) have remarked on the cited source. For an excellent introductory tutorial on "How to Shepardize," see http://helpcite.shepards.com/howtoshep/howto1.htm.

Before using these materials, it might be useful to review a brief pamphlet, *Understanding the Federal Courts*, that explains the jurisdiction of the various courts and whether a certain type of case will be heard at the federal or state level. This pamphlet can be found at http://www.uscourts.gov/UFC99.pdf, and the Administrative Office of the U.S. Courts maintains a page intended for "Educational Outreach" that offers lesson plans for high school teachers as well as other resources for the educational community.

There are vast amounts of government information available to the public through government and nongovernment Web sites. However, the lay public may be disadvantaged in the quest for public information from the courts because of a lack of a strong foundation in the conduct of legal research. Nonetheless, the courts and law schools have done an excellent job in presenting types of materials on their Web sites so that the lay public can easily find what is available. Electronic services, such as PACER, enable the public to keep abreast of new developments. At the same time, the legal sites serve a more specialized population, the law community. This community will also draw on the resources of the for-profit sector for their value-added enhancements. Carol M. Bast and Ransford C. Pyle, professors of criminal justice at the University of Central Florida, see a dramatic shift in legal research to reliance on online searching and online value-added enhancements.[18]

Clearly the Web continues to grow as an important resource for legal researchers. Researcher Robert C. Vreeland notes that "interface design is one of the few aspects of library Web sites that has been studied in detail." He then describes a citation study that identifies those Web servers linked most frequently from law library Web sites. The list includes LC's THOMAS and sites for both chambers of Congress, law schools, general portals (e.g., Yahoo!), GPO Access, other government agencies, newspapers, the for-profit sector, and so forth.[19] It is our hope that this chapter and book will assist in reshaping that list and the sites most frequently searched.[20]

NOTES

1. For a discussion of the resources of the Federal Judicial Center, see Barbara L. Fritschel, "An Index to Special Court Sessions in West's Federal Reporters," *Law Library Journal* 93 (Winter 2001): 109–10.

2. Examples of such sources are Robert C. Berring, *Finding the Law* (St. Paul, Minn.: West, 1995); Robert C. Berring and Elizabeth A. Edinger, *Finding the Law* (St. Paul, Minn.: West, 1999); Morris L. Cohen and Kent C. Olson, *Legal Research in a Nutshell* (Eagan, Minn.: West, 1996); J. Myron Jacobstein, Roy M. Mersky, and Donald J. Dunn, *Fundamentals of Legal Research* (New York: Foundation Press, 1998); Kendall F. Svengalis, *The Legal Information Buyer's Guide & Reference Manual, 1998–99* (Barrington: Rhode Island Law Press, 1998); Jerry Lawson, *The Complete Internet Handbook for Lawyers* (Chicago: American Bar Association, Law Practice Management Section, 1999); Christina L. Kunz, *The Process of Legal Research* (Boston: Little, Brown, 1996); Antje Mays, *Legal Research on the Internet: A Compendium of Websites to Access United States Federal, State, Local and International Laws* (Buffalo, N.Y.: William S. Hein, 1999); Erik J. Heels and Richard P. Klau, *Law, Law, Law, on the Internet: The Best Legal Web Sites and More* (Chicago: American Bar Association, Law Practice Management Section, 1998); Stephen Elias and Susan Levinkind, *Legal Research: How to Find & Understand the Law* (Berkeley, Calif.: Nolo.com, 1999); and Nancy P. Johnson, Robert C. Berring, and Thomas A. Woxland, *Winning Research Skills* (Eagan, Minn.: West, 1999).

3. See 3 Stat. 376.

4. See 42 Stat. 816.

5. Laurence F. Schmeckebier and Roy B. Eastin, *Government Publications and Their Use*, 2nd revised ed. (Washington, D.C.: The Brookings Institution, 1969), 283.

6. See 12 Stat. 117.

7. Schmeckebier and Eastin, *Government Publications and Their Use*, 285–87.

8. Associate Justice Stephen Breyer, "Our Democratic Constitution," The Fall 2001 James Madison Lecture, New York University Law School (October 22, 2001), 2–3, available at http://www.supremecourtus.gov/publicinfo/speech/sp_1022-01.html.

9. Jane E. Kirtley, ""Access to the Judicial Branch," in *Federal Information Policies in the 1990s: Views and Perspectives*, ed. Peter Hernon, Charles R. McClure, and Harold C. Relyea (Norwood, N.J.: Ablex, 1996), 67.

10. These observations are based on a comparison of Web sites from the first and second editions of *U.S. Government on the Web*.

11. "Judicial Conference Approves Recommendations on Electronic Case File Availability and Internet Use," *News Release* (September 19, 2001).

12. "Each of these lists [Sliplists] discloses the *U.S. Reports* volume and part numbers for a particular preliminary print; sets forth the name and citation of each case that will appear in that preliminary print; notes each case's docket number and date of issuance; specifies the sequential 'R' number assigned by the reported of Decisions to the slip opinion after it was issued; and includes a brief summary of the case's holding. As

new slip opinions are issued during the October term . . . . Sliplist entries for those opinions will be added here. As new bound volumes are published, their Sliplist entries will be deleted" (see http://www.supremecourtus.gov/opinions/sliplists.html).

13. "A counsel listing identifies all Supreme Court bar members who participated in a particular case argued before the Court. Each of the lists collected here cumulates in the counsel listings for a number of cases argued during October Terms . . ., setting forth the *U.S. Reports* volume and part number for the particular preliminary print in which the cases will appear; disclosing the docket number, name, and date of argument of each such case; identifying the counsel who argued each case; and specifying each individual attorney whose name appears on a brief on the merits if he or she was a member of the Court's Bar at the time the case was argued. As new opinions are issued during the . . . Term, counsel listing for those opinions will be added here. As new bound volumes are published, their Counsel Listings will be deleted here.

Caution: These electronic listings may contain computer-generated errors or other deviations from the official printed versions of the counsel listings as they will appear in the preliminary print or, about a year later, in the bound volume of the *U.S. Reports*. In case of discrepancies between the print and electronic versions of a counsel listing, the print version controls. Counsel are requested to report errors in these listings to the Reporter of Decisions" (see http://www.supremecourtus.gov/opinions/counsellist.html).

14. See "Search Supreme Court Decisions, 1937–1975" on GPO Access, http://www.access.gpo.gov/su_docs/supcrt/index.html.

15. *Per curiam* is a phrase that distinguishes an opinion of the whole court from that written by a single judge. It also refers to "an opinion written by the chief justice or presiding judge, or to a brief announcement of the disposition of a case by a court" without the accompaniment of a written opinion. See *Black's Law Dictionary*®, 6th ed. (St. Paul, Minn.: West, 1990), 1136.

16. Robert A. Mead, " 'Unpublished' Opinions as the Bulk of the Iceberg: Publication Patterns in the Eight and Tenth Circuits of the United States Courts of Appeals," *Law Library Journal* 93 (Fall 2001): 589.

17. Ibid.

18. Carol M. Bast and Ransford C. Pyle, "Legal Research in the Computer Age: A Paradigm Shift?" *Law Library Journal* 93 (Spring 2001): 285–302.

19. Robert C. Vreeland, "Law Libraries in Hyperspace: A Citation Analysis of World Wide Web Sites," *Law Library Journal* 92 (Winter 2000): 9–25.

20. Given the reliance of legal researchers on general portals and search engines, as Vreeland found (see note 19), the question arises as to how these tools can be improved. For that discussion, see Deanna Barmakian, "Better Search Engines for Law," *Law Library Journal* 92 (Fall 2000): 399–438.

URL SITE GUIDE

Federal Judiciary Home Page
http://www.uscourts.gov/

> Directory of Electronic Public Access Services ..
> http://pacer.psc.uscourts.gov/pubaccess.html
>
> Library
> http://www.uscourts.gov/library.html
>
> Links to Appellate and Trial Courts
> http://www.uscourts.gov/links.html
>
> The Third Branch
> http://www.uscourts.gov/ttb/index.html

Bankruptcy Courts
http://www.uscourts.gov/bankruptcycourts.html

http://www.uscourts.gov/links.html

Bernan
http://www.berman.com

Courts of Appeals
http://www.uscourts.gov/courtsofappeals.html

District Courts
http://www.uscourts.gov/districtcourts.html

http://www.uscourts.gov/links.html

Federal Judicial Center
http://www.fjc.gov/

FedLaw
General Services Administration
http://www.legal.gsa.gov/

FindLaw
http://www.findlaw.com/

Graphic Depiction (Federal Court System)
http://www.uscourts.gov/outreach/structure.jpg

How to Shepardize
http://helpcite.shepards.com/howtoshep/howto1.htm.

Judicial Conference of the United States
http://www.uscourts.gov/judconf.html

Judicial Resources (GPO Access)
http://www.access.gpo.gov/su_docs/judicial.html

Lexis-Nexis
http://www.lexis.com/research

Library of Congress
http://lcweb.loc.gov

Global Legal Information Network
http://lcweb2.loc.gov/law/GLINv1/GLIN.html

United States Judiciary: The Federal Court System and Decisions
http://www.loc.gov/law/guide/usjudic.html

U.S. Judicial Branch Resources
http://lcweb.loc.gov/global/judiciary.html

PACER
http://pacer.psc.uscourts.gov/pacerdesc.html

Directory of Electronic Public Access Services to Automated

Information in the United States Federal Courts
http://pacer.psc.uscourts.gov/pubaccess.html

U.S. Party/Case Index
http://pacer.uspci.uscourts.gov/

Supreme Court
http://www.supremecourtus.gov

About the Supreme Court
http://www.supremecourtus.gov/about/about.html

Case Citation Finder
http://www.supremecourtus.gov/opinions/casefinder.html

Counsel Listings
http://www.supremecourtus.gov/opinions/counsellist.html

Docket
http://www.supremecourtus.gov/docket/docket.html

Information about Opinions
http://www.supremecourtus.gov/opinions/info_opinions.html

Journal
http://www.supremecourtus.gov/orders/journal.html

Oral Arguments
http://www.supremecourtus.gov/oral_arguments/oral_
arguments.html

Orders
http://www.supremcourtus.gov/orders/01ordersofthecourt.html

Public Information
http://www.supremecourtus.gov/publicinfo/publicinfo.html

Related Web Sites
http://www.supremecourtus.gov/websites/websites.html

Rules
http://www.supremecourtus.gov/ctrules/ctrules.html

Search Supreme Court Decisions, 1937–1975

GPO Access
http://www.access.gpo.gov/su_docs/supcrt/index.html

Sliplists
http://www.supremecourtus.gov/opinions/sliplists.html

Slip Opinions
http://www.supremecourtus.gov/opinions/01slipopinion.html

Where to Obtain Supreme Court Opinions
http://www.supremecourtus.gov/opinions/opinions.html

The Third Branch
http://www.uscourts.gov/ttb/index.html

Understanding the Federal Courts
http://www.uscourts.gov/UFC99.pdf

Westlaw
http://www.westlaw.com/

Chapter 12

Intellectual Property

Article I , section 8, of the Constitution vests Congress with the "power . . . [t]o promote the progress of science and useful arts by securing for limited times to authors and inventors the exclusive right to their respective writings and discoveries." Herein is recognition for congressional legislation concerning "intellectual property," a broad term relating to products that originate in the creative mind and include patents, trademarks and service marks, copyrights, trade names, and trade secrets.[1] This chapter highlights federal policy concerning each of these types of intellectual property.

HISTORICAL COVERAGE

In 1802, the Superintendent of Patents, an official in the Department of State, was first placed in charge of patents, but in 1836, when patent law was revised, that office was displaced by the Commissioner of Patents and Trademarks, who headed the Patent and Trademark Office in the State Department. Then, in 1849, the Office was transferred to the Department of the Interior, and, in 1925, was relocated to the Department of Commerce, where the USPTO continues to reside.

Several copyright laws predate the currently effective 1976 Act. In 1906, the Copyright Office issued *Copyright Enactments of the United States, 1783–1906*, compiled by Thorvald Solberg, which included earlier federal copyright laws (1790–1906), proclamations (1891–1905), treaties (1899–1906), state laws (1895–1905), and attorney general rulings and decisions. As Laurence F. Schmeckebier and Roy B. Eastin point out, a 1963 revision of Bulletin No. 3 included that compilation. Issued in 1967, Bulletin 14 also covered copyright law.[2] Schmeckebier and Eastin devote limited attention to patents; for information on conducting an historical patent search, review the figures in this chapter, especially Figure 12.4 (page 287) and its inclusion of "Academic Research." The historical indexes discussed in Chapter 2 provide additional coverage, including the annual reports of the above-mentioned agencies.

The National Archives and Records Administration (NARA) contains related records, such as those of the Senate committees overseeing patents. For example, it has the records of the Committee on Patents and the Patent Office, which was established in 1837, and its successor, the Committee on Patents, which was in existence from 1869 to 1946. Beginning in 1947, jurisdiction reverted to the Judiciary Committee, which had dealt with matters related to patents prior to 1837.

For a more complete picture of earlier years, see Edward C. Walterscheld, *To Promote the Progress of Useful Arts: American Patent Law and Administration, 1787–1836* (Fred B. Rothman, 1998); Kenneth W. Dobyns, *A History of the Early Patent Offices: The Patent Office Pony* (Societies and Association, 1997), which includes a discussion of the Union and Confederate patent offices; Aubert J. Clark, *Movement for International Copyright in Nineteenth Century America* (Greenwood, 1960); Frank I. Schechter and Munroe Smith, *The Historical Foundations of the Law Relating to Trade-Marks* (Lawbook Exchange, 2000); Mark Rose, *Authors and Owners: The Invention of Copyright* (Harvard University Press, 1993); and Gillian Davies, *Copyright and the Public Interest* (Commercial, 1994).

PATENTS

Patents provide exclusive rights to produce, use, and offer for sale an invention for a limited time (a maximum of twenty years) and can be subdivided into three types. First, *utility patents* protect useful processes, machines, articles of manufacture, and compositions of matter. Examples include medications and computer hardware. Second, *design patents* guard against the unauthorized use of new, original, and ornamental designs for articles of manufacture. Third, *plant patents* protect invented or discovered, asexually reproduced plant varieties (by means other than from seeds, such as grafting, budding, or layering). A plant patent is granted on the entire plant. The Plant Variety Protection Act (PL 91-577), enacted in 1970, provides protection for sexually reproduced varieties for which protection was not previously provided, and is administered by the Plant Variety Protection Office of the Department of Agriculture.

The U.S. Patent and Trademark Office (USPTO), an agency of the Department of Commerce, serves the interests of inventors and the business community by granting patents and registering trademarks. It also advises and assists other agencies within the department and government on matters related to intellectual property. USPTO's home page provides access to every U.S. patent issued from 1790 to the present.[3] One page covers "Patents Legislation & Regulations" (http://www.uspto.gov/web/patents/legis.htm); some of these resources are available in PDF format.

As shown in Figure 12.1, USPTO has a Web page for "Patents" (http://www.uspto.gov/main/patents.htm) that covers "Services," "Patent Guides," "International Protection," "Patenting," and "Resources." One of the services includes the option of searching the *Official Gazette,* the official journal for both patents and trademarks. (Published since 1872, one part covers patents and the other addresses trademarks.) There is an "Electronic Filing System" (http://www.uspto.gov/ebc/efs/index.html) for submitting new utility patent applications; biosequence listings for applications already filed in paper; "pre-grant publication resubmissions for previously filed applications, where the applicant wants an amended, redacted, voluntary, or republication specification to be published rather than the application as originally filed"; and provisional applications; and multiple assignments (http://www.uspto.gov/ebc/efs/index.html).

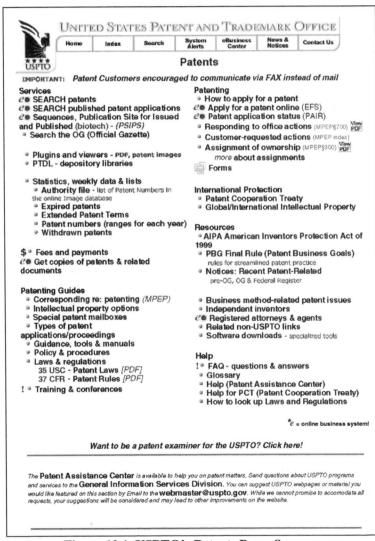

Figure 12.1. USPTO's Patents Page. *Source:*
http://www.uspto.gov/main/patents.htm.

USPTO's "Check Status" (http://www.uspto.gov/main/checkstatus.htm) permits individuals to check the status of a patent, look up registered patent attorneys and agents, track legislation and regulations, and so forth. One page covers patent grants and applications (http://www.uspto.gov/patft/), another leads to the Electronic Business Center (see Figure 12.2), and another page pertains to resources on the "American Inventor's Protection Act of 1999" (PL 106-113) (http://www.uspto.gov/web/offices/dcom/olia/aipa/index.htm). For example, there is the text of the legislation, related forms, and articles about the act.

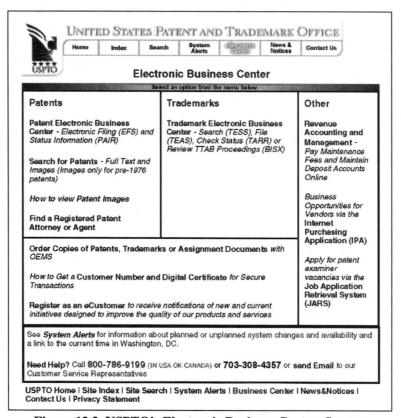

Figure 12.2. USPTO's Electronic Business Center. *Source:*
http://www.uspto.gov/ebc/indexebc.htm.

The National Agricultural Library of the Department of Agriculture has a Web page on "Ag Biotechnology Patents and New Technologies" (see http://www.nal.usda.gov/bic/Biotech_Patents). It provides the full text of biotechnology patents for the years 1994–1996 as well as links to pages within the department and elsewhere.

Legal Information Institute (LII) (http://www.law.cornell.edu/topics/patents.html) of the Cornell University School of Law provides an excellent introduction to various laws, court cases (Supreme Court and appellate court), and conventions and treaties, as well as other information (e.g., links to appropriate Web sites). The Community of Science, Inc., has "Search U.S. Patents" (http://patents.cos.com/), a "comprehensive bibliographic database containing records for . . . the patents issued since 1975" (http://patents.cos.com). Delphion (http://www.delphion.com) lets anyone search (by keyword or phrase) for patents (granted and applications) from its U.S. and European patent collections. It is also possible to search abstracts of Japanese patents. The Internet Patent News Service offers services, such as a Web site (http://www.bustpatents.com) "focusing on patent information—economics, legal analysis, statistics, court rulings, patent analysis tools and more."

The Process of Patent Searching

Anyone searching for patents or trademarks for the first time would be well advised to visit a patent and trademark depository library in person or virtually (via its Web site) (see Chapter 15). Louisiana State University has produced an excellent step-by-step guide for conducting a patent search online. There are even helpful notes; for example, under "finding the patents in the classification," there is mention that

> this is where the web gets patent searchers into trouble. Most web databases only cover from the mid-1970's to the present. You must search as far back in time as it was technologically possible for your invention to exist. (http://www.lib.lsu.edu/sci/ptdl/patsearch.htm)

Another page at this Web site identifies books on patents and trademarks (http://www.lib.lsu.edu/sci/ptdl/patbooks.htm; http://www.lib.lsu.edu/sci/ptdl/tmbooks.htm).

Finally, Eugene R. Quinn Jr. and Kathleen A. Portuán Miller provide an excellent introduction to patents and a bibliography listing looseleaf services, serials, treaties, illustrated texts, case law, nutshells, online sources, primary sources, general information on patent law, and such.[4]

Patent Law

The first patent law was enacted in 1790. The present law is a general revision of the one enacted in 1952 and is codified in Title 35, *United States Code*. The USPTO administers the law relating to the granting of patents, specifies the general subject matter that can be patented, sets the condition for patentability, and so forth. Under the Invention Secrecy Act of 1951 (66 Stat. 3, 35 U.S.C. 181), the government can prevent the granting of a patent, or publication or disclosure of an invention, if a defense agency maintains that publication or disclosure is detrimental to national security. The invention then remains secret, or a patent is not granted as long as "the national security requires" (35 U.S.C. 181).

Still, the decision to maintain secrecy is subject to annual renewal.[5] The Act also specifies an appeals process, and a claim for compensation for the damage caused by such secrecy order may be made through the proper federal court.

The Atomic Energy Act of 1954 (PL 83-703, 42 U.S.C. 2131–2139) excludes the patenting of inventions that apply solely to the utilization of special nuclear material or atomic energy for atomic weapons. The Government Research and Development Patent Policy Act of 1984 (PL 98-620) establishes uniform government policy regarding patent rights to inventions resulting from federally funded science and technology. The Federal Science and Technology Transfer Act of 1986 (PL 99-502) amends the Stevenson-Wydler Innovation Act of 1980 (PL 96-480) and changes government policy on patent rights for inventions created in federal laboratories and resulting from cooperative research and development (R&D) agreements with the federal government.

Finally, USPTO's "News & Notices" (http://www.uspto.gov/main/newsandnotices.htm) provides access to announcements, press releases, regulations (via the *Federal Register*), and other information related to patents and trademarks.

TRADEMARKS, SERVICE MARKS, AND TRADE NAMES

Trademarks protect words, names, symbols, sounds, or colors that distinguish goods and services. Unlike patents, trademarks can be renewed forever as long as they are used in business. One example is the shape of a Coca-Cola bottle. A service mark "is the same as a trademark except that it identifies and distinguishes the source of a service rather than a product.[6] The terms 'trademark' and 'mark' may be used to refer to both trademarks and service marks whether they are word marks or other types of marks. Normally, a mark for goods appears on the product or on its packaging, while a service mark appears in advertising for the services" (http://www.census.gov/mso/www/trade.html). Businesses and organizations may use names or designations to identify themselves and distinguish them from their competitors.[7]

The purpose of a trademark is to identify the source of products or services and to distinguish the trademark owner's goods and services from those of others. As long as a trademark fulfills these functions, it remains valid. Trademark ownership rights in the United States arise through use of a mark. Continued use of a mark is necessary to maintain trademark rights. The owner of a trademark is entitled to the exclusive right to use the mark. This entitlement includes the ability to prevent the use, by unauthorized third parties, of a confusingly similar mark. Marks used by unrelated parties are confusingly similar if, by their use on the same, similar, or related goods or services, the relevant consumer population would think the goods or services come from the same source.[8]

Unlike patent and copyright law, federal trademark law coexists with state and common-law trademark rights. Therefore, registration at either the federal or state level is not necessary to create or maintain ownership rights in a mark. For example, priority of trademark rights between owners of confusingly similar marks, regardless of whether the marks are federally registered, is based upon first use of the mark.[9]

At the federal level, the Lanham Trademark Act (15 USC 1051 et seq.), which is based on the commerce clause of the Constitution, regulates trade name infringement. In addition, the Trademark Law Reform Act of 1988 (PL 100-667, 102 Stat. 3935) amended the Lanham Act and established trademark rights that apply to the use of the mark in commerce (see specifically 15 U.S.C. 1051(b)).

Remedies against trademark infringement and unfair competition are available to trademark owners under both state and federal law (e.g., 15 U.S.C. 114–1121, 1125(a)). In this regard, the owner of a federal trademark registration has certain benefits. In a court proceeding, registration on the Principal Register constitutes *prima facie* evidence of the registrant's ownership of the mark (15 U.S.C. 1057(b)). Registration on the Principal Register may also be used as a basis to block importation of infringing goods (15 U.S.C. 1124) or to obtain remedies against a counterfeiter (15 U.S.C. 1116(d), 18 U.S.C. 2320). The Lanham Act provides that, under certain conditions, the right to use a registered mark may become incontestable (15 U.S.C. 1065). In addition, the Act provides for cancellation of registrations on certain grounds (15 U.S.C. 1064).[10]

Figure 12.3 is a reproduction of USPTO's Web page on "Trademarks" (http://www.uspto.gov/main/trademarks.htm). It covers "Services," "Trademark Guides," "International Protection," "Trademark Trial & Appeal Board," "Registration," and "Resources." There is also a Trademark Electronic Application System (TEAS) (http://www.uspto.gov/teas/index.html). This page also presents responses to frequently asked questions, a help desk, application forms, and "TEAS policy and technical hints." Other useful pages are entitled "Trademark Information" (http://www.uspto.gov/web/menu/tm.html), which provides access to TEAS, "Legal Resources," "General Information," the "Trademark Trial and Appeal Board," online application for a trademark, and trademark status; and "Frequently Asked Questions about Trademarks" (http://www.uspto.gov/web/offices/tac/tmfaq.htm). The latter page mentions that online trademark searches can be conducted at http://tess.uspto.gov. The thirty-four page guide to frequently asked questions also covers patents and copyrights. The previously-mentioned USPTO's "Check Status" (http://www.uspto.gov/main/checkstatus.htm) also covers trademarks.

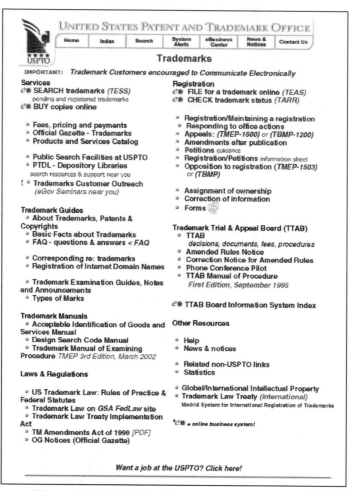

Figure 12.3. USPTO's Trademarks Page. *Source:*
http://www.uspto.gov/main/trademarks.htm.

TRADE SECRETS AND PROPRIETARY INFORMATION

According to section 1839 of the Economic Espionage Act of 1996 (PL 104-294, 110 Stat. 3488, 18 U.S.C. 1831–1839), trade secrets are

all forms and types of financial, business, scientific, technical, economic or engineering information, including patterns, plans, compilations, program devices, formulas, designs, prototypes, methods, techniques, processes, procedures, programs, or codes, whether tangible or intangible, and whether or how stored, compiled, or memorialized physically, electronically, graphically, photographically, or in writing if:

- The owner thereof has taken reasonable measures to keep such information secret; and

- The information derives independent economic value, actual or potential, from not being generally known to, and not being readily ascertainable through proper means by the public. (http://www.tscm.com/USC18_90.html)

Trade secrets refer to useful or valuable information that companies withhold to give themselves competitive advantage.[11] For the courts to regard such information as a commodity, it would have to have "a sufficient level of originality, novelty, or utility."[12] "There are several factors that are used to determine if subject matter qualifies as a trade secret. Among the factors considered are the extent of measures taken by the trade secret owner to guard the secrecy of the information and the ease or difficulty with which the information could be properly acquired or duplicated by others."[13] Thus, "the general rule is that subject matter cannot be successfully protected as a trade secret if it is widely distributed. However, if adequate security measures are taken to ensure that access to the subject matter being distributed is treated as secret, the subject matter may still be considered a trade secret."[14] Perhaps the most famous trade secret is the formula for making Coca-Cola.[15]

As Joe Morehead notes,

activities that the courts commonly treat as trade secret theft include

- Disclosures by key employees occupying positions of trust in violation of their duty of trust toward their employer;

- Disclosures by current and former employees in violation of a confidentiality agreement entered into with their employer;

- Disclosures by suppliers, consultants, financial advisors, or others who signed nondisclosure agreements with the trade secret owner, promising not to disclose the information;

- Industrial espionage; and

- Disclosures by any person owing an implied duty to the employer not to make such disclosure, such as directors, corporate officers, and other high-level salaried employees.[16]

"Unlike many of the other forms of intellectual property protection . . ., trade secrets are generally protected by state law, not Federal law. Trade secret protection is very limited. A trade secret holder is only protected from unauthorized disclosure and use of the trade secret by others and from another person obtaining the trade secret by some improper means."[17] In 1996, the Uniform Trade Secrets Act (PL 104-294, 110 Stat. 3488, 18 U.S.C. 1831) made the theft of trade secrets a federal criminal offense, gave the Department of Justice authority to prosecute trade secret theft inside and outside the United States, and broadened the definition of trade secrets to include new technologies for creating and storing these secrets.

The Federal Acquisition Regulation covers proprietary information and explains that

> contractors may have a legitimate proprietary interest (e.g., a property right or other valid economic interest) in data resulting from private investment. Protection of such data from unauthorized use and disclosure is necessary in order to prevent the compromise of such property right or economic interest, avoid jeopardizing the contractor's commercial position, and preclude impairment of the Government's ability to obtain access to or use of such data. (http://48C.F.R.27.402 Policy)

The purpose of this regulation is "to protect from disclosure outside the government proprietary information that is provided to the government during a bidding process" (http://48C.F.R.27.402 Policy). Furthermore,

> Exemption 4 of the Freedom of Information Act exempts from mandatory disclosure information such as trade secrets and commercial or financial information obtained by the government from a company on a privileged or confidential basis that, if released, would result in competitive harm to the company, impair the government's ability to obtain like information in the future, or protect the government's interest in compliance with program effectiveness. The law on Disclosure of Confidential Information (18 USC 1905) makes it a crime for a federal employee to disclose such information. (http://www.smdc.army.mil/SecurityGuide/S2unclas/Propriet.htm)

Created by the Small Business Administration, the National Partnership for Reinventing Government, and the U.S. Business Advisor interagency task force, the U.S. Business Advisor (USBA) was envisioned as "a one-stop electronic link to all the information and services government provides for the business community" (http://www.business.gov/busadv/pages.aboutus.cfm). One aspect of USBA is the Business Law Center and its BusinessLaw.gov, which "is an online resources guide and assistance tool . . . designed to help small businesses find legal information prior to startup or during expansion and other transitional phases" (http://www.businesslaw.gov/content_page.cfm?contentid=10031). It provides coverage of trade secrets, including a discussion of dangers, responses to frequently asked questions (http://www.business.gov/busadv/elccat.cfm?catid=10081), and patents and trademarks (http://www.business.gov/busadv/maincat.cfm?catid=85).

State government is a good resource on trade secrets, and a search of FirstGov (http://www.firstgov.gov) limited to state government produces more than 1,000 references.

COPYRIGHTS

Copyrights protect works of authorship (e.g., writing, music, and works of art). The Library of Congress (LC) currently registers copyrights for the life of the author plus seventy years:

> "Copyright" literally means the right to copy. The term has come to mean that body of exclusive rights granted by statute to authors for protection of their work. The owner of a copyright has the exclusive right to reproduce, distribute, and, in the case of certain works, publicly perform or display the work; to prepare derivative works; or to license others to engage in the same acts under specific terms and conditions. Copyright protection does not extend to any idea, procedure, process, slogan, principle, or discovery. (http://www.loc.gov/copyright/docs/circla.html)

"Under the law in effect before 1978, copyright was secured either on the date a work was published with a copyright notice or on the date of registration if the work was registered in unpublished form. In either case, the copyright endured for a first term of 28 years from the date it was secured" (http://www.copyright.gov/circs/circ1.html). During the final year (the 28th) of the first term, the copyright could be renewed. The 1976 Copyright Act extended the renewal term from twenty-eight to forty-seven years "for copyrights that were subsisting on January 1, 1978, or for pre-1978 copyrights restored under the Uruguay Round Agreements Act, making these works eligible for a total term of protection of 75 years" (http://www.loc.gov/copyright/circs/circl.html).

The Sonny Bono Copyright Term Extension Act of 1998 (PL 105-298) added another twenty years of protection, from seventy-five years to ninety-five years. The 1976 Copyright Act was also amended in 1992 by the Copyright Renewal Act (PL 102-307), which provided for automatic renewal of the term of copyrights secured between January 1, 1964, and December 31, 1997. Renewal registration was no longer required to extend the protection for ninety-five years. More recently, the Digital Millennium Copyright Act (PL 105-304, 112 Stat. 2860) updated copyright law for the digital age in preparation for ratification of World Intellectual Property Organization (WIPO) treaties.[18] Among the highlights of this 1998 public law are coverage of the circumvention of copyright protection systems, fair use in a digital environment, and online service provider (OSP) liability. The Act also requires the Register of Copyrights, after consultation with relevant parties, to submit to Congress recommendations regarding how to promote distance education through digital technologies while "maintaining an appropriate balance between the rights of copyright owners and the needs of users."[19]

Title 17 of the *United States Code* covers copyright and the protections for "original works of authorship (see http://www.loc.gov/copyright/title17 for the text of that title). Section 106 of the 1976 Act

generally gives the owner of copyright the exclusive right to do and to authorize others to do the following: to reproduce the work in copies or
phonorecords; to prepare derivative works based upon the work; to distribute
copies or phonorecords of the work to the public by sale or other transfer of
ownership, or by rental, lease, or lending; to perform the work publicly, in the
case of literacy, musical, dramatic, and choreographic works, pantomimes,
and motion pictures and other audiovisual works; to display the copyrighted
work publicly, in the case of literary, musical, dramatic, and choreographic
works, pantomimes, and pictorial, graphic, or sculptural works, including the
individual images of a motion picture or other audiovisual work; and in the
case of sound recordings, to perform the work publicly by means of a digital
audio transmission. (http://www.loc.gov/copyright/circs/circl.html)

Section 106A gives certain authors of visual art "the rights of attribution
and integrity," and section 107 covers "fair use" and the purposes for which the
reproduction of a particular work may be considered "fair use" (e.g., criticism,
news reporting, and teaching). The doctrine had its origins in common law and
provides four criteria for the determination of whether the unauthorized use of a
work is a "fair" use or an infringing use":

1. Amount and character of the use;

2. Nature of the copyrighted work;

3. Amount copied in relation to the whole copyrighted work; and

4. Effect of the copying on the potential market for the copyrighted
    work. (http://www.loc.gov/copyright/title17)

However, the distinction between fair use and infringement is neither totally clear nor easily defined. There is no specific number of words, lines, or
notes that may safely be taken without permission. Acknowledging the source of
the copyrighted material is no substitute for obtaining permission.

Internet users who view information and download it are copying. If the
material that is being copied is copyrighted, the possibility of infringement may
rest upon an application of the fair use doctrine to the circumstances surrounding
the unauthorized use of the material.[20] By viewing materials on the Internet, there
is a fixation of materials on a computer's random access memory (RAM). This
fixation may support an infringement claim based on the copyright owner's exclusive rights of reproduction.[21] However, if the copyright owner places work on
the Internet, it might be inferred that the owner expects other users to read and
download the copyrighted work. Legal complications arise when persons other
than the copyright owner publish copyrighted works on the Internet.

U.S. Copyright Office

The U.S. Copyright Office, which became a separate unit of LC in 1897,
has a Web site (http://lcweb.loc.gov/copyright/) that covers "What's New,"

"About the Office," "General Information," "Copyright Office Records," "Announcements," "Publications," "Legislation," "International," and "Copyright Links." Among these choices, there is coverage of Web casting, public laws, rules, proposed rules, and other notices appearing in the *Federal Register*. Those rules and regulations are retrievable in PDF and text format and are found at http://www.loc.gov/copyright/fedreg. The Copyright Office issues final regulations in Title 37 of the *Code of Federal Regulations* (CFR).

The Copyright Office provides additional information on specific sections of the Copyright Act and their application through Circulars, such as Circular 40, "Copyright Registration for Works of the Visual Arts"; Circular 15, "Renewal of Copyright"; Circular 15a, "Duration of Copyright"; and Circular 15t, "Extension of Copyright Terms." Circular 22 offers guidance in how "to investigate whether a work is under copyright protection, and if so, the facts of copyright" (http://www.loc.gov/copyright/circs/circ22.html).

It is possible to conduct a "Copyright Search" (http://www.loc.gov/copyright/search) from one of three databases containing "records of registrations and ownership documents since 1978":

- *Books, music, and so forth*: "Books music, films, sound recordings, maps, software, photos, art, and multimedia. Also includes renewals."

- *Serials*: "Periodicals, magazines, journals, and newspapers."

- *Documents*: "Copyright ownership documents, such as name changes and transfers." (http://www.loc.gov/copyright/search)

The purpose of CORDS, which is the Electronic Registration, Recordation, and Deposit System, is to

> enable copyright applicants to prepare their copyright applications and deposit materials in machine readable formats, to sign their submissions digitally using public key/private key encryption technology, and to send applications, deposits, and documents to the Copyright Office via the Internet. . . . This system will enable the Copyright Office to receive digital submissions via the Internet, verify that each one is authentic and complete, debit fees from the applicant's deposit account with the Copyright Office, create an electronic tracking record, acknowledge receipt of the application or document, provide for online processing of applications, deposits, and documents by examiners and catalogers, and notify applicants electronically that the registration or recordation has been completed. The Copyright Office digital repository will hold these digital copyright deposit materials in a secure and verifiable manner. (http://www.loc.gov/copyright/cords/cords.html)

There is also access to copyright legislation for the current Congress (see http://www.loc.gov/copyright/legislation).

Other Resources

The LII has an online collection of resources for copyright that includes the Copyright Act from the United States Code, Title 37 of the CFR, court decisions, conventions and treaties, and so forth (see http://www.law.cornell.edu/topics/copyright.html). The LII also has a searchable database of Supreme Court syllabi, which comprise "summaries of each case prepared by the Court's reporter of decisions" (http://www.law.cornell.edu/topics/copyright.html). It is possible to search for a topic, such as "copyright" and find references to cases such as *New York Times Co. v. Tasini*.

The Copyright Clearance Center, Inc. (Danvers, Mass.) (http://www.copyright.com/) serves as a clearinghouse for getting permission to produce copyrighted content in articles, books, coursepacks, and so forth. It does not provide the copyrighted content itself.

CASE LAW AND THE INTERNET[22]

American courts have been seeking equitable resolutions to copyright infringement actions over the unauthorized use of copyrighted works on the Internet. Court decisions applying the fair use principles to Internet use provide some legal guidance; however, case law precedent is still developing and certain issues remain unresolved. Still, the most recent cases have continued the traditional application of the fair use doctrine to Internet use of copyrighted materials.

An early case that dealt with fair use and online services involved an electronic bulletin board that was open to the public.[23] The scheme involved the electronic exchange of copyrighted Sega video games through the bulletin board. The bulletin board operators asserted a fair use defense that was based on the argument that the operators themselves did not download or retain copies of any Sega video games. The court applied the previously identified four fair use criteria to this situation and rejected the defendants' fair use defense. The court determined that the use was for a commercial purpose: to download the copyrighted games so as to avoid their purchase from the copyright owner. Considering the nature of the copyrighted work, the court observed that the work involved creativity, fiction, and fantasy. Since the entire work was copied, the one criterion—the amount of the work used—favored the plaintiff's claim. In considering the effect of copying on the potential market, the court concluded that the unauthorized copying of the copyrighted works would have an adverse impact on the potential market, as few persons would purchase the copyrighted works if they were available through the bulletin board. Therefore, the court concluded that the criteria favored the plaintiff and that the defendants' unauthorized use of the copyrighted works was an infringing use. Another subsequent decision that dealt with the fair use doctrine and Internet use involved the same parties and a similar factual situation. The court applied the four criteria to the facts at hand.[24] After balancing all of them, the court reached the same conclusion as in the earlier decision, finding that the fair use doctrine did not apply.[25]

Several online cases have involved the unauthorized use of certain written works of L. Ron Hubbard, founder of scientology. The simplified factual situation concerning these cases follows. In unrelated litigation, the Religious Technology Center (RTC) attempted to seal an affidavit concerning church ideology. Arnie Lerma, a former follower of Hubbard, obtained the affidavit and published it on the Internet through his Internet access provider, Digital Gateway Systems (DGS). The RTC brought an infringement action against Lerma, DGS, the *Washington Post*, and others. Another series of cases involved the RTC bringing an action for copyright infringement against a former minister, Dennis Erlich, for posting on an Internet bulletin board certain materials containing Hubbard's published and unpublished works. The RTC also named as defendants the bulletin board operator, Thomas Klemesrud, and the Internet access provider, Netcom. These cases are summarized here.

In *Religious Technology Center v. Lerma*,[26] the court dealt primarily with RTC's infringement actions against *The Washington Post*, certain reporters, and Lerma. This case did not deal chiefly with the Internet or online aspects of fair use. The action was based primarily on the unauthorized dissemination of information owned by the RTC and did not address substantive copyright issues.[27]

In another case involving the RTC's infringement action, the same defendants moved for summary judgment and the district court concluded that the fair use doctrine applied to the *Washington Post* and its reporters.[28] In reaching this conclusion, the court examined the four fair use criteria and applied them in a traditional copyright analysis. The court concluded that the purpose and character of the use of the material was for news gathering, and this favored the defendants. In evaluating the nature of the work, the court deemed it to be informational rather than creative, and that a broader fair use approach was appropriate. The court determined that the amount of the work used in relation to its entirety was not significant. Finally, the court found that the unauthorized use did not adversely affect the market value of the material. The court concluded that the unauthorized use of the copyrighted material by the *Post* and its reporters was a fair use.

In an unpublished opinion, the court subsequently examined the copyright infringement claim against Lerma.[29] Lerma first argued that the disputed works were not copyrightable. The court rejected this argument. He next raised the fair use defense for his unauthorized use of the copyrighted works. After examining each of the four fair use criteria, the court concluded that Lerma's use could not be construed as a fair use. Finally, Lerma argued that the RTC misused the copyright. The court concluded that the RTC had not done so and that Lerma's unauthorized use of the material was an infringing use. The RTC was awarded $2,500 in statutory damages.

In another series of cases, the RTC brought actions against Erlich, the bulletin board operator, and the Internet access provider. In two separate opinions, the district court for the Northern District of California addressed various copyright issues, including fair use.[30] Erlich did not dispute that he copied the works. He advanced a fair use defense.[31] The court granted, in part, the plaintiff's motion for a preliminary injunction against Erlich and concluded that his use of the RTC's materials was unlikely to qualify as fair use. In evaluating Erlich's purpose and the character of the use, the court determined that it was for criticism or comment and was, thus, for noncommercial use. Therefore, the fair use criterion was held to be slightly in Erlich's favor.[32] In looking at the nature of the copyrighted work, the court considered that some of the works were published, while others were unpublished. The court determined that the unauthorized use of the unpublished works favored the plaintiffs. In assessing the criterion about the amount of the work copied, the court favored the plaintiffs. As for the potential market for the work, the court concluded that Erlich's use would not have an adverse effect on the market. The court engaged in an "equitable balancing" of the criteria and found that Erlich did not assert a fair use defense for his copying.[33]

In *Religious Technology Center v. Netcom On-Line Communications*,[34] another action involving the RTC and Erlich's access provider and the bulletin board, the court granted, in part, and denied, in part, the defendants' motion for summary judgment and judgment on the pleadings and denied the plaintiffs' motion for a preliminary injunction. The district court applied the fair use analysis to the action of the Internet access provider, Netcom. The court determined that the access provider was not liable for direct infringement; rather, the court examined it as a case of contributory infringement on the part of Netcom and determined that the plaintiffs raised a genuine issue of fact concerning Netcom's contributory infringement.[35] Although Netcom was a commercial enterprise, the court found that its use of copyrighted work was of a different nature than the plaintiffs' use. In looking at the nature of the copyrighted works, the court determined that Netcom's use of the works was merely to facilitate its posting to the bulletin board, an entirely different use from the use of plaintiffs. and, therefore, favored Netcom. Regarding the amount of the copyrighted work copied, the court determined that Netcom copied no more of the plaintiffs' work than was necessary to function; thus, this factor did not favor the plaintiffs. The court concluded that Netcom's postings on the Internet raised a genuine factual issue as to whether the market for the plaintiffs' works was diminished. Because the court was not able to make a determination concerning the fourth fair use criterion—the market harm—the court decided that the fair use defense was not available to Netcom on motion for summary judgment.[36] In conclusion, the court determined that there were issues of fact to be determined in the case and that a fair use defense was not available for Netcom on summary judgment.

Later in 1997, the U.S. District Court for the Northern District of Illinois ruled that an Internet service provider was not liable for direct copyright infringement, despite the fact that materials were directly copied on a Web site that the service provider maintained for a subscriber.[37] However, the Internet subscriber was found to have infringed certain copyrighted "clip art" images by using them on the Internet. The court concluded that the subscriber's use of the clip art was primarily for commercial uses, for promoting his organizations, and for generating revenue. Hence, the fair use defense was not available for the defendant and the unauthorized use of the clip art on the Internet was an infringing use. In 1998, the same court reached a finding on infringement in a similar case involving the use of "shareware," copyrighted software that is loaned to potential purchasers under certain conditions.[38] The court went through an extensive fair use analysis within the context of shareware.[39]

In another case concerning fair use and the Internet, still images taken from a copyrighted videotape of a celebrity couple engaging in sexual activity were placed on the Internet without the couple's permission. Applying the fair use doctrine to a rather complex factual situation, the U.S. District Court for the Central District of California held that the unauthorized placement on the Internet of still images from a copyrighted videotape was not a fair use.[40] The court considered each fair use criterion within the context of the factual situation.[41]

The U.S. District Court for the Eastern District of Texas examined a unique case in which the plaintiff's copyrighted works—model legal codes—had been adopted as municipal laws by various communities.[42] The defendant then posted these copyrighted works on the Internet and was sued for infringement. The court applied the fair use analysis to the factual situation at hand and determined that the fair use defense was not applicable in this situation.[43] The copyrighted model codes, even when they had been adopted as municipal laws or ordinances, did not lose their copyright protection and could not be posted on the Internet without the permission of the copyright owner.

In *Kelly v. Arriba Soft Corp.*,[44] the court examined the fair use doctrine within the context of a "visual search engine" on the Internet. The defendant's visual search engine allowed a user to obtain a list of related Web content following a search inquiry. The visual search engine produced a list of reduced "thumbnail" pictures related to the inquiry.[45] The plaintiff argued that the use of the "thumbnail" copyrighted pictures obtained through the visual search was an infringement of his copyright interest. The court undertook an extensive fair use evaluation of the circumstances surrounding the visual search engine and the unauthorized use of the copyrighted photographs.[46] The court weighed all of the fair use criteria together and determined that the defendant's use of the copyrighted photographs as part of its visual search engine was a fair use of the plaintiff's images.[47]

The posting of copyrighted news articles on the Internet has been the subject of recent litigation.[48] The defendant posted copyrighted articles from newspapers on an Internet "bulletin board" Web site so that visitors to the site could comment on and criticize the articles. Applying the fair use criteria to the case, the court determined that the defendant's posting of full-length, copyrighted articles on the Internet was not a fair use of the copyrighted material. The court noted that the Web site operator could have avoided infringement if summaries of the articles had been posted or if hyperlinks to the articles on the newspapers' own Web sites had been provided.

The practice of "streaming"—the visual transmission of copyrighted television programming—on the Internet was the subject of a case in 2000. The defendant was transmitting portions of the plaintiff's copyrighted programming on the Internet. The plaintiff sought, and received, a temporary restraining order.[49] The U.S. District Court for the Western District of Pennsylvania did not examine the fair use doctrine or any other copyrighted defenses in its opinion.

In recent litigation, several motion picture studios brought an action to prevent the defendants from providing a computer program on their Web sites that allowed users to decrypt and copy the plaintiffs' copyrighted motion pictures from digital versatile disks.[50] Although the defendants argued that their activities were within the fair use exception, the court rejected this defense and granted the plaintiffs' motion for a preliminary injunction.[51]

The cases cited in this section illustrate the judicial process—the "equitable balancing"—that courts undertake in their evaluation of fair use claims. It appears that the courts are using the same analysis and criteria for Internet litigation as they have in making other intellectual property determinations. The courts have examined, in detail, the factual situation surrounding the litigation, and they have applied each of the fair use criteria to the case-by-case circumstances. The courts have then evaluated or weighed the statutory criteria and determined whether, on balance, the evidence favors a finding of fair use of the copyrighted material.

Although these cases provide judicial precedent, the use of copyrighted materials on the Internet is not entirely resolved. Factual circumstances may change the judicial outcome in various situations. In addition, various areas of fair use litigation and the Internet may still be developing. Examples of these subject areas are (1) possible liability for Internet server and bulletin board providers, (2) whether online use is legally distinguishable from the use of the printed form, (3) unintended or unintentional use of copyrighted materials, and (4) use of materials by schools and libraries.

INTERNATIONAL PERSPECTIVE

Figure 12.4, another page from the USPTO Web site, provides access to a wide assortment of material and Web sites on "international intellectual property." The page is intended "for those who wish to seek protection for their intellectual property beyond the borders of the United States of America as well as for those non-US customers who wish to seek patent or trademark protection in the United States of America."[52] Additional international coverage is available through the Web site of the Copyright Office.

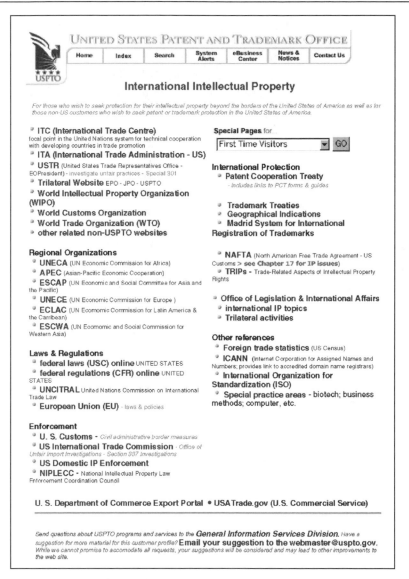

Figure 12.4. USPTO's International Intellectual Property Page. *Source:*
http://www.uspto.gov/main/profiles/international.htm.

Since the rights granted by a U.S. patent extend only to the United States and have no effect in other countries, an inventor who seeks patent protection elsewhere must apply for a patent in each of the other countries or in regional patent offices. The Paris Convention for the Protection of Industrial Property guarantees to citizens of the 140 signatory countries the same rights in patent and trademark matters that it gives to its own citizens. The treaty also guarantees that, on the basis of a regular first application filed in one of the member countries, the applicant may, within a certain period of time, apply for protection in all of the other member countries.

Another treaty, the Patent Cooperation Treaty, which came into force in 1978, facilitates the filing of applications for patent on the same invention in member countries by providing, for example, centralized filing procedures and a standardized application format. Clearly, intellectual property transcends national borders and takes into account international practices and obligations.

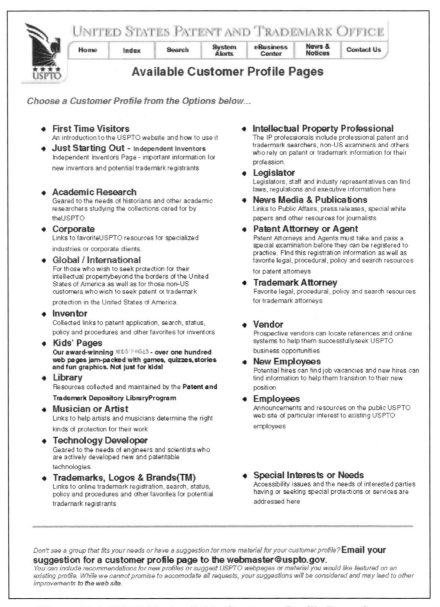

Figure 12.5. USPTO's Available Customer Profile Page. *Source:*
http://www.uspto.gov/main/profiles/customerprofiles.htm.

Goods and services to which a mark applies in a trademark registration are categorized according to the Nice Agreement Concerning the International Classification of Goods and Services for the Purposes of the Registration of Marks of June 15, 1957, as revised at Stockholm on July 14, 1967, and at Geneva on May 13, 1977 (International Classification). This treaty, of which the United States is a signatory, is administered by the World Intellectual Property Organization (WIPO).

CONCLUSION

As this chapter illustrates, the government entities engaged in intellectual property have a strong presence on the Web and provide the public with a diverse set of resources. Nevertheless, anyone dealing with patent searching, especially for the first time, is advised to rely on the services of patent and trademark depository libraries, as well as the service profiles identified in Figure 12.5. The staff of the depository libraries have the expertise to guide anyone in conducting a patent search.

The General Services Administration has a Web page that provides easy access to laws, regulations, Web links, and miscellaneous resources on "Patent, Trademark, Copyright, and Intellectual Property" (http://www.legal.gsa.gov/ legal23.htm). As already noted, FirstGov (http://www.firstgov.gov) provides access to intellectual property on both federal and subnational Web sites. Anyone searching for policy instruments and common law doctrines should not confine himself or herself to the resources presented in this chapter. Because FirstGov enables one to search beyond the federal level, it might be a good starting point for a broader search. Figure 12.5 is a reminder that the search can go beyond the borders of the United States.

NOTES

1. For an "Introduction to Intellectual Property Rights," see http://www.usinfo. state.gov/products/pubs/intelprp. A companion resource of the State Department covers "Selected Laws & Treaties" (http://usinfo.state.gov/usa/infousa/laws/intelpro.htm).

2. Laurence F. Schmeckebier and Roy B. Eastin, *Government Publications and Their Use* (Washington, D.C.: The Brookings Institution, 1969), 228–29.

3. Printouts and images can be viewed and downloaded. The images require the use of Alternatiff (see http://www.alternatiff.com/), which allows a browser to display files in a tagged image file format (TIFF).

4. Eugene R. Quinn Jr. and Kathleen A. Portuán Miller, "Understanding Patents: A Legal Overview and Research Bibliography," *Legal Reference Services Quarterly* 20 (2001): 85–110.

5. "An invention shall be ordered kept secret and the grant of a patent withheld for a period of more than one year. The Commissioner shall renew the order at the end thereof, or at the end of any renewal period, for additional periods of one year upon notification by the head of the department or the chief officer of the agency who caused the order to be issued that an affirmative determination has been made that the national interest continues so to require" (35 U.S.C. 181).

6. Examples of service marks include Blockbusters, which is the brand of a video rental service, and the U.S. Postal Service's eagle in profile, which is the brand of a package delivery service.

7. "Trade Name," in *West's Encyclopedia of American Law*, vol. 10 (Eagan, Minn.: West Group, 1998), 114–115.

8. Bruce A. Lehman, *Intellectual Property and the National Information Infrastructure*. The Report of the Working Group on Intellectual Property Rights (Washington, D.C.: Department of Commerce, Information Infrastructure Task Force, 1995), 168.

9. Ibid., 168–169. Priority may also be established by the filing date of a federal registration based on an intent to use a mark (15 U.S.C. 1051(b)) or a foreign filing (15 U.S.C. 1126).

10. Ibid., 170. See also 171–73.

11. For an excellent introduction to trade secrets, see Russell B. Stevenson Jr., *Corporations and Information: Secrecy, Access, and Disclosure* (Baltimore, Md.: The Johns Hopkins University Press, 1980), especially chapter 2. He discusses the development of trade secrets, the policies behind them, changes in trade secret protection for technology, and economic effects.

12. "Trade Secret," in *West's Encyclopedia of American Law*, vol. 10 (Eagan, Minn.: West Group, 1998), 115.

13. Lehman, *Intellectual Property*, 174.

14. Ibid.

15. See "Trade Secret," in *West's Encyclopedia of American Law*, 115–16, for more information about a trade secret.

16. Joe Morehead, *Introduction to United States Government Information Sources*, 6th ed. (Englewood, Colo.: Libraries Unlimited, 1999), 334.

17. Lehman, *Intellectual Property*, 173.

18. For the background of the Act, see Bruce Smith, Bruce T. Fletcher, and Charles R. McClure, "Federal Information Policy and Access to Web-based Federal Information," *Journal of Academic Librarianship* 26 (July 2000): 277–78. See also Lehman, *Intellectual Propert*.

19. PL 105-304, 112 Stat. 2860.

20. When a user pays a subscription fee for the use of particular information on the Internet, the service provider may have addressed the issues of copying/downloading in the access agreements with the users or the holder of a site license agreement. However, many Internet sites do not impose a user fee or contain copyright information concerning the material on the site.

21. See Christopher Wolf, "Net Users Could Face IP Liability," *National Law Journal* (May 20, 1996): C34–C35.

22. This section is taken from "The Copyright Doctrine of Fair Use and the Internet: Caselaw," an unpublished paper by Douglas Reid Weimer, Legislative Attorney, American Law Division, Congressional Research Service (Washington, D.C., March 2000).

23. *Sega Enterprises, Ltd. v MAPHIA*, 857 F. Supp. 679 (N.D. Cal. 1994).

24. Ibid. at 934–35.

25. Ibid. at 936.

26. *Religious Technology Center v. Lerma*, 908 F. Supp. 1353 (E.D. Va. 1995).

27. Ibid. at 1355–58.

28. Ibid. at 1361.

29. *Religious Technology Center* v. *Arnaldo Pagliariana Lerma*, 1996 U.S. Dist., LEXIS 15454 (E.D. Va. October 4, 1996).

30. The court examined other issues, such as trade secrets and tort claims, which are not discussed in this chapter.

31. *Religious Technology Center* v. *Arnaldo Pagliariana Lerma* at 1242–50.

32. Ibid. at 1244.

33. Ibid. at 1249–50.

34. *Religious Technology Center* v. *Netcom On-Line Commu.*, 907 F. Supp. 1361 (N.D. Cal. 1995).

35. Ibid. at 1373–75.

36. Ibid. at 1381. Apparently, the bulletin board provider did not assert a fair use defense; therefore, the court did not utilize the fair use analysis.

37. *Marobie-FL v. National Ass'n of Fire Equip. Distributors*, 983 F. Supp. 1167 (N.D. Ill. 1997).

38. *Storm Impact v. Software of the Month Club*, 13 F. Supp. 2d 782 (N.D. Ill. 998).

39. Ibid. at 787–90.

40. *Michaels v. Internet Entertainment Group, Inc.*, 5 F. Supp. 2d 823 (D.C. Cal. 1998).

41. Ibid. at 834–36. The final disposition of this case was reached in *Michaels v. Internet Entertainment Group*, 1998 U.S. Dist. LEXIS 20786 (1998).

42. *Veeck v. Southern Bldg. Code Congress Intern*, 49 F. Supp. (E.D. Tex. 1999).

43. Ibid. at 891.

44. *Kelly v. Arriba Soft Corp.*, 77 F. Supp. 1116 (C.D. Cal. 1990.

45. Ibid. at 1117.

46. Ibid. at 1118–21.

47. Ibid. at 1121.

48. *Los Angeles Times v. Free Republic* (C.D. Cal. No. CV 98-7840-MMM-AJWX, November 8, 1999).

49. *Twentieth Century Fox Film Corporation v. ICRAVETV* (2000 U.S. Dist. LEXIS 1013).

50. *Universal City Studios, Inc. v. Shawn C. Reimerdes*, 82 F. Supp. 2d 211 (S.D.N.Y. 2000).

51. Ibid.

52. See also Chapter 6 and coverage of the United States Trade Representative. This agency of the Executive Office of the President also deals with intellectual property.

URL SITE GUIDE

Ag Biotechnology Patents and New Technologies
National Agricultural Library
Department of Agriculture
> http://www.nal.usda.gov/bic/Biotech_Patents/

Alternatiff
> http://www.alternatiff.com

Copyright Clearance Center, Inc.
> http://www.copyright.com/

Delphion
> http://www.delphion.com/

FirstGov
> http://www.firstgov.gov/

Internet Patent Search System
Internet Patent News Service
> http://www.bustpatents.com

Introduction to Intellectual Property Rights
Department of State
> http://www.usinfo.state.gov/products/pubs/intelprp/

>> Selected Laws & Treaties
>> http://usinfo.state.gov/usa/infousa/laws/intelpro.htm

LII
Cornell University School of Law
> http://www.law.cornell.edu/

>> Copyright
>> http://www.law.cornell.edu/topics/copyright.html

>> Patents
>> http://www.law.cornell.edu/topics/patent.html

Patent Searching
Louisiana State University
> http://www.lib.lsu.edu/sci/ptdl/patsearch.htm

>> Patents and Trademarks Books
>> http://www.lib.lsu.edu/sci/ptdl/patbooks.htm
>> http://www.lib.lsu.edu/sci/ptdl/tmbooks.htm

Patent, Trademark, Copyright, and Intellectual Property
General Services Administration
> http://www.legal.gsa.gov/legal23.htm

Search U.S. Patents
Community of Science, Inc.
   http://patents.cos.com/

Trademarksaand Bureau Products
Bureau of the Census
   http://www.census.gov/mso/www/trade.htm

U.S. Business Advisor
   http://www.business.gov/

   About Us
      http://www.business.gov/busadv/pages/aboutus.cfm

   BusinessLaw.gov

   Business Law Center
      http://www.businesslaw.gov/content_page.cfm?contentid=10031

      Patents and Trademarks
         http://www.business.gov/busadv/maincat.cfm?catid=85

      Trade Secrets
         http://www.business.gov/busadv/e;ccat.cfm?catid=10081

U.S. Copyright Office
Library of Congress
   http://www.loc.gov/

   Brief History and Overview
      http://www.loc.gov/copyright/docs/circ1a.html

   Copyright Basics
      http:// www.copyright.gov/circs/circ1.html

   Copyright Law (17 U.S.C.)
      http://www.loc.gov/copyright/title17/

   Copyright Legislation
      http://www.loc.gov/copyright/legislation/

   Copyright Search
      http://www.loc.gov/copyright/search/

   CORDS
      http://www.loc.gov/copyright/cords/cords.html

   Federal Register Notices
      http://www.copyright.gov/fedreg/index.html

   How to Investigate the Copyright Status of a Work
      http:// www.loc.gov/copyright/circs/circ22.html

U.S. Patent and Trademark Office
   http://www.uspto.gov/

   American Inventor's Protection Act of 1999
      http://www.uspto.gov/web/offices/dcom/olia/aipa/index.htm

Available Customer Profile Pages
http://www.uspto.gov/main/profiles/customerprofiles.htm

Check Status (Patents & Trademarks)
http://www.uspto.gov/main/checkstatus.htm

Electronic Business Center
http://www.uspto.gov/ebc/indexebc.html

Electronic Filing System
http://www.uspto.gov/ebc/efs/index.html

Frequently Asked Questions about Trademarks
http://www.uspto.gov/web/offices/tac/tmfaq.htm

International Intellectual Property
http://www.uspto.gov/main/profiles/international.htm

News & Notices
http://www.uspto.gov/main/newsandnotices.htm

Patent Grants and Applications
http://www.uspto.gov/patft/

Patents
http://www.uspto.gov/main/patents.htm

Patents Legislation & Regulations
http://www.uspto.gov/web/patents/legis.htm

Trademark Electronic Application System
http://www.uspto.gov/teas/index.html

Trademark Information
http://www.uspto.gov/web/menu/tm.html

Trademark Search
http://tess.uspto.gov/

Trademarks
http://www.uspto.gov/main/trademarks.htm

 **Chapter 13**

Statistical Sources

In 1978, Joseph W. Duncan and William C. Shelton, both of the Office of Federal Statistical Policy and Standards, Department of Commerce, produced *Revolution in the United States Government Statistics, 1926–1976.*[1] In this seminal work, they discuss the evolution of the federal government's responsibilities beyond merely conducting the decennial census, which U.S. marshals originally supervised. As the powers of the federal government expanded, so did its factfinding. For the 1880 census, Congress established a census office in the Interior Department, with census supervisors appointed by the president, but subject to Senate confirmation. The changes that occurred between 1926 and 1976 in the increased sophistication of factfinding "reflect a basic shift in Government statistics from a clerical operation to a professional one."[2] At the same time, there was increased emphasis on "the drafting of the questionnaires, collection, editing, tabulation, analysis, presentation and use of accurate figures."[3]

Today, more than seventy agencies spend at least $500,000 annually on the collection and provision of statistical data, and eleven of them have such activity (combined with dissemination) as their primary mission. These agencies are

- Economic Research Service (Department of Agriculture);

- National Agricultural Statistics Service (Department of Agriculture);

- Bureau of the Census (Department of Commerce);

- Bureau of Economic Analysis (Department of Commerce);

- National Center for Education Statistics (Department of Education);

- Energy Information Administration (Department of Energy);

- Bureau of Justice Statistics (Department of Justice);

- Bureau of Labor Statistics (Department of Labor);

- National Center for Health Statistics (Department of Health and Human Services);

- Statistics of Income Division (Internal Revenue Service, Department of Treasury); and

- Bureau of Transportation Statistics (Department of Transportation).

They "ensure that the statistical information they collect, produce, and disseminate is accurate, reliable, and free from political interference and impose the least possible burden on individuals, businesses, and others responding to requests for data. Most of the other agencies that produce and disseminate statistical data do so as an ancillary part of their missions."[4] Examples of other agencies producing statistics are the Federal Reserve System (http://www.federalreserve.gov), Social Security Administration (http://www.ssa.gov), U.S. International Trade Commission (e.g., http://dataweb.usitc.gov), and the Department of Veterans Affairs (http://www.va.gov). The legislative and judicial branches also produce statistics. For example, there are management statistics for the district courts and the courts of appeals (see http://www.uscourts.gov/fcmstat/index.html). Clearly, government statistics constitute a significant resource that those in the government and others use on a regular basis. These statistics reflect most aspects of life within the United States, as well as the infrastructure of most countries. There is coverage, for instance, of agricultural production, the labor force, health care, transportation, economic well-being, and imports and exports.

THE ELEVEN PRINCIPAL AGENCIES

Because the eleven principal agencies maintain Web sites that cover a vast array of current statistical activity on a national, regional, and local basis, this section highlights those home pages. On a limited basis, those home pages may cover historical trends and issues. Additional historical information, as well as access to the products of other government bodies, is available through the indexes discussed later in this chapter, as well as in Chapter 2. At the same time, the home pages of other bodies (e.g., the National Archives and Records Administration and the Library of Congress) mention statistical resources, some of which are not available online.

Economic Research Service

The Economic Research Service (ERS) of the Department of Agriculture "provides economic analyses to support a competitive agricultural system; a safe food supply; a healthy, well-nourished population; harmony between agriculture and the environment, [and an] enhanced quality of life for rural Americans" (http://www.ers.usda.gov). To accomplish its mission, "ERS produces a range of data products available in different formats, including online databases, spreadsheets, and web files" (http://www.ers.usda.gov). (Access to these products is available through, for example, http://www.ers.usda.gov/Data). Further, ERS maintains "briefing rooms," which offer "an indepth discussion synthesizing

ERS research and the economic issues that frame the analysis" (http://www.ers.usda.gov). These briefing rooms also contain questions and answers, readings and data, and "a collection of other ERS products and services addressing . . . [an economic] issue" (http://www.ers.usda.gov/Briefing).

One Web page lays out the agency's publications produced since 1996 so that they are easily accessible (see http://www.ers.usda.gov/Publications). *Agricultural Outlook*, published ten times per year, is one of the most popular publications. It covers topics such as product market outlook, competition, developments in other countries, and farmers and e-commerce. There are also data on individual commodities, farm trade, and long-term analyses of U.S. agricultural policy.

National Agricultural Statistics Service

The National Agricultural Statistics Services (NASS), which is known as the factfinder of agriculture, provides "timely, accurate, and useful statistics in service to U.S. agriculture" (http://www.usda.gov/nass). Its home page (http://www.usda.gov/nass/) provides easy access to statistical information ("Publications," "Graphics," "Historical Data," "Search," "State Information," "Statistical Research," "Census of Agriculture," "On-Line Data Base," and "Today's Reports) and agency information (e.g., "News," "Customer Service," and "Other Links"). The On-Line Data Base, which is under construction, will include agricultural statistics for many commodities and data series at the national, state, county, and district levels. There will also be an identification of the agency's state offices, their addresses and telephone numbers, as well as an opportunity to subscribe (and unsubscribe) to e-mail-reports from these offices (http://www.usda.gov/nass/sso-rpts.htm).

Bureau of the Census

For a number of years, Congress authorized each census through a specific act. In 1954, Congress brought together in Title 13, *United States Code*, the laws upon which the Bureau of the Census operates. It takes censuses (population, housing, and economics) at regular intervals, as well as conducting related surveys. As Frederick G. Bohme and George Daily of the Bureau note:

> From its beginning, the decennial census has been more than a simple "head count." Gathering information on sex and age in 1790 was done . . . for the purpose of ascertaining the industrial and military strength of the Country . . . . The summary information gathered also had usefulness in unanticipated ways. For example, the General Post Office sent this note to the Secretary of State dated December 26, 1793:
>
>> If there be any spare copies of the Census of the Inhabitants of the U[nited] States in the Office of the Secretary of State, the Postmaster General requests Mr. Jefferson to favour him with one: it being proper to attend to the population of the country in forming an opinion upon applications for new post roads.[5]

Officially, census counts are used to determine the number of congressional representatives allowed each state and to align the boundaries of congressional districts so that each member of the House of Representatives represents approximately the same number of people. The information also serves as a basis for such things as grants-in-aid and revenue sharing programs for states and localities, market analysis, facilities planning (site location), studying environmental impact, and conducting research.

The first Economic Census, known as the Census of Manufacturers, was conducted in 1810. By 1953, when the Eisenhower administration failed to provide funding for the Economic Census, the Secretary of Commerce asked Ralph J. Watkins, director of research for Dun and Bradstreet, Inc., to form a committee to answer the question "Who needs this census?" The answer was "business, financial, professional, and government groups," and so the Economic Census was reinstated in 1954. "This was the first census to be conducted by mail, fully integrate the earlier economic censuses, and provide comparable census data across economic sectors."[6]

Conducted every five years, the most recent Economic Census (for 1997) covers manufacturers, business, governments, mineral industrials, housing and construction, and foreign trade, and it gives a detailed portrait of the economy from the national to the local levels. The latest census also replaced the Standard Industrial Classification (SIC) with the North American Industry Classification System (NAICS) that profiles "a fast-breaking, technologically driven, service-oriented, and increasingly international economy" in North America.[7]

Web Site

Figure 13.1 reprints the opening screen of the Bureau's Web site (http://www.census.gov/). This site, and the series of pages it provides, highlights both the decennial and economic censuses, and the site will become even more important because "there will be fewer printed reports from Census 2000 than from the 1990 census. Three printed report series will be produced, each containing one report per state, one for Puerto Rico, and a U.S. Summary."[8] Other files, ones containing more detailed tabulations for more geographical areas, will be released over the Web, followed by release on CD-ROM and DVD.

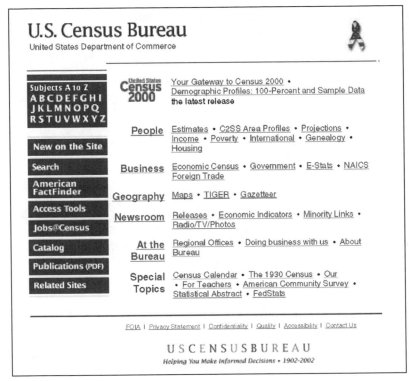

Figure 13.1. Web Site of the Bureau of the Census.
Source: **http://www.census.gov.**

Under "Business," there is now E-Stats, which focuses on "measuring the electronic economy." This section presents e-commerce statistics and E-Stats research papers. "Geography" leads to the TIGER (Topologically Integrated Geographic Encoding and Referencing System) database that was developed for the 1990 census. As John Kavaliunas of the Census Bureau notes:

> TIGER provides a digital or electronic representation of map features and other geographic information in a form that can be read and manipulated by a computer. The principal geographic products available to the public from the TIGER database are known as TIGER/Line Files, which are used for various applications from producing maps, to routing emergency vehicles, to coding a street address to a geographic area.
>
> To make use of these files, mapping or Geographic Information System (GIS) software that can import TIGER/Line data is required. The Census Bureau does not provide these data in any vendor-specific format. With the appropriate software, a user can produce maps ranging in detail from a neighborhood street map to a map of the United States. Many local governments have used the TIGER data in applications requiring digital street maps.

Software companies have created products for the personal computer that allow consumers to produce their own detailed maps. The TIGER/Line files themselves do not include demographic states.[9]

The American FactFinder provides useful information about communities, the economy, and society. "Users will be able to look up and view the boundaries of Census 2000 geographic areas through the American FactFinder and print maps at their desk-tops."[10] The Bureau will also make boundary, statistical, and thematic maps available on CD-ROM and DVD. In addition, the Bureau will plot some maps on demand. Users can view, print, and download statistics about the population, housing, industry, and business. FactFinder data sources include the decennial census, the economic censuses, and the American community survey.

American Community Survey (ACS), a monthly sample survey, produces a profile (economic, social, and housing indicators) of each community in the nation. The Bureau is looking at the possibility of replacing the long form in the 2010 census with results gathered through the ACS. "The questions are essentially the same as those on the long form, which seek information to manage and evaluate federal programs as required by federal law or court opinion."[11] Gregory J. Abbott and Cheryl V. Chambers of the Census Bureau explain that

> "community" refers to a broad range of groups. It includes geographic areas from states to census tracts, as well as population groups. For instance, eventually the American Community Survey will give policy makers a profile of teenage mothers, whether they are in school or working, living with their parents or living on their own. The survey also will reflect American's diverse population at the local level every year. Profiles will emerge for people of Hispanic origin such as Mexicans, Puerto Ricans, Cubans, and Dominicans, The major race groups also will [be] represented, including African Americans, American Indians, Whites, and Asians, with information provided separately for subgroups such as Chinese and Vietnamese. Information about ancestry groups such as Germans, Italians, Irish, Arabs, and French Canadians also will be available, as will data about the foreign born population.[12]

A useful page provides "quick and easy links to the latest data on racial and ethnic populations in the United States," in particular, "facts on the" Black/African American, Hispanic/Latino, Asian/Pacific Islander, and American Indian/Alaska Native populations (http://www.census.gov/pubinfo/www/hotlinks.html).

Other Sources

MapStats briefly profiles each state and county, as well as judicial and congressional districts, with a map and corresponding data (see http://www.fedstats.gov/qf/). Other products are the following:

- *Statistical Abstract of the United States* includes summary statistics on the social, political, and economic organization of the nation. Tables identify the source or sources from which the data are derived. Thus, information seekers can locate these sources for additional or updated statistics. The Web version provides "frequently requested tables," state profiles, state rankings, and a "Guide to State Statistical Abstracts."

- *State and Metropolitan Area Data Book* includes statistics on social and economic conditions in the United States at the state and metropolitan area levels. There are also selected data for countries and central cities of metropolitan areas.

- *USA Counties* is a CD-ROM product of more than 5,000 data items on counties.

- *County and City Data Book* presents a vast range of information for regions, divisions, states, counties, and cities of at least 25,000 people, and Minor Civil Divisions. Summary data come from various censuses, numerous other government agencies, and private agencies. (http://www.census.gov/statab/www/)

A feature of the Web site is access to the Data Bank ("data from Census 2000, product overviews and assistance in acquiring and using census information"), Newsstand ("news releases, webcasts, tipsheets, videos, photos and more"), Reference Room ("Count Questions Resolution Program . . . [for Census 2000, response rates, questionnaires and marketing"), and Group Corner ("information of interest to partners, teachers, customers, and elected officials") (http://www.census.gov/dmd/www/2khome.htm). In the Reference Room, we find that the national response rate for Census 2000 was 67 percent, which "exceeds the 65% response rate from the 1990 census and far exceeds the 61 percent response rate expected for the census. . . . More than 24 percent (9,294) of the local communities responded to the Census Bureau's challenge to increase their community's participation rates in this census by at least five percentage points over their 1990 response rate" (http://www.census.gov/dmd/www/rates.html).

State Data Center Program

Created in 1978, the State Data Center (SDC) Program is a cooperative program between the states and the Bureau. It provides the public with "easy and efficient access to . . . [census data and information . . . through a network of state agencies, universities, libraries, and regional and local governments. The Business and Industry Data Center Program . . . was added in 1988 to meet the needs of local business communities for economic data" (http://www.census.gov/sdc/www). The governor of a state appoints the SDC lead organizations.

The SDCs make "demographic, economic, and social statistics produced by the Census Bureau . . . accessible to state, regional, local and tribal governments, and non-government data users at no charge or on a cost-recovery or reimbursable basis as appropriate. Fees may be levied for customized products" (http://www.census.gov/sdc/www). For a discussion of the SDC program and links to each site, see http://www.census.gov/sdc/www.

The Bureau has twelve regional offices that provide services and maintain Census Information Centers for underserved communities (see http://www.census.gov/clo/www/cic.html).

Bureau of Economic Analysis

The Bureau of Economic Analysis (BEA) "seeks to strength the understanding of the U.S. economy and its competitive position by providing the most accurate and relevant GDP [gross domestic product] and economic accounts data in a timely and cost-effective manner" (http://www.bea.doc.gov/). The agency's home page offers news releases, publications and data, and regional catalogs of publications. As noted on the home page,

> The *national economic accounts* provide an aggregated view of the final uses of the Nation's output and the income derived from its production; two of its most widely known measures are gross domestic product (GDP) and gross domestic income (GDI). BEA also prepares estimates of the Nation's tangible wealth. The *industry economic accounts* provide detailed information on the flows of goods and services to industries for the production of gross output (input-output) and on the contributions by private industries and government to the nation's gross domestic product (GDP by industry). The regional economic accounts provide estimates and analyses of personal income, population. . . . The *international economic accounts* encompass the international transactions accounts (balance of payments) and the estimates of U.S. direct investment and foreign direct investment in the United States.

> BEA's current national, industry, regional, and international estimates usually appear first in news releases, which are available in a variety of formats. In addition, our monthly journal of record, the *Survey of Current Business* [http://www.bea.doc.gov/bea/pubs.htm], pulls together our estimates, analyses, research, and methodology into one comprehensive package. (http://www.bea.doc.gov/bea/role.htm)

STAT-USA/Internet, a subscription service (see http://www.stat-usa.gov) provides U.S.-produced information on the economy, business, and international trade. "STAT-USA services are not funded by the general taxpayer. Our only revenues are derived from the customers we serve" (http://www.stat-usa.gov/; http://www.stat-usa.gov/hometest.nsf/ref/What_STATUSA?OpenDocument). *State of the Nation*, one of the STAT-USA services, has "current and historical economic and financial releases and economic data," and *GLOBUS & NTDB*, another service, offers access to "current and historical trade-related releases, international market research, trade opportunities, country analysis, and . . . the *National Trade Data Bank (NTDB)*" (http://www.stat-usa.gov/hometest.nsf/ref/ What_STATUSA?OpenDocument). Through STAT-USA's Newsstand, popular reports can be purchased on an individual basis. Finally, there is free access to many STAT-USA products through the depository library program of the Government Printing Office (see Chapter 15).

National Center for Education Statistics

The mission of the National Center for Education Statistics (NCES) is "to collect, analyze, and disseminate statistics and other information related to education in the United States and in other nations" (http://nces.ed.gov). The home page (http://nces.ed.gov) reports on the numerous surveys and educational assessments that the agency makes (see http://nces.ed.gov/surveys). A feature of widespread interest is *The Nation's Report Card*. Information on it, as well as access to state profiles (where one can discover "how your state performed on the 2000 mathematics and other state NAEP [National Assessment of Educational Progress] assessments") can be found at http://nces.ed.gov/nationsreportcard. Other useful features are "NCES Fast Facts," "Quick Tables & Figures," "Global ED Locator," and "Encyclopedia of ED Stats (see http://nces.ed.gov). The NCES Electronic Catalog provides "customized searches to locate NCES publications and data products" (http://nces.ed.gov/pubsearch/index.asp).

Energy Information Administration

The Energy Information Administration (EIA), which collects information worldwide from the open literature, has a home page (http://www.eia.doe.gov) that provides access to energy information by geographical region, fuel, sector, or subject ("Process," "Environment," and "Forecasts"). It is also possible to find publications, historical data, press releases, and energy links. Some of the other options are "sign up for email updates," "contact experts," and "What's New." Topics addressed at this site include the energy supply, renewable energy, and international comparisons.

Bureau of Justice Statistics

At the home page of the Bureau of Justice Statistics (BJS) (http://www. ojp.usdoj.gov/bjs), there are statistics on "Crimes and Victims," "Criminal Offenders," "Special Topics" ("Sourcebook of Criminal Justice Statistics, Firearms and Crime, World Factbook of Criminal Justice Systems . . ."), "Crime and Justice Data from other Sources" (FBI's Uniform Crime Reports, Juvenile Justice Statistics, International Statistics, . . ."), and "The Justice System" ("Law Enforcement," "Prosecution," "Courts and Sentencing," "Corrections," and "Expenditure and Employment"). "Key Crime and Justice Facts at a Glance" presents trend charts with brief statements of findings (http://www.ojp.usdoj. gov/bjs/glance.htm). "Data for Analysis" offers federal district, state, and local data "assembled into spreadsheets from a wide variety of published sources. Intended for analytic use, the files include crime, justice and sociodemographic variables; and "online tabulations, source data & codebooks" (http://www.ojp. usdoj.gov/bjs/dtd.htm).

Bureau of Labor Statistics

The Bureau of Labor Statistics (BLS) is the principal fact-finding agency in the fields of labor economics and statistics. More specifically, it covers

- Employment and unemployment: Labor Force Statistics (Current Population Survey), Nonfarm Payroll Statistics at the national, state, and local levels (Current Employment Statistics), Covered Employment and Wages, Occupational Employment Statistics, and Local Area Unemployment Statistics;

- Prices and living conditions: Consumer Prices Indexes, Producer Price Indexes, International Price Indexes, and Consumer Expenditure Survey;

- Compensation and working conditions: National Compensation Survey, Employee Benefits Survey, Employment Cost Trends, Occupational Compensation Survey, and Safety and Health Statistics;

- Productivity and technology: Quarterly Labor Productivity, Multifactor Productivity, Industry Labor Productivity, and Foreign Labor Statistics;

- Employment projections: Employment Projections;

- International programs: Foreign Labor Statistics and International Price Indexes; and

- Other surveys: National Longitudinal Surveys.

The BLS has the database O*NET (The Occupational Information Network™), which replaces the *Dictionary of Occupational Titles*, first published in 1938 as a source of occupational information. It is possible to produce concise occupational profiles that give the most essential characteristics of an occupation, as well as the abilities, interests, and work values associated with workers in different occupations. There is also an identification of worker requirements (education, knowledge, basic skills, and cross-functional skills), occupation requirements (information on generalized work activities and organizational and work contexts), and experience requirements. Labor market characteristics cover employment projections and earnings data, and there is information specific to an occupation.

The Web site (http://stats.bls.gov/) provides easy and quick access to information under the following headings: "Economy at a Glance," "Career Guides," "Inflation and Spending," "Working and Looking for Work," "How Much People Earn," "Worker Safety and Health," "Productivity," "International Statistics," "Online Magazines," "Economic Analysis and Information Offices," and "Tools." The left side of the opening screen covers topics such as "Data," "Economy at a Glance," "News Releases," "Regional Information," "Publications and Research Papers," "Occupational Outlook Handbook," "Surveys & Programs," and "Other Statistical Sites."

As is evident, the home page leads to international, national, and regional information. The Bureau maintains economic analysis and information centers in Atlanta, Boston, Chicago, Dallas, Kansas City, New York, Philadelphia, and San Francisco. The page also identifies the "Most Requested Data" and "Other Types of Data Access" (http://www.bls.gov/data/). Furthermore, the "Surveys & Programs" provides resources under the headings "Employment and Unemployment," "Prices & Living Conditions," "Compensation and Working Conditions," and "Productivity and Technology."

Among the publications found at this Web site are the following:

- *Monthly Labor Review* features analytical articles on employment and unemployment, prices, compensation and working conditions, productivity, and other topics. There are also tables of current labor statistics, book reviews, and occasional columns on workplace performance and the law at work.

- *Employment and Earnings* covers developments in employment and unemployment as well as providing statistics on (1) national, state, and area employment and (2) hours and earnings.

- *Compensation and Working Conditions* includes articles on occupational pay, employee benefits, employer costs for employee compensation, occupational injuries and illnesses, and other workplace issues. The Bureau's compensation and working conditions programs present statistics.

- *CPI Detailed Report* reports on consumer price movements.

- *PPI Detailed Report* reports on producer price movements.

- *Occupational Outlook Handbook* and *Occupational Outlook Quarterly* provide information to guidance counselors, career planners, and anyone contemplating a specific career.

National Center for Health Statistics

The National Center for Health Statistics has a Web site (http://www.cdc.gov/nchs/) with a feature called "Data Warehouse," that provides access to the "Top 10 Links," "Micro-data Access," "Tabulated State Data," Information

Showcase," site index and site search, and so forth. The page lists numerous publications and survey results (e.g., the annual *Health United States*), many of which can be found in the "Information Showcase."

Statistics of Income Division

The Internal Revenue Service introduces the Statistics of Income (SOI) program and its data collection and reporting as follows:

> Remember what Mark Twain said about statistics? Well, obviously he hadn't heard about our Tax Stats page. There's a wealth of information about the financial composition of individuals, business taxpayers, tax exempt organizations and more. This data has been sampled from all kinds of returns and sorted in lots of interesting ways. These facts will amuse some of you. Others will find them worth their weight in gold. And everyone is happy, statistically speaking. (http://www. irs.ustreas.gov/taxstats/display/0,,i1%3D40%26genericId%3D16810,0)

Statistics are available on "Corporations," "Employment Taxes," "Estates/ Wealth/Gifts," "Excise Taxes," "Individuals," "International," "Partnerships," "Sole Proprietorships," "Tax Exempt/Employee Plans," and "Trusts."

Bureau of Transportation Statistics

Established in 1991, the Bureau of Transportation Statistics (BTS) collects, analyzes, and reports data relevant to ensuring the "most cost-effective use of transportation-monitoring resources. . . . [The agency strives] to increase public awareness of the nation's transportation system and its implications and improve the transportation knowledge base of decisionmakers" (http://www.bts.gov). The home page (http://www.bts.gov) has the following features: information about the agency, the *Journal of Transportation and Statistics*, a map gallery, press releases, products and research tools, searchable databases, a site map, what's new, the National Transportation Library ("contains documents and databases provided by the authors free of any restriction on reproduction" [http://ntl.bts.gov/browse.cfm]), surveys and programs, and so forth. Among the surveys and programs are

Airline information,

Airline on-time statistics,

Commodity Flow Survey,

International transportation,

Motor carrier information,

National Household Travel Survey (formerly the American Travel Survey),

OMNIBUS Survey,

Statistical policy and research,

Transportation indicators and statistics,

Transportation studies, and

TRIS Online.

TRIS Online is "the largest and most comprehensive source of information on published transportation research" (http://199.79.179.82/sundev/search.cfm).

The National Household Travel Survey is conducted every five years by the Department of Transportation. "Survey data are collected from a sample of U.S. households and expanded to provide national estimates of trips and miles by travel mode, purpose, and a host of other characteristics. The survey collects information on daily and local trips, and on long-distance travel in the United States" (http://ntl.bts.gov/nhts).

The OMNIBUS Survey "is a shared-cost survey that collects information from households in the United States on a monthly basis. [It] provides . . . data on issues related to safety, mobility, the human and natural environment, economic growth, and national security to support information planning and decision-making" (http://ntl.bts.gov/omnibus).

OTHER SOURCES

The Federal Interagency Council on Statistical Policy provides FedStats, which is an excellent Web site (http://www.fedstats.gov) for someone unfamiliar with the structure of government who wants access to the resources of more than seventy statistical reporting agencies "reporting expenditures of at least $500,000 per year in one or more statistical activities," including

- Planning of statistical surveys and studies, including project design, sample design and selection, and design of questionnaires, forms, and other techniques of observation and data collection;

- Training of statisticians, interviewers, or processing personnel;

- Collection, processing, or tabulation of statistical data for publication, dissemination, research, analysis, or program management and evaluation;

- Publication or dissemination of statistical data and studies;

- Methodological testing or statistical research;

- Data analysis;

- Forecasts or projections that are published or otherwise made available for government-wide or public use;

- Statistical tabulation, dissemination, or publication of data collected by others;

- Construction of secondary data series or development of models that are an integral part of generating statistical series or forecasts;

- Management or coordination of statistical operations; and

- Statistics consulting or training. (http://www.fedstats.gov/aboutfedstats.html)

There is a note that "all of the statistical information available through FedStats is maintained and updated solely by Federal agencies on their own web servers" (http://www.fedstats.gov/aboutfedstats.html).

FedStats has links to

- Statistics ("direct access to statistical data on topics of your choice," "statistical profiles of states, countries, congressional districts, and federal judicial districts," "international comparisons, national, state, county, and local," "published collections of statistics available online including the *Statistical Abstract of the United States*," and a "search across agency website"); and

- Statistical agencies ("agencies listed alphabetically with descriptions of the statistics they provide and links to their websites, contact information, and key statistics," "agencies by subject" (pull-down menu is provided), "press releases," and "selected agency online databases"). (http://www. fedstats.gov/aboutfedstats.html)

"More than 400 topics that range from acute conditions (colds and influenza) through weekly earning" are found in the section on "statistical data on topics of your choice" (http://www.fedstats.gov/aboutfedstats.html). This section of "links to statistics" is known as "Topic Links A to Z."

Other Government Agencies

The Office of Information and Regulatory Policy, Office of Management and Budget (OMB), within the Executive Office of the President, oversees the data collection process that executive agencies use. Relevant methodological and policy information is available at OMB's Web site (http://www. whitehouse.gov/omb). Within the legislative branch, congressional committees may ask the General Accounting Office (GAO) to investigate the plans and execution of statistical programs and surveys (see http://www.gao.gov).

Commercial Sources

American Statistics Index (ASI), published by the Congressional Information Service (CIS) since 1974, is the master guide and index to statistical publications of the federal government. It was created in response to the 1971 President's Commission on Federal Statistics, which called for a central source to locate data collected by the government. The monthly index, accompanied by a microfiche collection of the publications, is cumulated annually. (The microfiche set can be purchased as the complete collection or as nondepository materials only.)

The Statistical Universe is one of the suite of Universe Web-based products produced by Lexis-Nexis, which bought out CIS. The product provides full-text access to statistics from the federal government, as well as international, intergovernmental, and privately generated statistics, through a single interface. It includes coverage of *ASI* from 1973 to date; *Statistical Reference Index* (*SRI*), which is another product covering state government and privately published data from such institutions as think tanks, from 1980 to date; and *Index to International Statistics* (*IIS*), a resource for international and intergovernmental (IGO) organizational data, from 1983 to date. (Both *SRI* and *IIS* provide microfiche collections.) Users can search statistical tables by using the "Power Tables" feature, search summaries of statistical publications, or link to other Web sites that contain statistical information. Workable electronic formats allow users to view, download, and manipulate data using such applications as GIF images and spreadsheets. PDF is also available.

HISTORICAL COVERAGE

Anyone engaging in historical research for periods prior to the creation of the *American Statistics Index* in the early 1970s could check back issues of the *Statistical Abstract of the United States* (1897–). As an alternative, the Bureau of the Census issued *Historical Statistics of the United States: Colonial Times to 1970*,[13] a compilation that covers a broad range of topics, such as

Population;

Vital statistics, health, and medical care;

Migration;

Labor;

Prices and price indexes;

National income and wealth;

Consumer income and expenditures;

Social statistics;

Land, water, and climate;

Agriculture;

Forestry and fisheries;

Minerals;

Construction and housing;

Manufacturers;

Transportation;

International transactions and foreign commerce;

Financial markets and institutions; and

Government.

Coverage also extends to pre-1789 colonial and pre-national times. There is an introduction to each general topic that includes references to additional sources. Each data table has special notes on the scope or accuracy of the data.

In *The Statistical Work of the National Government*, Laurence F. Schmeckebier covers "current statistics," defined then as the mid-1920s; he also provides "a brief outline of the history of each class of data with sufficient bibliographic references to enable the reader to locate the publications."[14] This 574-page treatise has thirty-six chapters that cover topics such as the "Population" (including "Negroes, Indians, Chinese, and Japanese"), "Immigrants and Emigrants," "Occupations," "Births," "Education," "Labor and Wages," "Women and Children," "Imports and Exports," "General Statistics of Cities," "Foreign Countries," and "Land, Transportation and Communication." Adding to the value of this work for historical coverage—primarily from the end of the Civil War to the 1920s—is the coverage of both the executive branch and Congress. For example:

> In 1874 a select committee of Congress on transportation routes to the seaboard made a report, published as Senate Report 207, 43d Congress, 1st Session, which is largely devoted to testimony and a discussion of the transportation problem, but which contains some statistical material from unofficial sources on the grain movement, grain price, and freight rates on railroads in the United States, on ocean steamers, and on British canals and railroads.[15]

Using the historical indexes presented in Chapter 2, we would find this publication in the Serial Set (number **1586**). Schmeckebier issues a reminder about congressional testimony: Unofficial sources should be treated "with considerable caution and with due allowance for bias on the part of the witness."[16]

A search of the older indexes (see Chapter 2) might also disclose additional data. For example, the annual reports of executive departments and agencies provide data to explain and justify programs and actions. Another alternative is to consult the Web site of the National Archives and Records Administration (http://www.archives.gov/index.html) for its coverage of census (prior to the last seventy-two years) and other records.

The *Encyclopedia of the U.S. Census* covers topics related to the decennial census since the first one in 1790,[17] including those related to the cost of census taking and congressional reapportionment. A commercial edition is available on

CD-ROM, and the United States Historical Census Data Browser (http://fisher. lib.Virginia.edu/census) enables one to browse data created by the Inter-university Consortium for Political and Social Research (ICPSR), which requires institutional membership. Project data describe the population and economy within each state and county from 1790 to 1970.

CONCLUSION

Anyone starting a search for recent policy directives guiding statistical programs, services, and surveys should check the Web site of the agency in question. The home pages of OMB and GAO also merit examination. Because the Bureau of the Census produces approximately two-thirds of the government's statistics, its Web site (http://www.census.gov) might be a good starting point for current statistics. That site also provides hot links to other statistical bodies, within and outside the United States. FedStats is another useful starting point, as is *Statistical Abstract of the United States.*

NOTES

1. Joseph W. Duncan and William C. Shelton, *Revolution in the United States Government Statistics, 1926–1976* (Washington, D.C.: GPO, 1978).

2. Ibid., 1.

3. Ibid., 2.

4. Ibid.

5. Frederick G. Bohme and George Daily, "1990 Census: The 21st Count of 'We The People'," *Social Education* 53 (7) (November–December 1989): 422. For additional information on the history of the census, see Claudette Bennett, "Racial Categories Used in the Decennial Censuses," *Government Information Quarterly* 17 (2000): 161–80; Miriam D. Rosenthal, "Striving for Perfection: A Brief History of Advances and Undercounts in the U.S. Census," *Government Information Quarterly* 17 (2000): 193–208; William F. Micarelli, "Evolution of the United States Economic Censuses: The Nineteenth and Twentieth Centuries," *Government Information Quarterly* 15 (1998): 335–77.

6. Bureau of the Census, *The Economic Census—'97: Two Moments of Truth: 1954 and 1997* (Washington, D.C., June 1998), 1.

7. Ibid., 2. See also Carole A. Ambler and James E. Kristoff, "Introducing the North American Industry Classification System," *Government Information Quarterly* 15 (1998): 263–73.

8. John Kavaliunas, "Census 2000 Data Products," *Government Information Quarterly* 17 (2000): 215.

9. Ibid., 218.

10. Ibid.

11. Ann Quarzo, "Plans for Census 2000," *Government Information Quarterly* 17 (2000): 114.

12. Gregory J. Abbott and Cheryl V. Chambers, "Looking Toward an Information Base in the 21st Century: The American Community Survey," *Government Information Quarterly* 17 (2000): 224.

13. Bureau of the Census, *Historical Statistics of the United States: Colonial Times to 1970* (Washington, D.C.: GPO, 1970). SuDocs Number: C3.134/2:H62/789-970/pt. 1 and 2.

14. Laurence F. Schmeckebier, *The Statistical Work of the National Government* (Baltimore, Md.: Johns Hopkins Press, 1925), 3.

15. Ibid., 415.

16. Ibid., 3.

17. Margo J. Anderson, ed., *Encyclopedia of the U.S. Census* (Washington, D.C.: CQ Press, 2000).

URL SITE GUIDE

Bureau of Economic Analysis
Department of Commerce
 http://www.bea.doc.gov/

 STAT-USA/Internet
  http://www/stat-usa.gov/
  http://www.stat-usa.gov/hometest.nsf/ref/What_STATUSA?OpenDocument

 Survey of Current Business
  http://www.bea.doc.gov/bea/pubs.htm

Bureau of Justice Statistics
Department of Justice
 http://www.ojp.usdoj.gov/bjs/

 Crime and Facts at a Glance
  http://www.ojp.usdoj.gov/bjs/glance.htm

 Data for Analysis
  http://www.ojp.usdoj.gov/bjs/dtd.htm

Bureau of Labor Statistics
Department of Labor
 http://stats.bls.gov/

 Data Resources
  http://www.bls.gov/data/

Bureau of the Census
Department of Commerce
 http://www.census.gov/

 Census Information Centers
  http://www.census. gov/clo/www/cic.html

Data Bank
http://www.census.gov/dmd/www/2khome.htm

Key Publications
http://www.census.gov/statab/www/

MapStats
http://www.fedstats.gov/qf/

National Response Rate
http://www.census.gov/dmd/www/rates.html

Racial and Ethnic Populations
http://www.census.gov/pubinfo/www/hotlinks.html

Reference Room
http://www.census.gov/dmd/www/rates.html

State Data Center Program
http://www.census.gov/sdc/www/

Bureau of Transportation Statistics
Department of Transportation
http://www.bts.gov/

National Household Travel Survey
http://www.bts.gov/nhts/

OMNIBUS Survey
http://www.bts.gov/omnibus/

TRIS Online
http://199.79.179.82/sundev/search.cfm

Department of Veterans Affairs
http://www.va.gov/

Economic Research Service
Department of Agriculture
http://www.ers.usda.gov/

Briefing Rooms
http://www.ers.usda.gov/Briefing/

Data Products
http://www.ers.usda.gov/Data/

Publications
http://www.ers.usda.gov/Publications/

Energy Information Administration
Department of Energy
http://www.eia.doe.gov/

Federal Reserve System
http://www.federalreserve.gov/

FedStats
http://www.fedstats.gov/

General Accounting Office
   http://www.gao.gov/

Management Statistics (Courts)
   http://www.uscourts.gov/fcmstat/index.html

National Agricultural Statistics Service
   http://www.usda.gov/nass/

   On-Line Data Base
      http://www.usda.gov/nass/sso-rpts.htm

National Archives and Records Administration
   http://www.archives.gov/index.html

National Center for Education Statistics
Department of Education
   http://nces.ed.gov/

   Nation's Report Card
      http://nces.ed.gov/nationsreportcard/

   NCES Electronic Catalog
      http://nces.ed.gov/pubsearch/index.asp

   Surveys and Educational Assessments
      http://nces.ed.gov/surveys/

National Center for Health Statistics
Department of Health and Human Services
   http://www.cdc.gov/nchs/

Office of Management and Budget
   http://www.whitehouse.gov/omb/

Social Security Administration
   http://www.ssa.gov/

State Historical Census Data Browser
   http://fisher.lib.Virginia,edu/census

Statistics of Income Division
Internal Revenue Service
Department of the Treasury
   http://www.irs.ustreas.gov/taxstats/display/0,,i1%3D40%26genericId%
      3D16810,0

U.S. International Trade Commission
   http://dataweb.usitc.gov/

 Chapter 14

Maps and Geographical Information Systems

As Laurence F. Schmeckebier and Roy B. Eastin note, "maps have been published both independently and in connection with reports since the early days of the government but extensive systematic map publishing in series was developed in the last quarter of the 19th century."[1] They point out that "the early series which have been continued to the present time were devoted to navigation," and that, "for many years, the maps of land areas resulted almost entirely from exploring expeditions or from surveys made for a specific object and confined to limited areas. The maps generally formed part of the textual reports of the explorations or surveys."[2]

After the Civil War, four agencies within the Department of the Interior (Geological and Geographical Survey of the Territories—*Hayden Survey*, and the Geographical and Geological Survey of the Rocky Mountain Region—*Powell Survey*) and the War Department (Geographical Surveys West of the 100th Meridian—*Wheeler Survey*, and the Geological Exploration of the 40th Parallel—*King Survey*) conducted geologic and topographic surveys of the West. These efforts lacked coordination, and "no comprehensive plan for mapping the entire country existed until, in 1879, the United States Geological Survey"[3] (USGS) developed one and displaced those disparate agencies. Since that time, the mapping activities of the government have still not been confined to one department or agency. Some of the actors involved are the National Ocean Service, the National Imagery and Mapping Agency, the Forest Service, the Weather Bureau, the Central Intelligence Agency, the Environmental Protection Agency, the National Park Service, and the Natural Resources Conservation Service, all of which are discussed in the companion *U.S. Government on the Web*.[4]

Through the efforts of various agencies, the government has produced maps, atlases, surveys, gazetteers, guides, aerial and satellite photography, navigation charts, and so forth. A wide assortment of publications has resulted, and some of these works have been security classified (and, in some instances, declassified). The purpose of this chapter is to provide a general overview of government mapping products and services, as well as an introduction to geographic

315

information systems (GISs). A GIS is a computerized system that captures, stores, manipulates, analyzes, and presents geo-coded data—coded to a particular location on the earth's surface (e.g., latitude/longitude, census tract or block number, school or postal address, state, or town, voting or school district, postal code, congressional district, or hazardous waste site). A GIS allows users to overlay multiple digital images, such as roads and wetlands, to facilitate data analysis. A GIS can also integrate the attributes from each unique layer while maintaining spatial referencing. In essence, a GIS is both a tool and a process for bringing together, from various sources, data about boundaries (geographic coordinate data) and data about those features (attribute data) to query, manipulate, analyze, and present those data graphically to show patterns and perhaps trends.

Using a GIS, it is possible to produce images (maps, drawings, animations, and other cartographic products), engage in modeling and "what if" scenarios, provide customized output to address specific problems and questions, include more datasets, identify patterns and trends in spatial relationships, and gain more detailed insights into questions that previously might not have been answerable. Examples of questions that might be examined are:

- Does the outbreak of an infectious disease produce a pattern that correlates with the presence of nearby waste facilities?

- What is the demographic composition of a particular congressional district?

- What habitats of endangered species can be protected without imposing undue economic impact?

- How do problems related to forest fire control, economic impact, traffic flow, and environmental quality complicate the management of federal lands, including national parks?

HISTORICAL SOURCES

The historical and more current finding aids discussed in Chapter 2 include maps and mapping activities. The Serial Set, for example, contains numerous maps. Schmeckebier and Eastin mention that the charts found near the front of the *Checklist of United States Public Documents, 1789–1909* include maps. "The 'Notes' column [of those charts] generally indicates a book composed entirely of maps, although it does not always indicate their character. Maps are found in many other volumes for which there is no such notation, particularly in the reports on explorations and surveys."[5] The *Powell Survey* is covered under the SuDocs notation I.17., the *Hayden Survey* at I.18., the *King Survey* at W7.10: 18 (volumes 1–9), and the *Wheeler Survey* at W8. The notation I19. covers publications of the *Geological Survey*. Note that, when entries include a set of bracketed numbers (e.g., [4317–17]), those numbers refer to the Serial Set and volume numbers; in other words, Serial Set 4317 appears as volume 17.

Part XIV of the *CIS US Serial Set Index, 1789–1969* provides access to more than 50,000 maps that are embedded in Serial Set publications. The *Index and Carto-Bibliography of Maps, 1789–1969*, edited by Donna P. Koepp, with support from the University of Kansas, was issued in three segments, 1789–1897, 1897–1925, and 1925–1969. These maps cover a wide variety of topics, such as information on Native American tribes, economic conditions, inland transportation, and battlegrounds.

Both the *Monthly Catalog of United States Government Publications* and the biennial *Document Catalog* provide access to maps. In the latter source, "the detailed entry for each map was given under the publishing office, the maps being segregated after all other entries. There was no other detailed listing of maps, but there were cross references to the publishing offices from the names of states or specific areas."[6] Chapter 16 of Schmeckebier and Easton's *Government Publications and Their Use* covers maps, discusses information on a number of other historical sources on mapping activities, as well as the holdings of the National Archives and Records Administration and the Library of Congress (LC).

The Library of Congress's Geography and Map Division "has custody of the largest and most comprehensive cartographic collection in the world. . . . These cartographic materials date from fourteenth century portolan charts through recent geographic information systems data sets" (http://www.lcweb. loc.gov/rr/geogmap). Figure 14.1 (page 318) identifies map collections of the Division (1500–1999) that are available through the Web (http://lcweb2.loc.gov/ ammem/gmdhtml/gmdhome.html). Organized according to the seven major categories noted in the figure, a map appears in "only one category, unless it is part of more than one core collection. . . . These images were created from maps and atlases and, in general, are restricted to items that are not covered by copyright protection" (http://www.lcweb2.loc.gov/ammem/gmdhtml/gmdhome.html).

PRESENT DAY

Of the finding aids mentioned in Chapter 2, one of the best for beginning a search of government Web sites is FirstGov (http://www.first.gov.gov/). Inserting the search term "map" or "geographical information system," although they are very general, will suggest some initial sites to peruse. They lead to LC's Map Collections: 1500–1999. One might conduct a more focused search on a topic such as "sea-floor mapping." Also, LC's American Memory (http://memory. loc.gov/) includes maps, such as historical ones on the city of Boston. The Government Printing Office's Online Bookstore contains a set of Subject Bibliographies, number 102 of which covers "Maps and Atlases" (http://bookstore.gpo. gov/sb/sb-102.html).

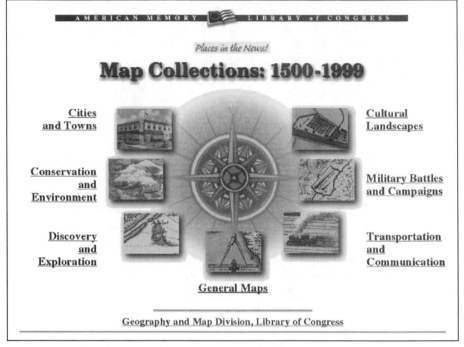

Figure 14.1. Library of Congress Map Collections, 1500–1999. *Source:*
http://lcweb2.loc.gov/ammem/gmdhtml/gmdhome.html.

In 1990, through Circular A-16, "Coordination of Surveying, Mapping, and Related Spatial Data Archives," the Office of Management and Budget (OMB) created the Federal Geographic Data Committee (FGDC), which was given responsibility for coordinating various surveying, mapping, and spatial data activities of federal agencies. In accordance with Executive Order 12906, "Coordinating Geographic Data Acquisition and Access: The National Spatial Data Infrastructure" (NSDI), which President Clinton issued on April 11, 1994, FGDC began to develop procedures and assist "in the implementation of a distributed discovery mechanism for digital geospatial data" (http://www.fgdc.gov/clearinghouse/clearinghouse.html). The NSDI's purpose is to make collections of spatial information searchable and accessible on the Internet using free reference implementation software developed by the Committee (http://www.fgdc.gov/clearinghouse/clearinghouse.html). The FGDC has seventeen federal agencies that are working with state, local, and tribal governments; the academic community; and the private sector to develop the NSDI and to address policies, standards, and procedures for organizations to cooperatively produce and share geographic data.

FGDC's Web site (http://www.fgdc.gov) provides news (including "Homeland Security and Geographic Information Systems"), the NSDI, access to standards, publications and special reports, data, metadata, a clearinghouse, and so forth. The Committee develops geospatial data standards for implementing the NSDI and reproduces standards directives, a standards reference model ("defines the expectations of FGDC standards, describes different types of geospatial standards, and documents the FGDC standards process"), standards documents by sponsoring organizations, and so forth (http://www.fgdc.gov/standards/standards.html).

FGDC's "Geospatial Data Clearinghouse is a collection of more than 250 spatial data servers that have digital geographic data primarily for use in Geographic Information Systems . . ., image processing systems, and other modeling software. These data collections can be searched through a single interface based on their descriptions, or 'metadata' " (http://130.11.53.184). It is also possible to "click on the name of a Clearinghouse Gateway" (http://130.11.53.184).

United States Geological Survey

The USGS, located within the Department of the Interior, "serves the Nation by providing reliable scientific information to describe and understand the Earth; minimize loss of life and property from natural disasters; manage water, biological, energy, and mineral resources; and enhance and protect our quality of life" (http://www.usgs.gov/stratplan/vision.html). Its Web site (http://www.usgs.gov) provides a useful introduction to the agency, its mission, and its resources. An excellent starting place is "About USGS" (http://www.usgs.gov/about_us.html), which discusses the organization and its personnel; provides links to a fax-on-demand service and other services, frequently asked questions, and Ask services (location of supplementary information); offers planning and budget documents; provides a history of the agency and its past directors; and contains a site map and an index of agency Web sites.

Before proceeding with a search of USGS's Web pages, it might also be beneficial to visit the U.S. Geological Survey Library (http://library.usgs.gov). This site includes databases, frequently asked questions, "Ask a Librarian" (submit e-mail reference questions), and similar features. The "USGS Web Mapping Portal" (http://gisdata.usgs.net), another general source, identifies different projects and sources and provides links to their Web pages (e.g., the National Land Cover Characterization Dataset, http://landcover.usgs.gov/nationallandcover.html, which is published on the Geography Network, http://landcover.usgs.gov/otherorganizations.html). In addition, there are lists of the "10 most . . . ," one of which is the "10 most downloaded files."

Maps

The USGS produces more than 80,000 different maps. These include the 1:24,000 scale topographic maps, known as the 7.5 minute quadrangles; topographic maps at smaller scales; maps of U.S. possessions and territories and of Antarctica; special maps of national parks, monuments, the moon, and planets; and geological and hydrologic maps. Perhaps the best known USGS maps are 7.5 minute quadrangles, which constitute the only uniform map series that covers the entire area of the United States in considerable detail. Mapfinder provides "a quick and easy way to find and order USGS 7.5 minute printed paper maps" (http://edc.usgs.gov/Webglis/glisbin/finder_main.pl?dataset_name=MAPS). One inch of these maps represents 200 feet on the ground, and the paper prints are approximately 22 by 27 inches (see http://edc.usgs.gov/Webglis/glisbin/finder_ main.pl?dataset_name=MAPS). For an introduction to the topographic maps, see http://mcmcweb.er.usgs.gov/topomaps, and for a listing of "Selected Federal Mapping Programs, Products, and Services," see http://mcmcweb.er. usgs.gov/topomaps/.

The USGS has a sixteen-page online booklet that "gives a brief overview of the types of maps sold and distributed by the USGS through its Earth Science Information Centers (ESIC) . . . " (http://mac.usgs.gov/isb/pubs/booklets/usgsmaps/ usgsmaps.html). For each type, there is an image and brief explanation of the scale, features, and what that type covers. As an example, a topographic-bathymetric map is shown, and it is noted that such maps "show in one format and one edition the data for a land-water area previously shown separately as a topographic map and a bathymetric map":

> On topographic-bathymetric maps, contour lines show elevations of the land areas above sea level, and isobaths (bathymetric contours) show the form of the land below the water surface.

> Some bathymetric maps show magnetic and gravity data in addition to water depths.

> Because coastal zones include both land and water, maps of such areas include both topographic and bathymetric data. In order to produce these coastal maps, the National Ocean service provided bathymetric data to be added to USGS topographic maps. The combined map serves the needs of oceanographers, marine geologists, land use planners, physical scientists, conservationists, and others having an interest in management of the coastal zone, the wetlands, and the offshore environment. Topographic-bathymetric maps at a scale of 1:24,000 are popular with people who enjoy fishing. Topographic-bathymetric maps are also available at 1:100,000 and 1:250,000 scale. (http://mac.usgs.gov/isb/pubs/booklets/usgsmaps/usgsmaps.html)

Other maps are orthophotoquads ("black-and-white, distortion free, photographic image maps that are produced in standard 7.5-minute quadrangle format from aerial photographs, but have no contours and only minimal cartographic treatment"), satellite image maps ("multicolor or black-and-white photograph-like maps made from data collected by Earth resources satellites"), and border maps ("203 natural color photoimage maps at a scale of 1:25,000 . . . [bracket] the U.S.-Mexico border and . . . [cover] the entire international boundary from the Pacific Ocean to the Gulf of Mexico") (http://mac.usgs.gov/isb/ pubs/booklets/usgsmaps/usgsmaps.html). The USGS has a business partner program to expand the diversity of maps and aerial photo images that information seekers can find online. For quick access to these partners and the types of services they offer, see http://mapping.usgs.gov/partners/viewonline.html.

Digital Raster Graphics are scanned images of a USGS "standard series topographic map, including all map collar information" (http://mcmcweb.er. usgs.gov/drg). This Web page covers software and sample data, standards and other technical information, access to USGS business partners, and so forth.

The National Geologic Map Database provides convenient and quick access to "information about maps and related data for: geology, hazards, earth resources, geophysics, geochemistry, geochronology, paleontology, and marine geology" (http://ngmdb.usgs.gov). There is coverage of "Geologic Maps" ("a catalog of paper and digital maps, and where to find them"), "Geologic Names" ("a catalog of lithologic and geochronologic names"), "New Mapping" ("places where geologic mapping is in progress"), "how to find topographic maps," "other earth science databases," and "other Web resources" (http://ngmdb.usgs.gov).

The USGS envisions the creation of *The National Map* that "will reestablish linkages between the topographic map series and the foundation digital data from which the maps will be derived" (http://nationalmap.usgs.gov/report/national_map_report_final.pdf). The purpose is to provide current information "measured in weeks and months, rather than years or decades." Thus, the National Map provides a "current, accurate, and nationally consistent base of geographic information, including digital data and derived topographic maps" (http://nationalmap.usgs.gov).

Atlases

The National Atlas of the United States®, which USGS maintains for the federal government "is designed to provide a reliable summary of national-scale geographical information" (http://www.nationalatlas.gov/federal.html). (For a twenty-five page description of participating government entities, see http://www.nationalatlas.gov/federal.html.) Although it cannot provide detailed map information, the Atlas directs users to other sources of this information (see national atlas.gov™, http://www-atlas.usgs.gov).

The Atlas of Antarctic Research, begun in December 1998, is "designed to promote greater geographic awareness of the continent and the digital geospatial data that describe it" (http://usarc.usgs.gov/antarctic_atlas). The Web site of this atlas reports some declassified images.

Mapping Program Standards

The USGS's "National Mapping Program Standards" (http://mapping. usgs.gov/standards/index.html) provides standards documents, an overview of program standards, and access to other standards information (that produced by the FGDC, as well as offering the Spatial Data Transfer Standard and links worldwide to other standards Web sites). The site notes that "standards set the criteria and specifications to ensure that all publications prepared by the USGS . . . National Mapping Program . . . reflect current mapping and data policies and are accurate and consistent in style and content" (http://mapping.usgs.gov/standards/index.html).

Geographical Information Systems

Geographical information systems combine technology with mapping and data services. For example, computer technology is combined with satellite imagery. As the USGS notes:

> [T]he condition of the Earth's surface, atmosphere, and subsurface can be examined by feeding satellite data into a GIS. GIS technology gives researchers the ability to examine the variations in Earth's processes over days, months, and years. As an example, the changes in vegetation vigor through a growing season can be animated to determine when drought was most extensive in a particular region. The resulting graphic, known as a normalized vegetation index, represents a rough measure of plant health. (http://www.usgs.gov/research/gis/application7.html)

For information about USGS global GISs, see http://webgis.wr.usgs.gov/globalgis/proj_desc.htm.

Other Products

The USGS offers convenient access to "Aerial Photographs," "Fact Sheets and Booklets," "Real-time Data," "Satellite Imagery," "Scientific Publications," "Software," "Maps," and "Digital Maps & Data" (see http://ask.usgs.gov/products.html).

The Geographic Names Information System (GNIS), which USGS developed in cooperation with the United States Board on Geographic Names (BGN)—an agency of the Department of the Interior created in 1890 and responsible for establishing and maintaining uniform geographic name usage throughout the national government (http://geonames.usgs.gov/bgn.html)—"contains information about almost 2 million physical and cultural geographic features in the United States. . . . The GNIS is our Nation's official repository of domestic geographic names information. Information about foreign geographic feature names can be obtained from the GEOnet Names Server" (http://geonames.usgs.gov/bgn.html) (see entry for the National Imagery and Mapping Agency) (GNIS is at http://geonames.usgs.gov). As noted at this Web page, GNIS is available on CD-ROM as *The GNIS Digital Gazetteer*.

The USGS's National Aerial Photography Program has Photofinder, which includes photographs "shot from airplanes flying at 20,000 feet. Each 9-by-9-inch photo (without enlargement) covers an area a bit more than 5 miles on a side" (http://edc.usgs.gov/Webglis/glisbin/finder_main.pl?dataset_name=NAPP).

Bureau of the Census

The Bureau of the Census developed the Topologically Integrated Geographic Encoding and Reference System (TIGER), a computerized mapping system that enables the public to visualize statistical information about the nation. It is possible to produce a map and see the dataset beneath it. The Bureau's "Mapping and Cartographic Resources" (see http://www.census.gov/geo/www/maps) and its Map Gallery (see http://www.census.gov/geo/www/mapGallery/index.html) include products drawing on the 1990 and 2000 decennial censuses. Using the American FactFinder (an interactive database engine for data from the latest economic census, the American Community Survey, and the decennial census of population), for instance, it is possible to build a search query, construct maps, and view the corresponding data tables. Other maps show population change from 1990 to 2000. Figures 14.2 (page 324) and 14.3 (page 325) illustrate the types of maps that the Bureau has produced based on recently published decennial census data. Figure 14.2 shows the 2000 population distribution in the United States. "The U.S. land area is shown in black against a midnight blue background in which the population locations are shown as if lights were visible during the night sky. White dots coalesce to form the urban population concentrations" (http://www.census.gov/population/www/cen2000/atlas.html). Figure 14.3 is an example of the geography of diversity; it is among the maps available at http://www.census.gov/population/www/cen2000/atlas.html.

Map Stats (http://www.census.gov/datamap/www) provides a visual profile of each state and its counties, together with a companion dataset for each state, county, and metropolitan area. The U.S. Gazetteer (http://www.census.gov/cgi-bin/gazetteer) links place names and zip codes to a computerized map of the area. There is a 1990 gazetteer of counties, places, and zip codes in the United States (http://ftp.census.gov/geo/www/gazetteer/places.html). The Bureau also has "The GIS Gateway" (http://www.census.gov/geo/www/gis_gateway.html), which provides links to numerous GIS resources available on the Web.

Forest Service

The Forest Service of the Department of Agriculture has a number of maps at http://www.fs.fed.us/links/maps.shtml. There is a map archive of fire danger, 1996–1999. Maps and literature citations are available at http://www.fs.fed.us/land/wfas/. *GEOMAC: Wildlife Fire Support* is a Web-based mapping tool for online maps of current fire locations and perimeters in twelve Western states. Fire personnel and the public can download information "to pinpoint the affected areas" (http://wildfire.usgs.gov/AboutGeomac/Public.html).

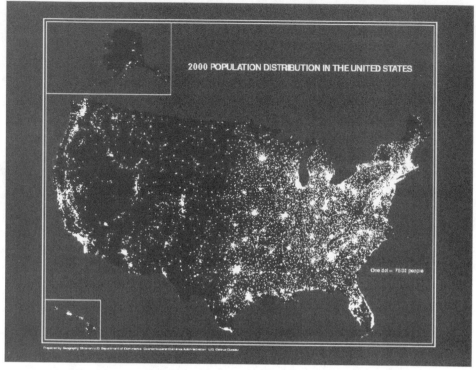

Figure 14.2. Population Density (Bureau of the Census). *Source:*
http://www.census.gov/geo/www/mapGallery/images/2k_night.jpg.

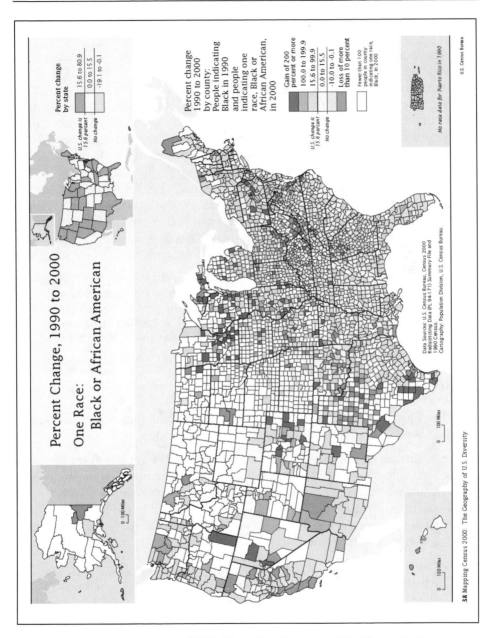

Figure 14.3. Geography of U.S. Diversity (Bureau of the Census). *Source:*
http://www.census.gov/population/www/cen2000/atlas.html.

Bureau of Transportation Statistics

The Bureau of Transportation Statistics (BTS)'s Geographic Information Services "are a national resource for transportation spatial data and GIS in transportation" (http://www.bts.gov/gis). The BTS provides geospatial data; a map gallery; state GIS resources; the National Spatial Data Infrastructure document on "a proposed identification standard for segmenting and identifying unique road segments"; and the Intermodal Network, which "represents an integration of different modal networks and contains special attributes that allow multimodal routing" (http://www.bts.gov/gis).

The National Transportation Atlas Databases (NTAD) "is a set of transportation-related geospatial data for the United States. The data consist of transportation networks, transportation facilities, and other spatial data used as geographic reference" (http://www.bts.gov/gis/ntatlas/ntatlas.html). The NTAD

> is distributed in shapefile format. A Shapefile is a simple, non-topological format for storing the geometric location and attribute information of geographic features. Distributing spatial data in shapefile format guarantees that the data will be easy to use and widely portable, as shapefiles can be easily imported into all major GIS software platforms. (http://www.bts.gov/gis/ntatlas/ntatlas.html)

Environmental Protection Agency

The Environmental Protection Agency (EPA) is another major producer of maps, atlases, and GISs. Its information sources include

- American Indian Lands Environmental Support Project, which "incorporates into a geographic information system . . . current multi-media contaminant releases, recent compliance and enforcement histories for facilities located on or near Indian lands, and other environmental data, such as stream reaches with fish consumption advisories, contaminated fish tissues and contaminated sediments";

- Better Assessment Science Integrating Point and Nonpoint Sources, which "integrates a geographic information system . . ., national watershed data, and state-of-the art environmental assessment and modeling tools into one convenient package";

- Geospatial Data Clearinghouse, which "provides access to geospatial data used in geographic information systems . . . to identify the location and characteristics of natural or man-made features and boundaries on the earth";

- Maps on Demand, which provide environmental information for the nation; and

• Spatial Data and Applications (Envirofacts), which coveys spatial data from various sources. (http://www.epa.gov/epahome/gis.htm)

Both Envirofacts and Maps on Demand are also available at http://www.epa.gov/epahome/gis.htm and http://www.epa.gov/enviro/html/mod/index.html. Envirofacts covers air, chemicals, facility information, hazardous waste, drinking water contaminant occurrence, and similar topics (see also http://www.epa.gov/enviro/html/ef_overview.html).

National Aeronautics and Space Administration

The National Aeronautics and Space Administration offers a rich array of photographs, animation, satellite imagery, atlases, and such. Its home page (http://www.nasa.gov) provides entry into assorted resources that, among other options, cover spacecraft and space probes. For example, Figure 14.4 shows a view of the Martian terrain: rock "Chimp" has "a large crack, oriented from lower left to upper right" (http://mars.jpl.nasa.gov/gallery/martianterrain/PIA01579.html).

Figure 14.4. Martian Terrain (National Aeronautics and Space Administration). *Source:* **http://mars.jpl.nasa.gov/gallery/martianterrain/PIA01579.html.**

National Imagery and Mapping Agency

An agency of the Department of Defense, the National Imagery and Mapping Agency (NIMA) offers numerous maps, images, geodata, and publications that are publicly available (see http://www.nima.mil). One of its resources, the GEOnet Names Server, is the official repository of foreign place-name decisions approved by the BGN. It covers names worldwide, except for the United States and Antarctica (see http://164.214.2.59/gns/html/index.html). Another resource is Earth-Info, a site that provides hyperlinks to worldwide imagery and geospatial information from both the government and private sectors (http://www.earth-info.org).

The Digital Nautical Chart®, which supports the worldwide navigation requirements of the U.S. Navy and the U.S. Coast Guard, "is an unclassified, vector-based digital database containing maritime significant features essential for safe marine navigation" (http://164.214.2.59/dncpublic). The Aeronautical Safety Center provides "timely, accurate, global aeronautical geospatial information and services for national, military, and civil aircrews" (http://164.214.2.59/dncpublic). It offers numerous reports, CD-ROMs, charts, and geospatial data (see http://164.214.2.62/products/digitalaero/index.html). Information about other NIMA products for public sale is available at http://164.214.2.59/poc/public.html.

National Oceanic and Atmospheric Administration

The Web site (http://www.noaa.gov) of the National Oceanic and Atmospheric Administration (NOAA) of the Department of Commerce provides statistics, maps, satellite imagery, research, and publications related to the weather (e.g., storm watches, drought, temperatures, and global warming), the ocean (e.g., coral reefs, tides and currents, and oil and chemical spills), fisheries (e.g., law enforcement and seafood inspection), and "charting & navigation" (nautical and aeronautical charts, ocean mapping, state navigation, and transportation). "Charting & navigation" links to the Electronic Navigational Charts (ENC), which "are essentially a database of vector chart features that can be intelligently processed and displayed by electronic charting systems. As 'smart charts', . . . they can be incorporated with Global Positioning System satellite data and other sensor information (water levels, winds and weather) to significantly improve navigation safety and efficiency by warning the mariners of hazards to navigation and situation where the vessels current track will take it into danger" (http://www.noaa.gov/charts.html).

The home page also provides links to "Cool NOAA Web Sites," and NOAA's National Weather Service provides weather forecast and past information for selected cities (http://www.wrh.noaa.gov/wrhq/nwspage.html).

The National Ocean Service (NOAA), a subunit of NOAA, provides numerous other maps, charts, images, and so forth. One example is MapFinder (http://mapfinder.nos.noaa.gov/mapfinderHTML3/surround/surround.html which contains coastal survey maps and raster GIS images.[7] It accurately depicts the shoreline features, such as rocks and tidal scale.

National Archives and Records Administration

"The holdings of . . . NARA . . . include over 15 million maps, charts, aerial photographs, architectural drawings, patents, and ship plans, constituting one of the world's largest accumulations of such documents" (http://www.archives.gov/index.html). Some of these are available online and others are housed in NARA facilities (see http://www.archives.gov/research_room/media_formats/cartographic_and_architecture). Descriptions of a small number of these resources are available through the NARA Archival Information Locator (NAIL) (http://www.archives.gov/index.html); while the majority of the descriptions are from the Special Media and Archives Division, National Archives II at College Park, Maryland.

Among NARA's mapping collections are

Exploration and scientific surveys,

Public land surveys and settlements,

Indian affairs,

Hydrography and navigation,

Topography and natural resources,

Census mapping,

Urban development,

Maps of foreign countries, and

Military campaigns.

General Information Leaflet No. 26, "Cartographic and Architectural Records," discusses each of these collections, along with architectural and engineering drawings, aerial photographs, reference services, public transportation, and finding aids (http://www.archives.gov/publications/general_information_leaflets/26.html). For example, under Indian Affairs, the leaflet states:

> Maps showing information about the Indians of the United States can be found among the records of many agencies, but the largest concentration is the central map file of the Bureau of Indian Affairs (RG 75). This body of over 16,000 maps, covering the period 1800–1939, includes items pertaining to Indian treaties, removal policy, reservations, settlements, and land use. Because of the vast extent of the Indian lands and the great variety of maps compiled or used by the Bureau, this file also contains much incidental information about other aspects of the physical, cultural, and historical geography of the United States. (http://www.archives.gov/publications/general_information_ leaflets/26.html)

THE PRIVATE SECTOR

The Environmental Systems Research Institute, Inc. (ESRI) offers the *Digital Chart of the World* on CD-ROM (http://www.esri.com), which is "a worldwide base map of coastlines, international boundaries, cities, airports, elevations, roads, railroads, water features, cultural landmarks, and much more" (http://www.esri.com). Pennsylvania State University Libraries provide additional information about the product (http://www.maproom.psu.edu/dcw/ dcw_about.shtml), and ESRI has additional GIS products, software, and datasets.

MapInfo Corporation (Troy, New York) (http://www.mapinfo.com) offers maps, GIS products, and e-services. Some of the products link census data to computerized mapping of the United States by state, census tract, and so forth. Using MapInfo's cross-platform mapping service, the National Cancer Institute provides online access to the *Atlas of Cancer Mortality* (http://www3.cancer. gov/atlasplus), which depicts cancer mortality data nationally and locally via electronic maps. The Department of Commerce has a U.S. Government Export Portal, which gives access to "general and industry specific trade statistics" (http://www.export.gov), and the Department's International Trade Agency uses MapInfo maps at http://www.ita.doc.gov.

GIS INFORMATION POLICY

Agencies collect and use spatial data for management and planning purposes. Those data might relate to ground or air transportation; cultural, economic, or demographic profiling (especially following the terrorist attacks of September 11); cadastral; vegetation; wetlands; soils; geology; and so forth. The data might be used for managing natural resources, environmental assessment and monitoring, emergency preparedness planning, nuclear safety and waste management, transportation planning, facilities and utilities planning and management, hazardous and toxic waste management, military preparedness and the conduct of military operations, or climate and atmospheric studies. Of course, government entities, especially the Department of Defense, might consider some GIS applications as internal (for use by the armed forces) and not for use by the general public or by those with whom the United States wages war.

A dataset that an agency releases in electronic form can be combined with other datasets of that or other agencies, or data files produced by the private sector, as long as there is a common element in each dataset that enables one to link or combine the files. On November 22, 1943, President Franklin D. Roosevelt signed E.O. 9397, which directed agencies to use Social Security numbers as their account numbers for individuals. By the 1960s, those numbers "became entrenched as essentially a universal identifier."[8] A connector might be a Social Security number or even a telephone number or street address that enables someone to link various datasets to individual households. In other words, it may not be sufficient to say that a particular census tract or voting district has so many households displaying certain characteristics: those related to social-demographic characteristics.[9] With the establishment of connections it becomes possible to go to the next level and identify those households with the desired characteristics.

Robert Gellman describes this dark side of GIS:

> [T]oday it is . . . easy to make a case for the private sector being the biggest threat [to an individual's privacy]. Companies collect, compile and resell as much personal information as they can. Every time you engage in a transaction that includes your name, phone number, credit card number or other identifier, you are likely to be added to someone's list without notice and without consent. If you call an 800 or 900 number, the person receiving the call can find out the number you called from and how the phone is registered.[10]

He further commented that "marketers want to know everything about you. Much demand for personal data is driven by the relentless appetite of companies to fine-tune their marketing of goods and services."[11]

Under these circumstances, the importance of the discussion of personal privacy in Chapter 9 becomes evident. Those policies may not speak directly to GISs, but they apply to the collection and use of data. The questions are, "How can different datasets be combined?," and, by combining data, "Is personal privacy imperiled?"

As Peter Hernon and Xavier R. Lopez discuss, intellectual property rights are an important mechanism that the public and private sectors use to regulate the diffusion of geographic databases. Since most public GIS databases are arrangements of factual data, copyright laws may have significant limitations in protecting the factual data in GIS datasets. It is critical to distinguish between the creation of finished hardcopy maps and the development of a GIS database. Unlike copyright for maps, which has a solid foundation in case law much akin to that for photography, the protection of factual content held in a database is uncertain. However, personal privacy law may take center stage as a policy instrument affecting some GIS systems.[12]

CONCLUSION

The types of resources highlighted in this chapter predate the foundation of the United States and provide a historical record of the development of the new nation into a superpower, one whose contributions to science have been profound. Using maps and GISs, researchers can engage in planetary research and monitor changing conditions on the earth (e.g., urban growth, snow disposal operations, public health, hazardous waste facilities, and site locations for business and industry). Government entities can also use these resources for planning and the accomplishment of their missions and to enable Congress to conduct better oversight.

Policy instruments relate to the development of a national spatial data infrastructure and the establishment of standards. In this regard, the Federal Geographic Data Committee plays a central role. However, the Department of

Transportationand other entities contribute to the infrastructure as they share digital images and let subnational government and the public have access to a number of these images. Clearly, the federal government plays a leadership role in international mapping and GIS activities. However, the availability of maps on government Web sites has undergone a reassessment after September 11, with maps being removed from Web sites of the Department of Defense and other government entities. Furthermore, the Federal Bureau of Investigation wants to restrict the availability of maps from the National Archives and Records Administration and the Library of Congress.

NOTES

1. Laurence F. Schmeckebier and Roy B. Eastin, *Government Publications and Their Use* (Washington, D.C.: The Brookings Institution, 1969), 406, 407.

2. Ibid.

3. Ibid.

4. A good introduction to map librarianship and a variety of government agencies that engage in mapping activities is Mary L. Larsgaard, *Map Librarianship: An Introduction* (Englewood, Colo.: Libraries Unlimited, 1998).

5. Schmeckebier and Eastin, *Government Publications and Their Use,* 407.

6. See http://www.noaa.gov/charts.html.

7. For an introduction to terms such as *raster,* see Allan B. Cox and Fred Gifford, "An Overview to Geographic Information Systems, *Journal of Academic Librarianship* 23 (November 1997): 449–61.

8. Robert Gellman, "Use of Social Security Number Is Out of Hand," *Government Computer News* (October 4, 1999): 17.

9. See Peter Hernon and Xavier R. Lopez, "Geographic Information Systems," in *Federal Information Policies in the 1990s: Views and Perspectives*, ed. Peter Hernon, Charles R. McClure, and Harold C. Relyea (Norwood, N.J.: Ablex, 1996), 246–54.

10. Robert Gellman, "Who Is Using IT the Most to Invade Our Privacy?" *Government Computer News* (September 13, 1999): 26.

11. Ibid.

12. Hernon and Lopez, "Geographic Information Systems," 240-43.

URL SITE GUIDE

American Memory
Library of Congress
    http://memory.loc.gov/

Bureau of the Census
    http://www.census.gov/

    Geography of U.S. Diversity
        http://www.census.gov/population/www/cen2000/atlas.html

    GIS Gateway
        http://www.census.gov/geo/www/gis_gateway.html

    Map Gallery
        http://www.census.gov/geo/www/mapGallery/index.html

    Map Stats
        http://www.census.gov/datamap/www

    Mapping and Cartographic Resources
        http://www.census.gov/geo/www/maps/

    Population Density Map
        http://www.census.gov/geo/www/mapGallery/2kpopden.html

    U.S. Gazetteer
        http://www.census.gov/cgi-bin/gazetteer

        Place and Zip Code Files
            http://ftp.census.gov/geo/www/gazetteer/places.html

Bureau of Transportation Statistics
    http://www.bts.gov/

    Geographic Information Services
        http://www.bts.gov/gis/

    National Transportation Atlas Data
        http://www.bts.gov/gis/ntatlas/ntatlas.html

Digital Chart of the World
    ESRI
        http://www.esri.com/

    Pennsylvania State University Libraries
        http://www.maproom.psu.edu/dcw/dcw_about.shtml

Environmental Protection Agency
    http://www.epa.gov/

    Envirofacts (and Maps on Demand)
        http://www.epa.gov/enviro/html/spatial_data.html
        http://www.epa.gov/enviro/html/mod/index.html
        http://www.epa.gov/enviro/html/ef_overview.html

    GIS
        http://www.epa.gov/epahome/gis.htm

Federal Geographic Data Committee
    http://www.fgdc.gov/

    Clearinghouse
        http://www.fgdc.gov/clearinghouse/clearinghouse.html

Clearinghouse Gateway
http://130.11.52.184/

Standards
http://www.fgdc.gov/standards/standards.html

FirstGov
http://www.firstgov.gov/

Forest Service
Department of Agriculture
http://www.fs.fed.us/

GEOMAC
http://wildfire.usgs.gov/AboutGeomac/Public.html

Maps
http://www.fs.fed.us/links/maps.shtml

Wild Danger Control
http://www.fs.fed.us/land/wfas/

GPO Access
Subject Bibliography 102
Maps and Atlases
http://bookstore.gpo.gov/sb/sb-102.html

Geography and Map Division
Library of Congress
http://lcweb.loc.gov/rr/geogmap/

Map Collections: 1500-1999
http://lcweb2.loc.gov/ammem/gmdhtml/gmdhome.html

MapInfo
http://www.mapinfo.com/

Use of Its Products

Atlas of Cancer Mortality
http://www3.cancer.gov/atlasplus

International Trade Agency
http://www.ita.doc.gov/

U.S. Government Export Portal
http://www.export.gov/

National Aeronautics and Space Administration
http://www.nasa.gov/

Martian Terrain
http://mars.jpl.nasa.gov/gallery/martianterrain/PIA01579.html

National Archives and Records Administration
http://www.archives.gov/index.html

Cartographic and Architectural Records
http://www.archives.gov/research_room/media_formats/cartographic_
and_architecture

Cartographic and Architectural Records

General Information Leaflet No. 26
        http://www.archives.gov/publications/general_information_leaflets/26.html

National Imagery and Mapping Agency
Department of Defense
        http://www.nima.mil/

Aeronautical Safety Center
        http://164.214.2.62/products/digitalaero/index.html

Digital Nautical Chart®
        http://164.214.2.59/dncpublic

Earth-Info
        http://www.earth-info.org

GEOnet Names Server
        http://164.214.2.59/gns/html/index.html

Public Sale (NIMA Products)
        http://164.214.2.59/poc/public.html

National Oceanic and Atmospheric Administration
        http://www.noaa.gov/

Charting & Navigation
        http://www.noaa.gov/charts.html

    MapFinder

    National Ocean Service
            http://mapfinder.nos.noaa.gov/mapfinderHTML3/surround/
            surround.html

    National Weather Service
            http://www.wrh.noaa.gov/wrhq/nwspage.html

United States Board on Geographic Names
        http://geonames.usgs.gov/bgn.html

United States Geological Survey
        http://www.usgs.gov/

About USGS
        http://www.usgs.gov/about_us.html

Atlas of Antarctic Research
        http://usarc.usgs.gov/antarctic_atlas/

Booklet (Mapping)
        http://mac.usgs.gov/isb/pubs/booklets/usgsmaps/usgsmaps.html

Digital Raster Graphics
        http://mcmcweb.er.usgs.gov/drg/

The Future of GIS
        http://www.usgs.gov/research/gis/application7.html

Geographic Names Information System
http://geonames.usgs.gov/

Geography Network
http://landcover.usgs.gov/otherorganizations.html

Global GISs
http://webgis.wr.usgs.gov/globalgis/proj_desc.htm

Mapfinder
http://edc.usgs.gov/Webglis/glisbin/finder_main.pl?dataset_name=MAPS

Maps (Booklet)
http://mac.usgs.gov/isb/pubs/booklets/usgsmaps/usgsmaps.html

Maps and Other Products
http://ask.usgs.gov/products.html

Mission
http://www.usgs.gov/stratplan/vision.html

National Atlas of the United States®

Nationalatlas.gov™
http://www-atlas.usgs.gov/

Participating Government Entities
http://www.nationalatlas.gov/federal.html

National Geologic Map Database
http://ngmdb.usgs.gov/

National Land Cover Characterization Dataset Published on the
Geography Network
http://landcover.usgs.gov/nationallandcover.html

National Map
http://nationalmap.usgs.gov/

Report
http://nationalmap.usgs.gov/report/national_map_report_final.pdf

National Mapping Program Standards
http://mapping.usgs.gov/standards/index.html

Partners
http://mapping.usgs.gov/partners/viewonline.html

Photofinder
http://edc.usgs.gov/Webglis/glisbin/finder_main.pl?dataset_
name=NAPP

Selected Federal Mapping Programs, Products, and Services
http://mapping.usgs.gov/html/connections.html.

Topographic Maps
http://mcmcweb.er.usgs.gov/topomaps

U.S. Geological Survey Library
http://library.usgs.gov/

USGS Web Mapping Portal
http://gisdata.usgs.net/

View USGS Maps and Aerial Photo Images Online
http://mapping.usgs.gov/partners/viewonline.html

 Chapter 15

Access to Government Information through Depository Library Programs

Depository library programs, which represent a partnership between a government agency that distributes or disseminates government information products and a group of libraries, exist at all levels of government in the United States, as well as in some other countries and international organizations. At the U.S. national level, the best known and largest program is operated by the Government Printing Office's (GPO) Superintendent of Documents. Examples of other programs include the census and the patent and trademark depositories. This chapter highlights all three, two of which date from the nineteenth century.

FEDERAL DEPOSITORY LIBRARY PROGRAM (GOVERNMENT PRINTING OFFICE)*

As discussed in Chapter 1, in 1789 the new government turned to newspapers to publish public laws, orders, and resolutions of Congress. Those newspapers that became official organs for a political party and that represented the interests of the party in power received special printing orders from the executive departments. The State Department, and its secretary, became the custodians of the acts of Congress and selected those newspapers that would publish authentic copies of laws and regulations. By 1795, copies of federal statutes were also distributed to the states, through their governors, in part so that rural areas inadequately served by newspapers could be informed of official policies and activities.

Any official publishing necessitated special legislation that permitted the printing of a sufficient number of copies of the journals of each house of Congress for distribution to state executives and state and territorial legislatures. Provision was made for the distribution of these journals, as well as acts, documents, and reports to incorporated universities, colleges, and historical societies.

On December 27, 1813, Congress adopted a resolution that incorporated the provisions that had theretofore been covered by special legislation and made them applicable to all future Congresses. The number of copies printed was limited to the usual number plus 200. The Librarian of the Library of Congress was authorized to distribute these publications, and government printing became a more profitable enterprise for printing firms. With this resolution, Congress became committed to the formal and regular distribution of its publications. On December 1, 1814, the American Antiquarian Society in Worcester, Massachusetts, became the first nongovernmental body to receive government-distributed publications.

The secretary of state continued to distribute publications, although his office had no specific authority to do so. By joint resolutions of 1840 and 1844, the number of copies of journals and documents printed was increased to 250 and then to 300.

Dissatisfaction with newspaper patronage, charges of misuse and corruption in printing contracts, concern about the cost of official printing, and criticism of presidential news organs led to various attempts to reform printing and distribution methods. At the 1853 Librarian's Conference, a resolution was adopted that precipitated Congress's first move toward a revision of the 1813 distribution system. As a result of various efforts, legislation of the late 1850s placed the emerging depository library program on a firm basis and also created GPO in 1860.

By resolutions of 1857 and 1858, the Library of Congress and the State Department transferred distribution authority to the secretary of the interior, who was charged with distribution to "such colleges, public libraries, atheneums, literary and scientific institutions, and boards of trade or public associations as may be designated to him by the Representatives in Congress from each Congressional district, and by the delegate from each Territory in the United States."[1] Depository designation was assigned by members of Congress, with those states having greater population density eligible for larger representation in the depository program. The framework for the present-day program was thus set.

An act of 1859 provided for depository designation by senators and for the permanent retention of depository publications by libraries. The secretary of the interior was charged with "receiving, arranging, safe-keeping, and distribution [of public documents] of every nature," printed or purchased for the use of the government, "except such as are for the special use of Congress or the Executive Departments."[2] The secretary could also retain or remove publications stored in the congressional library or deposited with the secretary of state.

By an act of March 1861, the secretary of the interior could decide which libraries received publications when there were insufficient copies for distribution to all depository libraries. Further, depository libraries were to receive publications, unless the secretary viewed them as no longer suitable to be recipients of these publications. According to LeRoy C. Schwarzkopf, a former documents librarian and depository library historian, this was the first indication of an inspection authority or a supervisory capacity of the depository program.[3]

In 1869, the Superintendent of Public Documents was created as an office within the Department of the Interior and was charged with the custody of government publications and their distribution. However, Congress and executive departments often maintained their own distribution practices and policies. These policies became so indiscriminate that the first Superintendent of Public Documents noted that many organizations, including depository libraries, received unwanted and duplicate publications. In his view, the receipt of unsolicited publications was counterproductive; these publications were "regarded with contempt" and publications of the federal government lacked credibility with the public.[4]

The demand for reform in printing and distribution practices resulted in the 1895 General Printing Act, which consolidated existing laws governing the printing, binding, and distribution of government publications. It transferred the Office of the Superintendent of Public Documents from the Department of the Interior to GPO. The office, renamed the Superintendent of Documents, was charged with directing efforts for bibliographic control, distributing public documents, selling these documents to the public, and administering the depository library program. To accomplish its charge, the office began to gather an extensive collection of government publications. (In 1972, these publications were transferred to the National Archives and Records Service, as it was then known.)

The act also specified that the number of legislative journals distributed would be limited to three per state and granted authority for the distribution of the *Congressional Record*. For the first time, publications of the executive departments—except those of a confidential, internal, or administrative nature—were eligible for depository distribution; in the past, however, a number of these publications had been republished as congressional documents, by order of Congress, and distributed to libraries as part of the Serial Set (see the discussion in Chapter 2 on the historical finding aids).

Because government printing, publishing, and distribution had become functions of both the legislative and executive branches, the act attempted to centralize government printing under GPO. Another provision stipulated that a catalog of government publications be prepared by the Superintendent of Documents on the first day of each month to identify the documents "printed" during the preceding month. The purpose was to keep the public and libraries informed of the publications that the national government issued. The Superintendent of Documents interpreted the word "printed" broadly so that it extended to material reproduced by any duplicating process.

The act also expanded the types of libraries that could become depositories. State libraries, libraries in executive departments, and libraries of the military academies all became eligible to join the program. Depository status could be gained either from designation by a member of Congress or by legal designation.

Section 70 of the act provided for the Superintendent of Documents to "investigate the condition of all" depository libraries and to remove any that were not maintained as public libraries or that allowed the number of books other than government publications to fall below 1,000; college libraries, however, were exempted from this minimal number. Irregularly thereafter, the *Annual Report of the Public Printer* summarized the results of a survey of depository libraries and their handling of depository publications.

After 1895, libraries still received vast quantities of publications and tended to treat many of them as second-class resources requiring minimal attention. The problems relating to the depository library program went beyond the fact that libraries could not make selection decisions but had to retain whatever they received. The intent was to ensure that each congressional district received a similar quantity of publications. With the increasing volume of publications distributed and the need for their permanent retention, many libraries let publications accumulate and stored them in separate areas of the library. However, high-use titles might appear elsewhere (e.g., in general reference collections).

The waste in printing, paper, and distribution, as well as in library handling and storage, was recognized, but not addressed, for years. Partial remedies considered, but not implemented, included a reduction in the number of depositories and in the flow of publications distributed gratis,[5] as well as revision of existing statutes to enable libraries to select the publications that they wanted to receive.

Under an act of 1905, depository distribution of reports on private bills (e.g., covering the relief of private parties, pensions, and the survey of rivers and harbors) and simple and concurrent resolutions was discontinued. An act two years later provided that libraries of land grant colleges could become depository libraries. This stipulation expanded the type of libraries that could receive depository status under a "law" designation. In 1913, legislation was enacted so that a member of Congress, at the beginning of a session, could no longer withdraw and reassign depository status at will. Depository designations had seldom been changed; however, this particular act guarded against the possibility of that occurring and stated that a library retained depository status unless it ceased to exist or voluntarily relinquished its privilege. The Superintendent of Documents could terminate the status of those libraries failing to comply with existing laws.

From 1913 until 1923, depository libraries returned to GPO some 1,226,558 publications for which they lacked storage space or that were not of interest to their publics.[6] Because depository libraries had to accept and retain whatever titles were distributed and were not allowed to discard them, they often tried to return unwanted publications to the Superintendent of Documents. The government not only had to pay for the printing of these unwanted publications, but also frequently absorbed the transportation costs to and from the libraries. There were even instances in which

> volumes with pretty bindings or attractive titles are taken out from the shipments and placed upon the shelves, and the remainder are dumped in attics or cellars to await an opportunity to return them to this office [that of the Superintendent of Documents]; and this sort of thing will continue so long as the government insists upon forcing upon libraries quantities of books for which they have no need.[7]

It was also estimated that, contrary to federal law, depository libraries discarded many publications, rather than returning them to the Superintendent of Documents.[8]

The high cost, in comparison to the low benefit, of these publications, as well as the "gross waste,"[9] led to a new policy. The appropriations act for fiscal year 1923 advanced the concept of selective depositories: Libraries could select those categories of publications suitable to the user community. When the act went into effect, fifty-one libraries did not submit selection profiles and were dropped from the depository program. On the other hand, 120 (out of 421) libraries wanted to receive either all publications available or two-thirds of those available. The others wanted to receive fewer publications—half or fewer of those previously received.[10] Libraries could now plan for collection growth, while the government saved on the cost of distributing publications to depository libraries.[11]

During the 1930s, both the Superintendent of Documents and the library community recognized the need to gather basic data on depository libraries (e.g., hours of service, number of users served, and the methods for classification and shelving depository publications). The Superintendent of Documents also wanted the opinions of depository librarians and members of the American Library Association's (ALA) Public Documents Committee on the number, types, and composition of libraries to participate in the depository program. Additional opinion was solicited on the procedure for designation of depository libraries and funding for depository inspection.[12]

The purpose for gathering assorted factual information and opinions was to provide a detailed, state-of-the-art assessment of the depository program for use in identifying and documenting existing problem areas, and for proposing further legislation. A survey was expected to indicate "the class of library eligible to become a depository, and where it should be located."[13] For the rest of the decade, the basic issues relating to the survey were how the data would be collected, by whom, and who would pay for data collection.

At this time, GPO had limited staff and travel funds to inspect the current condition of depository libraries. Moreover, it did not want to request an additional budgetary allocation from Congress for an inspection program or for gathering detailed factual information and opinions. As a consequence, GPO explored the use of a mail questionnaire to depository libraries as the best means to collect data and to let the libraries "express an opinion of the real value of the depository privilege and submit comments on the present service together with suggestions for improvements."[14] This survey was never initiated because it was realized that a voluntary solicitation of general views would not provide sufficient insights into the program as a whole.

The GPO turned to ALA's Public Documents Committee for assistance in drafting a questionnaire on current practices and conditions and for obtaining the necessary funding for data collection and analysis. If the Committee could not underwrite the cost, it was encouraged to seek outside funding for the survey. However, prior to the outbreak of World War II, the Committee was unable to attract the necessary funding.

An act of 1938 reversed the 1905 act and expanded the categories of congressional publications authorized for depository distribution to include reports on private bills and simple and concurrent resolutions. It also broadened distribution to include the journal of each house of Congress and all publications, except those of an administrative and confidential nature, ordered by a congressional committee; distribution of the House and Senate journals was no longer limited to three sets per state. In 1941, congressional hearings became available for depository distribution.

At the conclusion of World War II, attention reverted to the need for basic information on the depository program and the possible introduction of new legislation in Congress. It seems logical to assume that GPO was trying to cope with the increased volume of publications resulting from the war and to supply libraries with publications in the most cost-effective manner. Further, there was increased dissatisfaction with the depository program as then constituted. The Superintendent of Documents believed that a number of libraries regarded participation in the program "merely as an opportunity to obtain free publications." "Criticisms" even reached members of Congress that some "depositories are not being maintained as public libraries" and that "documents are stored in basements or are lost or destroyed instead of being made available for general public reference." Given the annual cost to the government of providing depository libraries with free copies, GPO and Congress wanted to see that funds were not wasted.[15]

The GPO recognized the need for an inspection of the condition of depository libraries as well as its responsibility to do so. However, it did not believe that all libraries had to be inspected in person. Its preference was to do the evaluation at the lowest cost. As a result, in its budget for fiscal year 1949, GPO requested funding for a regular survey of depository libraries. With the approval of the budget, the *Biennial Survey* was initiated in 1950.

The Depository Library Act of 1962 (PL 87-579, 79 Stat. 352) made some major modifications in the program. In the belief that there was a correlation between the number of depository libraries and public access, the potential number greatly increased. Now, members of the House could name two depositories per congressional district, and each senator could designate two per state. The number of federal (executive branch and independent agencies) depositories was also increased. For instance, the number jumped from 594 in 1962 to 1,045 in 1971 and 1,373 in 1983.

The act formalized pilot programs already in effect in both Wisconsin and New York (depository libraries in both states could transfer control of publications held at least twenty-five years to the State Library in New York or the State Historical Society of Wisconsin, with the permission of the Superintendent of Documents) and increased the system of regional libraries. Limited to two per state, these libraries were charged with the maintenance of comprehensive collections held permanently (some ephemeral and superseded publications could be discarded), the provision of reference and interlibrary loan service, and assistance to other depositories in the disposition of unwanted publications.

The overwhelming majority of libraries became selective depositories, meaning that they could limit their holdings to high-interest publications and, with the permission of a regional library, discard those not needed after a five-year retention period. Federal government depositories were exempted from the authority of regional libraries and could dispose of unwanted publications after first offering them to the Library of Congress and the National Archives.

All government publications, including those labeled as non-GPO publications—ones printed at field printing plants by federal agencies and not printed at GPO—became eligible for depository distribution. The only exceptions to this generalization related to publications intended only for official use, required for strictly administrative or operational purposes, classified for reasons of national security, and having no public interest or educational value. However, neither then nor subsequently were these exceptions defined in detail, with corresponding guidelines.

The wording of the 1895 act was modified so that depository collections should be "maintained so as to be accessible to the public," but the library need not be maintained as a public library. Further, there was an increase from 1,000 to 10,000 in the number of nongovernment publications that a library had to hold to qualify, minimally, as a depository. In addition, depository libraries were required to report "every two years on their condition;" the reporting took the form of the *Biennial Survey*. The Superintendent of Documents was, therefore, empowered to "make first hand investigation of conditions" and to include the results in his annual report. Any library having fewer than the required 10,000 books, not "properly maintaining" its depository holdings, or ceasing to be "maintained so as to be accessible to the public," could be removed from the roster of depositories if it did not correct the "unsatisfactory conditions within six months." These provisions still reflected a narrow vision of the inspection authority of the Superintendent of Documents; inspection was limited to those libraries "for which need is indicated."[16] The need for inspection was based on responses, or the lack thereof, to the *Biennial Survey*.

The Superintendent of Documents was, by the provisions of the 1962 act, required to "issue a classified list of Government publications in suitable form, containing annotations of contents and listed by item identification numbers"[17] to assist depository libraries in making their selections.

In subsequent years, the 1962 act has only been modified twice. First, an act of 1972 authorized special designation for the highest appellate court of each state; these libraries were exempt from the requirement of public access. Second, six years later, accredited law schools could become depositories under the "law," rather than by congressional designation. The purpose was to expand the number of depository libraries; law schools holding their status under a congressional designation could transfer their status to a law designation, thereby freeing a congressional designation in the district for another library—one that met the necessary requirements.

In 1975, a formal inspection program for all depositories was put in place, and three inspectors were charged with the inspection of each library at least every three years. In addition, there would be "a full investigation of any concern that is purported to be a violation of statutory law."[18] (Today, the inspection program has shifted: Libraries prepare a self-study report, the content of which is described at the FDLP Desktop (GPO Access; see below). The report could either serve as a substitute or document the need for an inspection.)

In July 1976, GPO requested approval from the Joint Committee on Printing (JCP) to start microform distribution to depository libraries. Approval was granted in March 1977. As government agencies and GPO produced CD-ROMs, there became a demand for depository distribution of this new format. Distribution was shifting from tangible publications (paper and microformat) to electronic products and access through the World Wide Web. GPO Access marked GPO's official entry into electronic publishing. In 1993, the Government Printing Office Electronic Information Access Enhancement Act (PL 103-40;107 Stat. 112; 44 U.S.C. 4101 et seq.) required the Superintendent of Documents to maintain an electronic directory of federal electronic information and provided for a system of online access to government information resources and for an electronic storage facility. With the inclusion of the fourth component—the Federal Bulletin Board, a service of SuDocs that enabled agencies to provide the public with self-service access to federal information in electronic form (see Senate Report 103-27)—GPO Access was created and tangible electronic products began to be disseminated to depository libraries.[19]

With the distribution of these products to depository libraries, some of them began to develop policies for the types of services they would provide. The Government Publications Department at the University of Nevada, Reno, developed three levels of service and decided which levels each public service staff member would provide:

1. Thorough knowledge (competency in using these tools and the ability to introduce patrons to their use). Thorough knowledge "is defined as the competency to instruct users in the major software features available in each product" distributed through the depository program.

2. General knowledge ("knowing what electronic products are available in the Department, and the ability to identify for patrons databases that may be appropriate for their research needs"). Staff would have general knowledge of specific products or software.

3. Rudimentary knowledge ("knowing where the product and its documentation are located, knowing which microcomputer workstation to use, knowing how to boot the product, and knowing how to exit from the product").[20]

DEPOSITORY PROGRAM TODAY

This section identifies some of the issues, resources, and challenges that currently face the depository program. The depository program has never received (or been entitled to receive) all publications that the government produces or sells. Chapter 19, Title 44, of the *United States Code* sets forth some exemptions to distribution. SuDocs also might conclude that some titles were too expensive to provide to depositories on a gratis basis. The depository program welcomed the introduction of microcards, and later microfiche, as formats that enabled the library community to gather more elusive publications. These elusive publications are known as fugitive documents, ones that depository libraries should receive but do not. In 1996, GPO estimated that approximately "50 percent of the government documents published in that year were not indexed, catalogued, and distributed to the depository libraries. . . . GPO asserts that these fugitive documents are increasing because of electronic dissemination of information via agency Web sites and decreasing agency compliance with the statutory requirements for printing through GPO."[21]

In fiscal year 2000, there were 1,328 libraries in the program, and 53 of them were designated as regional depository libraries. The regionals seek to develop comprehensive collections and receive all titles that GPO makes available to the depository program. They can withdraw superseded publications from their collections. The other libraries—selectives—select which *items*, or categories, they want to receive gratis, and they have limited retention responsibilities.

The Legislative Branch Appropriations Act of 1996 directed GPO to reassess the program's use of electronic publishing and dissemination technologies. It required GPO to examine the functions and services of the program, identify measures that were necessary to ensure a successful transition to a more electronically based program, and prepare a strategic plan for such a transition. The resulting study[22] and strategic plan[23] recommended a five-year transition to a more electronic program, identified a core of government publications that should continue to be distributed in paper, and established a schedule for the transition. By fiscal year 2000, about 57 percent of the depository titles were available online via GPO Access.[24]

The electronic delivery of publications supplements and selectively replaces the dissemination of information on paper or microfiche. The General Accounting Office (GAO) reported that the number of tangible titles—in paper, microfiche, or CD-ROM—distributed to depository libraries from fiscal year 1996 to fiscal year 2000 "remained relatively stable": 29, 373 titles (in 1996) to 28,848 (in 2000) titles. "A similarly modest decline was evident in the number of distributed tangible copies, from 13,472,946 copies distributed in fiscal year 1996 to 12,207,064 copies in fiscal year 2000."[25]

In fiscal year 2001, Congress reduced SuDocs funding for the program by $2 million, thereby accelerating the transition to a more electronic depository library program. The Superintendent issued a policy for the dissemination of publications to depository libraries that reaffirmed the commitment to online dissemination as the primary method of depository distribution and defined the conditions under which the program would continue to distribute tangible products, even if the publications are available online.[26] Specifically, the program will distribute a tangible version when any of the following conditions is met:

- There is a legal requirement to distribute the publication in tangible format;

- The paper publication is of significant reference value to most types of depository libraries;

- The paper publication serves a special needs population;

- The commonly accepted medium of the user community is tangible format; and

- The product is essential to the conduct of government.

Table 15.1 includes the titles that the Superintendent identified in 1996 as most essential to remain in paper format. It also shows which titles are available on the World Wide Web and provides the appropriate URL for each. There is no assurance of permanent retention of back issues of individual titles on an agency's Web site. However, GPO Access directs information seekers from the old Web address to the most recent one for an electronic publication.

Table 15.1 Essential Titles (Those Remaining in Paper Format)

Title	Current Title (Web Address)	SuDocs No.
Agricultural Statistics	http://www.usda.gov/nass/pubs/agstats.htm	A1.47:
Budget of the United States Government	http://www.whitehouse.gov/omb/budget/index.html	PrEx2.8:
Catalog of Federal Domestic Assistance	http://www.cfda.gov/default.htm	PrEx2.20:
Code of Federal Regulations	http://www.access.gpo.gov/nara/cfr/cfr-table-search.html	AE2.106/3:
Condition of Education	http://nces.ed.gov/pubsearch/pubsinfo.asp?pubid=2001072	ED1.109:
Congressional Directory	http://www.access.gpo.gov/congress/	Y4.P93/1:1/
Congressional Record (final bound edition)	Bound edition is unavailable; unbound can be found at http://www.access.gpo.gov/su_docs/aces/aces150.html	X1.1:

Table 15.1 (*cont.*)

Title	Current Title (Web Address)	SuDocs No.
Constitution of the United States, Analysis and Interpretation	http://www.access.gpo.gov/congress/senate/ constitution/index.html	X96-2: S.doc.26
Consumer Price Index Detailed Report	http://www.bls.gov/cpi/home.htm	L2.38/3:
Crime in the United States	http://www.fbi.gov/ucr/ucr.htm	J1.14/7:
Decennial Census	see http://www.census.gov/	[many variations]
Digest of Education Statistics	http://www.ed.gov/pubs/stats.html	ED1.326:
Economic Census	see http://www.census.gov/	[many variations]
Economic Indicators	http://www.access.gpo.gov/ congress/eibrowse/broecind.html	Y4.Ec7:Ec7/
Economic Report of the President	http://w3.access.gpo.gov/eop/	Pr__[# of President].9: Y1.1/7: congress#
Federal Register	http://www.access.gpo.gov/su_docs/ aces/aces140.html	AE2.106:
Foreign Relations of the United States	http://www.state.gov/www/about_state/ history/frus.html	S1.1:
Green Book (House Committee on Ways and Means)	http://www.access.gpo.gov/congress/wm001.html	Y4.W36:10-4/
Handbook of North American Indians	http://www.nmnh.si.edu/anthro/handbook.html	SI1.20/2:
Harmonized Tariff Schedule of the United States	http://www.usitc.gov/taffairs.htm	ITC1.10:

Table 15.1 (*cont.*)

Title	Current Title (Web Address)	SuDocs No.
Health United States	http://www.cdc.gov/nchs/products/pubs/pubd/hus/hus.htm	HE20.7042/6: formerly HE20.21:
Letters of Delegates to Congress	[on CD-ROM]	LC1.34:
List of Sections Affected—Code of Federal Regulations	http://www.access.gpo.gov/nara/lsa/aboutlsa.html	AE2.106/2:
Monthly Labor Review	http://stats.bls.gov/opub/mlr/mlrhome.htm	L2.6:
North American Industry Classification System, United States	http://www.census.gov/epd/www/naics.html	PrEx2.6/2:IN2 7/997
Occupational Outlook Handbook	http://www.bls.gov/oco/home.htm	L2.3/4:
Producer Price Index—Detailed Report	http://www.bls.gov/ppi/home.htm	L2.64:
Public Papers of the President	http://www.access.gpo.gov/nara/pubpaps/srchpaps.html	AE2.114:
Social Security Bulletin	http://www.ssa.gov/policy/pubs/SSB/index.html	SSA1.22:
Social Security Handbook	http://www.ssa.gov/OP_Home/handbook/	SSA1.8/3:
Sourcebook of Criminal Justice Statistics	http://www.albany.edu/sourcebook	J29.9/6:
Statutes at Large [public & private laws]	http://www.access.gpo.gov/nara/nara005.html	AE2.111:
State and Metropolitan Area Data Book	http://www.census.gov/statab/www/smadb.html	C3.134/5:
Statistical Abstract of the United States	http://www.census.gov/prod/www/statistical-abstract-us.html	C3.134:

Table 15.1 (*cont.*)

Title	Current Title (Web Address)	SuDocs No.
Treaties and Other International Agreements of the United States		S9.12/2:
Treaties in Force	http://www.state.gov/www/global/legal_affairs/tifindex.html	S9.14:
United States Government Manual	http://www.access.gpo.gov/nara/nara001.html	AE2.108/2:
United States Industry and Trade Outlook	http://www.ita.doc.gov/td/industry/otea/outlook/	C61.48:
United States Code	See http://lcweb.loc.gov/global/judiciary.html; see also GPO Access: http://www.access.gpo.gov/congress/cong013.html	Y1.2/5:
United States Congressional Serial Set	Parts are found at http://www.access.gpo.gov/su_docs/legislative.html; http://thomas.loc.gov	Y1.2/2:
United States Reports	For slip opinions, see http://www.loc.gov/law/guide/usjudic.html; http://www.supremecourtus.gov/opinions/opinions.html	Ju6.8:
World Factbook	http://www.odci.gov/cia/publications/factbook/index.html	PrEx3.15:

Public Access to Collections and Services

As previously discussed, with the exception of the highest appellate court library (44 U.S.C. 1915), all depositories, regardless of whether they have a congressional or by law designation, are supposed to serve the public. There have been reported incidents in which the public has been denied access to depository collections. In two instances, the courts placed limitations on public access and use. In the first case, *Commonwealth of Pennsylvania v. Downing* (1986), the Pennsylvania Supreme Court reversed a lower court decision and held that the Law School Library at Temple University did not have to permit entry to an unauthorized person. The "private nature of the . . . library is not changed by virtue of the fact that the law library has sought and received" depository status.[27] In the other case, *Carroll v. Temple University* (1995), a federal district court ruled that the same library could limit the use of the collection to normal business hours.[28]

Apparently, the latter decision conforms to the long-standing expectation of the Superintendent of Documents that private institutions can place reasonable limits on use by the general public. Those limits pertain to hours of collection use and the right to borrow titles.

Mistakes in Depository Distribution

Depository distribution is limited to publications that have educational value and widespread appeal as specified in 44 U.S.C. 1902. On occasion, agencies might inform the Office of the Superintendent of Documents, which, in turn, notifies the depository library community through *Administrative Notes,* that a title should not have been distributed to depository libraries because it was intended for internal use only. The Superintendent of Documents requests that the libraries holding this publication withdraw it from the collection and destroy it by any means to prevent disclosure of its contents. However, this same title would remain in the microprint or microfiche collection of any libraries gaining this title through the Readex program (see Chapter 2). In October 2001, GPO instructed depository libraries to destroy a CD-ROM put out by the United States Geological Survey because the information on water supplies posed a security risk in the aftermath of the September 11 terrorist attacks. The information was deemed too sensitive for public access. Agents of the Federal Bureau of Investigation (FBI) even visited some libraries to verify that the order had been carried out.

Depository Designation

By law and congressional designation, as well as the 1962 act, were all intended to increase the number of depository libraries. In the pre-Internet age, public access was equated with the number of member libraries; the more libraries in the program, the better was public access. In other words, members of the public need not travel far to use depository collections.

Even if congressional districts were redrawn, based on figures from the decennial census of population, there was no need to terminate depository status for any libraries, if the number exceeded the congressional requirement. However, no more libraries in those districts could be invited to join the program. On the other hand, if districts do not have the required number of depositories, other libraries (ones meeting the requirements) could enter.

Let us assume that a district has three depositories, two of which received a congressional designation. One of these libraries, a law library, could relinquish its congressional designation and pick up its status as a "by law" designation. Since the other depository is at a land grant university, the district now has two openings for a congressional designation, assuming the university library also switches to "by law" designation.

In the Internet age, it might be argued that there is not so great a need for all of these depository libraries. However, as shown, the law and historical precedent do not lead to a sharp reversal or decline in the number of member libraries. Why should a library surrender its status?

The last study to investigate this question was conducted in the early 1980s and showed that some libraries have left the program.[29] The major reasons for leaving the program appear to be the belief that government publications were not important to the institution's mission and that they were seldom used. One respondent to an unpublished survey noted that

> Prior to my coming . . . the only previous professional reference librarian was about 10 years before. In between one junior library clerk opened mail and tended to put material in a very haphazard subject classification developed in house years ago. The collection was not publicized, located on third floor and no catalog existed except in the clerk's head. A new director wanted the space for improvement and informed me that I was, among other things, in charge of the 75-year accumulation of documents—no weeding ever done! I recommended that the new four-year college in the area might be willing to become a depository and that the material could be transferred there.[30]

Another library noted that it stored documents in a house trailer. Once it was full, the library surrendered its depository status. These examples predate the emergence of the Internet, but show that libraries may no longer consider government publications essential in meeting their mission and the information needs of their publics. Apparently the public served by these libraries never voiced its opposition.

One library discussed in 2000 its departure from the depository program. It found unacceptable the new costs that it would have to absorb; the library was willing to replace those titles received gratis with the purchase of commercial packages and reliance on the Web. In fact, the Web might be "easier to use than those print, microfiche, or CD-ROM formats." Further, "although there were no substantial costs savings from personnel changes, staff assignments that have been altered were welcomed." Most important, withdrawal "has not created customer dissatisfaction," probably because the library had replacement sources in place before depository status was terminated.[31]

Library Inspection and Self-Study

From the 1970s to 1996, the staff of GPO's Library Programs Service conducted formal inspections of depository libraries, under 44 U.S.C. 1909. Those inspections resulted in "a snapshot of depository operations on that day," and they enabled the inspectors "to act as a consultant to aid the documents coordinator in increasing the efficiency and effectiveness of depository operations."[32] In subsequent years, a self-study prepared by the depository coordinator has served as "the initial part of the inspection process and a major determining factor whether a library will have an on-site inspection." The GPO maintains that the self-study "addresses many of the same issues as the inspection":[33] It highlights collection development, bibliographic control, maintenance, human resources, physical facilities, public service, cooperative efforts, and regional services, and offers a summary.

Instead of linking depository services to the overall library's strategic planning process or measuring *effectiveness* (defined as either the accomplishment of formal goals and objectives or the achievement of outcomes—behavioral changes in library users as a result of using library services and collections) and *quality* (as reflected through *service quality*),[34] a self-study emphasizes *inputs:* the number of resources and their allocation, and the development and implementation of policies (e.g., "are written public service guidelines for government information in electronic formats in place"). The self-study also focuses on collection and staff organization, the placement of signage, staff availability, interlibrary lending practices, the stability of funding for the depository collection and technological support, protection of the collection, the receipt and processing of the depository items, and so forth. The self-report, however, does not relate to the advancement of electronic government, as discussed in Chapter 16.

Nonetheless, based on the self-reports, GPO determines which libraries to audit. That decision is based on "when previous inspections were last conducted" as well as considerations such "as previous probationary status, ratings on previous inspections, length of time served as a depository library, and major changes in staffing or facilities."[35]

Restructuring the Depository Library Program

Since legislation resulting in the 1962 Depository Library Act was introduced in Congress, numerous conceptualizations of the federal information infrastructure and the depository library program have been advanced. Some of these have been associated with legislation; others have not.[36] The most recent proposal to reorganize that infrastructure was made in January 2001, when the National Commission on Library and Information Science proposed an agency, provisionally called the Public Information Resources Administration, to be located in the executive branch. It would have united under one management structure the National Technical Information Service, programs of the Superintendent of Documents (e.g., the depository program), and other information dissemination and sales programs from all three branches of the federal government. The basic structure of the depository program, renamed the Public Information Resources Access Program, would have remained unchanged.

Once the federal government began to view the Internet as a primary means of dissemination for information and services, as Congress began to rely on public laws such as the Government Performance and Results Act (PL 103-62) to achieve greater agency accountability, and as the Office of Management and Budget provided guidance for agencies to follow in managing their home pages, the depository program has been perceived as a less vital means of serving the public. In other words, the government could communicate directly with the governed without needing an intermediary, and it could expand the types of resources available to a worldwide public. This does not mean that the program does not have a role to play. It does mean that the library community and public laws must speak to the new role: a service role.

Government Information Locator Service and Metadata

Emerging in the 1990s, the Government Information Locator Service (GILS), to which GPO has been a party, "focused on the use of networking technologies, metadata, and standards to enable distributed, agency-based locator services searchable using a standard information retrieval protocol to assist users in identifying and accessing/acquiring government information resources."[37] In 1994, the National Institute of Standards and Technology adopted the GILS Profile (which relies on ANSI/NISO Z39.50, as Federal Information Processing Standard (FIPS) 192) and the Office of Management and Budget made GILS policy for the executive branch through Bulletin 95-01, which required agencies to establish locator services that conformed to FIPS. The Paperwork Reduction Act of 1995 (see Chapter 8) accepted the GILS as governmentwide policy.

The Dublin Core metadata initiative, and its resulting Dublin Core metadata element, "provided a simple, 15 element set that could be used for resource description to support resource discovery."[38] The question to answer is, "How will agencies use the initiative to improve access to government information, as FirstGov attempts to provide for integrated searching (tagging and pulling together content for improved searching) perhaps across locator services?"

Documentation Pertaining to Program Management

Library Programs Service (LPS), within the office of the Superintendent of Documents, administers the depository library program and the *Catalog of United States Government Publications*, as well as manages the distribution of publications for the International Exchange Service Program (Library of Congress). At the FDLP Desktop (http://www.access.gpo.gov/su_docs/fdlp/index. html), there are key documents, tools, a practical guide, and explanations relevant for librarians administering depository collections and services. For example, there is a brief discussion of content and service partnerships that increase the role of depository libraries in providing the public with access to electronic information products.[39]

Established in 1972, the fifteen-member Depository Library Council to the Public Printer assists LPS and GPO "in identifying and evaluating alternatives for improving public access to government information through the [depository program] and for optimizing resources available for operating the Program" (http://www.access.gpo.gov/su_docs/fdlp/libpro.html). The home page provides "a current and historical compilation of information dealing with the ... Council" (http://www.access.gpo.gov/su_docs/fdlp/council/index.html).

Sources Related to Depository Management

The FDLP Desktop presents the *Instructions to Depository Libraries*, the List of Classes (and related files) (http://www.access.gpo.gov/su_docs/ fdlp/pubs/loc/index.html), and an "Enhanced Shipping List Service" (for checking "your inclusion list against shipping lists, print Call Number labels or save the label file for your library to print label"; see http://ublib.buffalo.edu/libraries/ units/cts/acq/gpo). Further, "the electronic files of shipping list information are updated and uploaded to the Federal Bulletin Board twice weekly and can be found at http://fedbbs.access.gpo.gov/fdlp01.htm."

GPO Access provides "New Electronic Titles"—those added to the depository program's electronic collection during a four-week period (see http://www. access.gpo.gov/su_docs/locators/net/index.html).

What Remains to Be Done?

The GAO has noted that "electronic dissemination of government documents offers the opportunity to reduce the costs of dissemination and make government information more usable and accessible." However, it also pointed out that

> to move to an environment in which documents are disseminated solely in electronic format, a number of challenges would need to be overcome. These challenges include ensuring that these documents are (1) authentic, (2) permanently maintained, and (3) equally accessible to all individuals. In addition, certain cost issues—including the effect of shifting printing costs to depository libraries and end users—would need to be addressed.[40]

Given this environment, it is important that additional research explore the costs of participation in the depository program for both regional and selective depositories (see the accompanying CD-ROM product). Documents librarian Daniel C. Barkley would add that the program must address issues related to public access, deal with "external and internal forces," and provide the "average citizen [with] no-fee access to government information regardless of format."[41]

Over the years there have been various investigations of the use and non-use of government publications at depository libraries, primarily by faculty at academic institutions. The last major, or multiple institution, investigation was conducted in 1978, well before the emergence of the Internet and the significant changes it has produced in information-seeking behavior.[42]

There have been numerous counts of the number of hits on government Web sites. For example, the Bureau of the Census receives more than four million per week! On the other hand, the only valid count of depository users (per week) was done in 1989.[43]

Charles A. Seavey, a critic of the depository program, notes that standards exist for the depository program, but that these are not "carefully designed. . . . All . . . are weak in terms of quantifiable, measurable standards, or even normative data."[44] He asks for "an evaluation system based on measured phenomena, rather than subjective opinion." That system needs to "address the relationship of the depository with its public"—"service to the public [and] evaluation of collection-public interaction."[45]

Depository Library Cost Study

Regardless of the rhetoric concerning the availability of "free" federal government information accessible at a designated member of the Depository Library Program, there are substantial costs on the part of each member library to support the depository's functions. One study conducted during FY 1993 (July 1, 1992 through June 30, 1993) at the Joseph Mark Lauinger Library at Georgetown University estimated that, for each dollar of value received in federal government documents through the GPO program, the library expended more than four dollars.[46]

On the CD-ROM accompanying this book is a template for identifying and calculating the local costs for supporting depository library activities. This practitioner-based model is used to quantify the substantial financial commitments in terms of the direct, support, and overhead costs associated with providing public access to these materials; other models can be constructed based on local institutional characteristics. Direct costs identify those expenditures that exist only because of the depository's activities, such as staff, telephone, supplies, and information materials. Indirect or support costs are those costs that would exist even if the depository program did not but that can be directly attributed to the program's activities. Most often, these indirect costs are labor-related and handled by personnel in other departments; an example would be the costs related to processing the materials by library staff in technical services for public access and use. Overhead costs, often the most difficult to calculate, are based on formulas and ratios imposed by the parent institution to support the library. For example, overhead may include an assigned per square foot cost for utilities, facilities maintenance, and insurance against loss (e.g., fire).

The sum of identified and calculated direct support and overhead costs will provide an administrator with a good indication of the proportion of the entire library's budget allocation and expenditures used to support the depository library program's activities. It will also reveal the funding level necessary to support public access to "free" government information.

SuDocs Classification Scheme

Y4.P92/4:P92/phase 1/bk 7

The foregoing is an example of a retrieval number for a document arranged in the depository collection under the SuDocs Classification Scheme. This document is the Watergate hearings of the 1970s. For a detailed explanation of the system, see *An Explanation of the Superintendent of Documents Classification Scheme* (GPO, 1990) and the *GPO Classification Manual*.

Developed in GPO's Library between 1895 and 1903 by Adelaide Rossalie Hasse, the classification system, which is based on the current organization status of the authoring government body, shifts as the organizational structure of the government changes. Thus, as discussed in Chapter 2, publications of some issuing agencies (e.g., Women's Bureau and Children's Bureau) have been located in different places as these agencies moved within the structure of the government.

Executive Branch

The system begins with a letter (or letters) that refers to the department or independent agency. Thus, A stands for Department of Agriculture, C for Department of Commerce, S for Department of State, and so forth. Following the letter(s) is a number (or numbers), which refer to the parent organization or subordinate part; 1 stands for the Secretary's Office and any other number(s) refer to the subordinate bureau, office, or agency. Thus,

- A1. means the Office of the Secretary;

- A13. means the Forest Service; and

- A92. means the National Agricultural Statistics Service.

The system is expansive; in other words, not every number between A2 and A12, for instance, is currently assigned to a subordinate structure. Perhaps, at one time, some of these numbers had been so assigned. Herein is the value of Andriot's *Guide to U.S. Government Publications*; it identifies which ones had been assigned.

The number between the period and the colon specifies the type of publication distributed to depository libraries. Of course, the list varies from agency to agency and from time period to time period. We know that the Forest Service begins with A13. and we now see that the following number or set of numbers refers to the type of publication. For example,

- 2: refers to general publications;

- 3: refers to bulletins; and

- 28: refers to maps and charts.

As a consequence, A13.3: means bulletins of the Forest Service, which is situated within the Department of Agriculture. However, A13.40/2 refers to general publications of the Forest Service's Southern Forest Experiment Station. This example serves as a reminder of how vast and complex the government's organizational structure is.

The only exception to this patterns is the Public Health Service of the Department of Health and Human Services: HE20. refers to the Department's Public Health Service, and the letters between the period and the colon refer to the subordinate agency or institute and the type of publication. Thus, HE20.302 refers to the Indian Health Service (30) and general publications (2).

Next, PR refers to the president and the individual presidential number. PR 43, for instance, refers to George W. Bush and PrVp 43 refers to the current vice president. Note that a vice president operates largely behind the scenes and so few publications would appear here. In addition, little appears under PR for the president, who has various means by which to communicate policy and opinions. This system of designation began with President John F. Kennedy; for prior presidents see the collections of the Library of Congress and the National Archives and Records Administration.

The Executive Office of the President, which, among other agencies, includes the Office of Management and Budget, begins with PrEx, and the information that follows specifies the agency and the types of publications distributed through the program.

Everything following the colon specifies the individual publication. As is evident, it is critical that anyone using a depository library record all of the necessary retrieval information, from the opening letter to whatever follows the colon.

Judicial Branch

These publications fall within the JU area of the SuDocs Scheme. The number following JU specifies the court or the support agency (e.g., Administrative Office of the U.S. Courts). Thus, JU6. means the Supreme Court, and 2 refers to general publications. Which general publication? The information following the colon answers the question.

Legislative Branch

Documents beginning with Y4. are the working papers of Congress. Here are, for instance, committee prints (background information on basic policy matters) and congressional hearings. Following Y4. and up to the colon is an identification of the particular committee. The information following the colon refers to the particular publication.

Documents beginning with Y3. are from agencies reporting to Congress. The information that follows (up to the colon) specifies the particular agency. However, there are notable exceptions to the pattern, as some congressional agencies are not found here:

General Accounting Office (GAO),

Library of Congress (LC),

Government Printing Office (GP), and

Congressional Budget Office (Y10).

The Y section of the system does not cover all congressional publications. Other ones (bills, reports, and documents) are found in the Serial Set. With the 1980s, these Serial Set publications can be found in the Y1. area, but not for previous years. Thus, the numerically-arranged Serial Set is an extension of congressional-distributed publications (see Chapter 2).

Uncle Sam Migrating Government Publications

The University of Memphis Government Publications Department (http://www.lib.memphis.edu/gpo/mig.htm) is an excellent resource for finding the SuDocs number for government publications that have been converted to electronic format.

Item Numbers

Each stem part of the SuDocs Classification Scheme (the letters and numbers up to the colon) corresponds to a unique item number. That number serves as a tool by which selective depositories determine which categories they want to receive gratis through the depository program. Anything falling outside the scope of their selection parameters will not be supplied to depository libraries. Thus, it is important for them to reflect fully on the categories they want to receive. Wichita State University Library has Documents Data Miner© (http://govdoc.wichita.edu/ddm/), which provides

- List of Classes: ("search the current List of Classes by agency, item number, Sudoc stem, title, format and status (active/inactive)");

- Inactive or Discontinued ("access information about inactive or discontinued items, includes notes and annotations");

- Depository Selection and Directory (". . . search any depository profile. This feature merges profile data with List of Classes fields. It also provides depository directory and e-mail functions"); and

- Tools—Configuration (contains "union list configuration, home depository shortcut, colors-exports"). (http://govdoc.wichita.edu/ddm/)

Note that, when searching the *Catalog of United States Government Publications* on the Web (GPO Access), there is an option to "Locate Libraries." This refers to item numbers and the selection profile of each library so that information seekers can gain an idea about which library might contain a title.

CENSUS DEPOSITORY LIBRARY PROGRAM

There is no statutory base for the census depository library program in the *United States Code*, other than the role of the Bureau of the Census to collect, produce, and disseminate census data. Nonetheless, it seems that the program started in 1950 as part of the Bureau's efforts to disseminate census data, to support the use of those data, and to foster public awareness of the value of census data to their work, lives, and public policy. Obviously, the Bureau wants to obtain broad public support for participation in the completion of legally mandated censuses and surveys.

Six years later, there were 450 libraries in the program. With the Depository Library Act of 1962, the number of libraries in GPO's program expanded, and the Bureau of the Census encouraged libraries to seek membership in that program. Once libraries did so, they were removed from the roster of census depositories. As A. Ross Eckler, Director of the Census Bureau, explained, as the GPO "system is expanded to fill adequately the needs of more and wider areas, we may find it feasible to consider the eventual discontinuance of the Census Depository System."[47]

In 1977, the Bureau reviewed the program and reversed directions. It decided to expand the program to cities having a minimum population of 25,000, but the Bureau still asked each library already in the program if it wanted to remain. Furthermore, prior to 1977, census depositories, with few exceptions, received all publications automatically. Now they have to take seven titles (*Bureau of the Census Catalog, County and City Data Book, Historical Statistics of the United States, Congressional District Data Book, Statistical Abstract of the United States, Bureau of the Census Guide to Programs and Publications—Subjects and Areas*, and *Pocket Data Book*), but they could still determine other titles they wanted to receive. In addition, for the censuses of agriculture, construction industries, governments, housing, manufacturers, mineral industries, population, retail trade, selected services, transportation, and wholesale trade, these libraries were asked to select the publications for their state as well as the U.S. summary reports.

The libraries were also informed that they should "make Bureau publications available to the public." The publications should "be retained for 5 years or until superseded, whichever is sooner." Moreover, "should your library be designated in the future as a Federal Depository Library (GPO), you will automatically cease to be a Census Depository Library."[48]

By 1991, the program consisted of 130 libraries in thirty-eight states and the District of Columbia.[49] These libraries could now select CD-ROM products, if they so chose; still, the emphasis was on paper copies. The Bureau was still willing to entertain applications for depository library status. Any application would have to address the size of the community served, the size of the library and its collection, and the proximity of the library to the nearest GPO depository. Proximity would be a key factor in making the determination.

Although there is no mention of it at the Bureau's Web site (http://www.census.gov), the program, housed in the Customer Liaison Office, remains in existence. The number of participating libraries is small, and member libraries mostly receive CD-ROM products. However, although the "impact of the Internet . . . has ended the majority of printed census publications," these libraries receive "a few scattered printed publications."[50] Clearly, the Web site is the primary means of general dissemination to the public.

PATENT AND TRADEMARK DEPOSITORY LIBRARY PROGRAM

The U.S. Parent and Trademark Office (USPTO) of the Department of Commerce has a depository library program that, as authorized by 35 U.S.C. 13, disseminates patent and trademark information and supports the "diverse intellectual property needs of the public" (http://www.uspto.gov/web/menu/offices.html). The libraries in the program:

> . . . [R]eceive and house copies of U.S. patents and patent and trademark materials;

> . . .[M]ake them freely available to the public; and

> . . . [A]ctively disseminate patent and trademark information. To be designated, a library must meet the specific requirements and promise to fulfill the obligations outlined in the information brochure entitled *Notes on Becoming a Patent and Trademark Depository Library.* (http://www.uspto.gov/web/menu/offices.html)

A library must acquire and make freely available to the public a backfile of U.S. patents that covers at least the past twenty years, "protect the integrity of the collection, maintain classification system documents and related publications, . . . assist the public in efficient use of the collection, and retain all depository items until disposal is arranged through the . . . [program]" (http://www.uspto.gov/web/menu/offices.html). Furthermore, "the intellectual property collections of some libraries significantly exceed core requirements." Some have complete backfiles of all U.S. patents since 1790 (http://www.uspto.gov/web/menu/offices.html).

Begun in 1871, the program first provided for the distribution of printed patents to libraries for the public's use:

[D]uring the program's early years, twenty-two libraries, mostly public and all but several located east of the Mississippi River, elected to participate. Since 1977 the . . . network has grown to four times its original size. Currently, about half of the membership is academic libraries with nearly as many public libraries. There are also several state libraries and one special research library. All libraries regardless of size or mission must meet the same . . . requirements and obligations. (http://www.uspto.gov/web/menu/offices.html)

On its home page, the USPTO also identifies the benefits of depository status, the types of materials the libraries receive, and additional services and products that member libraries provide (http://www.uspto.gov/web/offices/ac/ido/ptdl/ptdlgen.htm). Additional coverage of the core collection and electronic databases can be found at http://www.uspto.gov/web/offices/ac/ido/ptdl/ptdlib_1.html.

Most important, the home page (http://www.uspto.gov/web/offices/ac/ido/ptdl/ptdlib_1.html) lists the member libraries, their addresses and telephone numbers, and identifies those in a geographical region. It also provides a seven-step strategy for patent searching and a strategy for trademark searching, contains *Notes on Becoming a Patent and Trademark Library,* describes how the patent collection can be used, and offers other resources as well.

CONCLUSION

Each of the depository programs discussed in this chapter has made the transition to the electronic environment. The GPO's program has not completed the transition, but it includes the largest number of libraries. The other two programs are more specialized and involve the resources of one executive branch agency. Both the GPO and USPTO programs are grounded in public law, whereas the census program is not. It is guided by the tradition of the Bureau of the Census to communicate with the public and aid in the use of census products. Undoubtedly, this service philosophy might make the public more supportive of the Bureau's data collection efforts. A depository library program provides a means by which the public should be able to receive guidance, direction, and instruction in the retrieval and use of government information products. A program is a partnership between a government agency and a set of libraries, with each gaining benefit and sharing in the cost of public access to information produced and disseminated by the federal government.

NOTES

*This section is partially adapted from Chapter 1, "Historical Background," in *GPO's Depository Library Program*, by Peter Hernon, Charles R. McClure, and Gary R. Purcell. Copyright © 1985 by Ablex Publishing Corp. Reproduced with permission of Greenwood Publishing Group, Inc., Westport, Conn.

1. Peter Hernon, Charles R. McClure, and Gary R. Purcell, *GPO's Depository Library Program* (Norwood, N.J.: Ablex, 1985), 5.

2. Ibid.

3. LeRoy C. Schwarzkopf, "Depository Libraries and Public Access of Government Documents," in *Collection Development and Public Access of Government Documents*, ed. Peter Hernon (Westport, Conn.: Meckler, 1982), 10.

4. *100 GPO Years, 1861–1961: A History of United States Public Printing* (Washington, D.C.: GPO, 1961),79, 90.

5. Ibid., 90.

6. *Annual Report of the Public Printer, 1923* (Washington, D.C.: GPO, 1924), 13.

7. *Annual Report of the Public Printer, 1907* (Washington, D.C.: GPO, 1907), 353.

8. *Annual Report of the Public Printer, 1923*, 13.

9. Ibid.

10. Ibid.

11. Ibid.

12. See *Annual Report of the Public Printer, 1931* (Washington, D.C.: GPO, 1931), 40–41.

13. *Annual Report of the Public Printer, 1938* (Washington, D.C.: GPO, 1939), 112.

14. *Annual Report of the Public Printer, 1932* (Washington, D.C.: GPO, 1932), 92.

15. *Annual Report of the Public Printer, 1947* (Washington, D.C.: GPO, 1947), 213.

16. Hernon, McClure, and Purcell, *GPO's Depository Program*, 14.

17. 79 Stat. 352.

18. Hernon, McClure, and Purcell, *GPO's Depository Program*, 14–15.

19. See *Managing the FDLP Electronic Collection: A Policy and Planning Document* (Washington, D.C.: GPO, Superintendent of Documents, Library Programs Service, 1998).

20. "CD-ROM Software & Policy on Assistance to the User," *Administrative Notes* [newsletter of the Federal Depository Library Program] 12, no. 17 (July 31, 1991): 18–19.

21. General Accounting Office, *Information Management: Electronic Dissemination of Government Publications*, GAO-01-428 (Washington, D.C.: General Accounting Office, March 2001), 5.

22. Government Printing Office, Superintendent of Documents, *Study to Identify Measures Necessary for a Successful Transition to a More Electronic Federal Depository Library Program* (Washington, D.C.: GPO, 1996).

23. Government Printing Office, Superintendent of Documents, *Federal Depository Library Program: Information Dissemination and Access Strategic Plan, FY 1996–2001* (Washington, D.C.: GPO, 1996).

24. General Accounting Office, *Information Management*, 6.

25. Ibid.

26. Government Printing Office, Superintendent of Documents, *Dissemination/Distribution Policy for the Federal Depository Library Program* (Washington, D.C.: GPO, Superintendent of Documents, January 2, 2001).

27. 511 A.2d 792, 795.

28. 1995 U.S. Dist. (LEXIS 7410).

29. Hernon, McClure, and Purcell, *GPO's Depository Library Program: A Descriptive Analysis*, 131–42.

30. Unpublished survey conducted by Peter Hernon in 1977.

31. Elizabeth M. McKenzie, Robert E. Dugan, and Kristin Djorup, "Leaving the Federal Depository Library Program," *Journal of Academic Librarianship*, 26 (July 2001): 285. For an opposing point of view, see Lorraine Kram, "Why Continue to Be a Depository Library if It Is All on the Internet," *Government Information Quarterly* 15 (1998): 57–71.

32. Government Printing Office, Superintendent of Documents, "Preparing for a Library Inspection"(n.d.,), 1, http://www.access.gpo.gov/su_docs/fdlp/selfstudy/prepare (2000).html.

33. Ibid., 2.

34. See, for instance, Peter Hernon and Ellen Altman, *Assessing Service Quality: Satisfying the Expectations of Library Customers* (Chicago: American Library Association, 1998); and Peter Hernon and Robert E. Dugan, *An Action Plan for Outcomes Assessment in Your Library* (Chicago: American Library Association, 2002).

35. Ibid.

36. See Peter Hernon and Charles R. McClure, *Public Access to Government Information: Issues, Trends, and Strategies*, 2d ed. (Norwood, N.J.: Ablex, 1988), 376–88; "Depository Library Council Recommendations to the United States Public Printer," *Administrative Notes* [newsletter of the Federal Depository Library Program] 16, no. 16 (December 5, 1995): 39–55; General Accounting Office, *Information Management*, 66–68.

37. William E. Moen, "The Metadata Approach to Accessing Government Information," *Government Information Quarterly* 18 (2001): 156.

38. Ibid., 157.

39. For a discussion of partnering, see Duncan Aldrich, "Partners on the Net: FDLP Partnering to Coordinate Remote Access to Internet-Based Government Information," *Government Information Quarterly* 15 (1998): 27–38; John A. Shuler, "Policy Implications of a Model Public Information Service: The DOSFAN Experience," *Government Information Quarterly* 17 (2000): 439–49.

40. General Accounting Office, *Information Management*, 2.

41. Daniel C. Barkley, "Public Service Guidelines in an Electronic Environment," *Government Information Quarterly* 15 (1998): 73–85.

42. See Peter Hernon, *Use of Government Publications by Social Scientists* (Norwood, N.J.: Ablex, 1979).

43. See Charles R. McClure and Peter Hernon, *Users of Academic and Public GPO Depository Libraries* (Washington, D.C.: GPO, Superintendent of Documents, 1989).

44. Charles A. Seavey, "Measurement and Evaluation of U.S. Federal Depository Collections," *Government Publications Review* 18 (1991): 147.

45. Ibid., 148.

46. Robert E. Dugan and Ellen M. Dodsworth, "Costing Out a Depository Library: What Free Government Information?" *Government Information Quarterly* 11 (1994): 261–84.

47. Undated letter from A. Ross Eckler, Director, Bureau of the Census, to Mr. Philip M. Burnett, Director of Libraries, University of Wisconsin, Madison.

48. Form letter from Raymond J. Koski, Chief, Publications Services Division, Bureau of the Census (September 1, 1977).

49. See Peter Hernon, "The Census Depository Library Program," *Government Information Quarterly* 8 (1991): 1–10.

50. E-mail message to Peter Hernon from the Webmaster of the Census Bureau (August 8, 2001).

URL SITE GUIDE

Documents Data Miner©
Wichita State University Library
    http://govdoc.wichita.edu/ddm/

Government Printing Office
    Depository Library Council
        http://www.access.gpo.gov/su_docs/fdlp/council/index.html

    Depository Library Publications
        http://www.access/gpo.gov/su_docs/fdlp/libpro.html

    Enhanced Shipping List Service
        http://ubib.buffalo.edu/libraries/units/cts/acq/gpo/

    Federal Bulletin Board
        http://fedbbs.access.gpo.gov/fdlp01.htm

    GPO Access
        http://www.access.gpo.gov/

        New Electronic Titles
            http://www.access.gpo.gov/su_docs/locators/net/index.html

GPO's Federal Depository Library Program Desktop
http://www.access.gpo.gov/su_docs/fdlp/index.html

Enhanced Shipping List Service
http://fedbbs.access.gpo.gov/fdlp01.htm
http://ublib.buffalo.edu/libraries/units/cts/acq/gpo

Instructions and Other Documents
http://www.access.gpo.gov/su_docs/fdlp/pubs/loc/index.html

Home Page
Patent and Trademark Office
http://www.uspto.gov/

List of Depositories
http://www.uspto.gov/web/offices/ac/ido/ptdl/ptdlib_1.html

Mission (Depository Program)

Patent Backfiles

Program Information
http://www.uspto.gov/web/menu/offices.html

Uncle Sam Migrating Government Publications
University of Memphis
http://www.lib.memphis.edu/gpo/mig.htm

 **Chapter 16**

Electronic Government

During the final decade of the twentieth century, a new concept began to emerge in American political and governmental parlance: *electronic government*. Initially, the term was little more than a general recognition of a confluence of information technology developments and the application and use of these technologies by government entities. Subsequently, it has often been used as a symbol, an ambiguous reference to both current applications of information technology to government operations, and a goal of realizing more efficient and economical performance of government functions. The dynamic concept has varying meaning and significance. This chapter reviews the emerging concept of electronic government, or e-government; describes the policy environment defining and shaping it; and discusses some of the components of e-government implementation.

A CONCEPTUAL OVERVIEW

A joint report of the National Performance Review and the Government Information Technology Services Board, *Access America: Reengineering through Information Technology*, issued February 3, 1997, introduced the term "electronic government."[1] Almost three years later, in a December 17, 1999, memorandum to the heads of executive departments and agencies, the president directed these officials to take certain actions in furtherance of "electronic government."[2] On May 18, 2000, Senators Fred D. Thompson (R-Tenn.) and Joseph I. Lieberman (D-Conn.), at that time the chair and ranking minority member, respectively, of the Senate Committee on Governmental Affairs, unveiled a Web site on e-government to collect ideas from citizens on how the government might offer more services and better information online.[3] During June 2000, the concept became part of the campaign offerings of the two major party candidates for the presidency.[4] On May 1, 2001, Senator Lieberman introduced the E-Government Act of 2001, a comprehensive proposal "to enhance the management and promotion of electronic Government services and processes" in various ways.[5]

369

The conditions contributing to the e-government phenomenon were recognized at least three decades ago. Observations offered by the authors of a report of the Commission on the Year 2000 of the American Academy of Arts and Sciences are informative in this regard. Concerning the executive branch, the report proffered the following:

> By the year 2000, despite the growth in the size and complexity of federal programs, the technological improvement of the computer, closed-circuit TV, facsimile transmission, and so on, will make it possible for the federal bureaucracy to carry out its functions much more efficiently and effectively than it can today, with no increase in total manpower.[6]

The use of information technologies was also seen as having critical importance for the legislative branch, constituting nothing less than "another aspect of congressional reform." Should "Congress continue to deny itself the tools of modern information technology and permit the Executive virtually to monopolize them," said the report, "Congress will ultimately destroy its power both to create policy and to oversee the Executive." Moreover, it was observed, the "technology revolution . . . promises greater accessibility of senators and congressmen to their constituents, individually and collectively, and vice versa." Regarding this latter consideration, the following warning was offered: "Communications may become too close and constant, and act as a constricting force. For instance, by 2000 it will be easy to have virtually up-to-the-minute polls of the electorate on any given issue. But where does this instant-opinion development leave the senator and congressman?"[7]

Such observations, however, should not obscure recognition that new information technologies have affected government operations in the past, as the following comment, penned in 1910, attests:

> Public officials, even in the United States, have been slow to change from the old-fashioned and more dignified use of written documents and uniformed messengers; but in the last ten years there has been a sweeping revolution in this respect. Government by telephone! This is a new idea that has already arrived in the more efficient departments of the Federal service. And as for the present Congress, that body has gone so far as to plan for a special system of its own, in both Houses, so that all official announcements may be heard by wire.[8]

The author, a respected Canadian editor and writer, also presciently noted that, "[n]ext to public officials, bankers were perhaps the last to accept the facilities of the telephone," because "[t]hey were slow to abandon the fallacy that no business can be done without a written record."[9] Subscription to such a "fallacy" constitutes a basis for the concerns of some regarding the paperless transactions of e-government.

Demand

E-government is operational in the United States today at the local, state, and national government levels. What has been the public reaction thus far? An answer to this question may be found in a survey commissioned by NIC, a commercial provider of Internet services and solutions for more than 100 American and global government partners, including twelve federal agencies.[10] Survey results were released at a July 26, 2000, news conference at the National Press Club in Washington, D.C.

For purposes of the survey, which was conducted by the Momentum Research Group of Cunningham Communication located in Austin, Texas, e-government was defined as "online government services, that is, any interaction one might have with any government body or agency, using the Internet or World Wide Web."[11] The survey methodology included 406 interviews, of which three-quarters fell into the citizen sector and one-quarter fell into the business sector.[12] Some of the findings follow:

- Almost two out of three online adults had conducted at least one e-government transaction.

- Almost one of five adults using the Internet had conducted an e-government transaction in the prior thirty days.

- Almost half of the citizen users reported that they would like to use the Internet to renew their driver's licenses, vote in major elections, and access one-stop shopping for all government services regardless of jurisdictions.

- Almost half of the business users reported that they would like to use the Internet to obtain or renew their professional licenses and access one-stop shopping to apply for all new business licenses and permits.

- When given a choice, almost three out of four citizens and three out of five businesses preferred to pay convenience fees for services over taxpayer-funded e-government initiatives.

- Business users expressed a strong preference for a single federal e-government portal, whereas citizens preferred to access information and services through their local e-government channels.

- Only one in three e-commerce users and only one in five non-e-commerce users trust that the government would keep their records confidential.[13]

Because "eGovernment is widely accepted and [is] seen as a growing trend and value to citizens and businesses nationwide," the following conclusions can be drawn:

- Citizens and businesses are more satisfied with their eGovernment experience than with traditional government service delivery.

- Citizens and businesses understand and expect certain eGovernment benefits, such as efficiency, time savings and cost-effectiveness.

- The growth of eGovernment depends on education and awareness.[14]

- Citizens favor eGovernment initiatives that are closer to home at the state or local level;

- The services offered online are appropriate to the needs of citizens and business users and are offered at a price that they are willing to pay.

- Trust is the most critical issue facing the adoption of eGovernment. Government must successfully address issues of public trust for eGovernment to be successful in the long term.

- Citizens and businesses who have conducted eCommerce transactions are much more confident that privacy and trust are maintained in the electronic environment. As users begin to interact with government online and experience the increased benefits, a greater degree of trust will be created.[15]

Updating that survey following the September 11 terrorist attacks, polls showed that the public wants e-government to serve as "an easier way to communicate with elected officials."[16] They also see it "as a key tool for catching and prosecuting terrorists and for coordinating government responses to bioterrorism attacks." Furthermore, e-government "provides citizens with easy-to-use services," "improve[s] communication among government levels," "enable[s] citizens to stay informed and voice opinions," and "help[s] businesses use resources/comply with regulations."[17] According to reporter William Matthews, "the most surprising finding" is "the public's belief that e-government can improve accountability."[18]

POLICY ENVIRONMENT

A variety of policy instruments support and shape the e-government concept. In brief, they seek to promote the use of new information technology by government entities with a view to improving the efficiency and economy of government operations. In addition, they seek to ensure the proper management of these technologies and the systems they serve, their protection from physical harm, and the security and privacy of their information.

The policy environment centers on the following instruments that were discussed in Chapters 7–9: the Privacy Act, the Paperwork Reduction Act (PRA), the Computer Security Act, the Computer Matching and Privacy Protection Act, the Electronic Freedom of Information Amendments, the Clinger-Cohen Act, E.O. 13011 on federal information technology management (July 16, 1996),

PDD 63 on critical infrastructures protection (May 22, 1998), the Rehabilitation Act Amendments,[19] the Government Paperwork Elimination Act, the Children's Online Privacy Protection Act, Office of Management and Budget (OMB) memoranda on federal Web site privacy, electronic commerce guidance, Government Information Security Amendments, and the Children's Internet Protection Act.

For example, the Clinger-Cohen Act (110 Stat. 3009-393) comprises the Federal Acquisition Reform Act of 1996 (110 Stat. 642) and the Information Technology Management Reform Act of 1996 (110 Stat. 679). Repealing a section of the Automatic Data Processing Act (79 Stat. 1127), the Clinger-Cohen Act makes each agency responsible for its own information technology (IT) acquisition and requires the purchase of the best and most cost-effective technology available (110 Stat. 186). It also contains several provisions that either amend or gloss provisions of the PRA of 1995 as set out in chapter 35 of Title 44 of the *United States Code*.[20] Among the amendments is one establishing a chief information officer (CIO) in each agency, replacing the designated senior official mandated by the PRA at 44 U.S.C. 3506. Additional duties and qualifications of the CIO are prescribed in the Clinger-Cohen Act.

Other Clinger-Cohen Act provisions gloss the responsibilities prescribed in the PRA. The capital planning and investment control duties assigned to the OMB director by the Clinger-Cohen Act are to be performed, according to that statute, in fulfilling the director's IT responsibilities under 44 U.S.C. 3504(h) of the PRA. Similarly, the director is to "encourage the use of performance-based and results-based management" in fulfilling these same responsibilities. The Clinger-Cohen Act requires agency heads, in fulfilling their counterpart IT responsibilities assigned under 44 U.S.C. 3506(h) of the PRA, to "design and implement . . . a process for maximizing the value and assessing and managing the risks of the information technology acquisitions of the . . . agency" and to perform certain prescribed duties. Also, agency heads are to "identify in the strategic information resources management plan [44 U.S.C. 3506(b)(2)] required under any major information technology acquisition program, or any phase or increment of such a program, that has significantly deviated from the cost, performance, or schedule goals established for the program."[21]

Among the 1998 amendments to the Rehabilitation Act of 1973 (PL 93-112) adopted by Congress is a new subsection requiring federal agencies to procure, maintain, and use electronic and information technology that provides individuals with disabilities, including both federal employees and members of the public, with accessibility comparable to what is available to individuals without disabilities.[22] The Architectural and Transportation Barriers Compliance Board, known as the Access Board, was tasked with developing access standards to implement the new requirement. The amendments anticipated that the board would issue final access standards in February 2000 and the electronic and information technology access requirement would become effective on August 7, 2000. However, the Access Board did not publish proposed standards for electronic and information technology for public comment until March 31, 2000.[23]

Provision was subsequently made in the Military Construction Appropriations Act for Fiscal Year 2001 to delay the effective date of the electronic and information technology access requirement until six months after the date of the publication of the board's final standards (114 Stat. 555), which were issued on December 21.[24] Federal agencies actively prepared to ensure that not only their Web sites, but also their internal software programs, were in compliance by June 21, 2001.[25] Since late 2000, free software for testing Web site accessibility has been available to ease agency burden and cost.[26]

Electronic Commerce Guidance

The convergence of computer and telecommunications technologies has not only revolutionized the storage, retrieval, and sharing of information, but also, in the considered view of many, produced an information economy resulting from commercial transactions on the Internet. The federal government is a participant in e-commerce, and statutes such as the GPEA, discussed previously, reflect encouragement of this development.

Among the first Clinton administration initiatives in furtherance of government participation in e-commerce was the June 15, 1995, unveiling of the U.S. Business Advisor (http://www.business.gov), a new online computer service directly linking the federal government to American business. The new service was announced by the president and vice president during the White House Conference on Small Business held at the Washington Hilton Hotel. An upgraded and improved version of the U.S. Business Advisor, providing users with one-stop electronic access to more than sixty different federal organizations that assist or regulate businesses, was announced by Vice President Al Gore on February 13, 1996.

On July 1, 1997, President William Clinton released a report, *A Framework for Global Electronic Commerce*, expressing five operating principles that the administration would follow in fostering e-commerce and designating lead federal agencies in key policy areas:[27]

- The private sector should lead.

- Governments should avoid undue restrictions on electronic commerce.

- Where government involvement is needed, its aim should be to support and enforce a predictable minimalist, consistent, and simple legal environment for commerce.

- Governments should recognize the unique qualities of the Internet.

- Electronic commerce on the Internet should be facilitated on a global basis.

In his remarks announcing the release of the report, the president indicated that he was directing all federal department and agency heads to review the policies of their organizations that affect global electronic commerce with a view to ensuring that they were consistent with the five core principles of the report. Cabinet members were directed to achieve some of the administration's key objectives within the next year, and relevant agencies were called upon to work with the Department of Commerce, industry, and law enforcement agencies to ensure that Americans conducted their business affairs in a secure environment. The assistance of the private sector was sought to meet "one of the greatest challenges of electronic commerce: ensuring that we develop effective methods of protecting the privacy of every American, especially children who use the Internet" (http://clinton6.nara.gov/1997). Specific assignments and tasks in these regards were made in a July 1 presidential memorandum to the heads of executive departments and agencies on the subject of electronic commerce. A November 30, 1998, memorandum to the heads of executive departments and agencies assigned additional responsibilities to the assistant to the president for economic policy, the secretaries of commerce and state, and the administrator of the Small Business Administration.

On January 24, 1999, the president and vice president announced an Information Technology for the 21st Century (IT2) initiative for which $336 million was proposed to fund three kinds of activities:

1. Long-term information technology research that will lead to fundamental advances in computing and communications, in the same way that government investment beginning in the 1960s led to today's Internet;

2. Advanced computing for science, engineering and the Nation that will lead to breakthroughs such as reducing the time required to develop life-saving drugs; designing cleaner, more efficient engines; and more accurately predicting tornadoes; and

3. Research on the economic and social implications of the Information Revolution, and efforts to help train additional IT workers at our universities. (http://clinton6.nara.gov/1999)

The significance of IT2 was underscored in a February report of the President's Information Technology Advisory Committee, which, in a relevant part, stated:

While the importance of information technology to the future of the economy and the government is clear, it may not be immediately obvious that government investment is needed to ensure continued progress.

We cannot rely on industry to fund the needed research because they necessarily focus, in view of economic realities, on the short term. Industry cannot and will not invest in solving problems of importance to society as a whole unless such investments make sense from a business perspective.

Information technology research is essential for the continued growth of the economy and for the solution of some of the most critical problems facing the Nation. Unless steps are taken now to reinvigorate Federal research in this critical area, we are very likely to see a significant reduction in the rate of progress over the coming decades. The cost to the Nation of such a reduction will be significantly greater than the investment needed to address the problem.[28]

In a November 29, 1999, memorandum to the heads of executive departments and agencies, President Clinton directed each federal agency, including independent regulatory agencies, to assist a working group on electronic commerce with identifying any provision of law administered by the agencies, and any regulation issued by them, that may impose a barrier to electronic transactions or otherwise impede the conduct of commerce online or by electronic means. They were also tasked with recommending how such laws or regulations might be revised to allow electronic commerce to proceed while maintaining protection of the public interest. The working group conducted a similar exercise with representatives of state and local government.

The heads of executive departments and agencies were informed of Clinton administration efforts to address the so-called digital divide in a December 9, 1999, presidential memorandum. *Digital divide* is a reference to the perceived disparity that results from portions of the population not having the ability to use IT due to a lack of access and/or skill. Among the actions directed, the memorandum indicated, were the development of a national strategy for making computers and the Internet accessible to all Americans; expansion of the federal community technology centers network to provide low-income citizens with access to IT; encouragement of the development of IT applications that would help enable low-income citizens to start and manage their own small businesses; and use of training to upgrade the IT skills of the American workforce, particularly workers living in disadvantaged urban and rural communities.

A December 17, 1999, memorandum to the heads of executive departments and agencies directed them, among other actions, to make available online, by December 2000, to the maximum extent possible, the forms needed for the top 500 government services used by the public; to make transactions with the federal government performable online, with online processing, by October 2003; and to promote the use of electronic commerce, where appropriate, for faster, cheaper ordering on federal procurements.

IMPLEMENTATION COMPONENTS

As discussed in Chapter 15 of *U.S. Government on the Web*, the principal components of electronic government are communication between an agency and the public, information access, service delivery (including, for example, the dissemination of forms, buying and paying for goods and services, and applying for licenses, grants, and benefits), procurement (submitting bids and proposals), security, privacy, management (e.g., through OMB's leadership for the executive branch), maintenance (of IT systems), the digital divide (the perceived disparity that results from portions of the population not having the ability to use IT due to a lack of access and/or skill), emergency response, and oversight. In essence, these components define government responsibilities under the rubric of electronic government. The intent clearly is to improve the efficiency and economy of government operations.

It would seem that

> the challenge for policymakers in the long run will be to determine whether any continuing disparities in the availability and use of the Internet among different groups of Americans threaten to offer citizens separate levels of service and access. . . . Multiple access methods to government services and processes—in person, by phone, via fax, using public kiosks—may be essential to supplement Internet use.

> The Congress has taken action to address the digital divide that confronts people with disabilities. Specifically, the Workforce Investment Act of 1998 [P. L. 105-22] (section 508 of the Rehabilitation Act, 29 U.S.C. 794d) requires federal departments and agencies and the U.S. Postal Service to procure, develop, maintain, and use electronic and information technology that is accessible for people with disabilities—including both federal employees and members of the public—unless an undue burden would be imposed on the department or agency.[29]

Emergency Response

In the American governmental experience, an expectation has long existed that the president will exert leadership when a sudden crisis threatens the nation. Such thinking may be traced to the seventeenth-century British philosopher John Locke, who argued that occasions may arise when an executive must exert broad discretion in meeting special exigencies or "emergencies" for which the legislative authority has provided no relief or existing law does not grant necessary remedy. As the federal government has evolved during the past two centuries, a number of developments have occurred regarding presidential response to national emergencies, resulting in a less drastic situation than the one envisioned by Locke. Special institutions, such as the current Federal Emergency Management Agency (FEMA), have been created to respond to, coordinate the efforts of other agencies to respond to and plan for national emergencies. Such institutions have coordinated, and contributed to, the preparation and maintenance of emergency plans, such as the Federal Response Plan for the delivery of federal disaster assistance,[30] and standby directives, such as E.O. 12656 of November 18, 1988, assigning emergency preparedness responsibilities among the federal departments and agencies.[31] In addition, Congress has enacted various laws that provide the president with ready authority to address an emergency, as well as some standby statutory powers that may be selectively activated under the terms of the National Emergencies Act of 1976, as amended.[32]

Responding to an emergency arising from severe disruption of computer-based critical infrastructures and e-government operations both draws upon and builds upon this legacy of developments. Experience has shown that severe weather conditions produced by a hurricane or tornado can damage or destroy communications systems and critical infrastructures in a geographic area. Consequently, the restoration of communications damaged or destroyed by severe weather is addressed in the Federal Response Plan. A recently added plan annex concerning terrorism indicates that the Department of Justice is responsible for "crisis management," defined as "measures to identify, acquire, and plan the use of resources needed to anticipate, prevent, and/or resolve a threat or act of terrorism," such as damaging or destroying critical infrastructures. The annex specifies that FEMA is responsible for "consequence management," defined as "measures to protect public health and safety, restore essential government services, and provide emergency relief to governments, businesses, and individuals affected by the consequences of terrorism."[33] This plan will be subsequently supplemented with a national strategy for combating terrorism being developed by former Pennsylvania Governor Tom Ridge and his Office of Homeland Security.

Critical infrastructure protection planning and preparation is also addressed in PDD 63. In addition to creating new institutions and assigning responsibilities regarding these matters, the directive establishes a public-private partnership structure, recognizing that, because "the targets of attacks on our critical infrastructure would likely include both facilities in the economy and those in the government, the elimination of our potential vulnerability requires a closely coordinated effort of both the government and the private sector."[34] Among the first fruits of these partnerships is the National Plan for Information Systems Protection, made public on January 7, 2000.[35] An October 1999 General Accounting Office (GAO) report reinforced the value of these public-private partnerships and offered various recommendations for critical infrastructure protection based on recent experiences of addressing the year 2000 computing problem.[36]

On October 18, 2001, President George W. Bush issued E.O. 13231, "Critical Infrastructure Protection in the Information Age" (see 66 FR 53063–53071), which notes that

> the information technology revolution has changed the way business is transacted, government operates, and national defense is conducted. Those three functions now depend on an interdependent network of critical information infrastructures. The protection program authorized by this order shall consist of continuous efforts to secure information systems for critical infrastructure, including emergency preparedness communications, and the physical assets that support such systems. Protection of these system is essential to the telecommunications, energy, financial services, manufacturing, water, transportation, health care, and emergency services sectors.

It is the policy of the United States to protect against disruption of the operation of information systems for critical infrastructure and thereby help to protect the people, economy, essential human and government services, and national security of the United States, and to ensure that any disruptions that occur are infrequent, of minimal duration, and manageable, and cause the least damage possible. The implementation of this policy shall include a voluntary public-private partnership, involving corporate and nongovernmental organizations.[37]

The OMB's director was given "the responsibility to develop and oversee the implementation of government-wide policies, principles, standards, and guidelines for the security of information systems that support the executive branch departments and agencies, except those noted in section 4(b) [relating to national security information systems] of this order."[38] The director would be assisted by the establishment of the President's Critical Infrastructure Protection Board.

Ultimately, in the event that severe disruption of, or damage to, critical infrastructure results in public disorder in a locale, the president may resort to the deployment of armed forces personnel, military technicians, the Ready Reserve, or federalized National Guard units to support federal law enforcement officials.[39] These troops would function under federal civilian direction; no condition of martial law would necessarily result.

Oversight

Electronic government is subject to oversight by both executive branch officials and legislative branch entities. The OMB director is a principal executive branch overseer of e-government, monitoring agency compliance with relevant statutes, presidential directives, and OMB and National Institute of Standards and Technology (NIST) guidance. Within departments and agencies having them, CIOs performing statutory responsibilities and duties for ensuring compliance with the requirements of the PRA and monitoring the performance of IT programs also play an oversight role.[40] Also, in departments and agencies having them, inspectors general (IGs) exercise an oversight capability, particularly with regard to protecting the transmission, storage, and processing of sensitive data in electronic forms and formats.[41]

Congressional committees and subcommittees, assisted sometimes by congressional support agencies such as GAO, conduct oversight of executive entities and activities for various purposes: to ensure executive compliance with legislative intent; to improve the efficiency, effectiveness, and economy of government operations; to evaluate program performance; to investigate alleged instances of poor administration, arbitrary and capricious behavior, abuse, waste, dishonesty, and fraud; to assess agency or officials' ability to manage and carry out program objectives; to review and determine federal financial priorities; to ensure that executive policies reflect the public interest; and to protect individual rights and liberties, among other functions.

For Congress, oversight of electronic government may prove to be particularly daunting. With potentially thousands of daily electronic transactions—for information, benefits, services, and goods—occurring, rapidly and invisibly, overseers will have to be alert to the development of administrative or managerial problems that could quickly snowball, resulting in unnecessary hardship, waste, misfeasance, or worse. Careful attention will have to be given to the creation, maintenance, preservation, security, integrity, and accessibility of the records of these transactions for possible audit and review by overseers. When agency leaders and program managers are consulted or brought before a congressional committee or subcommittee for an oversight proceeding, the agency CIO and IG may also be consulted or otherwise be found to be important participants. Moreover, for congressional and executive overseers alike, FirstGov, the single federal portal, may prove to be a useful tool for scrutinizing governmentwide compliance with certain e-government policies, such as Web site privacy notices, and other uniform requirements for federal Web sites.

Concerns and Developments

Congress passed amendments to two appropriations bills regarding Web site information practices. Section 501 of the FY2001 Transportation Appropriations Act (PL 106-346) prohibited funds in the FY2001 Treasury-Postal Appropriations Act from being used by any federal agency to collect, review, or create aggregate lists that included personally identifiable information (PII) about an individual's access to, or use of, a federal Web site or enter into agreements with third parties to do so, with exceptions. Section 646 of the FY2001 Treasury-Postal Appropriations Act (PL 106-554) required IGs to report to Congress on activities by those agencies or departments relating to the collection of PII about individuals who access any Internet site of that department or agency, or entering into agreements with third parties to obtain PII about use of government or nongovernment Web sites. (The discussion in Chapter 8 covers the FY2002 treasury bill and thereby updates the privacy issue.)

Some software products include, as part of the software itself, a method by which information is collected about the use of the computer on which the software is installed. When the computer is connected to the Internet, the software periodically relays the information back to the software manufacturer or a marketing company. Software that collects and reports is called "spyware." Software programs that include spyware can be obtained on disk or downloaded from the Internet. They may be sold or provided for free. Typically, users have no knowledge that the software product they are using includes spyware. Two bills in the 107th Congress (H.R. 112 and S. 197) would require that users be notified if the software they are using includes spyware.

Another concern has been the extent to which e-mail exchanges or visits to Web sites may be monitored by law enforcement agencies or employers. In the wake of the September 11 terrorist attacks, the debate over law enforcement monitoring has intensified. Previously, the issue had focused on the extent to which the Federal Bureau of Investigation (FBI), with legal authorization, uses Carnivore (now called DCS 1000), a software program, to intercept e-mail and monitor Web activities of certain suspects. Privacy advocates are concerned about whether Carnivore-like systems can differentiate between e-mail and Internet usage by the subject of an investigation and those of other people. To help oversee the extent to which the FBI uses Carnivore/DCS 1000, the FY2002 Department of Justice authorization bill (H.R. 2215/S. 1319) as passed by the House and reported from the Senate Judiciary Committee requires the Justice Department to report to Congress on its use of DCS 1000 or any similar system. Following the terrorist attacks, however, Congress passed antiterrorism legislation, the USA PATRIOT Act (PL 107-56), that expands law enforcement's ability to monitor Internet activities.[42]

Another concern relates to whether the widespread use of computers for storing and transmitting information contributes to identity theft, in which one individual assumes the identity of another using personal information such as credit card and social security numbers. It may be that businesses are careless in handling PII. At any rate, the Federal Trade Commission has a toll free number (877-ID-THEFT) to help victims of identity theft. The 105th Congress passed the Identity Theft and Assumption Deterrence Act (PL 105-318), and the 106th Congress passed the Social Security Number Confidentiality Act (PL 106-433) and the Internet False Identification Act (PL 106-578). Additional legislation was introduced into the 107th Congress regarding Internet privacy, for example, H.R. 89, the Online Privacy Protection Act, which would require the Federal Trade Commission to prescribe regulations to protect privacy of personal information collected from and about individuals not covered by the Children's Online Privacy Protection Act (PL 105-277), and H.R. 237, the Consumer Internet Privacy Enhancement Act, which would require Web site operators to provide clear and conspicuous notice of their information practices and provide consumers with easy methods to limit use and disclosure of their information.

In a notice seeking comments on a proposal to issue documents in electronic format, the Federal Energy Regulatory Commission asked the public for comments on the following questions:

- Would adopting issuances via e-mail be easier for recipients than receiving paper service?

- Although the agency's Web site offers documents in multiple formats (e.g., ASCII and WordPerfect), should even more formats be offered— such as portable document format (PDF)?

- Would e-distribution reduce the number of parties filing motions to intervene simply to remain aware of a proceeding's developments?

- Would it be beneficial for the agency to e-mail Web links to other documents in addition to its own issuances?[43]

Clearly, the agency is using public comment as a means to improve electronic service delivery of the commission's issuances and of the electronic services for parties filing documents, as well as to respond to the public's needs in lieu of conducting a more expensive needs assessment.

With the September 11 terrorist attacks, there was "a record number of visitors" to federal Web sites. "Undoubtedly, the World Wide Web has become one of the places people turn to for information. As well, the agencies also used their sites to collect information."[44] The FBI, for example, transformed its Internet Fraud Complaint Center into a focal point for tips about the terrorists (http://www.ifccfbi.gov) and received more than 54,000 tips in the week following the attacks. The FEMA responded to the emergency by posting current information. However, most other "agency Web sites trailed media sites and often provided little more than background data and links to other sites."[45]

At the same time, a number of agencies have shut down Web sites due to viruses such as the Code Red worm or have removed material from their sites so that material does not reach terrorists.[46] With the national concern over anthrax, the Internal Revenue Service anticipates a sharp increase in the electronic filing of tax returns; it has projected at least forty-six million such filings.[47]

In the aftermath of the attacks, the departments of Energy and Transportation and the Environmental Protection Agency removed information from their Web sites.[48] The Nuclear Regulatory Commission (http://www.nrc.gov) announced that, "in support of our mission to protect public health and safety,. . . [it] is performing a review of all material on our site. In the interim, only select content will be available" (http://www.nrc.gov). The redesigned home page is more selective in the content provided. It provides news and information; a public meeting schedule; Webcasts; regulations; "What's New;" information about the agency; selective coverage of nuclear reactors, nuclear materials, and radioactive waste; an electronic reading room; and so forth.

Unrelated to the terrorist attacks, due to a federal judge's concern about the security of financial accounts held in trust for Native Americans, most Web sites of the Department of the Interior (DOI) were shut down during much of the winter and spring of 2001–2002. A notice on DOI's Web site reads:

> Access to the DOI website has been restricted in compliance with a court order. Select DOI webpages will be made available to the public through USGS [United Stats Geological Survey], who has received court approval to reconnect to the Internet. All information posted on this version of DOI.GOV will be certified not to contain or provide access to individual Indian trust data. (http://www.doi.gov/index.html)

The shutdown is linked to alleged government mismanagement of Native American trust accounts and the money the government collected for Native Americans from oil, gas, and mineral leases on their lands. U.S. District Court

Judge Royce Lamberth ordered DOI to disconnect from the Internet all computers that had access to trust fund information. Thus, the suspension of Internet access not only affected communication between DOI and the public but also the conduct of departmental business; use of faxes, "snail mail," and the telephone replaced use of the Internet.

THE BUSH ADMINISTRATION: MAJOR PROPOSALS AND INITIATIVES

Shortly after the inauguration of President George W. Bush, the Council for Excellence in Government, a nonpartisan, nonprofit organization seeking to improve the performance of government at all levels, issued *E-Government: The Next American Revolution*. The report "proposes the fundamental challenge of bringing e-government into being, sets out specific principles and proposals to meet it, and identifies the resources required."[49] The report provides something of an overview of current proposals that have been offered from various quarters for realizing e-gov. Among its specific recommendations are the following:

Presidential Initiatives

- Establish an Assistant to the President for Electronic Government within the White House staff, with Cabinet rank, to confirm the President's personal leadership role;

- Create a Council on Electronic Government, chaired by the President's new electronic government assistant and including members representative of federal, state, local, and tribal governments, Congress, and relevant private sector and research community interests;

- Designate the OMB Deputy Director for Management as Deputy Director for Management and Technology, with responsibility for supporting the development of e-government through the President's budget and management processes;

- Through the OMB Deputy Director for Management and Technology, create an Office of Electronic Government and Information Policy within OMB, headed by a presidentially-appointed and Senate-confirmed Federal Chief Information Officer, who would chair an interagency Chief Information Officers Council; and

- Insist that nominees to top-level executive branch positions "make a commitment to the strategic development of e-government in their departments and agencies."

Congressional Initiatives

- Create a Congressional Office of E-Government to "guide congressional action" on using e-gov to achieve policy goals and to provide the public "maximum electronic opportunity to receive information from and interact with all members, committees, and agencies of the Congress," with the head of such office serving on the President's Council on Electronic Government and providing liaison with state and local government legislatures on e-gov; and

- Ascertain, during Senate confirmation proceedings, nominees' commitment to e-gov; insist, during oversight and appropriations hearings, "that agencies demonstrate their actions to implement e-government."

Judiciary Initiatives

- Through Web sites, make "[c]ourt calendars, rules, case assignments, sentencing guidelines, decisions, and an easy-to-use guide to the judicial process . . . available to and searchable by the public," and enable citizens "to ask and get answers to questions online;" and

- Both the Administrative Office of the United States Courts and the National Center for State Courts should appoint a liaison to the President's Council on Electronic Government.[50]

Among other innovations recommended by the report was the creation of a $3 billion Strategic Investment Fund to support, through collaborative ventures with the private sector and other levels of government where possible, "e-government program and service delivery initiatives that are both cross-sector and multi-agency, as well as research and development for solutions to enterprise-wide problems of privacy, security, and interoperability."[51] The report also offered various recommendations regarding collaborative efforts by government at all levels and the private sector in furtherance of e-gov; building an e-gov workforce, largely among civil servants rather than contracted personnel; and improving privacy, security, and interoperability.[52] The report concluded with the results of a public opinion poll regarding various aspects of e-gov.

Electronic Government Fund

In advance of his proposed budget for FY2002, President Bush, through OMB, released, on February 28, 2001, *A Blueprint for New Beginnings: A Responsible Budget for America's Priorities*. Intended as a ten-year budget plan, the *Blueprint*, among other innovations, proposed the establishment of an electronic government account, seeded with "$10 million in 2002 as the first installment of a fund that will grow to a total of $100 million over 3 years to support interagency electronic Government . . . initiatives."[53] Managed by OMB, the fund was foreseen as

- Supporting "projects that operate across agency boundaries" and build upon FirstGov, "the online information portal that provides 24 hours a day/seven days a week access to all Government online information";

- Facilitating "the development of a Public Key Infrastructure to implement digital signatures that are accepted across agencies for secure online communications"; and

- Furthering "the Administration's ability to implement the Government Paperwork Elimination Act of 1998, which calls upon agencies to provide the public with optional use and acceptance of electronic information, services and signatures, when practicable, by October 2003."[54]

About one month later, on March 22, OMB Deputy Director Sean O'Keefe announced that the Bush administration had decided to double the amount to be allocated to the e-gov fund, bringing it to $20 million, and outlined some standards for the types of projects that would qualify for the fund. Being an interagency endeavor was mandatory; supporting FirstGov was desirable. Having a capital planning element that spelled out costs, benefits, and future projections was another requirement for funded projects, and having available budgeted funds for a project, which monies from the e-gov fund would supplement, was also highly desirable.[55]

As included in the president's budget submitted to Congress on April 9, the fund was established as an account within the General Services Administration, to be administered by the Administrator of General Services "to support interagency projects, approved by the Director of the Office of Management and Budget, that enable the Federal Government to expand its ability to conduct activities electronically, through the development and implementation of innovative uses of the Internet and other electronic methods." The initial request for the fund was $20 million, to remain available until September 30, 2004.[56]

As approved by Congress, the Treasury, Postal Service, and General Government Appropriations Act (PL 107-67, 115 Stat. 514) allocates only $5 million to the fund, to remain available until expended. The House committee report accompanying the bill recommended that the administration work with the House Committee on Government Reform to "clarify its authorization."[57] The Act stipulates that transfers of monies from the fund to federal agencies may not be made until ten days after a proposed spending plan and justification for each project to be undertaken using such monies has been submitted to the House and Senate Committees on Appropriations.

The president's budget for FY2003 seeks $45 million for the e-gov fund, and acknowledges that this amount is "a significant increase over the $20 million requested in 2002," but notes that the request "is supported by specific project plans" and "would also further the Administration's implementation of the Government Paperwork Elimination Act (GPEA) of 1998, which calls upon agencies to provide the public with optional use and acceptance of electronic information, services, and signatures, when practicable, by October 2003."[58]

E-GOVERNMENT ACT OF 2001

Described by proponents as "a bipartisan effort to maximize the organization, efficiency, accessibility, and quality of the federal government's online resources, while reducing overall cost," the E-Government Act of 2001 was initially introduced in the Senate (S. 803) by Senator Lieberman for himself and eleven cosponsors on May 1, 2001.[59] An identical version of the bill was offered in the House (H.R. 2458) by Representative Jim Turner for himself and thirty-six cosponsors on July 11. Designated "a work in progress" by Senator Lieberman at the time of introduction, the initial version of the bill offered several innovations. It would, for example,

- Establish a federal chief information Officer (FCIO) within OMB to head a new Office of Information Policy and to promote e-gov and implement governmentwide information policy set by the Paperwork Reduction Act, the Clinger-Cohen Act, and the Government Paperwork Elimination Act, among other laws; foster inter-organizational dialogue (interagency, cross-branch, federal-state-local, and public-private sector) concerning IT applications for e-gov; and pursue improved standards, protocols, and procurement regarding IT;

- Statutorily mandate a federal Chief Information Officer (CIO) Council, chaired by the FCIO, to assist with the development of information policies and multi-agency IT initiatives; coordination with NIST on the development of IT standards; and partner with the Office of Personnel Management to address the shortage of IT professionals in the federal executive branch;

- Under the direction of the FCIO and building on FirstGov, establish, maintain, and promote a centralized online government portal allowing Internet users to access all online federal government information and services through a single, functionally arranged Web page;

- Upgrade regulatory activities by posting on agency Web sites the same information published in the *Federal Register* related to an administrative proceeding; require agencies to accept submissions related to administrative proceedings by electronic means, including e-mail and fax; and mandate the FCIO to work with the regulatory agencies to establish electronic dockets for administrative rulemaking;

- Require federal courts to establish Web sites containing opinions, docketing information, and other specified information about the courts and individual cases, unless they elect to opt out of some of these arrangements; and

- Prescribe other refinements and innovations regarding privacy and security practices, electronic signatures compatibility, agency Web site management, online access to federally-funded research and development activities, online crisis management, and disparities in access to the Internet.

The legislation met with administration opposition but illustrates the types of changes to e-government that might emerge in the coming years.

Bush Administration Action Plan

In a July 18, 2001, memorandum to executive department and agency heads, OMB Director Mitchell E. Daniels Jr., on behalf of President Bush, apprised executive department and agency heads of administration efforts to develop an electronic government action plan using an interagency task force under the leadership of OMB Associate Director Mark Forman. The latter, a former Unisys vice president for e-business, joined OMB on June 25, where he was given primary responsibilities for IT and e-gov matters. In a July 27 interview with *GovExec.com*, Forman was highly critical of current government efforts at implementing e-gov. He indicated that a lack of communication between IT specialists and agency senior program officials was the principal reason that bigger e-gov gains had not occurred. Consequently, his e-gov action plan task force will scrutinize agency performance plans with a view to realizing the goals and objectives of those plans better through IT and e-business applications modeled after best practices in the private sector. "The key is to align a lot of buzzword-type technologies with where they provide the greatest strategic improvement," said Forman.[60]

In his interview, Forman also indicated that, in the following eighteen months, a steering committee of representatives from the President's Management Council would provide twenty-sixty project ideas for improving and facilitating e-gov implementation. Originally created by President Clinton in October 1993, the council was reconstituted by President Bush on July 11, 2001, with OMB Deputy Director O'Keefe designated as chair, and the panel held its first meeting that same day.[61] The presidential memorandum rechartering the council continued the panel's oversight of the federal management role, but also created CIOs in the federal departments and agencies to facilitate implementation and oversight of management initiatives and other performance, resource allocation, and mission responsibilities. (As of the writing of this chapter, no funds have been appropriated for these projects.)

In his August 25, 2001, weekly radio address to the nation, President Bush announced the release of *The President's Management Agenda*, a report identifying fourteen management problems in the federal government and offering specific solutions to address them. In language reminiscent of the National Performance Review launched by the Clinton administration, the report urged "rethinking government," called for a reduction of middle management, and championed "results-oriented" and "market-based" administration. It proposed five governmentwide initiatives: strategic management of human capital, competitive outsourcing, improved financial performance, expanded electronic government, and budget and performance integration. The e-gov initiative seeks to secure greater services at lower cost as well as measurable gains in public-sector worker productivity for the IT investment.

The report's nine specific program initiatives included a reiteration of support for reducing barriers to the delivery of federally funded social services by faith-based and community groups. Some proposals in support of the agenda, such as "Freedom to Manage" legislation, creating a fast-track arrangement to eliminate agency-identified statutory barriers to efficient management, are expected to be controversial.

CONCLUSION

By 2001, electronic government meant the use of technology, particularly the Internet, to enhance the access to and delivery of government information and services to citizens, businesses, government employees, and other agencies at the federal and state levels.[62] Mitchell E. Daniels Jr., OMB's director, identified four priority areas of service to reform "the government so that it is citizen-centered":

- Service to *individuals*: Deploy easy to find one-stop shops for citizens, including single points of easy access entry to access high quality government services.

- Service to *businesses*: Reduce burden on businesses by using Internet protocols and consolidating the myriad of redundant reporting requirements.

- *Intergovernmental affairs*: Make it easier for states to meet reporting requirements, while enabling better performance measurement and results, especially for grants.

- *Internal efficiency and effectiveness*: Improve the performance and reduce costs of federal government administration by using e-business best practices in areas such as supply chain management, financial management, and knowledge management.[63]

Although "the Internet opens new opportunities for streamlining processes and enhancing delivery of services," responsibilities and challenges accompany those opportunities. There are nine challenges, including

> (1) sustaining committed executive leadership, (2) building effective e-government business cases, (3) maintaining a citizen focus, (4) protecting personal privacy, (5) implementing appropriate security controls, (6) maintaining electronic records, (7) maintaining a robust technical infrastructure, (8) addressing IT human capital concerns, and (9) ensuring uniform service to the public.[64]

Clearly the government recognizes "the individual citizen and citizen 'community of interest' as customers. However, translating this growing awareness into better, efficient, and friendly services can be challenging."[65]

Despite the terrorist attacks of September 11, the government is still proceeding with the continued development and implementation of e-government. However, the broadening concept of national security and homeland protection have called for rethinking what information agencies place on the Web. Some Web sites have been redesigned and maps—and other information—potentially useful to terrorists removed from their pages. E-government remains a movement toward government without boundaries, and as FirstGov illustrates, it brings together services and sources at the national and subnational levels.

A significant problem remains, however, There needs to be more stability in the URLs for agency Web presentations. For the first edition of *U.S. Government on the Web*, we periodically run a spider to monitor changes in URLs and to provide readers with updated access. Between the first and second editions (1999 to 2001), 25.4 percent of the URLs listed changed. For the second edition, we ran a spider at page proof stage and updated published URLs. In the following three months, 6.1 percent of the URLs changed. One of the agencies producing the most changes was the Government Printing Office, which made the URLs longer and more complex.

Complicating matters, a number of the e-government efforts of agencies inadequately serve the public's needs. The OMB has assigned color grades (green, yellow, or red) to agency performance. Green, the top grade, means that a project meets the White House's criteria for success and is considered at least 90 percent effective. To date, no agency has received this rank. Yellow signifies that some of the criteria are met, and red—the color received by most agencies—indicates inadequacy. Yet the president's proposed FY 2003 funding for IT does not relate directly to the scores. Clearly the scoring and the improvement of Web site performance are linked to more than the design, layout, and usability of a home page. E-government provides a means by which the public can interact directly with government and obtain information and services. It also affords government a means to increase its efficiency, effectiveness, and responsiveness to the public.[66]

The complex environment addressed in this book suggests that e-government remains a puzzle, the size, shape, and content of which has yet to be resolved. It is our hope that this book and its companion, *U.S. Government on the Web*, help to navigate this environment, while at the same time placing the digital era within a larger context: more than two centuries of government publishing.

NOTES

1. Office of the Vice President, *Access America: Reengineering through Information Technology; Report of the National Performance Review and the Government Information Technology Services Board* (Washington, D.C.: GPO, 1997).

2. The White House, Memorandum for the Heads of Executive Departments and Agencies, *Electronic Government* (Washington, D.C., December 17, 1999).

3. See Ben White, "Senators Go Looking for E-ideas," *Washington Post,* May 19, 2000, A29; the Web site may be accessed directly at http://cct.georgetown.edu/development/ eGov or through the committee Web site at http://gov_affs.senate.gov. See also Shruti Date, "Senators' E-gov Site Comes to Fruition," *Government Computer News* 19 (July 24, 2000): 62.

4. See, for example, Christopher J. Dorobek, "Gore and Bush Make E-gov a Campaign Issue," *Government Computer News* 19 (June 19, 2000): 6.

5. See *Congressional Record* (daily edition) 147 (May 1, 2001): S4101–15.

6. William M. Capron, "The Executive Branch in the Year 2000," in *The Future of the U.S. Government: Toward the Year 2000*, ed. Harvey S. Perloff (New York: George Braziller, 1971), 307.

7. John Brademus, "Congress in the Year 2000," in *The Future of the U.S. Government*, 319–21.

8. Herbert N. Casson, *The History of the Telephone* (Chicago: A. C. McClurg, 1910), 201–02.

9. Ibid., 203.

10. NIC, *Benchmarking the eGovernment Revolution: Year 2000 Report on Citizen and Business Demand*, by the Momentum Research Group of Cunningham Communication (Reston, Va.: NIC, 2000).

11. Ibid., 34.

12. Ibid.

13. NIC, *Benchmarking the eGovernment Revolution*, 3.

14. For example, a $10,000 kiosk, recently installed in a District of Columbia supermarket and offering a wide variety of federal, state, and local government information and services, was almost totally ignored by passing shoppers, who were largely unaware of its purpose. See Manny Fernandez, "E-Government Not on Shopping List," *Washington Post,* August 4, 2000, B4; Jennifer Surface, "Few Notice $10,000 Kiosk Set Up to Make Government Accessible," *Washington Times,* July 31, 2000, C2.

15. NIC, *Benchmarking the eGovernment Revolution*, 4.

16. "GSA Debuts Friendlier FirstGov," *Federal Computer Week* 16, no. 5 (March 4, 2002): 8.

17. Ibid.

18. William Matthews, "Perception of E–gov Shifting," *Federal Computer Week* 16, no. 6 (March 4, 2002): 39.

19. The Rehabilitation Act Amendments of 1998 constituted Title IV of the Workforce Investment Act of 1998, 112 Stat. 936; the electronic and information technology access requirement was appended to the Rehabilitation Act as section 508, 112 Stat 1203, at 29 U.S.C. 794(d); the Rehabilitation Act was originally enacted in 1973, 87 Stat. 355, at 29 U.S.C. 701 et seq.

20. The Clinger-Cohen Act provision (110 Stat. 680) repealed a section (40 U.S.C. 759) that had been appended to the Federal Property and Administrative Services Act by the Automatic Data Processing Act, which is popularly known as the Brooks Act; the repealed provision authorized the Administrator of General Services to coordinate and provide for the procurement, maintenance, and utilization of federal automatic data processing equipment.

21. 110 Stat. 3009–393.

22. The Rehabilitation Act Amendments of 1998 constituted Title IV of the Workforce Investment Act of 1998, 112 Stat. 936; the electronic and information technology access requirement was appended to the Rehabilitation Act as section 508, 112 Stat 1203, at 29 U.S.C. 794(d); the Rehabilitation Act was originally enacted in 1973, 87 Stat. 355, at 29 U.S.C. 701 et seq.

23. *Federal Register* 65 (March 31, 2000): 17346–67; the proposed standards also are available from the Access Board Web site at http://www.access-board.gov/sec508/508index.htm.

24. Associated Press, Guidelines to Force Federal Agencies to Redesign Web Sites," *Washington Times,* December 22, 2000, A5.

25. Carrie Johnson, "Agencies Act to Ease Use of Internet by Disabled," *Washington Post,* August 24, 2000, A23; William Jackson, "Agencies Face June Deadline for Meeting Section 508," *Government Computer News* 20 (January 8, 2001): 1, 13; Karen Robb, "Work on IT Access for Disabled Advances," *Federal Times* (January 15, 2001): 1, 18; Karen Robb, "Agencies Scramble to Accommodate Disabled, *Federal Times* (June 25, 2001): 1, 17.

26. Steve Graves, "Bobby Blows Whistle on Inaccessible Web Pages," *Government Computer News* 19 (September 4, 2000): 1, 60–61.

27. President's Information Infrastructure Task Force, *A Framework for Global Electronic Commerce* (Washington, D.C., July 1, 1997), available from the National Institute of Standards and Technology Web site, http://www.iitf.nist.gov/eleccomm/ecomm.htm.

28. U.S. President's Information Technology Advisory Committee, *Report to the President: Information Technology Research: Investing in Our Future* (Washington: February 1999), 6–7; the report is available at http://www.ccic.gov/ac.

29. General Accounting Office, "Electronic Government: Challenges Must Be Addressed with Effective Leadership and Management," testimony of David L. McClure, before the Senate Committee on Governmental Affairs, GAO-01-959T (Washington, D.C.: General Accounting Office, July 11, 2001), 26.

30. The text of the Federal Response Plan is available at http://www.fema.gov/r-n-r/frp.

31. See *Federal Register* 53 (November 23, 1988): 47491–512.

32. See 50 U.S.C. 1601 et seq.

33. U.S. Federal Emergency Management Agency, *Federal Response Plan* (Washington, D.C.: Federal Emergency Management Agency, April 1999), TI-1.

34. The full text of PDD 63 is available at http://www.fas.org/irp/offdocs/pdd/pdd-63.htm.

35. The full text and executive summary of the national plan are available from the Critical Infrastructure Assurance Office Web site (http://www.ciao.gov) in the "CIAO Document Library."

36. General Accounting Office, *Critical Infrastructure Protection: Comprehensive Strategy Can Draw on Year 2000 Experiences*, GAO Report GAO/AIMD–00-1 (Washington, D.C.: General Accounting Office, October 1999).

37. E.O. 13231, "Critical Infrastructure Protection in the Information Age," October 18, 2001.

38. Ibid.

39. See 10 U.S.C. 332, 372, 374–375, 12301–12302, and 12406.

40. See 40 U.S.C. 1425(c)(2) and 44 U.S.C. 3506(a)(2).

41. See "Security, Information Technology and Facilities," *Journal of Public Inquiry* (Spring–Summer 2000): 28–30.

42. Title II of the USA PATRIOT Act expands the scope of subpoenas for records of electronic communications to include records commonly associated with Internet usage, such as session times and duration (section 210); allows Internet service providers to divulge records or other information (but not the contents of communications) pertaining to a subscriber if they believe there is immediate danger of death or serious physical injury or as otherwise authorized, and requires them to divulge such records or information (excluding contents of communications) to a government entity under certain conditions (section 212); and adds routing and addressing information (used in Internet communications) to the information a government agency may capture using pen registers and trap and trace devices as authorized by court order, while excluding the content of any wire or electronic communications (section 216). The latter section also requires law enforcement officials to keep certain records when they use their own pen registers or trap and trace devices and to provide those records to the court that issued the order within thirty days of expiration of the order. To the extent that Carnivore-like systems fall within the new definition of pen registers or trap and trace devices provided in the Act, that language would increase judicial oversight of the use of such systems and allow a person acting under color of law to intercept the wire or electronic communications of a computer trespasser transmitted to, through, or from a protected computer under certain circumstances.
Section 223 sets a four-year sunset period for many of the Title II provisions, but among the sections excluded from the sunset are sections 210 and 216.

43. Dan Caterinicchia, "Agency Seeks E-document Comments," *Federal Computer Week* 15 (October 15, 2001): 14.

44. Christopher J. Dorobek, "Web Sites That Worked," *Federal Computer Week* 15 (October 1, 2001): 18.

45. Ibid.

46. See, for example, George I. Seffers, "DOD Defends Web Site Shutdown," *Federal Computer Week* 15 (September 3, 2001): 54.

47. Judi Hasson, "IRS E-filing, Bio Fears Clash," *Federal Computer Week* 15, no. 38 (November 12, 2001): 12.

48. J. Timothy Sprehe, "Perils of Public Access," *Federal Computer Week* 15, no. 43 (December 10, 2001): 46.

49. Council for Excellence in Government, *E-Government: The Next American Revolution* (Washington, D.C.: Council for Excellence in Government, February 2001), 6; the report is available at http://www.excelgov.org.

50. Ibid., 7–10.

51. Ibid., 10–11.

52. Ibid., 11–14.

53. U.S. Office of Management and Budget, *A Blueprint for New Beginnings: A Responsible Budget for America's Priorities* (Washington, D.C.: GPO, 2001), 179–180; available at http://www.gpo.gov/usbudget/index.html.

54. Ibid.

55. William Matthews, "Bush E-gov Fund to Double," *Federal Computer Week* 15 (March 26, 2001): 8.

56. Office of Management and Budget, *Budget of the United States Government, Fiscal Year 2002: Appendix* (Washington, D.C.: GPO, 2001), p. 994.

57. House Committee on Appropriations, *Treasury, Postal Service, and General Government Appropriations Bill, 2002*, a report to accompany H.R. 2590, 107th Cong., 1st sess., H.Rept. 107-152 (Washington, D.C.: GPO, 2001), 74-75.

58. FY2003 Budget. See http://www.whitehouse.gov/omb/budget/index.html.

59. *Congressional Record* (daily edition) 147 (May 1, 2001): S4101–16.

60. Shane Harris, "OMB Official Outlines His Plan for Overhauling E-Government," *GovExec.com* daily briefing, July 27, 2001, available on the GovExec.com Web site at http://govexec.com/dailyfed/0701/072701h1.htm.

61. The original mandate of the President's Management Council may be found in 3 C.F.R., 1993 Comp., 788–91.

62. The Center for eGovernance, developed by the National Academy of Public Administration and Virginia Polytechnic Institute and State University, is a clearinghouse to foster partnerships and an exchange of ideas among government, academic institutions, and other organizations (see http://www.napawash.org/ce).

63. Mitchell E. Daniels Jr., "Memorandum for the Heads of Executive Departments and Agencies: Citizen-centered E-government: Developing the Action Plan," M-01-28 (Washington, D.C.: Office of Management and Budget, July 18, 2001), 1–2 (see http://www.whitehouse.gov/omb/memoranda/m01-28.html).

64. General Accounting Office, *Electronic Government*, 1–2.

65. Ibid., 13.

66. Office of Management and Budget, *E-Gov Strategy: Simplified Delivery of Services to Citizens* (Washington, D.C.: GPO, February 27, 2002); available at http://www.whitehouse.gov/omb/inforeg/egovstrategy.pdf.

URL SITE GUIDE

Center for eGovernance
http://www.napawash.org/pc_egovernance/index.html

Citizen-centered E-government
Office of Management and Budget
http://www.whitehouse.gov/omb/memoranda/m01-28.html

Federal Response Plan
Federal Emergency Management Agency
http://www.fema.gov/r-n-r/frp/

FirstGov
http://www.firstgov.gov/

Nuclear Regulatory Commission
http://www.nrc.gov/

PDD63
http://www.fas.org/irp/offdocs/pdd/pdd-63.htm

Senators Thompson/Lieberman
E-government Experiment
http://gov_affairs.senate.gov

http://www.senate.gov/~gov_affairs/egov/

U.S. Business Advisor
http://www.business.gov/

# Appendix

The Literature on Government Information Policy

The scholarly literature pertaining to government information policy is both interdisciplinary and cross-disciplinary. As the chapters imply, that literature comes from a wide variety of disciplines and fields within those disciplines. Examples include agricultural science, economics, environmental studies, geography, government and political science, law, public policy, and library and information science, but that literature might also come from medicine and other disciplines, and cover topics such as the public's right to know, the concept of the information life cycle, hazardous waste, global warming, government publishing, information access and secrecy, privacy, intellectual property, and information technology.

The purpose of this appendix is not to address each discipline, field, or topic, but rather to identify some key sources, finding aids, and publishers, thereby supplementing the coverage in the book. Readers can consult these resources to find additional literature, both historical and present day.

Although not covered below, complementary source material includes national newspapers (e.g., the *New York Times* and the *Washington Post*), discipline-specific newspapers (e.g., *The Chronicle of Higher Education*), and technology-focused periodicals (e.g., *Government Computer News* and *Federal Computer Week*), which provide up-to-date coverage of developments in information technology and related changes in information policy and government management of information resources. There are also the products of think tanks, professional associations (other than those discussed below), nonprofit organizations (e.g., Rand®, http;//www.rand.org), and public interest groups (e.g., OMB Watch; http://www.ombwatch.org). Some of these groups and organizations reflect a specific political ideology, whereas others strive for neutrality.

395

The focus of this appendix is on the scholarly literature, especially that appearing as books, articles, and dissertations. The intent is to be suggestive, rather than comprehensive. These writings cover the entire information life cycle—some aspects more than others (e.g., in particular, protection, use, and preservation)—and management of that life cycle. There is some coverage of organizations and groups that try to affect the political process.

Before listing those sources, it is useful to identify some guides whose intent is to identify a wide range of resources and, in a few instances, illustrate their use:

- *Introduction to United States Government Information Sources*, 6th ed., by Joe Morehead (Libraries Unlimited, 1999).This is the classic text for identifying and describing the bibliographic and textual structure of federal government information for depository librarians and students in schools of library and information science. The focus is on the GPO's depository library program.

- *Accessing U.S. Government Information: Subject Guide to Jurisdiction of the Executive and Legislative Branches*, by Jerrold Zwirn (Greenwood, 1996). This book links the executive and legislative branch entities with their respective jurisdictions.

- *Locating United States Government Information*, 2d ed., by Edward Herman (William S. Hein, 1997). This practical guide, in a workbook format, provides illustrations from finding aids and offers questions and answers.

- *Subject Guide to U.S. Government Reference Sources*, 2d ed., by Gayle J. Hardy and Judith Schiek Robinson (Libraries Unlimited, 1996). This work covers both print and electronic reference sources. The content is now dated.

- *Tapping the Government Grapevine: The User-Friendly Guide to U.S. Government Sources*, by Judith Schiek Robinson (Oryx Press, 1998). This complements the work by Herman, identifies key source material, explains the use of this material, and offers tips on conducting research.

- *Using Government Information Sources: Electronic and Print*, 3d ed., by Jean L. Sears and Marilyn K. Moody (Oryx Press, 2001). First published in 1985, this tool examines a wide variety of information sources for all three branches of government. Each chapter includes a search strategy, background information on print and electronic sources, discussions, bibliographies, and other information.

The Bowker Annual: Library and Book Trade Almanac™ (Bowker) and the *Annual Review of Information Science and Technology* (Information Today; published for the American Society for Information Science and Technology) include coverage of government information. The former source, which is published annually, covers "Legislation" and "Federal Agency and Federal Library Reports," which includes agencies such as the National Technical Information Service and the Government Printing Office. The latter source often contains scholarly articles on government information policies, including those related to the information superhighway. Each article contains a substantial bibliography.

MONOGRAPHS

A number of publishers have been active in the publication of works related to government information policy. First, in the 1980s and 1990s, Ablex Publishing Corp. (then in Norwood, New Jersey; now part of Greenwood Publishing Group), published a number of works in the book series edited by Peter Hernon and Charles R. McClure and later by Hernon alone. The series was discontinued in 2000 when Hernon retired as series editor. Some of the works are

- *Federal Information Policies in the 1980's: Conflicts and Issues*, edited by Peter Hernon and Charles R. McClure (1986), which was based on a report for the congressional Office of Technology Assessment;

- *Public Access to Government Information: Issues, Trends, and Strategies*, by Peter Hernon and Charles R. McClure (1984, 1988);

- *United States Government Information Policies: Views and Perspectives*, edited by Charles R. McClure, Peter Hernon, and Harold C. Relyea (1989);

- *United States Scientific and Technical Information (STI) Policies: Views and Perspectives*, edited by Charles R. McClure and Peter Hernon (1989);

- *The National Research and Education Network (NREN): Research and Policy Perspectives*, by Charles R. McClure, Ann P. Bishop, Philip Doty, and Howard Rosenbaum (1991);

- *Silencing Science: National Security Controls and Scientific Communication*, by Harold C. Relyea (1994);

- *Federal Information Policies in the 1990s: Views and Perspectives*, edited by Peter Hernon, Charles R. McClure, and Harold C. Relyea (1996);

- *Deep Information: The Role of Information Policy in Environmental Sustainability*, by John Felleman (1997); and

- *The Impact of Information Policy: Measuring the Effects of the Commercialization of Canadian Government Statistics*, by Kirsti Nilsen (2001).

Second, the National Research Council, which "was organized by the National Academy of Sciences in 1916 to associate the broad community of science and technology with the Academy's purposes of further knowledge and advising the federal government" (http://www.nas.edu/nrc) offers publications through the National Academy Press. The NAP has issued various works on information technology and scientific information policy, such as the following:

- *A Question of Balance: Private Rights and the Public Interest in Scientific and Technical Databases* (1999). New legal initiatives threaten to compromise public access to scientific and technical data. This book examines how policymakers are attempting to find a balance between the rights of database rights holders and public interest users of the data such as researchers, educators, and libraries.

- *Bits of Power: Issues in Global Access to Scientific Data* (1997). The book makes recommendations about access to scientific data from public funding, examines trends in electronic transfer and management, and discusses the need for improved access to scientific data.

- *The Digital Dilemma: Intellectual Property in the Information Age* (2000). This is an analysis of current trends in copyright law, including such topics as individual access to information resources, public access to resources, and protection of intellectual property.

A more complete list is available at the Web site of the National Academy Press (http://www.nap.edu/index.html).

Third, university presses have produced works, such as

- *The Press, Politics, and Patronage: The American Government's Use of Newspapers, 1789–1875*, by Culver H. Smith (University of Georgia Press, 1977);

- *Protecting Privacy in Surveillance Societies*, by David Flaherty (University of North Carolina Press, 1989);

- *Regulating Privacy: Data Protection and Public Policy in Europe and the United States*, by Colin J. Bennett (Cornell University Press, 1992);

- *Legislating Privacy: Technology, Social Values, and Public Policy*, by Priscilla M. Regan (University of North Carolina Press, 1995);

- *Managing Privacy: Information Technology and Corporate America*, by H. Jeff Smith (University of North Carolina Press, 1994);

- *Presidential War Power*, by Louis Fisher (University Press of Kansas, 1995);

- *Constitutional Conflicts between Congress and the President*, by Louis Fisher (University Press of Kansas, 1997);

- *Technology and Privacy*, edited by Philip E. Agre and Marc Rotentberg (MIT Press, 1997);

- *Visions of Privacy: Policy Choices for the Digital Age*, edited by Colin J. Bennett and Rebecca Grant (University of Toronto Press, 1999); and

- *Who Owns Academic Work? Battling for Control of Intellectual Property*, by Corynne McSherry (Harvard University Press, 2001).

Fourth, a number of publishers have produced occasional works that, although not dedicated solely to the study of government information policy, address various information policy issues, including intellectual policy, data privacy, freedom of information, and networking technologies. Examples follow:

- *Science as Intellectual Property: Who Controls Scientific Research?*, by Dorothy Nelkin (MacMillan, 1984).

- *Who Owns Information? From Privacy to Public Access*, by Anne W. Branscomb (Basic Books, 1994).

- *Shamans, Software, and Spleens: Law and the Construction of the Information Society*, by James Boyle (Harvard University Press, 1996).

- *Code and Other Laws of Cyberspace*, by Lawrence Lessig (Basic Books, 1999).

- *Federal Information Disclosure*, 3rd ed., edited by James T. O'Reilly (West Group, 2000).

- *The Social Life of Information*, by John Seely Brown and Paul Duguid (Harvard Business School Press, 2000).

- *Evaluating Networked Information Services: Techniques, Policy, and Issues*, edited by Charles R. McClure and John Carlo Bertot (Information Today, 2001).

Fifth, government entities have produced numerous policy studies. For example, these publications might come from Congress, the Office of Management and Budget, the now defunct congressional Office of Technology Assessment, or the National Commission on Libraries and Information Science. Examples follow:

- *Electronic Collection and Dissemination of Information by Federal Agencies: A Policy Overview*. Report (99-560) by the House Committee on Government Operations (Washington, D.C.: GPO, 1986).

- *Intellectual Property Rights in an Age of Electronics and Information*, OTA-CIT-302 (Office of Technology Assessment (1986). (SuDocs:Y3. T22/2:2 IN8/3). Although the publication date might indicate an outdated work, this report is prescient in its thorough examination of the effects of technology on intellectual property from the standpoints of economics, politics, and law, and how all these factors affect society and its access to information.

- *Public Information in the National Information Infrastructure*, by Henry H. Perritt (Office of Management and Budget, 1994). (SuDocs: PrEX 2.2:IN 3/3). This document outlines the basic technology, economic, legal, and policy questions that lawmakers need to address when making policy decisions regarding digital government information.

Of course, some agencies, such as the General Accounting Office and the Congressional Research Service (see Chapter 4), issue numerous reports and policy analyses of varying public availability.

As the new century unfolds, there is no leading publisher of works related to government information policy. Instead, a number of publishers have produced some works. As a result, it is essential to conduct a broad search for books and to consult book reviews appearing in the periodicals and indexing services identified below.

BIBLIOGRAPHIES

Bibliographies are particularly useful for gathering citations on various historical aspects of government information policy. Some examples follow:

- *Annotated Bibliography of Bibliographies on Selected Government Publications and Supplementary Guides to the Superintendent of Documents Classification System*, by Gabor Kovacs (Greeley, Colo.: G. Kovacs). Alexander Body began publishing this work in 1967, and five supplements were issued through 1977. Beginning in 1980 with the sixth supplement, the work was supplemented by Gabor Kovacs. In 1990, Mary L. Alm compiled the eleventh and last edition of this work. What distinguishes it from other similar publications are the lengthy and meticulous annotations.

- "Recent Literature on Government Information," in *Journal of Government Information*, by Dena H. Hutto. This is an annual bibliography of primary and secondary source materials, with some annotations.

- *The Scout Report* is a weekly, annotated publication highlighting new and newly discovered online resources of interest to researchers, educators, and others. It generally has a section for government information. The *Report* is available both on the Web site (see http://scout.cs. wisc.edu) and in e-mail form via mailing list subscription. The Internet Scout Project is located at the Department of Computer Sciences at the University of Wisconsin-Madison and is funded by a grant from the National Science Foundation.

JOURNAL LITERATURE

Articles and various studies about government information can be found in numerous journals in the social sciences and law. Of particular interest to information professionals are *Government Information Quarterly* (*GIQ*) and the *Journal of Government Information* (*JGI*) (formerly titled *Government Publications Review*). These scholarly journals are devoted to the publications and information activities of governments, including the federal government. Each is a research-oriented journal that contains peer-reviewed articles. *GIQ* features coverage of information policies—those discussed in this book—more than does *JGI,* which is reflected in the composition of the editorial boards of both journals. *GIQ*'s board is much broader and has included government policymakers and policy analysts, lawyers, journalists, librarians and library school educators, and information policy consultants.

GIQ features an editorial and review section, together with in-depth articles that analyze information policies and practices. Occasionally an entire issue is devoted to one topic (e.g., metadata) for a comprehensive examination of a subject and how it affects policy.

JGI is published six times per year. The final issue of the year is devoted to "Notable Documents," which can serve both as a selection tool and a review of the literature on government information for the preceding year. It also features the annual "Recent Literature on Government Information" section discussed above.

Two journals in library and information science should not be overlooked as sources of articles on government information policy and its literature. The *Journal of Academic Librarianship* (*JAL*), published bimonthly, features a column entitled, "Information Policy," which highlights issues related to the topic. *Library Journal*, published monthly, has an annual "Notable Documents List," which can serve as a selection tool and updating service.

D-Lib Magazine is a monthly Web-based periodical (http://www.dlib.org) whose focus is innovation and research being done in digital libraries. It often has articles on and about government information policy as it relates to the digital library.

Coverage of government information policy appears in journals outside library and information science, such as *Public Administration Review* and *Administrative Law Review*. To locate these journals and their coverage of information policy, it is best to rely on the finding aids discussed in the following section.

INDEXES, ABSTRACTS, AND DATABASES

PAIS International is available both in online and print formats. It indexes public policy and public affairs literature in books, periodicals, government documents, and reports. Both citations and abstracts of contents indexed are available.

Social Sciences Index is also available in both online and print formats. It indexes articles in all areas of the social sciences, including government policy. Only citations to journal articles are provided.

Dissertation Abstracts International represents the work of authors from over 1,000 North American and European universities on a full range of subjects. It includes abstracts from a number of dissertations that relate to information policy. The online equivalent is entitled *Digital Dissertations*.

Index to Legal Periodicals and Books contains citations from journals and law books published. Topics covered include information policy and regulatory issues. It is available in both online and print formats.

PA Research II is an online resource that indexes periodicals in the social sciences, humanities, general sciences, business, and general interest. Approximately half of the articles indexed are available full-text. Otherwise, the content is in citation and/or abstract form.

Lexis-Nexis *Academic Universe* and *Government Periodicals Universe* are two of the suite of Web-based products available from this company. *Academic Universe* provides full-text content from newspapers, periodicals, wire services, and broadcast transcripts on a variety of topics. Of particular interest are the policy papers and law reviews that often contain in-depth analysis of information policy issues. *Government Periodicals Universe* indexes periodicals on a variety of topics published by agencies and departments of the federal government. The disciplines covered include information policy and information technology. Only citations to periodical articles are included.

The National Journal Group of databases provides very current news and analysis of politics, policy, and government topics. The suite of titles consists of, among others, *Congress Daily*, *The Hotline*, and *Technology Daily*. National Journal Group, Inc.'s online sources provide briefings that are updated on a daily or weekly basis, with a focus on news from Washington, D.C. and Capitol Hill (see http://nationaljournal.com).

PolicyFile is a Web-based product that indexes research and publication abstracts addressing the complete range of public policy research. It draws its content from public policy think tanks, university research programs, research organizations, and publishers (see http://www.policyfile.com).

Finally, both *GIQ* and *JGI*, as well as other periodicals of Reed-Elsevier, including those produced by Pergamon Press, are included in ScienceDirect. This database provides extensive coverage of information policy issues on a global basis.

INTERNET RESOURCES

This section is illustrative of the Internet resources that both serve as a gateway to materials on information policy and/or address policy issues directly through the work that they are doing. The list highlights the spectrum of projects underway that explore and analyze information policy, often as they relate to digital technologies.

The Berkeley Center for Law and Technology fosters the advancement of technology by guiding the development of intellectual property and related fields of law and policy as they intersect with technology, business, and science. The Center sponsors research and lectures (see http://www.law.berkeley.edu/institutes/bclt).

The Berkman Center for Internet and Society is a research program at the Harvard University Law School, founded to explore cyberspace and policy issues ranging from governance to privacy, to intellectual property, to content control, to government information access. The Center has an active research mission and sponsors, among other things, free online lectures, workshops, and discussions (see http://cyber.law.harvard.edu).

The Center for Democracy & Technology (CDT) is a nonprofit public policy organization whose mission is to conceptualize, develop, and implement public policies to preserve and enhance access to the Internet. One of its areas of focus is to support use of the Internet to permit citizens' immediate and broad access to government information. Besides its own policy publications, CDT compiles and identifies testimony, speeches, and legislation related to its mission (see http://www.cdt.org).

The Center for Public Integrity (http://www.publicintegrity.org/dtaweb/home.asp) provides the public "with the findings of its investigations and analyses of public service, government accountability, and ethics-related issues . . . [F]ounded . . . in 1990, [it] is a non-profit, non-partisan educational organization that is supported in part by your contributions" (http://www.publicintegrity.org). The Web site provides assorted reports and information that enable the center to serve as "a watchdog in the corridors of power" (http://www.publicintegrity.org).

The Center for the Public Domain is a philanthropic foundation dedicated to the preservation of a healthy and robust public domain. Through grant making, research, conferences, and collaborative programs, the Center focuses on the importance of the public domain, particularly as it relates to policy discussions (see http://www.centerforthepublicdomain.org).

A related Web site, opensecrets.org (http://www.opensecrets.org), focuses on "money in politics." It presents news and information, issues, and assorted resources.

The Digital Promise, a project of the Century Foundation, seeks to develop public policies concerning public interest needs in the networked environment (see http://www.digitalpromise.org).

The Harvard Information Infrastructure Project identifies key issues and seeks to guide policy as it relates to the dynamic information infrastructure. It provides an interdisciplinary forum addressing a wide range of emerging issues relating to information infrastructure policy. The Project disseminates publications, organizes seminars and lectures, coordinates a research fellowship program, and provides several graduate level courses in fulfillment of its mission (see http://www.ksg.harvard.edu/iip).

The Center for Strategic and International Studies provides press releases, current news, publications, and so forth on global issues (see http://www.csis.org). Headquartered in Washington, D.C., the center is private, bipartisan, and tax-exempt. It assesses political risk; analyzes regional affairs; identifies long-range "consequences of current practices and policies and . . . [carries] out a range of contingency and scenario-based analyses;" "builds structures and partnerships for policy solutions;" crafts "targeted policy solutions;" and is "committed to developing current and future leaders" (http://www.csis.org/about/index.htm).

The well-known Freedom of Information Center at the University of Missouri has a home page (http://www.missouri.edu/~foiwww) that provides a media law guide, current developments, and "Quick Reference Links" to the "First Amendment," "FOIA Guides," "FOI Advocate Newsletter," "Index/Historical Files," "Links," "Media Law Research," "Official Secrets Act," "Terrorism & FOI Access," and so forth.

ASSOCIATIONS AND ORGANIZATIONS

Numerous organizations work to affect government information policy as part of their mission. They often publish position papers and other documents, which may be of interest to those seeking information on those topics. The following list is by no means comprehensive.

Common Cause "is a nonprofit, nonpartisan citizen's lobbying organization promoting open, honest and accountable government" (http://www. commoncause.org). Its Web site (http://www.commoncause.org) includes news, policy coverage, information about Congress, and so forth on any "corruption in government and [on] big money special interests" (http://www. commoncause.org).

The Electronic Privacy Information Center (http://www.epic.org/) provides resources and guides, as well as current information, related to privacy and other information policy issues (e.g., encryption and surveillance). Annually, the Center issues *The Privacy Law Sourcebook*, which "is the first one-volume resource . . . [for those] who need a comprehensive collection of US and International privacy law, as well as a fully up-to-date section on recent developments" (http://www.epic.org/pls).

The Reporters Committee for Freedom of the Press is "a nonprofit organization dedicated to providing free legal help to journalists and news organizations since 1970" (http://www.rcfp.org). Its home page (http://www.rcfp.org) provides news articles, amicus briefs, and other information on issues such as the First Amendment, the Freedom of Information Act, and the protection of classified information.

The Society of Professional Journalists, Sigma Delta Chi (SDX), provides "resources for journalists and the public on issues involving access to government records and activities and freedom of information education" (http://spj. org/foia.asp).

The Software & Information Industry Association has a home page (http://www.spa.org) that relates news and covers topics such as "Government Affairs," which includes recent statements and reports, some of which are limited to association membership.

The National Academy of Sciences' Computer Science and Telecommunications Board (CSTB) provides independent assessments of technical and public policy issues relating to computing, information, and communications. The CSTB takes an interdisciplinary approach to technical, economic, social, and policy issues (see http://www4.nationalacademies.org/cpsma/cstb.nsf).

EDUCAUSE is a nonprofit association whose mission is to advance higher education by promoting the use of information technology. It sponsors projects and tracks issues that affect information policy (see: http://www.educause.edu).

The Brookings Institution's home page (http://www.brook.edu/dybdocroot) leads to research studies and Policy Briefs, which "are timely, short and informative papers that bring background and recommendations on current issues to policymakers, journalists, and the general public. The views expressed in policy briefs are those of the author alone" (http://www.brook.edu/comm/policybriefs/archive.htm).

The American Bar Association has been an active participant in government information policy, and its Web site includes publications, "policy & advocacy" (e.g., coverage of the issues on which the Association lobbies), news releases, and similar items. As noted on its home page, "As the world's largest voluntary professional membership association, the ABA has access to expert opinions, quality research and objective, high-quality reports—information you can trust" (http://scratch.abanet.org).

The American Library Association's (ALA) Washington, D.C. office comprises of two offices, the Office of Government Relations (OGR) and the Office for Information Technology Policy (OITP). The OGR acts as the link between ALA members and the federal government; OITP promotes the development and utilization of electronic access to information as a means to ensure the public's right to a free and open information society (see http://www.ala.org/washoff).

The Association of Research Libraries (ARL) has a Federal Relations and Information Policy program that tracks activities of legislative, regulatory, and government agencies that have an impact on research libraries. The program analyzes, responds to, and seeks to influence information, intellectual property, and telecommunications policies (see http://www.arl.org/info/index.html).

Finally, the University of Michigan Documents Center has a Web page for "Government Documents Librarianship Government Information Policy" that provides access to policy statements, laws, and so forth (see http://www.lib.umich.edu/govdocs/).

# About the CD-ROM

The CD-ROM is a self-contained resource to supplement the text and figures of the book. CD-ROM users need not have a connection to the Internet; all of the files are on the CD. The files are keyed to the chapters of the book and include

- Federal government documents in text and image formats,

- Pages from federal Web sites that have been modified to be accessible from the CD-ROM,

- Charts and tables,

- Examples of searches, and

- Some 100 review/study questions and answers .

TECHNICAL REQUIREMENTS FOR USING THE CD-ROM

The CD-ROM has been designed to work with either Microsoft's Windows-based or Apple Macintosh computer systems. Two software applications must be installed properly on each computer used with the CD-ROM:

- A Web browser such as Microsoft's Internet Explorer or Netscape, and

- Adobe's PDF Reader (many of the files are formatted using Adobe's "portable document format," with an extension of .pdf).

If your computer workstation has both of these applications installed, you are ready to use the CD-ROM. Place the CD-ROM in the drive, access the CD-ROM, and open its Table of Contents by clicking on the file named **cd-toc.htm**. If you lack either of the necessary applications, see the following.

Microsoft Windows-Based Computers

- A standalone, freeware version of Netscape Navigator (version 4.08) is included on this CD-ROM in the Windows folder.

Step 1: Copy the file winnet4.exe to your hard drive.

Step 2: Then install winnet4.exe onto your hard drive, following the defaults offered.

- A freeware version of Adobe Reader 5.0.5 is included on this CD-ROM in the Windows folder.

Step 1: Copy the file reader5.exe to your hard drive.

Step 2: Then install reader5.exe onto your hard drive, accepting the defaults offered.

Apple Macintosh Computers

- A standalone, freeware version of Netscape Navigator (version 4.08 in MacBinary format) is included on this CD-ROM in the Mac folder.

Step 1: Copy the file macnet4.bin to a folder on your hard drive.

Step 2: Then install macnet4.bin onto your hard drive, following the defaults offered.

- A freeware version of Adobe Reader 5.0.5 (in MacBinary format) is included on this CD-ROM in the Mac folder.

Step 1: Copy the file reader5.bin to a folder your hard drive.

Step 2: Then install reader5.bin onto your heard drive, accepting the defaults offered.

ACKNOWLEDGMENTS

Most of the documents and several of the charts included on the CD-ROM are federal government documents in the public domain. A few of these documents and charts have been modified for presentation on this CD-ROM, such as removing Web-based graphics or images or by removing active links to Web sites. However, please note that the document and chart text contents were not altered in any document. Other charts, and all of the illustrated search examples, have been created specifically for this CD-ROM and include graphics viewable inside a Web browser.

The questions and answers included on the CD-ROM were inspired and, for the most part, created and contributed by **Joe Morehead**, the author of the six editions of *Introduction to United States Government Information Sources*. A graduate library science, federal government, or law course may find these questions challenging when exploring the research process concerning federal government information and sources. Other authors of the work in hand contributed questions and answers to supplement Professor Morehead's original work.

About the Authors

Peter Hernon is Professor, Simmons College Graduate School of Library and Information Science, Boston, where he teaches courses on government information, the evaluation of library services, and research methods. He received his Ph. D. from Indiana University in 1978 and has taught at Simmons College, University of Arizona, and Victoria University of Wellington (New Zealand). He is the founding editor of *Government Information Quarterly,* the current editor of the *Journal of Academic Librarianship,* and the co-editor of *Library & Information Science Research.* He is the author of more than 160 articles and thirty-seven books, including the co-authored *U.S. Government on the Web*, now in its second edition.

Harold C. Relyea is a Specialist in American National Government with the Congressional Research Service (CRS) of the Library of Congress. An undergraduate of Drew University, he received his doctoral degree in government from The American University. Since joining CRS in 1971, he has produced a number of major studies for Congress, including analyses of the office and powers of the president, executive branch organization and management, congressional oversight, and various aspects of government information policy and practice. Dr. Relyea has testified before congressional committees and subcommittees on various occasions and also recently appeared before a committee of the European Parliament. He currently is a member of the CRS Systems Security Team and was formerly the editor of the *CRS Review* and the head of the executive and judiciary section of the CRS Government and Finance Division.

In addition to his CRS duties, Dr. Relyea has authored numerous articles for scholarly and professional publication in the United States and abroad. Currently preparing a book on national emergency powers, his recently published titles include *Silencing Science: National Security Controls and Scientific Communication* (1994), *Federal Information Policies in the 1990s* (1996), and *The Executive Office of the President* (1997). He has served on the editorial board of *Government Information Quarterly* since its founding in 1984 and has held similar positions with several other journals in the past.

Robert E. Dugan is the Director of the Mildred F. Sawyer Library at Suffolk University in Boston. During a nearly thirty-year career, he has been a reference librarian, director of public libraries, head of statewide library development, a state librarian, an associate university librarian, and college library director. He has authored and co-authored three other books and over fifty articles on topics such as information policy, technology, outcomes assessment, and library management and operations.

Joan F. Cheverie is the Head of the Government Documents and Microforms Department at Georgetown University. She has a B.A. from Mount Holyoke College, M.S.L.S. from Catholic University, and M.A. from Georgetown University, She has been an adjunct instructor at the School of Library and Information Science at Catholic University, as well as a Visiting Program Officer at the Coalition for Networked Information.

INDEX

411